To my students, past and present

FIFTH EDITION

Anatomy
of Film

For Bedford/St. Martin's

Developmental Editor: Carina Schoenberger
Senior Production Supervisor: Joe Ford
Production Associate: Chris Gross
Project Management: DeMasi Design and Publishing Services
Senior Marketing Manager: Richard Cadman
Text Design: Claire Seng-Niemoeller
Cover Design: Lucy Krikorian
Cover Photo: Alfred Hitchcock Directing Rear Window. Universal Photofest.
Composition: Macmillan India Inc.
Printing and Binding: Haddon Craftsmen, an RR Donnelley & Sons Company

President: Joan E. Feinberg
Editorial Director: Denise B. Wydra
Director of Marketing: Karen Melton Soeltz
Director of Editing, Design, and Production: Marcia Cohen
Manager, Publishing Services: Emily Berleth

Library of Congress Catalog Card Number: 2004107339

For information, write: Bedford/St. Martin's, 75 Arlington Street, Boston, MA 02116
(617-399-4000)

ISBN: 0-312-41516-8
EAN: 978-0-312-41516-7

Published and distributed outside North America by
PALGRAVE MACMILLAN
Houndmills, Basingstoke, Hampshire RG21 2XS and London
Companies and representatives throughout the world.

ISBN: 1-4039-4631-0

A catalogue record for this book is available from the British Library.

Preface

Little did I suspect as I wrote the first edition of *Anatomy of Film* in 1976 that it would be going into a fifth edition in 2005. After its first publication, I realized that subsequent editions had to reflect an ever-changing medium, the needs of an increasingly diverse student population, and fluctuations of taste as one generation yields to another. Yet despite these changes, the essential goal has always remained the same: to help students develop an appreciation and critical awareness of film with a brief, clear, and enjoyable text. This book introduces film as a text that should be "read" as any other and helps students identify the components of a film in order to interpret it.

The fifth edition of *Anatomy of Film* offers new features that make it applicable to today's students, while retaining those features that have made it a successful classroom tool for over a quarter of a century.

Features

- **A solid foundation of film fundamentals.** In order to offer students a gradual introduction to film, I begin with basic terminology and move on to more complex topics such as genre, subtext, auteurism, film analysis, and finally film theory and criticism.

- **Rich examples from the past and present.** I have tried to maintain the same balance between the films of the past and those of the present that has existed since the first edition. To present the past and present as a continuum, I often use examples from the past, such as *Seven Brides for Seven Brothers* (1954), to help analyze recent films, such as *Moulin Rouge* (2001) and *Chicago* (2002).

- **In-depth coverage of genre.** I have designed Chapter 5 to provide students with a thorough understanding of some of the most important genres: musicals, westerns, crime film, film noir, combat film, comedy, women's films, horror, and science fiction. This edition also includes a new section on the documentary.

To respond to the ever-changing art form of film, the fifth edition of *Anatomy of Film* also offers several new features.

New to this edition

- **Greater attention to independent film.** It is important to acknowledge the contributions of independent filmmakers—those who work outside of mainstream Hollywood—to the art of film. In Chapter 1, the section on the independent film has been considerably augmented. It explores how "independent film," once self-explanatory, has become increasingly difficult to define, especially now that the major studios have created "boutique" divisions such as Sony Pictures Classics, Paramount Classics, and Fox Searchlight to distribute the kind of films that would not ordinarily show up at the local multiplex.

- **New section on documentary as a genre.** In response to requests from instructors, I have included a section on documentary in Chapter 5 that includes recent documentaries that have attracted mass audiences, such as *Spellbound*, *The Kid Stays in the Picture*, and *Capturing the Friedmans*.

- **More adaptations.** Because so many teachers of literature use *Anatomy of Film*, I have increased the number of film adaptations by using Virginia Woolf as a point of departure for two films in which the author figures: *Mrs. Dalloway* (1998), a faithful adaptation of her novel of the same name, and *The Hours* (2002), an equally faithful film version of Michael Cunningham's novel. Because science fiction writer Philip K. Dick's work continues to inspire films (for example, *Blade Runner* [1982], *Paycheck* [2003]), I have added an analysis of Steven Spielberg's *Minority Report* (2002), which is based on Dick's story of the same name.

- **Deeper coverage of international film.** Before the 1940s, moviegoers in the United States distinguished between "American" and "foreign" films. The end of the Second World War saw the emergence of a truly international cinema. I have combined discussions of some international films of the past, now deemed classics (for example, Kurosawa's *Rashomon* [1950], Bergman's *The Seventh Seal* [1957] and *Wild Strawberries* [1957]) with such contemporary examples as *Russian Ark* (2003), *Monsoon Wedding* (2002), and *Crouching Tiger, Hidden Dragon* (2001).

- **More on the visual nature of film.** I have included 30 percent more images to demonstrate how a filmmaker's decisions affect what the audience sees. I have also added a newly conceived chapter on color and visual effects that emphasizes how filmmakers use visual cues to establish mood, character, and setting.

- **New examples of analysis and criticism.** In Chapter 9, "Film Analysis," I now examine five films that are truly representative of film art: *Casablanca* (1942), *Raging Bull* (1980), *The Truman Show* (1998), *A.I. Artificial Intelligence* (2001), and *Crouching Tiger, Hidden Dragon* (2001). Two student papers provide readers with additional models of criticism.

- **Updated guide to online resources.** In Appendix 3, I alert students to various Internet sources and at the same time explain how they should be used. I have offered advice on how to properly cite online material when it is used as a source.

Acknowledgments

I would like to express my thanks to instructors who continue to use this text. I am also grateful for the suggestions for improvement that I have received from Karen Fulton at Missouri Western State College; Candyce Leonard at Wake Forest University; Manuel F. Medina at University of Louisville; Martin F. Norden at University of Massachusetts; David Popowski at Minnesota State University, Mankato; Timothy Shary at Clark University; Julie Steward at Samford University; Richard Terrill at Minnesota State University, Mankato; and additional readers who choose to remain unnamed. Many of these suggestions are reflected in the fifth edition.

Bernard F. Dick
Professor of Communication and English
Fairleigh Dickinson University
Teaneck, New Jersey

Contents

Film, Space, and Mise-en-Scène   49

CHAPTER 3

The Film Director   223

Film and Literature   254

Film Analysis   297

Film Theory and Criticism   320

CHAPTER 1

Understanding the Medium

*F*iction is a widely understood term; it means the invented, the imaginative, the fanciful—the opposite of fact. There is also historical fiction, as well as historical drama: terms for works of the imagination that draw on history for narrative or dramatic purposes. Thus, a novel or a play can still be considered fiction even though it is derived from fact. There are other forms of fiction as well—gothic, romantic, picaresque, detective, stream-of-consciousness, to name a few. Fiction, then, is an umbrella term—one with many different spokes.

Film is another word that means different things in different contexts: roll film, film stock, *a* film, *to* film. We were all exposed to some kind of film before we saw our first example of classic moviemaking. It may have been something we saw on television: a cartoon, a music video, a *Lassie* rerun. Perhaps it was an educational film we saw in school, or a **theatrical film** intended to be shown in movie theaters. Yet, asked to define film, many of us would hesitate. But so would professional filmmakers. Animators, documentary filmmakers, Hollywood directors, and experimental filmmakers perceive themselves as all working in the same medium—film. The films they produce, however, differ totally in look, subject matter, and style. To the general public, film means "movie"—a perfectly acceptable term that the noted American critic Pauline Kael always championed.

Unfortunately, the word *movie* suggests popular culture rather than art. An alternative term, *cinema*, suggests art rather than popular culture. Ironically, *cinema*, though it is a French word, is derived from the Greek *kinein* (to move); thus, whether we say *cinema* or *movie*, we are talking about an art form that was once known as "moving pictures"—appropriately named because the pictures really moved. There is nothing pejorative about the word *movie*; certainly some of the greatest examples of film art ever produced (many of which are discussed in this text) are, and always will be, movies. Although Kael found the word *cinema* pretentious, it is commonly used to categorize films according to kind—contemporary cinema or world cinema, for example; and origin—American cinema, French cinema, and so on. Calling a film a movie implies nothing about artistic worth. Whether we use the word *movie* or *cinema*, we are discussing the same "spoke" of the umbrella term *film*.

Film as a Hybrid Art

Movies should be treated as texts—works to be analyzed and interpreted. They are similar to any other text, including a textbook. *Text* comes from the Latin *textus*, meaning "to weave." A text weaves the material together in an orderly and coherent fashion. A movie is also a text, but a special kind of text—an audiovisual one, as the American playwright, screenwriter, and critic John Howard Lawson described it. Once it was a written text, either in the form of a screenplay or a plot synopsis, as was often the case during the silent era. Or, if it were not written down, it consisted of an idea in the mind of the filmmaker, who then transformed it into an audiovisual text.

Like opera, film is a hybrid art. Opera draws on other arts: theater, painting, music, and, depending on the opera, dance and mime. Film can draw on all of these, and it is also an outgrowth of another art: photography. Film is often called a collaborative art, in the sense of requiring the talents of a vast number of specialists, all of whom are generally acknowledged in the **end credits**. It is also an art in which one person, the director, is expected to integrate all of these contributions into a totality. Throughout this book, we will be anatomizing film—viewing the elements that make up, as Pauline Kael would want us to say, a movie. It is important to remember, however, that all of the elements work together to realize an artistic vision.

The Creation of the Narrative Film

In the late nineteenth century, going to a movie often meant going to an arcade or a kinetoscope parlor, where there were rows of coin-operated peep shows called kinetoscopes. They looked like cabinets and provided about a minute's worth of moving pictures: galloping horses, speeding trains, a couple kissing, a man sneezing, waves crashing on the beach, kangaroos boxing. Today, such entertainment hardly seems revolutionary; in fact, kinetoscope fare does not seem like entertainment at all. However, to our forebears, whose idea of a photographed image was a picture in a family album, seeing people in motion or nature in action was a revelation.

We will be dealing almost exclusively with the **narrative film,** one that tells a story. The narrative film came about when filmmakers discovered that the medium could do more than just record whatever was in front of the camera. The next step was not only to capture the real but to re-create it: to show what could or might be; in other words, to tell a story.

In 1895, the Lumière brothers, Louis and Auguste, photographed scenes of real life in France or *actualités*: a train arriving at a station; workers at quitting time; a mischievous boy stepping on a gardener's hose, causing water to squirt into the gardener's face. Another French movie pioneer, Georges Méliès, who had been a magician, preferred to tell more elaborate stories. Méliès's *A Trip to the Moon* (1902) is a series of "artificially arranged scenes," to use his phrase, that were highly theatrical and followed each other sequentially, so that there was a beginning, a middle, and an end. The narrative film was beginning to take shape. But the best narrative is not so much sequential as causal. It is not a matter of A happening first, B second, and so forth; but, rather, A's happening first causes B to happen second, with C as the result.

The best of the early narrative films was E. S. Porter's *The Great Train Robbery* (1903), which pretty much follows the situation-complication-resolution model. Outlaws enter a railroad telegraph office and tie up the operator. They board a train, rob the passengers, and run off into the woods. Meanwhile, back at the telegraph office, the operator's daughter arrives with her father's lunch and unties him. A posse is formed, and the outlaws are killed—all in less than twelve minutes. Although the fourteen episodes that make up *The Great Train Robbery* seem to unfold sequentially, cause-effect is also at work. Because the operator's daughter has brought her father his lunch, she can untie him; because the operator has been untied, a posse can be formed; and because a posse has been formed, the bandits can be tracked down.

Train robberies were common in the early twentieth century. However, it would have been impossible to film one. So why not imagine what one might have been like in 1903? And so, with *The Great Train Robbery*, the narrative film came into its own.

Narrative Film

In attempting to define film, John Howard Lawson wrote the following: "A film is an audiovisual conflict; it embodies time-space relationships; it proceeds from a premise, through a progression, to a climax or ultimate term

Playwright, screenwriter, and critic John Howard Lawson, whose book *Film: The Creative Process*, is a seminal work of film criticism. *(Courtesy AMPAS/FSA)*

of the action."[1] Note that Lawson has not described film as such; he has described one of its particular forms: the narrative film.

To Lawson a movie is narrative, told through sound and image, that builds to a climax and culminates in a resolution. Lawson does not make dialogue part of the definition; he merely says that a movie is audiovisual. A movie does not need spoken dialogue to tell a story. The silent films had no spoken dialogue; piano or organ accompaniment was common, and sound effects were necessary to complement the action on the screen. Even with the advent of sound, filmmakers who were truly creative knew that parts of the action could be told visually without any dialogue.

In a film, the images themselves can tell part of the story, independently of language. Some of the most unforgettable moments in film are wordless. The burning sled in Orson Welles's *Citizen Kane* (1941) that reveals the meaning of "Rosebud"; a man, destined to be a loner, standing in the doorway of a house that everyone but himself enters, in John Ford's *The Searchers* (1956); an astronaut clearing the window of his spacecraft at the same time that his wife is looking out the window of their home, so that it seems as if they see each other, in Ron Howard's *Apollo 13* (1995). The great filmmakers have always known that the difference between theater and film is the difference between a play and a screenplay; the latter is precisely what the term implies: a play designed for the screen, where images can carry as much weight as words.

Bette Davis (left) as Margo Channing; Marilyn Monroe as an aspiring actress; and George Sanders as a formidable critic in *All About Eve* (1950). *(Courtesy Twentieth Century-Fox)*

Joseph L. Mankiewicz's *All About Eve* (1950) illustrates the way images advance or enhance the action without the use of dialogue. *All About Eve* is the story of an aspiring actress, Eve Harrington (Anne Baxter), who deceives the Broadway star Margo Channing (Bette Davis) into befriending her. After she betrays Margo and becomes a star herself, Eve becomes the victim of a similar scheme: Phoebe, a starstruck student, will do to Eve what Eve did to Margo. As Phoebe stands in front of a three-way mirror, bowing to an imaginary audience as if she were accepting an award, her image is multiplied until the screen is filled with what seems to be an infinity of Phoebes. The final sequence is entirely without dialogue. None is needed; the visuals themselves make the point. As long as there are stars, there will be the starstruck, some of whom will stop at nothing to achieve fame.

Alfred Hitchcock's *Psycho* (1960) will always be remembered for the shower murder of Marion Crane (Janet Leigh). The episode is completely wordless, although the music seems to shriek. As Marion prepares for a shower in her room at the Bates Motel, Norman Bates (Anthony Perkins), in the adjacent parlor, removes the painting *Susanna and the Elders* from the wall to watch Marion undress through a peephole. She goes into the shower, luxuriating in the spray of water. Suddenly a shadow, presumably of an elderly woman, appears against the shower curtain. The woman pulls the curtain aside and proceeds to stab Marion repeatedly, as blood mingles with the water and swirls down the drain. Although the entire episode lasts less than a minute, a great deal of information has been imparted. Hitchcock's choice of painting was not arbitrary; it depicts the biblical story of the Elders who spied on Susanna entering her bath. Marion's privacy has been invaded. Instead of relaxing in the shower, she experiences the repose of death. Instead of her body being cleansed, it is defiled. Actually, it is the shower stall that must be cleansed, because it has been splattered with blood.

Writing down everything that happens in that episode takes longer than it does to see it. In his *Filmguide to Psycho*, James Naremore devotes five pages to a description of those forty-five seconds of film.[2]

A shower about to be interrupted by a murderous intruder in Hitchcock's *Psycho* (1960). *(Courtesy Museum of Modern Art/Film Still Archive, hereafter abbreviated as MOMA/FSA)*

Time-Space Relationships

Like any narrative, a good movie involves conflict: personalities clash, goals differ, interests diverge, characters are at odds with each other or with society. In a movie, however, the conflict is audiovisual: it is heard and seen rather than written and read. A movie "embodies time-space relationships." While a written narrative can suggest that two events are occurring at the same time in different places, a movie can do more than suggest: it can show them occurring.

Time Code (2000) went beyond juxtaposing two simultaneous events. In this highly experimental film, the screen is partitioned into four parts, so that it resembles a grid. In each part, a story about infidelity unfolds, so that the audience is able to experience four interlocking narratives on the same subject, taking place on the same day and in the same general part of Los Angeles. Since *Time Code* was never intended for multiplexes, it did not attract wide audiences. It was the director Mike Figgis's attempt to illustrate how film can depict four actions occurring at the same time without the director's having to cut from one to the other. Because it is a method that is so at odds with what the public expects of a movie, *Time Code* does not represent the wave of the future.

Yet it does illustrate a major difference between film and fiction. At the beginning of Iris Murdoch's novel *Henry and Cato* (1976), one character is pacing up and down a bridge in London "at about the hour" that another is on a jet over the Atlantic. Then Murdoch reminds us that "at about the hour" the first two characters were on their respective bridge and jet, two more were in their library, and another was elsewhere, rereading his daughter's letter. Although Murdoch manages to interweave the destinies of all these individuals, she has to keep repeating "at about the hour" until they have been introduced. A filmmaker could capture the simultaneous action of the novel's opening by turning it into a prologue, using a split screen or a gridlike screen on the order of *Time Code*, then switching to a more traditional form of narrative for the rest of the film. For the novelist, it is not so easy. Apart from

Simultaneous action in *Time Code* (2000). *(Courtesy MOMA/FSA)*

splitting the page, a novelist has no other choice but to use temporal references such as "at the same time" or summary statements implying that while event A was occurring in one place, event B was occurring in another.

Movie Time

A movie must tell a story within a certain period of time. Anyone who attends movies regularly checks the movie timetable in the newspaper. Television programmers are especially conscious of a movie's running time, since films are often cut to fit into a particular time slot. Running time, however, is real time—90 minutes, 105 minutes, and so on. Movie time is not; movie time manipulates real time.

Movie time is elastic. In a movie, an entire day can be compressed into a few minutes or even seconds; likewise, a few minutes or seconds can be prolonged into what seems to be an entire day. In the famous Odessa Steps sequence in *Potemkin* (1925), the Russian director Sergei Eisenstein distorts real time. He makes the massacre seem longer than it was because he wants to emphasize the atrocities the czarist troops committed against the people of Odessa. Toward the end of the sequence, a soldier swings his saber, striking the right eye of a woman wearing a pince-nez. In reality, the soldier would have slashed her eye with one movement of his arm, but Eisenstein fragments the act. First, we see the soldier, his arm raised with the blade behind his head; then we see his savage face, but not the saber; now his face dominates the screen. Next, he shouts something as his raised arm begins to descend. Finally, we see the woman—her mouth gaping, the right lens of her pince-nez shattered, blood spurting from her eye and running down her face.

Removing a key from a key ring is a simple operation. In Alfred Hitchcock's *Notorious* (1946), however, the action is prolonged to create suspense. Alicia (Ingrid Bergman) is an American intelligence agent whose job requires her to marry Sebastian (Claude Rains), an ex-Nazi. She has the keys to every room in their house except the wine cellar. Since her coworker (Cary Grant) suspects that the cellar contains more than wine, Alicia must remove that key from her husband's key ring while he is in the bathroom getting ready for a party they are giving that evening. The moment is stretched out, making the audience wonder whether she will succeed; and if she does, what will happen when her husband discovers that the key is missing. In real life, a wine bottle perched too close to the edge of the shelf will simply fall and shatter. Later in *Notorious* a wine bottle does shatter, but first it lingers on the edge, causing us to wonder whether it will fall, and if it does, what its contents will reveal.

In Frank Capra's *Meet John Doe* (1941), a cross-country political campaign occurs in a few seconds. The climax of *Nickelodeon* (1976) is the premiere of D. W. Griffith's *The Birth of a Nation* (1915). To make the premiere as credible as possible, clips from the actual film are used. The premiere is so authentic, and the audience's reaction so spontaneous, that we forget that Griffith's three-hour epic has been reduced to a few minutes of screen time. Likewise, Robert Altman's *Nashville* (1975), which runs two and a half hours, is so absorbing that we forget we have spent five days with twenty-four people, whose destinies have been interconnected. If the film engages our attention, as James Whale's *Show Boat* (1936) does, we are oblivious to the fact that a story that spanned three generations took only 113 minutes to tell.

A few films exhibit perfect unity of time: the running time coincides with the story time. Such films, admittedly, are rare, but Robert Wise's *The Set-Up* (1949) and Fred Zinnemann's *High Noon* (1952) run seventy-two and eighty-four minutes, respectively. Clocks are important markers of time in both films; as a result, we realize that there was no difference between the time it took to see the film and the time it took for the plot to unfold.

The Diversity of the Medium

Even within narrative films, there is such great diversity that it is nearly impossible to generalize about the nature of the medium. Not every movie is offered by a major film studio. Not every film is made in Hollywood. To get a sense of the many different kinds of movies, we will examine two types that are quite different from the mainstream films shown at multiplexes. **Independent film** can be viewed in art houses or on the Independent Film Channel (IFC) or the Sundance Channel (SUN) on cable television. **International film** from such countries as Hungary, China, France, Iran, and Sweden can be rented on DVD or read about in *Variety* each week.

Independent Film

To most of us, "independent" means, among other things, "unaffiliated," "self-supporting," "free of external control or influence," "unwilling to be part of the mainstream," and so forth. In the movie business, "independent" has a more specialized meaning, although the reason men and women are drawn to independent filmmaking is precisely their unwillingness to be part of a product-driven industry like corporate Hollywood with its committee decision making. Instead, they desire to have the freedom to make their own movies without interference from studio executives interested only in the commercial success of the project.

The independent film, or "indie," is not a new phenomenon. Ever since movies began, there have been independent filmmakers—mavericks who chose to go their own way because they sized up the system and decided they wanted to work outside of it. The studio that is now Universal was once called IMP, which stood for Independent Moving Pictures. IMP was independent because its head, Carl Laemmle, refused to let it be swallowed up by a powerful trust, the Motion Pictures Patents Company (MPPCo), which sought to dominate production by making it difficult for independent moviemakers to function unless they became MPPCo members. In 1912, the MPPCo was declared a violation of the Sherman Anti-Trust Act and within a few years ceased to exist. But in the meantime, life was not easy for the "indies."

In 1919, three actors, Mary Pickford, Charlie Chaplin, and Douglas Fairbanks, and the director D. W. Griffith founded United Artists, often thought of as a studio but really a distribution company formed to produce and distribute their films and those of others. Over the next few decades, a number of independent producers arrived on the scene, each different from the others. One of the greatest, Samuel Goldwyn, distributed some of his films through United Artists (e.g., *Dead End*, 1937), but many through RKO Radio Pictures, a major studio until its demise in 1957. Goldwyn never wanted a studio base; he used a studio only to distribute his films.

However, there were self-styled independent producers who wanted a studio affiliation for security. In 1944, Hal Wallis left Warner Brothers, where he had been production chief, because he wanted to select only the films he wanted to make rather than have to put a slate of twenty-odd films a year into production. He relocated to Paramount, where he remained until 1970, during which time he gave the studio such masterpieces as *Come Back, Little Sheba* (1952), *The Rose Tattoo* (1955), *Becket* (1964), and *True Grit* (1970), in addition to less prestigious but popular films such as the Dean Martin and Jerry Lewis comedies and many of Elvis Presley's films. After leaving Paramount, he did the same at Universal for five years. *Anne of the Thousand Days* (1969) and *Mary, Queen of Scots* (1971) are highly regarded for their historical accuracy; and *Rooster Cogburn* (1975), Wallis's last production, will always be remembered as the only pairing of John Wayne and Katharine Hepburn.

Another independent producer of the period, Sam Spiegel, had a long-term arrangement with Columbia Pictures, resulting in such classics as *On the Waterfront* (1954), *The Bridge on the River Kwai* (1957), and *Lawrence of Arabia* (1962). But to call *Sheba* or *On the Waterfront* "independent films" is to ignore the distinction between films made outside the system and those made within it. Wallis and Spiegel produced within the system. A contemporary example is Jerry Bruckheimer, who found a niche for himself at Disney, for which he produced, among other films, *Armageddon* (1998), *Pearl Harbor* (2001), and *Pirates of the Caribbean: The Curse of the Black Pearl* (2003). Wallis and Spiegel worked within the studio system without becoming part of it; Bruckheimer produced for studios long after the studio system had ended. Yet the three of them had something in common: they made movies that were distributed by major studios. It all comes down to being *in* the business, but not *of* it; or functioning within the system on one's own terms versus being part of it on someone else's. Wallis, Spiegel, and Bruckheimer used studios as outlets; to use an analogy, they were like circus performers who insisted on a safety net when doing their high-wire act.

The independent film has radically changed since the days of Goldwyn and Wallis. Rather than generalize, let us consider specific examples:

- If the term "independent film" is limited to films that are totally self-financed, few films would qualify. In 2003, Mel Gibson put up his own money to make *The Passion of the Christ* (2003), a movie in both Latin and Aramaic, dealing with the last hours of Jesus Christ's life. As a superstar, Gibson could afford $25 million to make this highly personal film through Icon, his production company. But a typical film school graduate could never come up with anything approximating that amount. *The Passion of the Christ* is literally an independent film.

- More representative of real independent moviemaking is *The Blair Witch Project* (1999), which is impossible to confuse with a studio-produced film. Shot with a 16-mm camera and a camcorder at a cost of $30,000, it went on to gross $140 million. A fluke? Perhaps. An independent film? Definitely. But *The Blair Witch Project* still needed a distributor: Artisan, which Lions Gate Entertainment purchased in 2003.

- Although Miramax was once an independent film company, it is now part of the Walt Disney Company. Still, Miramax claims to be "independent" (that is, of Disney) — or so the co-chairman, the flamboyant Harvey Weinstein, insists, noting that Miramax is autonomous in matters of production and distribution and can pursue cooperative ventures with other studios without getting Disney's approval. For example, *Shakespeare in Love* (1998) was a coproduction between Miramax and Universal; *The Hours* (2002), between Miramax and Paramount. Although *Gangs of New York* (2002) and *Chicago* (2002) were released under the Miramax banner, they were not really independent films like *The Passion of the Christ*; if one were to ask, "Did Miramax produce either film on its own?" the answer would be "no." Obtaining accurate information about movie financing is virtually impossible, since the industry becomes tight-lipped when it comes to divulging costs and profits (gross or net). But the credits speak for themselves: Seven production companies, including Miramax, were involved in financing *Gangs of New York*, which Miramax distributed in the United States; Miramax was one of three companies responsible for *Chicago*, which it also distributed in the United States. Are both films "independent productions"? It is difficult to say, but the production values are a good indication: both films, especially *Gangs of New York*, epitomize big-budget moviemaking and star power (Leonardo di Caprio and Cameron Diaz in *Gangs*; Renée Zellweger in *Chicago*) — hardly the values usually associated with an "indie" movie.

- *My Big Fat Greek Wedding* (2001) was an independent film without very recognizable names that became a crossover hit, attracting audiences that would ordinarily bypass independent films in favor of standard Hollywood fare. Budgeted at $5 million, *Greek Wedding* grossed over $100 million. According to the ads, the movie was an IFC Films release. IFC, however, was the distributor. The film itself was the result of a joint venture between Gold Circle Films, which provided what in the business is known as P & A (Print & Advertising), thus acquiring the North American distribution rights; MPH Entertainment; HBO; and Playtone, Tom Hanks and his wife Rita Wilson's company.[3] Hanks and Wilson became involved in the production after Wilson, a screenwriter of Greek descent, saw Nia Vardalos perform her one-person show about her eccentric Greek-American family in Los Angeles and encouraged her to turn her act into a screenplay. Vardalos did — with herself in the leading role. An independent film? Given its production history, it could be nothing else.

The major studios have created specialty divisions for producing independent films and distributing those they have acquired, known as "pickups," thus increasing their output and perhaps gaining some prestige if the releases find favor with the critics. Sony Pictures has Sony Pictures Classics; Twentieth Century-Fox, Fox Searchlight; Paramount, Paramount Classics; Warner Bros., Warner Independent Pictures. Compare, for example, Fox's *Moulin Rouge* (2001) and Fox Searchlight's release, *Bend It like Beckham* (2002). The former is unmistakably a studio film, lavishly produced and photographed, starring Nicole Kidman. The latter is a small British film without recognizable actors. Although *Beckham* found a mass audience, as it deserved, it was never intended to be anything other than a Fox Searchlight acquisition.

Far from Heaven (2002) and *The Pianist* (2002) came out under the Focus Features trademark. In Hollywood, Focus Features is considered an indie. However, Focus is the specialty films arm of Vivendi Universal, the present corporate parent of Universal Pictures. Trade publications regard Focus Features as an independent company in the same way that they do Miramax. *Far from Heaven* and *The Pianist* feature relatively well-known actors (Julianne Moore and Dennis Quaid in *Far from Heaven*, Adrien Brody in *The Pianist*). Both films had high budgets. Are they indies? To the *Hollywood Reporter*, yes. To the industry, yes. In the same way as *Greek Wedding*? Hardly. *Greek Wedding* did not have a conglomerate like Vivendi Universal behind it.

As an executive at the former Artisan Entertainment, which distributed *The Blair Witch Project*, once remarked, "We are all independents today, and at the same time no one is independent."[4] Every filmmaker is dependent on financing, whether it comes from one's own pocket, a bank, a studio, or friends. Once the money is available, the next step is to make the movie as envisioned; if that happens, a filmmaker can claim to be "independent" in the sense of having realized his or her intentions.

As you can see, independent films are incredibly diverse. There are good, mediocre, and unbelievably bad movies that can either be studio releases or independent films. No one can claim that independent cinema is superior to mainstream cinema, but only that independent films generally offer an experience quite different from the typical Hollywood product. John Sayles's *Passion Fish* (1992), a well-regarded independent film, has the texture of a short story. After an accident leaves soap opera star May-Alice (Mary McDonnell) paralyzed, she becomes an embittered woman and a potential alcoholic. Her caregiver, Chantelle (Alfre Woodard), refuses to allow May-Alice to succumb to self-pity. To say that nothing happens in the film is untrue. Actually, much happens, but it is internal because the change is psychological. In the final scene, the two women are in a rowboat on a lake. Although May-Alice can return to the soap (with her disability becoming part of the character), she refuses to become a plot peg. She realizes that Chantelle needs her, just as she needs Chantelle. Is there a resolution? Is closure reached? The final image is of May-Alice and Chantelle in a boat that is not moving toward the shore; if it were, we would feel real closure. But Sayles is suggesting that there has been a resolution: two people have made a decision affecting each of them—for how long is uncertain. If *Passion Fish* seems open-ended, it is because Sayles has caught the certainty of a commitment as well as the uncertainty of its permanence.

International Film

The early 1950s were dire years for the American movie business. A familiar scenario was occurring throughout the country. A local movie theater would be functioning on a Saturday night. The next day, the marquee would be bare. Soon, the theater would become a drugstore or a food market. Movie attendance dropped from 90 million in 1946, then a banner year for the industry, to almost half that ten years later. Hollywood began to take a "bigger is better" approach to try to win back the audiences that it had lost to television. First there were 3-D movies, which required audiences to wear Polaroid glasses with cardboard frames to experience the illusion of depth. The first 3-D film, *Bwana Devil* (1953), startled audiences, especially when a snake, its tongue flickering, slithered down a tree and, so it seemed, on to the viewer. Next came attempts to expand the size of the screen; thus, the standard format of 1.33:1 (the old **aspect ratio** in which the screen was approximately $1\frac{1}{3}$ times as wide as it was high) underwent various changes from 2.5:1 ($2\frac{1}{2}$ times as wide as it was high) to 1.85:1 (almost twice as wide as it was high), which is now standard in the United States.[5]

Far from taking film seriously, for the most part American intellectuals took a dim view of "the movies." Few academics at the time would have believed that film study would become a discipline, as rigorous in its own way as any object of study. That mentality began to change as more international filmmakers arrived on the scene, validating the art of film. What were called "foreign films" in the 1950s and 1960s captured the attention of academics as well as serious undergraduates, who had written off American movies as the cinema of the marketplace.

Shortly after World War II ended in 1945, international films began to be shown with some regularity in American movie theaters. Until that time, they had been seen primarily in major cities like New York, where there were a few movie houses that specialized in such films; or in communities that supported occasional showings of non–English language films in their neighborhood theaters.

After the war, Americans were exposed to an entirely different kind of moviemaking. The films that came out of Italy between 1944 and the early 1950s, now termed *Italian neorealism*, were shot on the streets, in apartments, trattorias, and so forth, since there were no soundstages in Rome. The rubble left by the war provided an authenticity that no Hollywood studio could replicate. These films often dealt with survival and loss: the plight of women working in the Po Valley rice fields was shown in *Bitter Rice* (1948); a father whose bicycle is stolen, making it virtually impossible for him to find work, constituted the story line of *The Bicycle Thief* (1947); street children struggling to survive on their own were depicted in *Shoeshine* (1946). Many of these films did not have happy endings and thus had a sobering effect on audiences that expected such endings.

American intellectuals were drawn to European cinema because of the profundity of so many of the films, particularly those of Swedish director Ingmar Bergman, whose work had the richness and density of great literature. Bergman's films lent themselves to serious discussion. One could argue at length about such Bergman masterpieces as *The Seventh Seal* (1957) and *Wild Strawberries* (1957), which are not easily summarized. Superficially, *The Seventh Seal* deals with a medieval knight returning from the Crusades and the various people he encounters just as the Black Plague is breaking out. But on a much deeper level the film is about the knight's crisis of faith, his quest for God, his attempt to find some meaning in life, and his eventual acceptance of his mortality. It is also about innocence versus experience, life versus death, and reason versus faith. In *Wild Strawberries* a doctor is traveling by car to receive an honorary degree. But the trip is really a death trip. The film abounds in images of death: smashed eyeglasses; a pocket watch without hands; a hearse that loses a wheel, causing a coffin to fall onto the street. The film moves between past and present, between the visionary and the real, a time of innocence and of innocence betrayed. The subtleties of such serious topics were not easily handled by mid-twentieth-century Hollywood.

Bergman's films are not what, in Hollywood, are called "high concept"—a misleading term for a movie that can be summed up in twenty-five words or less or described with familiar titles: "*Lake Placid* (1999) is *Jaws* (1975) with crocodiles"; "*Gladiator* (1999) is an R-rated *Fall of the Roman Empire* (1963) with decapitations." Many international films are not so easily classified; they resist the kind of labels that studio executives use when discussing a film they plan to put into production: "erotic thriller," "action-adventure," "slasher," "chick flick."

Today, international film, like independent film, often resists pigeonholing. For example, note how the topic of rape is handled in the French film *Humanité* (1999). The movie opens with the discovery of the body of an eleven-year-old girl who has been brutally murdered and raped. Yet we never witness the act, only its aftermath, suggesting that the film goes beyond a child's violation and murder. *Humanité* is essentially a study in bleakness, set in a town in northern France where people lead aimless lives. One could easily imagine a studio executive, too busy to read the script but intrigued by the subject matter, turning it over to an assistant and saying, "Find out who the rapist is and why he did it." The rapist's identity is discovered at the end, yet we never discover why he did it. The film is not a whodunit; *Humanité* depicts the impact of a tragedy on people whose lives are too empty to allow them to respond to it as they should. To sum up *Humanité* as a film about the search for a child's rapist is to minimize the real point of the film.

French cinema, of course, is only one of many kinds of cinema. The international film scene, once almost exclusively European (with the exception of Japan and India, where the films of Akira Kurosawa and Satyajit Ray, respectively, made their way into art houses), has now become truly global, making the word "foreign" obsolete. You have only to check the Sunday Arts & Leisure section of the *New York Times*, with its array of movie listings that makes New York seem like a cinematic United Nations. In the summer of 2003 one could see British, Indian, French, Italian, German, Russian, Italian, Chinese, Japanese, Spanish, and Bulgarian films.

Still, there is always a temptation to reduce the films of a particular country to a list of conventions. This is like subjecting a literary movement, such as the Romantic movement, to a list of characteristic features applicable to any nineteenth-century poem. It does not always work; Wordsworth is not Byron, and Shelley is not Coleridge. Rather, you should try to discover what makes an international film unique, even if it seems to be similar to the kinds of movies that you know.

Take, for example, **Bollywood,** the term for the popular cinema of Bombay, India, in which musical sequences are common. They even occur in a drama like *Armaan* (2003), in which one of the main characters dies of a heart attack. Song-and-dance sequences are a convention of the Bollywood film, just as car crashes are a convention of American action films and grisly murders of slasher films. The typical Bollywood film recycles familiar plot points from Western films; apart from song-and-dance sequences, there are love triangles, unyielding fathers, star-crossed lovers, and an array of villains ranging from criminals to womanizers.[6]

If Mira Nair's *Monsoon Wedding* (2002) resonated so deeply with American audiences, it was largely because most people can identify with the problems involved in preparing for a wedding. The impending wedding is a familiar plot peg, seen in *Father of the Bride* (1950, 1991) and *Betsy's Wedding* (1990). Often the bride bolts from the altar when she is about to say "I do" and rushes off to her true love, as in *It Happened One Night* (1934), or the bride explains that she cannot say "I do" because she loves someone else, expecting the bridegroom to understand, as in *Cover Girl* (1944); or the bride, realizing she still loves her ex-husband, who luckily is nearby, goes through with the wedding — but with her ex-, not her fiancé, so the guests will not be disappointed, as in *The Philadelphia Story* (1940).

In *Monsoon Wedding*, we do not have the typical American mother and father about to marry off their daughter. Unlike the Hollywood wedding movie, *Monsoon Wedding* involves an arranged marriage and includes a case of sexual abuse that had been kept secret and finally erupts amid the wedding preparations.

Monsoon Wedding (2002), Triptych: The cast (top left); director and screenwriter Mira Nair (bottom left); bride and groom Vasundhara Das and Pavin Dabas (right). *(Courtesy USA Films)*

In an American wedding movie, English is the vehicle of communication. In *Monsoon Wedding*, most of the characters know English but do not always speak it, alternating between English, Hindi, and Bengali. In American films, a major fear is a wedding in the rain. In *Betsy's Wedding*, a reception in a tent is interrupted by a heavy downpour that leaves the guests, including the father and his newly wedded daughter, dancing in the mud. In *Monsoon Wedding*, the rain is a symbol of renewal and fertility; it does not mar the "perfect day" that American parents want for their children and the bride wants for her wedding. Instead, rain is nature's way of making the day even more perfect by washing away—at least momentarily—the problems that existed previously.

There will always be those who patronize only Hollywood movies with big-name stars, those who vary their moviegoing with independent and international films, and those who avoid Hollywood releases altogether, believing independent and international films have greater depth. Those in the first and third categories are limiting their moviegoing. The best films, regardless of origin, take us on a journey into a realm where we have never been. Restricting one's moviegoing to a particular kind of film is the equivalent of reading only one genre of literature. Film encompasses a huge variety of texts, all of which deserve some degree of examination.

Shakespeare (Joseph Fiennes) and his muse, the fictional Viola (Gwyneth Paltrow), in the multiple-Oscar-winning *Shakespeare in Love* (1998). *(Courtesy MOMA/FSA)*

Examining a Film Text

Before we begin to anatomize the different elements that appear in all types of film—be they narrative, independent, international—let's examine a moment in film to see how those elements weave together into a single text.

Like an opera, the opening of *Shakespeare in Love* (1998) employs many forms of art: print, dialogue, music, camera movement, settings, costumes, and performance. Even before the action begins, a printed title, "London—Summer 1593," appears on the screen in white lettering on a black background. Another title follows in the same monochrome: "In the glory days of the Elizabethan theatre two playhouses were fighting it out for writers and audiences." Then, without our noticing it, black and white changes to color, and soothing music is heard—not period music, but, rather, music that transcends time, evoking neither present nor past. Against a blue sky, a third title materializes: "North of the city was the Curtain Theatre, home to England's most famous actor, Richard Burbage." As the camera slowly descends from the sky, the thatched roof of what turns out to be a typical Elizabethan theater comes into view, along with more text: "Across the river was the competition, built by Philip Henslowe, a businessman with a cash flow problem." The competition is the Rose.

The camera is now inside the Rose, gradually revealing a theater with three galleries and an apron stage. Even if we did not know that Henslowe's theater has been reconstructed with painstaking accuracy, the detail confirms it. The thatched roof covered only the galleries, leaving the groundlings, who paid a penny for what today would be called standing room, exposed to the elements. Thus, the theater has a dirt floor, on which we see the tattered poster of a play that was produced there.

A scream is heard as the camera zooms over to a curtained area behind which Henslowe is being tortured because he has been unable to pay his bills. The opening dialogue is typical of what is heard throughout the film. The language is not exactly Elizabethan, but it has an authentic ring because the actors look and speak as if they were in London in 1593. Once Henslowe tells his creditor that he has a new play by Shakespeare, the music returns, as if to assure us that all will be well.

Finally, the film proper begins after the names of the production companies — Miramax, Universal, and Bedford Falls — come on. Someone with ink-stained hands and ink-encrusted nails is practicing his signature. From the various spellings (Will Shagsbeard, W. Shakspur), we conclude that it is Shakespeare. Then, in the same script, the movie's title appears on the screen.

The setting now changes to a marketplace where vendors ply their wares. Henslowe makes his way through the teeming crowd to Shakespeare's untidy room. Shakespeare's first words could not be more authentic: "Doubt thou the stars are fire, doubt that the sun doth move." Even though the audience may not know that the lines are from *Hamlet* (II, 2), they sound as if they were written by Shakespeare, and that is what matters.

Shakespeare owes Henslowe a play, but the playwright is suffering from writer's block and needs to consult a therapist, a combination pharmacist-alchemist-astrologer. On the way to his "weekly session," Shakespeare hears a Puritan preacher fulminating against two of London's best-known playhouses, the Curtain and the Rose, and calling for "a plague on both their houses." Shakespeare takes note of the phrase "a plague on both their houses," filing it away in his memory. Anyone familiar with *Romeo and Juliet* would appreciate the allusion supplied by the script's coauthor, Tom Stoppard, one of Britain's best-known playwrights.

In the therapist's office, the camera slowly begins circling the couch, executing a 180-degree turn that ends with Shakespeare's being face-to-face with the therapist, who, true to his profession, is taking notes. In this scene, the director John Madden has chosen to make the camera an active participant in the narrative, not a passive recorder of the action.

Within the first ten minutes of the film, we have been introduced to a cross-section of Tudor society. The merchants wear aprons and caps; the gentlemen, doublets and circular collars called ruffs. At the queen's palace at Whitehall, where Shakespeare's *Two Gentlemen of Verona* is to be performed, we see the nobles, splendidly dressed—but none more so than Queen Elizabeth (Judi Dench), whose richly embroidered gown is so massive that she looks imprisoned in it, and who, given the condition of her teeth (another historically accurate touch), could have used a good dentist. The lords and ladies look more comfortably dressed; the gown of Viola (Gwyneth Paltrow), in particular, has fluidity and grace. If the Whitehall audience is dressed more fashionably than the theatergoers in the galleries of the Rose, the reason is that *Two Gentlemen of Verona* is not being performed at a theater but in a banqueting hall for the queen and her guests. Elizabeth, taken with a bit of comic relief involving a dog, laughs raucously and throws the animal a sweet.

Suddenly, we are aware that the sound has been muted, as often happens in movies when a character sees someone so captivating that he or she becomes oblivious to everyone else. Shakespeare has just caught sight of Viola—a typical case of love entering through the eyes, which is a recurring theme in Elizabethan poetry and validated in *Romeo and Juliet*. The camera cooperates in the mood by reducing the rest of the characters to a blur so that Viola stands out as the object of Shakespeare's attention. The movie continues, with the audience properly set up for a romance set in a specific time period.

In the opening scenes of *Shakespeare in Love*, print, setting, costumes, color, camera movement, and performance mesh seamlessly. The same elements that make up the opening keep reconstituting themselves throughout the film, making *Shakespeare in Love* a true film text.

NOTES

1. John Howard Lawson, *Film: The Creative Process* (New York: Hill & Wang, 1967), 292.
2. James Naremore, *Filmguide to Psycho* (Bloomington: Indiana University Press, 1977).
3. *Variety*, 16–22 September 2002: 9.
4. Stephen Galloway, "When Worlds Collide," *Hollywood Reporter*, Independent Producers & Distributors edition, August 2000: 9.
5. Most film texts explain the various widescreen processes (Cinerama, CinemaScope, VistaVision, and so forth); see, for example, David A. Cook, *A History of the Narrative Film*, 3rd ed. (New York: Norton, 1996), 463–479.
6. See Sheila J. Nayar, "Dreams, Dharma, Mrs. Doubtfire," *Journal of Popular Film and Television* 31 (Summer 2003): 73–82, who illustrates how Bollywood incorporated plot devices from Hollywood movies.

CHAPTER 2

Graphics and Sound

A movie's running time and the speed at which the action progresses are among the many decisions that are made before or after production. Who has made these decisions is not the point; often we do not know who was responsible for a particular image or line of dialogue. Some directors— Woody Allen and Robert Altman, for example—allow actors to improvise certain scenes. Several writers worked on the *Casablanca* (1942) screenplay, but the final line, "Louis, I think this is the beginning of a beautiful friendship," never appeared in any of the drafts. It was the inspiration of the producer, Hal Wallis, who also decided that the film (originally called *Everybody Comes to Rick's*) would be entitled *Casablanca*.

Although Victor Fleming is credited as the director of *Gone with the Wind* (1939), Sam Wood and George Cukor also worked on the film. But none of these directors was responsible for the impressive burning-of-Atlanta sequence; that was the work of the film's art director, William Cameron Menzies. Thus, in writing about film, we use the general term *filmmaker* because it is often difficult to know who was responsible for what effect.

Examples of Studio Logos

TOP RIGHT: Universal's globe. Universal is now a subsidiary of MCA (Music Corporation of America), a diversified entertainment and leisure company. *(Copyright by Universal Pictures, a Division of Universal City Studios, Inc. Courtesy MCA Publishing Rights, a Division of MCA, Inc.)*

BOTTOM RIGHT: A 1940s version of the Columbia logo, which is only slightly different today. *(Courtesy Sony Pictures Entertainment and MOMA/FSA)*

Graphics

As many different people as there are making decisions when producing a film, there are even more different decisions that can be made. Such decisions include where and how to use graphics—the combination of print and design. Graphics can appear in films as logos, titles, credits, or wherever a filmmaker chooses to convey information through the printed word.

Logos

Every film is intended to begin and end with a certain image. In American films, the first image to appear on the screen is generally the studio's logo or the distributor's name.

A logo is a studio's trademark. Although studios have certainly changed since Hollywood's golden age of the 1930s and 1940s, the logos of such studios as MGM, Warner Bros., Columbia, Paramount, Twentieth Century-Fox, and Universal have either remained the same or have been only slightly modified. Universal's globe still spins in the sky, but it is no longer encircled by an airplane as it was in the early 1930s; nor is it made of Plexiglas, as it was from

A 1940s version of the Paramount logo, which still remains a star-spangled mountain. *(Courtesy Paramount Pictures and AMPAS/FSA)*

1936 to 1946. Columbia's Lady with a Torch is intact, though the torch shines more brightly and the lady is slimmer.

In *Transparent Things*, Vladimir Nabokov claimed that contained within each word is its own history; if this is so, we might also say that encapsulated within each logo is the studio's history. In the 1930s and 1940s, moviegoers knew the difference between the studios. When they heard MGM's lion roar its greeting, they knew they could expect a well-produced film with an outstanding cast; at that time, MGM was Hollywood's biggest studio, boasting of "more stars than there are in the heavens." When an audience saw the Republic eagle, they knew they would be seeing a B-movie; Republic was known for "programmers" (for example, Gene Autry and Roy Rogers westerns)—movies that filled out the second half of a double bill. Whether they are studying films of the past or attending those of the present, students of film should be able to distinguish between the studios.

Although filmmakers have no control over the logo, they often try to integrate it with the film so that it is not merely a trademark. Steven Spielberg's *Indiana Jones and the Temple of Doom* (1985) opens with Paramount's snowcapped mountain, which appears concurrently with the Indiana Jones theme on the soundtrack. The combination of logo (Paramount's mountain) and music (the familiar Indiana Jones theme) says that what follows is both a Paramount picture and an Indiana Jones movie.

Moulin Rouge (2001) identifies itself as a Twentieth Century-Fox film in an unusual way. Since most of the action takes place in the legendary Paris music hall of the same name at the turn of the twentieth century, we first see a red curtain that parts to reveal the Fox logo. Another Fox release, *Down with Love* (2003), does it differently. Set in 1962, the film is a throwback to the romantic comedies of the 1960s, especially the Doris Day–Rock Hudson *Pillow Talk* (1960) that inspired it. However, *Down with Love* does not open with the contemporary Twentieth Century-Fox logo, which is much more massive and imposing than the earlier versions, but with the kind that movie-goers would have seen in the 1960s.

In the Universal release *Waterworld* (1995), the logo is directly related to the film's setting: the earth sometime in the future, when it is completely covered with water. The first image to appear is the blue Universal globe in a sky of much darker blue. Gradually the globe begins to fall from the sky, filling the screen with an expanse of blue that resembles an ocean. Next comes the title, *Waterworld*; there are no further credits until the end of the movie.

Has the moviegoer missed anything by arriving just as *Waterworld* appears on the screen? Nothing in terms of plot, but certainly something in terms of a filmmaker's desire to establish a mood by using the studio's logo as more than a trademark.

Main Titles, Credits, Precredits, Sequences, and End Credits

The main reason for being seated when the movie begins is that it is impossible to know exactly how it will begin. Take, for example, the **main title** — the film's title and, usually, the opening credits. If you miss the main title when it consists only of the film's name, cast, key personnel, producer, and director, you will not have missed any of the plot. But you will have missed a certain part of the film — a part that is often imaginatively executed. Main titles can be quite creative and even witty. In Preston Sturges's *The Lady Eve* (1941), in which a female cardsharp pursues a timid herpetologist, the main title appears as a snake slithering across the screen; in Billy Wilder's *The Seven Year Itch* (1955), the main title — designed by Saul Bass, who is renowned for his main titles — consists of credits popping out of a jack-in-the-box. *Psycho's* main title was also designed by Saul Bass; here, the credits intersect, coming onto the screen horizontally and vertically as the actors' first and last names split apart. The main title prepares the viewer for a movie about a split personality, as well as one in which slashing and cutting figure prominently.

The main title of Hitchcock's *Vertigo* (1958), created by John Whitney and Saul Bass, is one of the most evocative in all film. First, a woman's eye looks out at us from a reddish haze. The camera then moves down to her mouth and back to her eyes. The title, *Vertigo*, seems to emanate from one of her eyes. Next, reddish and blue-green spirals spin out of the eye, until, by the end of the main title, the spirals have disappeared, and superimposed above the eye are the words "Directed by Alfred Hitchcock." The *Vertigo* main title was not simply flashy artwork; it was integral to a film in which a man becomes obsessed with a woman who resembles his lost love. The relationship literally spirals out of control, resulting in tragedy.

A main title can also be educational. *The Front* (1975), which deals with one of the most shameful periods in American history (the McCarthy-inspired

TOP LEFT: *Cry of the City* (Robert Siodmak, 1948) opens with the Twentieth Century-Fox logo. *(Courtesy Margaret Herrick Library of the Academy of Motion Picture Arts and Sciences)*

BOTTOM LEFT: After the logo, the main title begins with the movie's name, often against an appropriate background. *(Courtesy MOMA/FSA)*

witch-hunt as it affected television in the early 1950s), begins with a 1950s montage of film clips of the Korean War; Marilyn Monroe's wedding to Joe DiMaggio; President Eisenhower and his wife, Mamie; and Ethel and Julius Rosenberg (whose execution as Soviet spies is still a controversial subject) being led away by the police—all to the musical accompaniment of "Young at Heart" as sung by Frank Sinatra.

Although a main title basically functions as a program or a playbill, it can also establish the mood of the film, especially when it is artistically executed and appropriately orchestrated. Missing a main title like *Psycho*'s, which is accompanied by Bernard Herrmann's tense musical score, is like arriving at a performance of Wagner's opera *Die Meistersinger* after the prelude, which is a major piece of music in its own right. And to miss the main title of Martin Scorsese's *The Age of Innocence* (1993), designed by Saul and Elaine Bass and consisting of roses opening to the sun, is to miss a title that is both elegant and prefigurative. Here, the main title not only implies a privileged existence but also anticipates the way flowers are used both as decorations and as expressions of love.

Sometimes a film dispenses with graphic design, starting immediately with a **credits sequence,** in which the credits are integrated with the main action. *The Four Seasons* (1981) opens with a credits sequence in which one couple picks up two other couples in their car. The credits come on during the sequence. By the time the sequence is over, and the last credit has appeared, we have been introduced to three couples whose trips together constitute the plot.

The Hours (2002) depicts one day in the lives of three women — one, a historical figure; the other two, fictional characters — in three different years. The historical figure is the author Virginia Woolf in 1923; the second is a Los Angeles wife and mother in 1951; and the third is a New York book editor in 2001. The credits sequence starts with a prologue depicting Virginia Woolf's suicide in 1941, after which the title, *The Hours,* comes on the screen. More credits follow as the scene switches to 1951 Los Angeles, then back to 1923 and on to 2001. The final credits coincide with the end of the sequence, as each woman awakens to a day that will radically change her life. To miss the credits sequence is to miss the ingenious way in which the lives of three women have been so well integrated that they seem to be unfolding at the same time, rather than in three different years.

Sometimes a credits sequence involves an image or an object that takes on greater meaning in the course of the film. As the *Forrest Gump* (1994) credits start to roll, a feather floats through the air, eventually resting on Forrest's (Tom Hanks) left shoe. Forrest retrieves the feather and places it in a children's book that he has been reading. Anyone who was not present during the sequence will not appreciate the ending, in which Forrest reopens the book and the feather is released, returning to the sky from which it originally fell. The feather symbolizes the interconnection of chance and destiny, which is one of the film's themes.

Sometimes a film opens cold with a **precredits sequence** — a sort of prologue preceding the credits. In this kind of sequence, the title does not appear until after the sequence is over. If such a technique seems like a gimmick, remember that film is an art form, but it is also a business. And just as businesses experiment with various ways of attracting customers, so does Hollywood. One way to get an audience's attention is to vary the logo/main title/film proper format and offer the unexpected.

Exactly who was the first to alter the format is unknown, but film historians tend to credit Lewis Milestone, who directed the movie version of John Steinbeck's *Of Mice and Men* (1939). The film opens with neither logo nor title but with two men in flight, followed by a posse. The men manage to hop a freight train and scramble into an open boxcar, joining others riding the rails in search of work during the Great Depression. Someone pulls the door shut; then verses from Robert Burns's poem "To a Mouse," which inspired the title, appear, as if they had been inscribed on the door. The key phrase, "Of Mice and Men," is highlighted, thus becoming the title. The remaining credits follow.

A filmmaker might choose a precredits sequence to keep the audience guessing about the identity of the characters or the nature of some pivotal event that is later dramatized. After the Twentieth Century-Fox logo, *Phone Call from a Stranger* (1951) begins with a man rushing out of his home in the rain and entering a waiting cab. "Airport, hurry!" he instructs the driver. Then the credits come on. The man becomes one of the main characters, and the plot hinges on a flight during a rainstorm. *Picnic* (1955) begins with Columbia's logo, the Lady with the Torch. However, the title does not come on the screen until we see a man jump off a freight car. He seems to be a drifter; it is only after he washes himself off in a nearby reservoir that the title comes on the screen. The man, Hal (William Holden), becomes a pivotal character. In *Hustle*'s (1975) precredits sequence, a body is washed up on a beach; we expect to learn the corpse's identity—and eventually do.

Another reason for choosing a precredits sequence is to capture the viewer's attention with the hope of sustaining it for the film's duration. Thus some filmmakers deliberately attempt to draw the viewer into the action at the outset. After the Columbia logo, *Postcards from the Edge* (1994) begins without title or credits. The setting seems to be a Latin American country; a female tourist is stopped at customs, then brought to a police station, where she is brutalized. The viewer is shocked at this treatment but then discovers that the tourist is an actress and her beating is merely a scene in a movie being shot. Once the sequence ends, the title appears, and *Postcards from the Edge*—which dramatizes the difficult relationship between the actress in the precredits sequence and her famous mother—starts.

Some films begin without a credits or precredits sequence. Anyone who missed *The Matrix* (1999) and was unfamiliar with the plot was out of luck if he or she decided to see the sequel, *The Matrix Reloaded* (2003). Immediately after the Warner Bros. logo, the title appears, and the movie begins without credits—or, more important, without any kind of prologue. John Sayles's *Sunshine State* (2002) has an even more radical opening. After the name of the distributor, Sony Pictures Classics, comes on the screen, we see a boy setting fire to what looks like a float. His action will eventually be explained, but there will be no title or credits until the end. You cannot accuse John Sayles of breaking the rules, because there are no rules, only traditions. And when tradition is ignored in favor of a new approach, something nontraditional is the result.

If viewers lose important information by arriving after the film has formally begun, they may also lose significant elements by leaving before it has formally ended. In the 1930–1950 period, **end credits** consisted only of the cast of characters. Today the end credits acknowledge everyone from the star's fitness trainer to the caterers. While comics joke about end credits being longer than the movie and mock such job titles as **"gaffer"** and **"best boy,"** the end credits show the complexity of contemporary filmmaking and prove conclusively that film is a collaborative art in which the gaffer (chief electrician) and best boy (the gaffer's first assistant) are among the collaborators.[1]

Since the end credits are prepared by the studio's legal department and must follow a specific format, they do not figure among the filmmaker's decisions. Filmmakers, however, have learned to use the end credits to the movie's advantage so that they are not just the cue to exit the theater. End credits can also function in the following ways:

- *As epilogue.* In *Sweet Liberty* (1986), which depicts the filming of a book about the American Revolution, the end credits are interspersed with scenes from the movie's premiere. Until the very end, the author (Alan Alda) is appalled at what is being done to his book. During the end credits, he is interviewed by a reporter who congratulates him on writing history as it should be written. At that moment, a disclaimer appears on the screen to the effect that any similarity between the film and American history is purely coincidental. Anyone who leaves during the end credits misses the point that in the movies, historical truth may have to be sacrificed for the sake of entertainment.

- *As an informational or educational source.* *The Front* is a highly accurate portrayal of blacklisting in the 1950s. The end credits not only list the actors, the director, and the writer but also identify those participants who themselves had been blacklisted—the actors Herschel Bernardi, Zero Mostel, and Lloyd Gough; the screenwriter Walter Bernstein; and the director Martin Ritt. Since *Chaplin* (1992) is based on fact, the end credits consist of shots of the main actors, along with a brief account of what happened to the historical figures they portrayed. The end credits of *Rumble in the Bronx* (1996) show audiences the risks actors face when they perform their own stunts. Outtakes, or shots that were deleted from the movie, show martial arts actor Jackie Chan sustaining bodily injuries while making the film.

- *As a musical postlude.* The end credits of Woody Allen's *Radio Days* (1987), which is set in 1941, are orchestrated with the music of the 1940s, thereby allowing a nostalgic mood to linger. During the end credits of Martin Scorsese's *GoodFellas* (1989), the popular song "My Way" is heard, suggesting that the narrator, who from childhood has aspired to be a gangster, has no regrets about his profession. Those who automatically got up and left during the end credits of *Postcards from the Edge* missed the opportunity to hear Meryl Streep, who is known primarily as a dramatic actress, deliver a completely uninhibited rendition of "I'm Checkin' Out."

- *As postcredits epilogue.* *Priscilla, Queen of the Desert* (1994), which recounts the adventures of three drag queens touring the Australian outback, has not only end credits worth staying for but an additional scene as well. The end credits roll as one of the performers lip-synchs "Save the Best for Last." When the credits are over, a short scene comes on that does not add to the narrative but is a delightful touch in its own way. Early in the film, the trio launches a kite made of pink crepe paper into the sky. In what can only be called a post-credits epilogue, the kite lands somewhere in Japan, piquing the curiosity of the locals who discover it.

The end credits are similar to a curtain call, except that in a theater the cast—not the crew—takes the bows; in a movie, everybody does. A serious theatergoer would never leave during a curtain call, and a serious moviegoer should not leave during the film equivalent of that. One might argue that such curtain calls are extraneous to the plot. That may be true, but they are not extraneous to the films in which they appear. The process of making a film entails many decisions. A filmmaker may choose to begin with a main title that consists of nothing but words on a plain background, an elaborate main title that foreshadows the action or includes part of it, or no title at all. End credits may simply satisfy legal requirements or may add to the plot. No matter how a film begins or ends, it should be seen as it was intended to be seen—in its entirety. To miss the titles and credits is to miss part of the text.

Opening Titles and End Titles

There are titles other than main titles. A **title** is simply printed matter that appears in a film. Often, after the main title, there is an **opening title** that can function as:

- *A time-place designation.* "Shanghai, 1935" is the opening title of *Indiana Jones and the Temple of Doom*; "Phoenix, Arizona. Friday, December the Eleventh. Two Forty-Three, P.M." is *Psycho*'s quite specific opening title. Even more precise is the opening title of Gus Van Sant's *Psycho* remake (1998), which changes the date and specifies the day: "Friday, December 11, 1998."
- *A confirmation of the film's authenticity.* "This film is based on a true story" is from *GoodFellas*; "Inspired by a true story" is from *Catch Me If You Can* (2002), which was suggested by the autobiography of con artist Frank Abagnale.
- *A preface explaining an event with which the audience might be unfamiliar.* Although most World War II moviegoers knew the history of the conflict, later generations might not. Thus, in Steven Spielberg's *Empire of the Sun* (1987), the opening title explains the significance

of December 7, 1941, and, more important, what Japanese aggression meant to British subjects living in Shanghai. *Shakespeare in Love* (1998) is prefaced by three titles that explain the state of the theatre in the late sixteenth century.

- *An epigraph* (literary excerpt) *or a quotation.* When Warner Bros. was about to release *Little Caesar* (1930), the first major crime movie of the sound era, the studio expected a backlash from groups that would claim the film glorified criminals. Anticipating such criticism (which happened anyway), the studio added an opening title from Saint Matthew's gospel: "For all they that take the sword shall perish with the sword."

   George Santayana's "Those who do not remember the past are doomed to relive it" is the epigraph to *Lacombe, Lucien* (1974), which shows how a French boy's apathy has made him a pawn of the Nazis. The opening title of *King Kong* (1933) — "'And the Beast looked upon the face of Beauty and lo! his hand was stayed from killing and from that day forward he was as one dead.' — An Old Arabian Proverb" — invites us to look at the movie in terms of the proverb and to regard *King Kong* as a version of Beauty and the Beast.

- *A disclaimer.* Since *The Public Enemy* (1931) was even more violent than *Little Caesar*, Warner Bros. added a disclaimer, stating that the film was intended "to honestly depict an environment that exists today in a certain strata of society, rather than glorify the hoodlum or the criminal." *Hennessy* (1975), which dramatizes an attempt to blow up the Houses of Parliament on Guy Fawkes Day, incorporates newsreel footage of the royal family. The opening title is quite explicit: "This motion picture incorporates extracts from a news film of the Queen at a State Opening of Parliament which, when photographed, was not intended for use in a fictional context." Similarly, the opening title of Martin Scorsese's *The Last Temptation of Christ* (1988) makes it clear that the film is based on a novel and is not a historical account of the life of Christ.

An opening title can be stationary, as in *Empire of the Sun*; it can also roll up or down the screen, in which case it is known as a **roll-up title** or a **crawl.** Roll-up titles were common in the serials of the 1930s and 1940s. To evoke that era, director George Lucas chose a roll-up title for *Star Wars* (1977), now one of the most famous and often-parodied examples of a roll-up title.

Just as an opening title can serve as a preface or a prologue, an **end title** can function as an epilogue. An end title is particularly useful as a means of informing the audience of the fate of the characters, especially if extending the action would prove anticlimactic, destroy the mood the ending was

The end title of the World War II documentary *Prelude to War* (Frank Capra, 1942). *(Courtesy National Archives)*

supposed to create, or, from a more pragmatic standpoint, send the film over budget.

At the end of Hitchcock's *The Wrong Man* (1957), which is based on a true incident, a musician's wife becomes mentally unbalanced after her husband is falsely accused of theft and imprisoned. The end title informs us that she was eventually cured and is living in Florida. The title is a bald statement of fact and nothing more; when it appears on the screen, it has the effect of a case stamped "Closed." Had Hitchcock shown the wife basking in the Florida sun, he would have shattered the film's somber mood. The title he chose, however, provides neither a happy ending nor a triumph for the wrong man, even though he is now free.

Dog Day Afternoon (1975) is a film about a Vietnam vet (Al Pacino) with two children who holds up a Brooklyn bank to finance a transsexual operation for his second wife — a man he married in a wedding ceremony complete with celebrant and bridesmaids. The film ends on a Kennedy Airport runway, a few feet from the jumbo jet the vet has ordered to fly him to Algeria. Then three titles appear on the screen without any fanfare, as if they were being typed by someone concerned only with the accuracy of the transcription, not with its implications: the vet is serving a twenty-year prison sentence; his first wife is on welfare; and his second wife has become a woman and is living in New York.

In Samuel Fuller's *Shock Corridor* (1963), the opening and end titles are identical: "Whom the gods wish to destroy, they first make mad." The double-duty quotation is appropriate for a movie about an ambitious reporter who feigns madness in order to solve a murder and ends up going mad himself. The end title of Martin Scorsese's *Kundun* (1997), a solidly researched film about the fourteenth Dalai Lama, is particularly moving: "The Dalai Lama has not yet returned to Tibet. He hopes one day to make the journey." *Kundun* ends in 1959 with the Dalai Lama, unable to accept a Tibet under Chinese Communist control, going into exile in India.

The opening and end titles of a Chinese film, Wong Kar-wai's *In the Mood for Love* (2000), complement each other. First, we read the following:

"It is a restless moment. Hong Kong. 1962." The restless are not only the characters (a man and a woman who discover that their spouses are having an affair with each other) but also the director, who wants both to evoke and to transcend the Hollywood model for movies of this kind. Wong Kar-wai would like us to think of the movies of the 1950–1960 period (for example, *September Affair*, 1950; *Love Is a Many-Splendored Thing*, 1955; *A Summer Place*, 1959; *Strangers When We Meet*, 1960), in which adultery was glamorously transformed into grand passion through exotic settings, lush photography, and romantic music. However, the end title makes it clear that 2000 is not 1962; Hong Kong is not Hollywood; and Wong Kar-wai has a profound knowledge of American movies as well as a style of his own: "That era has passed. Nothing that belongs to it exists anymore."

Intertitles

The silent film made great use of **intertitles**—printed material that appeared on the screen periodically during the course of the movie. The intertitle was one of the ways in which the silent filmmaker supplemented the narrative or clarified the action; it is also a reminder of film's early dependence on the printed word. D. W. Griffith used intertitles for a variety of purposes, not just to reproduce dialogue and identify characters. He used them (1) to attest to the accuracy of a particular setting: "An historical facsimile of Ford's Theater as on that night, exact in size and detail with recorded incidents, after Nicolay and Hay in *Lincoln, a History*" introduces the assassination-of-Lincoln sequence in *The Birth of a Nation*; (2) to comment on the action or to play on the audience's emotions: the intertitle "Dying, she gives her last little smile to a world that has been so unkind" accompanies the heroine's death in *Broken Blossoms* (1919); (3) to define terms with which the audience may be unfamiliar: *Pharisee* and *Sanhedrin* in the film *Intolerance* (1916); and (4) to reveal a character's thoughts: the intertitle "The Inspiration" appears after Ben Cameron sees some white children frighten black children with a sheet in *The Birth of a Nation*; the "inspiration" is the use of bedsheets to make the robes for the cross-burning Klansmen. Griffith treated intertitles as images, integrating them with the film so they would be part of the narrative.

    A Woman of Affairs (1928) shows how silent filmmakers used punctuation, especially the dash, to suggest how the lines would have been spoken:

> My nerves have gone to pieces—I'm going out—somewhere—I didn't mean to come here—I started driving—Why should a man—happy as David was—take his own life? David died—for decency.

Intertitles did not die with the advent of sound. Martin Scorsese used them in *Raging Bull* (1981) and *GoodFellas*, both of which are based on fact,

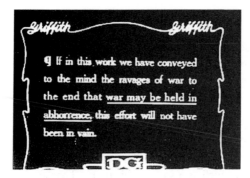

An intertitle from *The Birth of a Nation* (D. W. Griffith, 1915). Note the underscoring for emphasis and the DG trademark as a sign of authorship. *(Courtesy MOMA/FSA and Epoch Producing Corp.)*

to achieve a sense of authenticity. Each sequence in *Raging Bull,* which is told in flashback, is introduced by an intertitle ("New York, 1964"; "The Bronx, 1941"; "La Motta vs. Robinson, 1943"). Scorsese does the same in *GoodFellas* ("Brooklyn, 1953"; "June 11, 1970"; "Idlewild Airport, August 1963").

Woody Allen may well have chosen to use intertitles in *Hannah and Her Sisters* (1986) because, in addition to being an actor, a director, and a screenwriter, he is also a playwright and a short-story writer. Allen's stories are often vignettes, and *Hannah and Her Sisters* is a series of vignettes about three sisters. Thus, Allen segments the film, introducing each vignette with an intertitle that can be (1) a line of dialogue repeated in the segment (the opening intertitle, "God, she's beautiful!," is also the first line of dialogue, spoken offscreen); (2) a character introduction ("The Hypochondriac" introduces the Woody Allen character); (3) a vignette title ("The Abyss" is the intertitle of the episode in which Allen thinks he has a brain tumor); and (4) a quotation (" 'The only absolute knowledge attainable by man is that life is meaningless' — Tolstoy"). By using intertitles in so many different ways, Allen allies himself not only with the venerable tradition of the intertitle but also with the written word.

Since Philip Kaufman was both the screenwriter and the director of *The Unbearable Lightness of Being* (1988), he clearly intended the titles to serve a purpose. The film opens like a fairy tale. The first intertitle, "In Prague in 1968 there lived a young doctor named Tomas," is followed by a scene showing Tomas in a less than fairy-tale situation: making love to a nurse. The second intertitle, "But the woman who understood him best was Sabina," is followed by another lovemaking scene, this time between Tomas and Sabina. After the third intertitle, "Tomas was sent to a spa town to perform an operation," the film turns serious, as one might expect of a film about the Soviet-backed invasion of the former Czechoslovakia in 1968. The intertitles, with their storybook connotations, run counter to the erotic scenes that succeed them. Once the intertitles end, the eroticism continues, but within a historical, not a storybook, context.

Subtitles

The **subtitle** shares one of the main functions of the intertitle: the transmission of dialogue. Although subtitles—in which the translation of dialogue appears at the bottom of the screen—are common in international films shown in the United States, they are also used in American films in which there are scenes that require the characters to speak in a language other than English. For such scenes, filmmakers now prefer to have the actors use the characters' native tongue rather than simulate an accent that suggests their nationality—which was the case until about 1970. *Tora! Tora! Tora!* (1970) is unusual among films about World War II because it was apparently the first Hollywood production in which the Japanese spoke their own language, with subtitles providing the translation. Since then, it has become standard to use subtitles whenever a foreign language is spoken—Russian (*Red Dawn*, 1985), Sicilian (*The Godfather Part II*, 1974), French (*The Last of the Mohicans*, 1992), Sioux (*Dances with Wolves*, 1990), Hindi (*Monsoon Wedding*). When a hearing-impaired character uses sign language in *Four Weddings and a Funeral* (1994), the translation is given in subtitles. In context, the translation is quite funny, since the character is expressing sentiments about someone who, if he understood sign language, would not be amused.

Other Uses of the Printed Word

Printed matter in a film is a visual; as such, it can make a valuable contribution to the narrative. The entire plot of *Citizen Kane* revolves around an attempt to discover the meaning of Charles Foster Kane's dying word, "Rosebud!" Until the end, no one—neither the characters nor the audience—knows what "Rosebud" means. The characters never find out, but the audience eventually does. After Kane's funeral, workmen begin clearing out his cluttered basement, throwing what they consider to be junk into a blazing furnace. One of them tosses in a sled, which, as it burns, allows us to see that it bears a name: Rosebud. The film's resolution is a word, but one that must be seen—a word that symbolizes Kane's lost childhood.

Another example of the symbolic use of print occurs in *Casablanca* when Rick (Humphrey Bogart), standing in the rain, reads a letter from Ilsa (Ingrid Bergman) informing him that she cannot leave with him for Marseilles. As Rick reads the letter, the rain falls on it, causing the ink to run, tearlike, down the page. The running ink provides the tears that the stoic Rick cannot show; it also signals the end of an affair that has faded like the words of the letter. In both films, print has been dramatically embellished—by flames in *Citizen Kane* and by rain in *Casablanca*.

Naturally, print does not always operate so symbolically. Generally, print is a visual shorthand that enables the filmmaker to identify locales and

The ironic juxtaposition of print and image in *Taxi Driver* (1976), in which Travis Bickle (Robert De Niro) may be ready for the unexpected but is not exactly sane. *(Courtesy Sony Pictures Entertainment and MOMA/FSA)*

impart important information without having to resort to awkward exposition. Thus signposts, street signs, newspapers, and plaques are used to pinpoint setting. Since much of *The Grapes of Wrath* (1940) consists of a drive from Oklahoma to California along Highway 66, signs along the way tell the audience which state the Joads are in. A San Francisco newspaper seen at the opening of Hitchcock's *The Birds* (1963) immediately identifies the setting.

It is possible to formulate a general rule about the best use of print in film: print should be used as a means of supplying information that either cannot be imparted in any other way or that will reduce the amount of exposition. Sometimes the script calls for print. In *Dark Victory* (1939), Judith Traherne (Bette Davis) learns that she is terminally ill when she comes across her medical file and sees the words "prognosis negative." When Bob Woodward (Robert Redford) realizes that Carl Bernstein's (Dustin Hoffman) apartment is bugged in *All the President's Men* (1976), he turns up the stereo in the apartment and types:

Deep Throat says our lives may be in danger. SURVEILLANCE. BUGGING.

The computer screen has also become an important narrative tool, capable of advancing the plot in the same way the typewriter once could. The computer that the villain in *Ghost* (1990) uses to transfer funds becomes the means of revealing his identity; *The Net* (1995) revolves around an attempt to use computer technology to alter a character's identity.

Film, then, uses print in a variety of ways. Signs, plaques, posters, headlines, ticker tape, letters, notices, invitations, telegrams, notes, e-mail, and other written texts can perform an important narrative function; as visual shorthand, print minimizes the need for expository dialogue.

Sound

Seeing a narrative film without sound would be an abomination. Even the silent films (which were silent only in the sense that there was no spoken dialogue) had some kind of sound effects as well as musical accompaniment. *Nickelodeon* illustrates the importance of sound in the silent film by showing the world premiere of *The Birth of a Nation*, in which men fire cap pistols backstage to simulate the gunfire in the battle scenes.

Gunfire, a staple in westerns, war films, and crime movies, is one of many sound effects used in films. Under the heading of sound effects come all the sounds heard in a film except dialogue, music, and offscreen narration. Noise is an important sound effect in a film, and it can be a legitimate, even powerful, device. Jacques Tourneur's *Cat People* (1942) would not be the horror classic it is without sound effects in two crucial scenes. As Alice (Jane Randolph) walks home at night, she hears the ominous sound of footsteps. Just when we think that whatever is following her will catch up with her, we hear the sound of brakes; a bus has pulled up alongside Alice, and she quickly boards it. Later, as she is swimming in an indoor pool, she hears growling sounds, as if a ferocious beast were nearby.

The noise in *Cat People* is atmospheric, intended to heighten suspense. In many films, however, noise is essential to the plot. There is a scene in Hitchcock's *Marnie* (1964), for example, that requires noise—a noise that the audience and Marnie must hear but that another character in the same scene cannot hear. After taking money from her employer's safe, Marnie (Tippi Hedren) stealthily leaves the office. In the adjacent area, a cleaning woman is washing the floors. In order not to be heard, Marnie removes her shoes, placing them in the pockets of her jacket. One of the shoes falls to the floor. Anyone in the vicinity would have heard the sound, yet the cleaning woman does not look up from her work. As we wonder whether Marnie will be discovered, the janitor calls to the cleaning woman in an unnaturally loud voice, making it clear that she has difficulty hearing.

Ordinarily, the sound of rain beating against a window would be audible, but in *And Now Tomorrow* (1944) it is not. When Emily Blair (Loretta

Young) wakes one morning, she sees the windowpanes streaked with rain but does not hear the rainfall. The audience discovers that Emily has lost her hearing at the same moment that she does: when the rain silently beats upon the window.

There are times when sound is expected, and instead there is silence. At the end of Neil LaBute's *In the Company of Men* (1997), two misogynistic executives, who have had unsuccessful relationships with women, decide to take their revenge on the female sex by tricking a hearing-impaired woman into thinking that they are interested in her. When one of the men realizes the injustice he has committed, he returns to beg forgiveness. As he pleads, no sound comes from his lips. Another director might have wanted the man's words to be heard, but LaBute decided otherwise. By indicating that the woman cannot hear him, LaBute also makes it clear that, to her, he no longer exists.

Actual and Commentative Sound

As a form of sound, noise can emanate from a source that is either on- or off-screen. We do not have to see the source of the noise; we only have to know that there is a source. We never see the foghorns in *Long Day's Journey into Night* (1962), but we hear the sound they make, and we know it is coming from nearby ships. In Joseph L. Mankiewicz's *A Letter to Three Wives* (1949), everything in the Finney kitchen shakes when the train passes by. We never see the train, but we hear it and witness the results of the vibrations it causes.

Sound, then, can be **actual** (or natural), in the sense of coming from a real source that we may or may not see. Sometimes there is a face to go with the voice; at other times, the voice is faceless. Thus we do not always have to see a character to be aware of his or her existence. In *Sorry, Wrong Number* (1948), a woman, while making a phone call, overhears two men plotting a murder, which turns out to be her own. The murderers are heard, not seen — except at the end, when one of them appears in silhouette as he ascends the stairs to the bedroom of his terror-stricken victim. At the end of Hitchcock's *Saboteur* (1942), an enemy agent falls to his death from the Statue of Liberty, producing a scream from below. There is no reason to show the witness; the scream makes it clear that someone saw the body hit the pavement.

Sound can also be **commentative,** in that it may come from a source outside the physical setting of the action. Perhaps the most familiar type of commentative sound is background music — the recurring motifs or signature themes that can identify a character (Lara's theme in *Dr. Zhivago*, 1965), a place (the Tara theme in *Gone with the Wind*), a physical state (the blindness theme in *Dark Victory*), or an obsession (the power theme in *Citizen*

Barbara Stanwyck as the terrified wife who overhears plans for her own murder in *Sorry, Wrong Number* (1948). *(Courtesy Paramount Pictures/Hal Wallis Productions)*

Kane). In *Dark Victory*, when Judith Traherne discovers that she will experience a short period of blindness prior to death, the blindness theme is heard on the soundtrack. Judith cannot hear the music because it is not coming from a source within the action, but the audience hears it and, having heard it before in various forms, recognizes it as a sign of Judith's fate.

Synchronization and Asynchronization

Another way of approaching sound is from the perspective of **synchronization** and **asynchronization**. In synchronization, sound and image are properly matched; the sound comes from within the image or from an identifiable source. Synchronization is not limited to a literal correlation of sound and image. In many films, characters may be in transit and the audience will see the car on the freeway or the plane in the air but not see the characters. Yet we hear their conversation. In postproduction, the dialogue has been added and synchronized with the image.

There are, however, more sophisticated forms of synchronization. For example, a nonhuman sound may be combined with the image of a person. In *Cat People*, Irena (Simone Simon) tactfully tells her husband on their wedding night that she is not ready to consummate their marriage. As they retire to separate rooms, Irena, who is a descendant of a Serbian cat cult and periodically reverts to panther form, falls to her knees, assuming an animal posture. At that moment, the roar of a panther is heard. The audience knows the source of the sound: the Central Park Zoo, which Irena frequents. However, within the new context of an unconsummated wedding night, the combination of a sound coming from an identifiable source and the image of the crouching Irena adds another dimension to the narrative: her repressed sexuality is given voice. In *The Godfather* (1972), just before Michael kills the drug dealer Sollozzo and the crooked police captain McCluskey in a Bronx restaurant, a screeching sound is heard. We have no idea where it came from, but obviously it is outside. Given the restaurant's location in the Bronx and the time of the action in the late 1940s, it would have to be coming from the nearby elevated subway, the now-defunct Third Avenue el. The sound is appropriate for another reason: it reflects Michael's vengeful frame of mind, which is quite the opposite of his expressionless face.

While sound and image have been synchronized in each of these instances, we know the sound source and see the image before us; it now seems as if the image were making the sound. The combination of a growling panther and a crouching woman suggests that within Irena there is something waiting to be unleashed; vengeance combined with screeching brakes tells the audience that an apathetic face masks Michael's pent-up anger that erupts in violence.

Synchronization, then, can be quite imaginative. It can be particularly effective when a character remembers the past. The voice of the person who's remembering can be combined with the image of what is remembered, or the face of the person remembering can be combined with the sound that is remembered. In *A Streetcar Named Desire* (1951), Blanche DuBois (Vivien Leigh) periodically recalls the music that was played on the night that her husband committed suicide. At the end of *Forever Amber* (1947), Amber (Linda Darnell) watches her son go off with his father, never to see either of them again. Earlier, the child's father—Amber's former lover—had said, "May God have mercy on both of us for our sins." In the final scene, Amber, standing at the window, recalls his words—her image synchronized with the sound of his voice.

In synchronization, sound and image are related contextually, spatially, and temporally. In asynchronization, sound and image are related symbolically, metaphorically, or ironically. With the latter, the image the viewer expects to see after hearing a particular sound turns out to be something quite different. Asynchronization allows filmmakers to contrast sound and image, substitute a sound for an image, or juxtapose sounds and images that would not normally occur at the same time.

In Fritz Lang's *M* (1931), Mrs. Beckmann is waiting anxiously for her daughter Elsie to return from school. She leans out the window, calling, "Elsie! Elsie!" On the screen we do not see Elsie but, rather, a series of

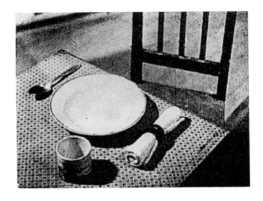

Asynchronization in *M* (1931). When Mrs. Beckmann calls "Elsie!," the response is not verbal but visual: a place setting never to be used again. *(Courtesy MOMA/FSA and Janus Films)*

images: an empty stairwell, an empty attic, Elsie's place at the dinner table, her ball on the grass, and, finally, a balloon that is momentarily caught in some telephone wires and then floats away.

The asynchronization is remarkably subtle. Ironically, Mrs. Beckmann's call is heard, but she is answered only by images that denote absence and emptiness. Elsie will never return. Like the balloon that was caught in the wires and then blown skyward by the wind, she was enticed by a child molester and led away to her death.

Overlap

What might seem to be asynchronization could be **overlapping sound**—sound or dialogue that either carries over from one scene to the next or anticipates the new scene by starting at the end of the previous one. Thus, overlapping sound is really synchronous, since it emanates from a known source. Bridging scenes through sound was rare in the 1930–1950 period, mainly because such a device would have struck audiences as illogical. If *The Age of Innocence* had been released in 1943 instead of in 1993, there would never have been a scene like this: Newland Archer (Daniel Day-Lewis) stands in front of a flower shop. Before he even enters, we hear a voice saying, "Oh, Mr. Archer. Good evening." In a 1943 version, the florist would have extended the greeting *after* Archer had entered. Today, however, overlapping sound has become so commonplace that it is just a cue for a scene change. Thus, it is the equivalent of a sound bridge, connecting two scenes aurally.

Still, there are instances in which the scenes being bridged are connected in ways that develop the narrative instead of merely linking segments of it together. In Spike Lee's *Malcolm X* (1992), as Malcolm walks along a street thronged with prostitutes, we hear the words "What has happened to our women?" Is this what Malcolm is thinking? The next scene clarifies the situation: the question is part of a sermon that is about to end. The incident in the first scene inspired the subject matter of the sermon in the second, with the question becoming the link between them.

In *Three Days of the Condor* (1975), a CIA official in Washington is asking questions about an agent, who at that moment is hiding out in a Brooklyn Heights apartment. The official's voice carries into the next scene, which takes place in the apartment. The overlapping voice gives us the unsettling impression that the CIA is present everywhere, including Brooklyn Heights.

At the end of *Medium Cool* (1969), set in Chicago during the 1968 Democratic Convention, the director, Haskell Wexler, allows the audience to hear about an event before it happens. As a TV cameraperson and an Appalachian schoolteacher are driving away from a bloody confrontation between the police and Vietnam War protesters, a newscaster's voice describes their death in a car crash before it is actually shown. Like the film, the untimely newscast is disturbing; it is not just a matter of overlap but of omniscience. It is as if the "cool medium," as media critic Marshall McLuhan called television, knew our destiny and could therefore compose our obituary before we died.

Voice-Over Narration

Voice-over, off-camera narration or commentary, has been a standard feature of film since the beginning of the sound era and is now so common in film and television that we scarcely notice it. We have become accustomed to the television voices of unseen individuals promoting products, reading labels, or attesting to the miraculous results of a headache remedy. In airports and train stations, we continually hear voices announcing arrivals and departures. We seldom inquire about the source or identity of the voice because we are usually interested only in the information the voice is conveying. Because disembodied voices are everywhere, we tend to give little thought to voice-over narration in film. It is another case of accepting the familiar uncritically.

Voice-over is also one of the most frequently abused techniques in film. A gifted filmmaker like Woody Allen uses voice-over intelligently; in *Radio Days*, Allen makes voice-over integral to the film, which is a reminiscence by a narrator whose younger self appears as a character. Unfortunately, voice-over can also be a convenience for writers who cannot think of any other way to impart information. In John Ford's *When Willie Comes Marching Home* (1950), the main character's voice keeps intruding even though there is no reason for him to tell his own story.

Historically, when the movies learned to talk, filmmakers seized upon voice-over as a narrative device and attempted to use it the way they had used titles. As often happens, the quest for novelty led to eccentricity, and soon voice-over narration was being entrusted to everyone—and everything. *The First Time* (1952), narrated by an unborn baby, dramatizes the disruptions that come with the birth of a first child. A variation on the same device occurs in *Look Who's Talking* (1989), which is told from the point of view of a newborn baby (with Bruce Willis providing the voice-over). The film had a certain charm, unlike the 1990 and 1993 sequels, which had little audience appeal, suggesting that once may have been enough.

Since voice-over has become so widespread, its appropriateness deserves assessment. Is it a convention, like a soliloquy in a play? Does it function as an expository prologue, in which a voice relates what we should know before the movie starts? Or is it an emergency cord that a filmmaker pulls when he or she is unable to think of another way to convey information? There is no manual a filmmaker can consult to determine whether to use voice-over or titles, or whether to use neither and work the exposition into the dialogue. Sometimes voice-over needs some kind of aural reinforcement: a few sounds, some chords, a musical theme. Sometimes the necessary information can be incorporated into the dialogue, so that neither voice-over nor titles are necessary.

The best filmmakers know intuitively when to use voice-over and when to use some kind of title. They also know that in some instances a combination is required. The 1935 adaptation of Charles Dickens's *A Tale of Two Cities*, directed by Jack Conway, is a good example of the sensible use of print and voice-over. The novel includes two of the most famous lines in English literature: the opening line ("It was the best of times, it was the worst of times") and the closing line ("It is a far, far better thing that I do, than I have ever done; it is a far, far better rest that I go to than I have ever known"). The opening appears as a title without voice-over. This is fitting because these are the words of Dickens, not one of his characters; thus, the text alone is sufficient. At the end, however, voice-over is necessary. The last words of the film, like those of the novel, are the thoughts of Sydney Carton, the main character; they are not Dickens's reflections. Since these are Carton's thoughts, the audience must hear them. Since Carton does not verbalize his thoughts, the audience hears them through voice-over.

The dominant forms of voice-over are the narrating "I" and the voice of God.

The Narrating "I".   The narrating "I" tells the story, or a portion of the story, that we see on the screen. There can be one "I" or several. Some films are narrated by one character (*Murder, My Sweet,* 1944); others by multiple narrators (*Citizen Kane; Sorry, Wrong Number*). Since anyone can tell a story in the movies, even a corpse has the opportunity in Billy Wilder's *Sunset Boulevard* (1950). In the film, Norma Desmond (Gloria Swanson), a former silent-screen star half crazed by memories of a past that will never return, believes she can make a comeback in a movie about Salome. She hires an out-of-work screenwriter, Joe Gillis (William Holden), to help her with the script in which she plans to star. When Gillis decides to leave her, Norma kills him. *Sunset Boulevard* begins with Gillis's body floating in a pool; Gillis's voice then proceeds to tell the story of his fatal association with Norma Desmond. The narration is ironically fitting: a corpse talking about the living dead.

On the other hand, the voice-over prologue of *American Beauty* (1999) consists of the main character's startling admission that he will be dead by the end of the film—and knows it: "My name is Lester Burnham. This is my neighborhood. This is my street. This is my life. I'm forty-two years old. In less than a year, I'll be dead." Lester (Kevin Spacey) is right, and his voice returns at the end. Now at peace, he recalls his favorite childhood memories, realizing how little we appreciate the inexhaustible sources of beauty that exist in the world. "You have no idea what I'm talking about, I'm sure," Lester adds. "But don't worry. You will someday." Even in death, Lester has not lost his sardonic sense of humor.

Billy Wilder's *Double Indemnity* (1944) is considered a classic of "I" narration. It opens with Walter Neff (Fred MacMurray) entering a Los Angeles office building shortly before dawn. Neff describes himself as having "no visible scars"—none, that is, that can be seen *now*. Actually, he has just been shot by his lover, whom he then killed. While Neff still has the strength, he recites his whole story into a dictaphone. The film then becomes a flashback in the form of a testimony that is being recorded and dramatized at the same time.

In "I" narration, if there is only one narrator the narrator's voice will recur periodically throughout the course of the film. This kind of narration is more difficult, since the narration must unify the film, bridging the scenes as the action shifts from present to past. Neff's narration in *Double Indemnity* succeeds because the flashbacks frequently end with a cue line—a line that triggers the next bit of dialogue so that the action can return to the present without an awkward transition. When Neff and Phyllis Dietrichson (Barbara Stanwyck) are in a supermarket plotting her husband's murder, Phyllis says, "Remember, we're in it together." "Yes, I remember," Neff answers into the dictaphone.

Sometimes the "I" tells his or her story in the hope of learning from it. Robert Bresson's *Une Femme Douce* (1969) opens with a suicide. Someone rushes to the veranda, a chair is overturned, a white shawl flutters through the air, and a woman's body falls to the pavement. A man, later revealed to be the woman's husband, begins to speak of her. Bresson keeps returning to her body, which now lies on a bed, to remind us that her husband is narrating the film. The approach is psychologically valid, for the husband is not so much recalling his wife as trying to understand why she committed suicide. At the end, he knows no more than he did at the beginning.

Walter Neff (Fred MacMurray) as the narrating "I" in *Double Indemnity* (1944), one of the finest examples of first-person narration in film. *(Copyright Paramount Pictures. Courtesy MCA Publishing Rights, a Division of MCA, Inc.)*

The voice of the "I" in *Badlands* (1973) has a distancing effect that works well in the context of a film narrated by the fifteen-year-old Holly (Sissy Spacek) as she accompanies her boyfriend Kit (Martin Sheen) on a killing spree. Holly's voice is coolly impersonal, totally without feeling, as if she were merely narrating what she had witnessed.

The Voice of God. Between 1945 and the early 1950s, the **semidocumentary** was a popular type of film. While a documentary is a nonfiction film, as we have already seen, a semidocumentary is a fiction film based on fact (e.g., *The House on 92nd Street*, 1945; *Boomerang*, 1947; *The Naked City*, 1948). In the semidocumentary, the credits often appear in a "typewriter" typeface to give the movie a "case history" look. An authoritative voice delivers the prologue, reminding the audience that the film sprang from today's headlines or from the FBI's files and that it was shot on location. Since the voice belongs to no character, it is completely disembodied. As a result, it can weave in and out of the action, commenting, reflecting, even questioning. In the semidocumentary, the disembodied voice, or **voice-of-God** technique, as it is sometimes called, has two advantages: it can impart a feeling of objectivity, which is required by a film of this kind; and it can insinuate itself

This scene from *Barry Lyndon* (1975) between Barry (Ryan O'Neal) and his son (David Morley) was introduced by the off-camera narrator, who said: "Barry had his faults, but no man could say of him that he was not a good and tender father. He loved his son passionately, perhaps with a blind partiality. He denied him nothing." *(Courtesy Warner Bros., Inc.)*

into the characters, noting their moods and emotional states. The voice in *The Naked City* speaks directly to the characters as if it were an alter ego, a confidant, and a conscience combined. "How are your feet holding out, Alan?" it asks, or, "Lieutenant Muldoon, what's your hurry?" It even speaks to the audience: "Ever try to catch a murderer?" Since the voice had the first word, it is fitting that it should have the last: "There are eight million stories in the naked city. This has been one of them."

The disembodied voice is not restricted to the semidocumentary. Stanley Kubrick used it ingeniously in his 1975 adaptation of Thackeray's novel *Barry Lyndon*. Both the novel and the film have a narrator; however, in the film the narrator is not Lyndon — as it was in the novel — but a voice behind the scenes, very much like the one in *The Naked City* but wittier and more urbane. It is actually the voice of the British actor Michael Hordern, which, like the traditional voice of God, is omniscient. The voice tells us about something before it happens, or informs us of the outcome of an event without dramatizing it for us. When Lyndon is about to die, the voice even reads his obituary. The voice can speak with authority at this moment because it has been speaking with authority since the film began.

Voice-over is often used in movies that are not narrated by one of the characters but that, for purposes of plot, require a character's voice to be heard. Such voices are variously labeled the epistolary voice, the subjective voice, the repetitive voice, and the voice from the machine.

The Epistolary Voice. Advancing the plot through letters is a device common to both fiction and film. The epistolary novel has a long tradition that reaches back to Samuel Richardson's *Pamela* and *Clarissa*, which were written in the mid-eighteenth century. In film, the letter is a familiar means of setting the plot in motion (William Wyler's *The Letter*, 1940; *A Letter to Three Wives*, 1949) or of bridging the years (*Sea of Grass*, 1947). When an exchange of letters is used to mark the passage of time, voice-over is sufficient. In *About Schmidt* (2002), the title character corresponds with an African child whom he has sponsored. The **epistolary voice** allows the audience to hear that Schmidt uses letter writing as a means of venting his frustration and anger, instead of as a vehicle of communication.

In an era of film censorship, the epistolary voice was one way of having a character repent by voice-over confession. Robert Anderson's play *Tea and Sympathy* was considered unfilmable in the 1950s because of its subject matter: Tom Lee, a prep-school student thought to be gay because of his fondness for music and poetry, is initiated sexually by Laura Reynolds, the headmaster's wife. The play is best remembered for the final scene, in which Laura comes to Tom's room and slowly begins to unbutton her blouse. Pressing his hand against her breast, she makes one request: "Years from now, when you talk about this, and you will, be kind." When MGM decided to film the play in 1956, the Johnston Office* felt that any woman who would offer her body to an adolescent should die. After much wrangling, the director, Vincente Minnelli, decided to make the plot a flashback occasioned by a class reunion at which Tom discovers a letter Laura had written to him. As Tom reads the letter, Laura's repentant voice is heard, urging him to forget what they have done (which is "wrong") and go out into the world and write edifying novels.

What we have been discussing are films in which the letter is a plot device whose contents must be heard. There are few films that are totally epistolary; that is, in which the entire film is a dramatization of a letter or a series of letters. In *A Walk in the Sun* (1945) and *Platoon* (1986), the narrator is writing letters to his sister and grandmother, respectively; however, it does not follow that each film is a dramatization of the letter the character is writing.

If a film is totally epistolary, it really is an example of the narrating "I," since the epistolary voice is used only to tell the contents of a letter. Max Ophüls's *Letter from an Unknown Woman* (1948), which revolves entirely around a letter Lisa (Joan Fontaine) has written to her former lover as she lay dying, is totally epistolary. Because the letter is such a personal document, we see only its powerful beginning ("By the time you read this letter I may be dead") and its unfinished ending. Otherwise we hear Lisa's voice and experience the visualization of her words. Yet the letter that is being dramatized is also being read by Lisa's lover, who never even bothered to learn her name. Thus, the audience and the lover learn about Lisa at the same time.

The Subjective Voice. Movies abound with examples of the inner voice that literally speaks its mind—the subjective voice—because the audience requires access to the character's thoughts. Pip in *Great Expectations* (1946)

---

*The Motion Picture Producers and Distributors of America, Hollywood's self-censorship organization, was called the Johnston Office when it was headed by Eric Johnston from 1945 to 1963; previously it had been called the Hays Office and the Breen Office.

wonders how Joe Gargery, the blacksmith, will greet him when he returns home dressed as a gentleman. In *The Accused* (1948), we hear what a psychology professor, who has killed a student in self-defense, is thinking when she realizes the consequences of her act. During her flight from Phoenix in *Psycho*, Marion Crane imagines what her employer will say on Monday morning when she fails to report for work.

A more complex form of the subjective voice appears in the stream-of-consciousness film. Although **stream of consciousness** has been applied to everything from inarticulate rambling to incoherent prose, it is really the unbroken flow of thoughts, memories, and associations in the waking mind. *Hiroshima, Mon Amour* (1959), a stream-of-consciousness film, opens with a man and a woman making love. At first their skin looks charred, like that of the Hiroshima victims; then it becomes dewy, as though cleansed by the act of love. She is a French actress, and he is a Japanese architect she meets in Hiroshima while making a film. As their bodies move toward fulfillment, we hear their voices—his denying that she knows the significance of Hiroshima, hers insisting that she does. But these are not their actual voices; they sound distant, anesthetized. We are hearing the rhythms of poetry, not prose. It is each character's interior that we hear, an interior expressing itself in the language of memory, which is made up of both words and images. When the architect's voice says, "You know nothing of Hiroshima," her consciousness replies with pictures of the artifacts she has seen at the museum and with newsreel footage of the bombing of Hiroshima. When the woman says, "Who are you?," instead of a verbal reply we see a street in Hiroshima. The man is Hiroshima, the only name she will ever associate with him.

The Repetitive Voice. A character, often the hero or the heroine, tosses restlessly in bed while someone's voice reverberates in his or her unconscious, repeating key dialogue from an earlier scene (in case the audience missed its significance). This kind of repetition, called the repetitive voice, occurs in Hitchcock's *Rebecca* (1940) when some comments made about Rebecca give Joan Fontaine's character a sleepless night. The same technique appears in *Cat People* when Irena keeps hearing the voice of her psychiatrist as Halloween cats prowl across the screen.

The repetitive voice has become so familiar that it runs the risk of becoming a cliché. Yet at times some kind of recapitulation is necessary, and the filmmaker must decide whether the repetition should be aural or visual. If the character's words are important, then it is necessary to hear only what he or she has said. At the end of *Gone with the Wind*, Scarlett recalls the words her father had spoken earlier about the value of land and the importance of Tara. Hearing his words is sufficient. On the other hand, in *Murder on the Orient Express* (1974), the repetition is visual. Since the film is a whodunit, crucial shots are repeated: guilt is often a question not of what one says but

Francis Dee as Betsy the nurse and James Ellison as the tortured Wesley who chooses suicide in the Val Lewton production *I Walked with a Zombie* (1943). *(Courtesy RKO Radio Pictures)*

of how one reacts, so the passengers' reactions, not just their words, are recalled for us visually.

The Voice from the Machine. Some filmmakers regard voice-over as the modern equivalent of the deus ex machina, or god from the machine, of Greek theater. In certain Greek tragedies, particularly those of Euripides, a god would descend from a crane to resolve the action and bring the play to a conclusion. Some movies feature a "voice from the machine"; it belongs to none of the characters and materializes near the end to tie up any loose plot threads or offer some commentary on the action. The voice from the machine is not the voice of God, which is consistent throughout the film; the voice from the machine is heard only at the end. At the end of *The Lady and the Monster* (1944), a voice intrudes to remind us that Patrick Cory (Richard Arlen) has been sent to prison for his role in an experiment to keep a dead man's brain alive. The voice also reminds us that this is to be a film with a happy ending, and that Cory will emerge from jail to find his beloved waiting for him. Since no voice has been heard up to this point, we wonder whose it is. It must belong to a supernatural power that knows more about the script than the screenwriter does.

Despite its title, Jacques Tourneur's *I Walked with a Zombie* (1943) is a superior horror film. Initially, the movie is narrated by the "I" of the title—a Canadian nurse who has come to the West Indies to tend to a woman who turns out to be a zombie. At the end, the zombie is killed by her brother-in-law, who then commits suicide. Suddenly, a male voice asks God to pardon the unholy couple. The switch from the nurse's voice to the voice from beyond imparts a moralistic tone to a film that has otherwise remained aloof from moral issues. Perhaps the coda was a sop to the Legion of Decency, a Catholic organization that rated films along moral lines from 1934 through the mid-1960s and frowned on suicide. Still, it mars the artistry of an unusually intelligent B-movie.

Voice-over, then, is not just faceless sound; it is a narrative device that can serve different purposes. It can be personal, like the narrating "I," or impersonal, like the voice of God; it can reveal the contents of a letter or the contents of the unconscious; it can refresh a character's memory or our own. Because of its versatility, voice-over is often abused; although it is now a well-established narrative tool, it should not be taken for granted.

NOTE

1. For a guide to all the individuals involved in the making of a movie, see Eric Taub, *Gaffers, Grips and Best Boys* (New York: St. Martin's Press, 1987). Even more detailed is Ira Konisberg, *The Complete Film Dictionary* (New York: Meridian/Penguin, 1989).

CHAPTER 3

Film, Space, and Mise-en-Scène

A long with sound, every film text requires illustrations. As with time, film can manipulate space to communicate information or convey a feeling. Images of people, places, and things can be near or far, partial or full, stationary or moving. They can flash by quickly or linger on the screen, follow each other chronologically or appear in a symbolic order. Which images we see and how we see them are the result of the filmmaker's choices.

The Shot

A film, of course, is a moving picture, not a series of still photographs. Yet we have all seen photos or frame enlargements of one particular moment in a movie. This moment, or **shot,** is like an excerpt. And like an excerpt, it is only part of a work. It is easy to become enamored of particular shots, especially those that are strikingly photographed. Some can have an impact, even if you have not seen the films in which they appear. A shot, however, should be viewed as part of the total film in which its meaning resides. It is important to examine a shot specifically, but not in isolation. A shot takes on its deepest meaning within the context of the film.

Types of Shots

A shot is simply what is recorded by a single operation of the camera. Shots can be defined in terms of distance, area, or the subjects they contain.

Does the camera appear to be close to the subject? If so, the shot is a **close-up (CU)**—in terms of human anatomy, a shot of the head, for example. Perhaps it is a head-and-shoulders shot, in which case it is a **close shot (CS)**. If the shot is of a specific part of the body—an eye, a mouth— it is an **extreme close-up (ECU)**. A shot of the complete human figure, with some of the background visible, is a **long shot (LS)** or a **full shot (FS)**. If the camera is so far away that the result is a broad, panoramic view, it is an **extreme long shot (ELS)**. A shot that is neither a close shot nor a long shot but something in between is a **medium shot (MS),** showing, for example, the subject from head to waist or from waist to knees. These definitions, however, are fluid and are, at best, approximate. What is a medium shot to one director may be a medium close-up to another. The director may have used the term *close-up*, but on the screen, it becomes an extreme close-up. In other words, these are relative descriptions.

If a shot defines an area—say, a dining room with a family gathered around a table—it is called an **establishing shot (ES)**. This is a type of long shot that is often broken down into its components, as Frank Capra did in the dinner table scene in *Mr. Smith Goes to Washington* (1939), in which he first showed Jefferson Smith's (James Stewart) family, followed by individual shots of the various members. An establishing shot can also identify the setting by using a familiar landmark, such as San Francisco's Golden Gate Bridge or Paris's Eiffel Tower. In short, it "establishes" the location so that the viewer knows where the action is taking place.

Shots can also be defined by what they contain. A **two-shot** includes two characters; a **three-shot**, three characters. **Shot/reverse shot** is the principle of alternating shots of characters in a conversation so that we see first one character, then the other. An **over-the-shoulder shot** functions in the same way, except that we look over the shoulder of character A into the face of character B; and then, over the shoulder of character B into the face of character A.

Close-ups and Long Shots. French director Jean-Luc Godard was fond of saying that the close-up was invented for tragedy, the long shot for comedy. This is something of an oversimplification, but Godard succeeds at suggesting that filmmakers have reasons for choosing one shot over another depending on the kind of movie they are making or the type of scene they are shooting. A close-up can reveal a particular emotion that a long shot might not capture. When Lucy (Lillian Gish) is denounced by her father in *Broken Blossoms*, D. W. Griffith uses a close-up to express her fear.

The close-up is also a means of emphasis. Hitchcock found it ideal for objects like a suspicious glass of milk in *Suspicion* (1941), an envelope dropped by a Nazi agent in *Saboteur* (1942), a wine bottle filled with uranium ore in *Notorious* (1946), and a necklace worn by a woman who should not have had it in her possession in *Vertigo*. These objects were so crucial to the plot that Hitchcock used close-ups to make sure the audience could not miss them.

Hitchcock also used the extreme close-up to provide the proverbial chill up the spine. The extreme close-ups of Marion Crane's screaming mouth and staring eye in the shower sequence help make *Psycho* a horror film. Extreme close-ups of the eye are, in fact, standard in horror films, especially if it is the eye of the killer spying on a prospective victim through a peephole, as is the case in *Psycho* and *The Spiral Staircase* (1946).

Like any shot, an extreme close-up can have a direct bearing on the plot. The words "prognosis negative," which confirm Judith Traherne's terminal condition in *Dark Victory*, must be visible, and that can be done only in extreme close-up. If a scar identifies a murderer, as it does in *A Stranger Knocks* (1963), the scar needs to be photographed in ECU.

The ECU should be used with discretion; it is such a dramatic form of emphasis that a preponderance of such shots is like the speech pattern of someone who gives equal emphasis to every word, including *a* and *the.*

While a close-up can express moments of intense emotion, a long shot can be as effective in a different way. For example, a death in long shot is less painful to watch. The death of Santiago (Arthur Kennedy) in Edgar G. Ulmer's *The Naked Dawn* (1955) is photographed in long shot. Santiago is on horseback when the bullet strikes him; we see neither stunned eyes nor spurting blood. Instead, the shot has a formalized beauty, reminiscent of a painting like Brueghel's *Fall of Icarus*, in which the death of Icarus is made part of the setting.

Westerns are known for their long shots and extreme long shots, which make the subject part of the environment in addition to conveying the awesome vastness of nature. In George Stevens's *Shane* (1953), a deer laps water from a stream, with snow-fringed mountains in the background. A man bids farewell to a woman who merges with the landscape as he rides off in John Ford's *My Darling Clementine* (1946). Many of Ford's long shots have an intensely pictorial quality. In *Clementine*, we see a stretch of sky brooding over the dusty main street of Tombstone; a bar thronged by men—sometimes in silhouette, sometimes illuminated by the kerosene lamps that hang overhead; and Monument Valley with its cliffs and mesas rising skyward from a flat plain and dwarfing all who pass beneath them.

High-Angle and Low-Angle Shots. Shots are also defined by the position of the camera in relation to the subject. When Lillian (Jane Fonda) looks out of her hotel window in *Julia* (1977), what she sees on the street below

Robert Redford and Dustin Hoffman prepare for the Library of Congress scene in *All the President's Men* (1976). The camera is set for a high shot. *(Courtesy Warner Bros., Inc.)*

is rendered as a **high-angle shot.** In a high-angle shot, the camera is positioned above, or sometimes "high above," the subject. This is occasionally referred to as a **God's eye shot** or bird's eye shot, a type favored by Hitchcock to suggest entrapment. As the insurance investigator in *Psycho* mounts the staircase of the Bates home, a high-angle shot makes him look smaller and therefore vulnerable—as indeed he is, as a figure rushes out of a room off the landing, ready to end his snooping with a knife. This kind of shot has not gone out of fashion; in *The Others* (2001) a stunning high shot shows a mother (Nicole Kidman) at the bottom of a staircase, terrified at the thought of confronting the "intruders" on the floor above.

A high-angle shot can also convey a feeling of frustration. The high-angle shot of the president pacing the floor in D. W. Griffith's *Abraham Lincoln* (1930) reminds us that the burdens of the office dwarf even the great. In *All the President's Men* (1976), as reporters Bob Woodward and Carl Bernstein sort out library slips, the camera watches them from above; indeed, the men seem to grow smaller as they realize the enormity of their task. The scene ends with the camera peering down at the reading room of the Library of Congress, which looks like a magnified snowflake.

Orson Welles prepares for a low-angle shot, below floor level, in *Citizen Kane* (1941). *(Courtesy MOMA/FSA and RKO)*

If the camera shoots up at the subject from below, it is a **low-angle shot.** Serving the opposite function of a high-angle shot, a low-angle shot makes the subject appear larger than it actually is. Such a shot can suggest dominance or power, as it does in *Citizen Kane* when Kane's guardian hovers over him as he presents the young Kane with a sled.

Sometimes the script requires a high- or low-angle shot for the sake of consistency rather than for symbolism or imagery. In *Julia*, the shot following the one of Lillian at the window had to be a high-angle shot; an eye-level shot would have made no sense. If a man is waiting at the foot of a staircase for a woman to descend, as Gabriel (Donal McCann) is for Gretta (Anjelica Huston) near the end of John Huston's *The Dead* (1987), the woman must be photographed in a low-angle shot to match the man's angle of vision. The context of the action can determine the nature of the shot.

The same holds true of other types of shots; their nature is the result of a filmmaker's decisions based on his or her interpretation of the screenplay.

Subjective Camera. An **objective shot** represents what the camera sees; a subjective shot, what the character sees. This is sometimes referred to as a

A low-angle shot of Gretta (Anjelica Huston) descending the stairs in *The Dead* (1987). *(Frame enlargement courtesy Vestron Pictures)*

subjective camera. As the Joads drive into Hooverville in John Ford's *The Grapes of Wrath*, the residents are looking straight ahead as they step aside for the truck. At whom are they staring? Actually, they are staring at the Joads, whom we cannot see. However, in terms of what appears on the screen, they are staring at us; Ford has put us behind the wheel in order to see poverty and squalor through the Joads' eyes.

Sometimes in a film we experience sheer motion without a corresponding image. In Hitchcock's *Marnie*, for example, Mark (Sean Connery) is seated at his desk when Marnie enters the room. Mark looks straight into the camera, acknowledging Marnie's presence. We do not see her, however; we only experience some sense of movement toward the desk. For a moment we have become Marnie, but we cease to be Marnie when she comes into view.

Because subjective camera offers a one-sided take on reality, it should never dominate a film as it did in *Lady in the Lake* (1946)—the textbook case of how not to make the audience a participant in the action. The main character in the film, Philip Marlowe (Robert Montgomery), is never seen except in a mirror. As a result, there are scenes in which the other characters, supposedly looking at him, stare straight into the camera, which represents Marlowe and, by extension, us. When a woman kisses Marlowe, she has to purse her lips into the lens, which makes it seem as though she were kissing us. To light Marlowe's cigarette, she thrusts the lighter into the lens as if

Philip Marlowe's (Robert Montgomery) reflection in *Lady in the Lake* (1946), the subjective-camera film in which Marlowe is visible only when a mirror catches his image. *(Courtesy WCFTR)*

she were about to ignite the viewer. When Marlowe is socked in the jaw, it seems that the camera, and, therefore, the viewer, is the one getting punched.

Subjective camera should be restricted to specific scenes or sequences, as it is in *Dark Passage* (1947), in which Vincent Parry (Humphrey Bogart) escapes from San Quentin to track down his wife's murderer. Parry escapes by concealing himself in a barrel that has been loaded onto a prison truck. The camera is totally subjective, jostling us as Parry maneuvers the barrel from the truck and making us reel with dizziness as it rolls down a hill. When the barrel comes to rest, we peer out of it cautiously but get no more than a tunnel-like view of the outside. Parry is now a presence. When he hitches a ride, the driver speaks to the presence. When the driver recognizes him, the presence knocks him unconscious. Later, the presence scans the highway and climbs into Irene Jansen's (Lauren Bacall) waiting car.

When the presence showers, a hand adjusts the showerhead and a jet of water sprays the camera lens. Camera movements express the presence's emotional state. When the presence is wary, the camera darts in the same direction as his apprehensive eyes. Gradually, there is a switch from subjective to objective camera, from Parry as a presence to Parry as a character. The transition begins when a sympathetic cabdriver recommends plastic surgery and refers Parry to a reliable doctor. Once we see Parry after the operation, the camera ceases to be subjective.

Related to subjective camera is the **point-of-view (POV)** shot. A POV shot represents the point of view of the character, or what the character sees. There is a famous POV shot at the end of Hitchcock's *Spellbound* (1945) when Dr. Murchison (Leo G. Carroll) is unmasked as a murderer. Murchison aims a gun at his accuser and then turns it around to fire at himself. The close-up of the gun with which Murchison commits suicide is a POV shot, representing the way he saw the gun when he turned it on himself. One of the most unusual — and unsettling — POV shots occurs in Jean Renoir's *The Woman on the Beach* (1947), when a blind painter shaves in front of a mirror that does not reflect his image. Although the character's blindness had been established earlier, we did not experience his point of view until that moment.

An entire film can be a study in point of view. In Hitchcock's *Rear Window* (1954), a professional photographer (James Stewart) is confined to a wheelchair because of a broken leg. His apartment in a Greenwich Village complex allows him to look across the courtyard into the windows of his neighbors and observe their activities — which he does, out of a combination of boredom and voyeurism. Gradually, he reaches certain conclusions about the residents, even giving some of them names (he dubs a dancer "Miss Torso"; a woman who entertains an imaginary suitor, "Miss Lonelyhearts"). Therefore, we see only what he sees; lacking any other source of information, we have no other choice but to accept his point of view.

The Moving Shot.   Movement in film can be deceptive. When the camera rotates on a fixed axis, either for a horizontal **pan shot** or a vertical **tilt shot,** it is not, strictly speaking, moving. The camera itself is probably on a tripod. Only the camera head moves. For **mobile camera** shots, the camera is on a moving vehicle such as a dolly, a truck, or a crane, or on specially built tracks. The mobile camera has the advantage of being able to add to the narrative by opening up more space, thereby augmenting what is seen. The pan and the tilt can add to our knowledge, too.

When the camera pivots horizontally left to right or vice versa, it is a pan shot. Through panning, a filmmaker can have the camera comment on a situation, thus making it almost a character. In *The Thin Man* (1934), when Nora Charles (Myrna Loy) opens a door on the right, the camera pans right to left, from the doorway to the interior, where her husband is comforting a weeping girl. When the husband catches sight of his wife, the camera pans left to right, back to Nora in the doorway, as if it, too, were embarrassed at what it has discovered.

In *The Others*, the daughter tells her excessively religious mother (Nicole Kidman) that there are "others" in the house. Her mother punishes her by having her read from scripture. Writer-director Alejandro Amenábar

James Stewart as a photographer who spies on his neighbors and Thelma Ritter as a visiting nurse in Alfred Hitchcock's *Rear Window* (1954), filmed almost exclusively from the photographer's point of view. *(Courtesy MCA)*

begins a slow pan from right to left, from the daughter to her mother embroidering, inverting the usual cause-effect relationship by starting with the effect (the punishment) and ending with the cause (the mother). By starting with the daughter doing her penance, and ending with the one who imposed it, Amenábar has established a connection between the punished and the punisher, which takes on greater meaning at the end when we learn that the daughter was right about "the others."

As David Locke (Jack Nicholson) in Michelangelo Antonioni's *The Passenger* (1975) cries aloud in desperation because his Land Rover is stalled in the sand, the camera answers by panning the indifferent desert. Martin Scorsese uses slow, almost languid pans of the characters' living rooms in *The Age of Innocence*—the slow panning suggesting lives of leisure. A **swish pan,** which is unusually rapid and produces a momentary blur, can suggest a sudden change or a transformation. In Rouben Mamoulian's *Dr. Jekyll and Mr. Hyde* (1932), there is a swish pan immediately after Dr. Jekyll drinks the potion and becomes Mr. Hyde.

When the camera pivots vertically, the result is a tilt shot, which is sometimes called a vertical pan; hence the expression pan up/down, which has become increasingly common among filmmakers. Tilting can mimic the eye's movement, perhaps up the face of a building to take in its height, or down a column of names. In *Jane Eyre* (1944), the camera tilts down from a plaque that reads "Lowood Institution" to the figure of the sleeping Jane Eyre, who is being carried into it. In *Citizen Kane*, the camera pans up to the entrance gate of Kane's estate, Xanadu, past the No Trespassing sign, reminding us that the warning applies to everyone but itself. At the end of the film, the camera pans down the gate to the No Trespassing sign as it returns to its starting point.

Like the horizontal pan, the tilt shot can be a silent spectator, commenting visually on a situation. As the vampire is about to sink her teeth into a victim's neck in *Dracula's Daughter* (1936), the camera pans up the wall, leaving the rest to the viewer's imagination.

As the camera pans or tilts, it guides the eye horizontally or vertically, determining both the direction and the object of the audience's vision.

Tilt-pan and pan-tilt combinations are also possible, to direct the viewer's or the character's gaze across one surface and up or down another. In Hitchcock's *Stage Fright* (1950), a combination of panning and tilting occurs in the notorious flashback, which is later revealed to have been a total lie. Jonathan Cooper (Richard Todd) is explaining to his bewildered girlfriend how Charlotte Inwood (Marlene Dietrich) begged him to go to her flat and bring her a new dress. As Cooper enters the flat, the camera pans across the room to the body of Charlotte's husband and then tilts up a closet door. At first the camera's tilting up a clothes closet seems odd, but it is part of Hitchcock's plan to make Cooper's story believable. Thus, Hitchcock has the camera guide Cooper to the closet, as if Cooper did not know where the closet was. If Cooper had headed straight for the closet, the audience would sense that he was more familiar with Charlotte's flat than he should be and would not accept his story.

As we have seen, in panning and tilting the camera itself does not move. In a moving shot, the camera moves with, toward, alongside, or away from its subjects. There are several kinds of moving shots, depending on the way in which the camera moves. If it moves on tracks, what you have is a **tracking shot;** if it is mounted on a dolly, a **dolly shot;** if it moves up and down, in and out of a scene on a crane, you have a **crane shot,** which is easily identified by its ascending or descending motion, although a crane can move laterally as well.

In *North by Northwest* (1959), Hitchcock uses a crane shot to suggest what may lie in store for one of the characters. When Philip Vandamm (James Mason) discovers that his mistress is an American agent, he decides to kill her aboard a plane. "This matter is something that is best disposed of at a great height—over water," he remarks. At the mention of height, the camera cranes upward.

Some writers use the terms *dolly shot* and *tracking shot* interchangeably; the camera dollies in (tracks in) when it moves toward the subject and dollies out (tracks out) when it moves away from the subject. Other writers

Preparing for a crane shot in *Cover Girl* (1944), with the camera in a mechanical arm. *(Courtesy MOMA/FSA)*

simply call any shot in which the camera is moving on a vehicle a tracking shot, which is identified by the direction of the camera: forward tracking shot, vertical tracking shot, diagonal tracking shot.

Tracking shots have distinct advantages over other shots because they can encompass a greater area and supply more detail; thus, they can sustain a mood for a longer period of time. While the pan and the tilt can act as a silent commentator, the track can be a character's alter ego or unseen companion. Max Ophüls was a master of the moving shot. In his films, the camera seems to waltz and glide; it can rush up the stairs with the breathless lovers or accompany them on a stroll, occasionally slipping behind a fountain so as not to be conspicuous. In *Letter from an Unknown Woman* (1948), Ophüls makes the camera almost human. As a provincial band ruins Wagner's "Song to the Evening Star," the camera, unable to stand the tinny sound, rises up fastidiously and leaves the square. In the same film, the camera accompanies the operagoers up the grand staircase as if it were escorting them.

The moving camera can physically draw viewers into the action, and it can even lure them into a character's consciousness, as it does in the film version of Eugene O'Neill's *Long Day's Journey into Night* (1962). The crane shot that ends the film is one of the great feats of moviemaking; in it Sidney Lumet manages to incorporate almost all of Mary Tyrone's great monologue. Mary (Katharine Hepburn) is in her parlor with her husband and their two

sons. She recalls how a nun had dissuaded her from entering a convent—
something she was contemplating because she claimed to have visions of Our
Lady of Lourdes. If regression could be visualized, it would consist of gradual diminution. Almost as soon as Mary begins her monologue, the camera
starts pulling back from her; then it rises up as her thoughts leave this world.
As Mary grows smaller, so do her husband and sons. As the monologue draws
to a close, Mary appears in close-up as she speaks the final lines: "That was
in the winter of senior year. Then in the spring something happened to me.
Yes, I remember. I fell in love with James Tyrone and was so happy for a
time." Mary's close-up is followed by close-ups of the other Tyrones; then
there is one last close-up of Mary's face, now strangely peaceful.

Zooms and Freezes. Some filmmakers prefer the **zoom** to the moving
shot because it is both economical and timesaving. Technically, the zoom is
not a moving shot because the camera does not move—a cameraperson
employs a lens of variable **focal length,** the distance from the center of the
lens to the point where the image is in focus. The adjustable lens gives the
impression of the camera moving close to, or far away from, the subject,
hence the terms **zoom in/zoom out.** A zoom can single out someone in
a crowd, pinpoint a criminal's hiding place in the woods, or capture a facial
expression without the person's being aware of the camera's presence.
Zooming can also flatten an image, creating an unreal sense of depth and
generally resulting in the loss of detail. Some filmmakers may prefer such a
two-dimensional effect. Stanley Kubrick clearly did in *Barry Lyndon,* in
which he deliberately zoomed out of close-ups to reveal scenes that resem-
bled paintings—a technique in keeping with his purpose of portraying the
eighteenth century as if it were a museum exhibit.

The zoom represents deceptive motion and distorts size; the **freeze
frame,** on the other hand, is a form of stopped motion and suggests stasis.
In a freeze frame, all movement suddenly halts, and the image "freezes" as it
turns into a still photograph. At the end of François Truffaut's *The 400 Blows*
(1959), Antoine Doinel (Jean-Pierre Léaud), having escaped from a reformatory, heads toward the ocean. When he reaches the water's edge, he walks
into the shallows; then he turns and faces the shore. At that instant Truffaut
freezes the frame, trapping Antoine between the reformatory and the ocean,
between the past and the present. The freeze implies immobility, helplessness, or indecision.

The freeze can also suggest the immobility that comes with death. At
the end of the shower sequence in *Psycho*, Hitchcock freezes the close-up
of Marion's staring eye, as the camera draws back, distancing itself from the
eye that no longer sees and thus bringing to a close one of the most shock-
ing yet artistically done sequences in film.

The zoom and the freeze are similar in that they can call attention
to details more dramatically than other devices do. Because of their strong

The most famous freeze frame in film: the final shot in *The 400 Blows* (1959). *(Courtesy MOMA/FSA and Janus Films)*

underscoring power, they are as easily misused as italics are by inexperienced writers. There was a time in the 1970s and 1980s when many American films ended with a freeze frame, which then became the background for the end credits. However, examples of the intelligent use of the freeze frame are hard to come by. A great filmmaker will freeze for a reason; a mediocre one will freeze for effect.

Combining Shots: The Sequence

In film, shots combine to form sequences, or what we generally think of as scenes. Note that some writers prefer to distinguish between a scene and a sequence. A scene, they would say, is a unit of action that takes place in the same location and is made up of one shot or many shots. A **sequence** is a group of shots forming a self-contained segment of the film that is, by and large, intelligible in itself.

From the above definitions, *scene* and *sequence* appear to be virtually synonymous, and for all practical purposes they are. The chief difference is that there can be scenes within a sequence, but not sequences within scenes. In the key sequence in *Notorious*, there are several scenes. The sequence begins in the bedroom with Alicia's removing the key to the wine cellar from

Alex's key chain (scene 1); next, she gives the key to Devlin downstairs (scene 2); finally, Devlin and Alicia go down to the wine cellar (scene 3).

There are several kinds of sequences. In Chapter 2 we discussed credits and precredits sequences. Sequences can also be identified as linear, associative, and **montage**. Linear sequences have a beginning, a middle, and an end. When a sequence is designated as associative, it means that the links between beginning, middle, and end are visual rather than narrative. A montage consists of a series of shots related by some theme or mood, like the New York montage that accompanies the credits of Woody Allen's *Manhattan* (1979). Note that these types of sequences are not mutually exclusive. An associative sequence can be linear; a linear sequence can contain a montage.

The Linear Sequence

In a linear sequence, one action links up with another, creating a miniature drama. Let us return to the key sequence in *Notorious*. The beginning of the sequence initiates the action: Alicia removes the key. The middle adds to the action: Alicia slips the key to her coworker, Harry Devlin, during the party at Alicia's house; they proceed to the wine cellar, where they discover that one of the bottles contains uranium ore; meanwhile, the champagne supply dwindles, and Alicia's husband and the wine steward go down to the cellar. The end follows and completes the action: the husband discovers his wife with Devlin. In a linear sequence, then, the connections between the incidents are like links in a chain.

After *The Age of Innocence*'s main title, with its rose motif, the action begins with a shot of a basket of daisies — another instance of the role flowers play in the film. A hand plucks one of the daisies; it is the hand of the soprano, singing Marguerite in a performance of Gounod's *Faust*. The setting, then, is an opera house. Everyone is elegantly attired, as is indicated by shots of bejeweled hands and necks. And the audience is less interested in the opera than in who is sitting next to whom, as the camera imitates the way gossipmongers might use their opera glasses. Newland Archer is seated in a box, wearing a white rose in his lapel. In another box are three women, two of whom will play important roles in his life: his fiancée, May (Winona Ryder), and the Countess Olenska (Michelle Pfeiffer), whose colorful past has made her an object of speculation and, among the self-righteous, scorn. Although Newland insists that his engagement be announced at the ball following the performance, he chooses to sit behind the countess. Indifferent to the opera, they recall their childhood together.

Faust, which will be heard again, was not an arbitrary choice on Scorsese's part. In the opera, Faust gives up his soul to possess Marguerite. In the film, Archer sells his soul, one might say, to respectability by choosing to marry the conventional May rather than the unconventional countess, whom he really loves. Although the opening sequence lasts only a few minutes, it establishes the setting (New York in the 1870s) and introduces the characters (New York society), three of whom (Archer, May, and the countess) become the principal ones. The beginning introduces us to a privileged world; the middle, to a world where appearances alone count; and the end, to a world where a man who cannot wait to announce his engagement to an innocent young woman chooses to sit next to a woman whose innocence is questionable.

In some linear sequences, however, a few links may be missing; in such cases, the sequence is elliptical. In an elliptical linear sequence certain details are omitted because viewers are expected to make the connections for themselves. The "Wedding of Angharad" sequence in John Ford's *How Green Was My Valley* (1941) comprises three episodes that appear, on the surface, to be loosely related: "The Courting of Angharad," "The Visit to Gruffydd," and "The Wedding." In the first episode, Evans, a wealthy mine owner's son, comes to court Angharad (Maureen O'Hara). Since Angharad displays a mind of her own, there is little likelihood that Evans will win her despite his wealth. Thus, we do not take the courting seriously. In the second episode, Angharad calls on Mr. Gruffydd (Walter Pidgeon), the minister, whom she really loves. There is something disturbing about this episode—it hints at love never to be consummated. Angharad speaks of her affection for the minister, but his only concern is his low salary, which makes marriage impossible. In the third episode, Angharad steps ghostlike into a carriage, her bridal veil billowing in the breeze.

The three episodes become linked by the impressions they create in the audience's mind. Initially, there seems to be no connection between the courting and Angharad's visit to Gruffydd, but the link becomes clear with the final episode: money, which means nothing to Angharad but means a great deal to the minister. In choosing Evans, she chose what Gruffydd considered the prerequisite for marriage. The folly of her choice is a mirthless wedding. The tragedy of her choice is mirrored in the minister's face as he watches the wedding party drive away.

The Associative Sequence

In an associative sequence, the scenes are linked together by an object or a series of objects. In another sequence in *Notorious*, Alicia, who has fallen in love with Devlin, plans an intimate dinner for the two of them. As Devlin leaves for headquarters, Alicia asks him to pick up some wine. In the next scene, Devlin enters his supervisor's office with a bottle of champagne, which he leaves on the desk. When he discovers that Alicia's assignment requires her to seduce Sebastian, he is so disturbed that he forgets the champagne. Scene 2 ends with a close-up of the bottle. In the third scene, Devlin

Harry Devlin (Cary Grant) on the verge of forgetting the champagne in *Notorious* (1946). Hitchcock ends the scene with a close-up of the bottle, the object that unifies the entire sequence. *(Courtesy ABC Picture Holdings, Inc.)*

is back in Alicia's apartment, where the dinner is burned and there is not even any wine to salvage the evening. He looks around for the champagne. "I guess I left it somewhere," he mutters. These three episodes coalesce into a sequence that might be entitled "The Ruined Dinner," whose three scenes might be called "The Bottle Suggested," "The Bottle Purchased," and "The Bottle Forgotten." The bottle is an object that unifies the sequence: the close-up of the bottle in scene 2 links scenes 1 and 3, bringing them into dramatic focus.

In the sequence that ends another Hitchcock film, *North by Northwest*, Eve Kendall (Eva Marie Saint) is holding on to the hand of Roger Thornhill (Cary Grant) to keep from sliding off Mount Rushmore. Thornhill encourages her to "hang in there," having recently proposed marriage. In one of the smoothest transitions in film, the hand to which Eve was just clinging is now helping her climb to the upper berth of a compartment on the Twentieth Century Limited. Without the audience's suspecting it, the scene changed from Mount Rushmore to the train compartment. Thornhill's hand was the unifying image; it rescued Eve from death and saved her for marriage.

The Montage Sequence

Montage is a word that has many meanings. When it is used to describe a sequence, montage can be defined as a series of shots arranged in a particular order for a particular purpose. In a montage sequence, the shots are arranged so that they follow each other in rapid succession, telescoping an event or several events into a couple of seconds of screen time. *A New Life* (1988) contains a montage that shows a newly divorced woman trying to resume dating for the first time in twenty-five years. A specific kind of montage, called **American montage** because it was so prominent in American films of the 1930s and 1940s, collapses time as shots blend together, wipe each other away, or are superimposed on each other. A typical American montage might consist of calendar pages blowing away as one month yields to another, while over the blowing pages are superimposed headlines giving the main events that took place during that time period. Another American montage might be newspapers spinning across the screen announcing a murder trial as one headline obliterates the other. During the trial, one shot would wipe away another. The face of the judge would dissolve into the defendant's; superimposed over the defendant's face would be that of his anguished wife and, over hers, the face of the real murderer. When the montage ends, the action resumes.

A montage sequence can have features of both the linear and the associative sequence. A montage sequence compressing a decade into ten seconds could be linear in its chronological arrangement. The World War II montage was common in films of the 1940s. First, one would see a headline announcing the Japanese attack on Pearl Harbor; then subsequent headlines would enumerate key battles, and the last headline would proclaim the Japanese surrender.

A montage can also be unified by images. For example, the tour-of-Washington montage in *Mr. Smith Goes to Washington* combines shots of the Capitol, the White House, the Washington Monument, the Lincoln Memorial, and excerpts from Lincoln's Second Inaugural Address and the Gettysburg Address, all of which are associated with American democracy.

From Shot to Shot

In order to create sequences and scenes, filmmakers must decide how to arrange a series of shots so that one replaces another. Filmmakers can move from one shot to another by either using a **cut** or a **transition**.

Cuts

Cut is one of the most commonly used terms in film. It can be a verb a director shouts to terminate a shot ("Cut!") or a noun meaning a strip of film or a joint between two separate shots. It can also be a version of a movie in its various stages—a **rough cut** is one of the earliest versions, a **director's cut** is the film as the director envisioned it, and a **final cut** is the version audiences will see.

In the context of this chapter, a cut is the joining of two separate shots so that the first is instantaneously replaced by the second, showing something the preceding shot did not. There are six basic kinds of cuts: straight, contrast, cross (parallel), jump, form, and match.

In a **straight cut,** one image instantaneously replaces another. Straight cuts are the most common kind of cuts: shot B replaces shot A. In *The Lady Eve* (1941), Preston Sturges cuts from Charlie Pike (Henry Fonda) sitting at a table in a ship's dining room (shot A) to a group of women staring in his direction (shot B).

In a **contrast cut,** the images replacing each other are dissimilar in nature; for example, the cut from the manacled feet of slaves to the galloping hooves of horses in *Slaves* (1969) contrasts the enslaved and the free.

The **crosscut,** or **parallel cut,** presents two actions that occur simultaneously. In *Saboteur*, an attempt to sabotage a battleship at a christening is crosscut with the ceremony itself. In *Moonstruck* (1987), a mother is having dinner with a university professor, while her daughter is at the Metropolitan Opera with her lover.

The Godfather ends with one of the most chilling examples of crosscutting in film. Scenes from the baptism of Michael Corleone's nephew are crosscut with a series of killings Michael has ordered to take place. At the same time that Michael is witnessing the religious ceremony, and officially becoming his nephew's godfather, the audience witnesses the Mafia assassinations that result in the deaths of Michael's enemies, including his brother-in-law Carlo, the baby's father.

A break in continuity that leaves a gap in the action constitutes a **jump cut.** In *Darling* (1965), a shot of a couple about twenty yards from the entrance to a building is followed by a shot of them going through the door to the interior of the building. Obviously, not everything has to be shown in a particular scene or sequence, but excessive jump-cutting can give a film the continuity of a comic strip. On the other hand, when a knowledgeable director jump-cuts, there is probably a reason. In Jean-Luc Godard's *Breathless* (1959), the main character shoots a police officer in Marseilles, runs across a field, and emerges in Paris. Godard is too talented a filmmaker to break continuity without a reason. *Breathless* is the kind of movie that calls attention to itself as a movie. It is dedicated to Monogram Pictures, which produced low-budget films during the 1930s and 1940s, and re-creates the style of the low-budget American film in which a character can move from one location to the other without being seen in transit.

A **form cut** is a cut from one object to another that is similarly shaped. In *Detour* (1946), there is a cut from a record in a jukebox to a drumhead—one circular object replaces another.

Similar in principle to the form cut is the **match cut,** in which one shot complements or "matches" the other, following it so smoothly that there seems to be no break in continuity as far as time and space are concerned, although there often is. However, if the match is designed to bring us into a different time frame, it should be done so naturally that we barely notice it. For example, in *Indiana Jones and the Last Crusade* (1989), Steven Spielberg uses a match cut to bring Indiana from youth to adulthood. In the first shot, Indiana the boy (River Phoenix) bows his head to receive the famous hat; as the head lifts in the second shot, it is Indiana the man (Harrison Ford) who is wearing the hat. Probably the most famous match in film is the one in Stanley Kubrick's *2001: A Space Odyssey* (1968), when an ape hurls a bone into the air in one shot and a space shuttle appears in the next. The match condenses the history of evolution into two images.

Transitions

In a cut there is no bridge between shots; one shot simply replaces another. Just as writers use transitional words and phrases like *however, moreover,* and *in fact* to bridge ideas, filmmakers use transitions to bridge scenes. And just as one can spot transitional phrases, one can also spot transitional devices in film because they are more noticeable than cuts. The following are the chief transitional devices used in film.

The Fade.   The **fade-out** is the simplest kind of transition: the light decreases, and the screen goes dark or to a particular color. The opposite is the **fade-in,** where the light increases as the picture gradually appears on the screen. In general, the term *fade* refers to a fade-out. Most fade-outs are no more profound than a blank screen, but some can bring an action to an artful close, much the way a gifted orator rounds out a sentence. A good illustration is the first fade-out in William Wyler's *Mrs. Miniver* (1942). The first sequence covers a day in the lives of the Minivers. Both husband and wife feel guilty for having purchased something the other might find frivolous: Kay (Greer Garson) has bought a new hat, and Clem (Walter Pidgeon) a new car. At the close of the day, the camera pans the bedroom, pausing at the hat smartly perched on the bedpost. The scene fades out with the hat in silhouette. Fading out on the hat brings the sequence full circle: it began with Kay's buying the hat and ends with the hat's being displayed. We smile at the fade because it provides the same pleasure of recognition we receive when a speech begins and ends with the same image. But we also smile at

Harry Devlin as the uninvited guest at Alicia's (Ingrid Bergman) party in *Notorious*. Hitchcock will fade out on the back of Grant's head and fade in on his face. *(Courtesy ABC Picture Holdings, Inc.)*

its wisdom, for it represents one of those little domestic triumphs that seem more meaningful at the end of the day than at the beginning.

In the theater, the stage may go dark between scenes, or the curtain may even descend between them, to mark the passage of time. In film, a fade can function in the same way. The first fade in *Notorious* occurs at a particularly dramatic moment. There is an unidentified guest at Alicia's party, sitting with his back to the camera. Curiously, he remains after everyone else leaves. Hitchcock fades out on the back of the man and fades in on his face, which is none other than Cary Grant's. Hitchcock interrupts the party with a fade to indicate a lapse of time; but the fade is also a clever way of introducing the male lead by linking two scenes in which he appears—one ending with his back to the camera, the other beginning with his face coming into view. The fade helps produce a natural rhythm.

A fade can also be commentative. In *Mr. Skeffington* (1944), the aging Fanny Skeffington (Bette Davis) reassembles her former suitors, who are now either married or going bald. The scene fades out as the men enter the dining room and fades in on a gentleman's hat and gloves. The hat and gloves belong to Edward (Jerome Cowan), an impoverished suitor who has returned to court Fanny. The fade-out allows us to see a connection between the two scenes. In the first, Fanny has invited her suitors to dinner to reassure herself that she is still beautiful. However, Edward is not interested in her beauty, which is nonexistent, but only in her money, which is also nonexistent although he does not know it. One charade fades out and another fades in. A cut would not have conveyed the idea of one farce rising out of another.

The Dissolve. A fade denotes demarcation — it indicates the end of a narrative sequence. A **dissolve** denotes continuity by the gradual replacement of one shot by another. This kind of transition, in which the outgoing and incoming shots merge, serves a variety of functions. Sometimes a dissolve simply has the force of "in the meantime" or "later." In *North by Northwest*, Hitchcock dissolves a shot of Roger Thornhill bribing his mother to get a key from the desk clerk at a hotel to a shot of the two of them walking down the corridor toward the room Thornhill was so anxious to enter.

A dissolve can also mean "no sooner said than done." The Mother Superior in *The Song of Bernadette* (1943) no sooner asks to see Bernadette than the shot dissolves into Bernadette's room. In Max Ophüls's *Caught* (1949), a shot of a woman gazing at a picture of a model in a mink coat dissolves into a shot of the woman, who has become a model herself, wearing a mink.

When is a dissolve a transition, and when is it more than a transition? This is like asking, when is a word simply a conventional sign and when is it a symbol? Water can simply be a liquid, or it can be a sign of birth, rebirth, or fertility. It depends on the context: in T. S. Eliot's poems, water is never just water. It is the same with a dissolve. What a dissolve means — if, in fact, it means anything — is determined by the context. The dissolve in *North by Northwest* was just a way of getting two characters from the hotel lobby to one of the floors.

When two images blend in such a way that their union constitutes a symbolic equation, however, the result is a metaphorical dissolve. This is a visual form of **synecdoche** (or **metonymy,** to which synecdoche is very similar). Synecdoche is a species of metaphor in which the part is substituted for the whole — the term "wheels" for car, for example — or a sign replaces the thing signified, as in green meaning "go." We often use this figure of speech without knowing it — saying "All hands on deck" when hands = crew, or "He addressed his comments to the chair" when chair = chairperson.

In *The Two Mrs. Carrolls* (1947), Geoffrey Carroll (Humphrey Bogart) is a wife poisoner. Early in the film, Sally (Barbara Stanwyck) discovers a letter he dropped, addressed to his wife. Because Sally is in love with Geoffrey, she questions him about his marriage. He replies that he is getting a divorce. The letter dissolves into a neatly wrapped package of poison Geoffrey has just purchased from a pharmacist. The merging of the two images, the letter and the package, results in the equation: Mrs. Carroll + package = death. Dissolving an envelope bearing a woman's name into the means that will make her only a name is an ingenious touch.

The dissolves in George Stevens's films have an effect similar to the homogenization of cream and milk. In *Shane*, when Starrett (Van Heflin) and Shane (Alan Ladd) succeed in uprooting a stubborn tree trunk, Stevens slowly merges their triumphant faces into the landscape, making the men one with nature. Later, when Starrett watches a homesteader's property go up in flames, Stevens dissolves his vengeful face into the burning house. The resulting equations — man + nature = natural man; face + burning house = consuming rage — do not advance the plot; their purpose, rather, is to illustrate one of the film's main themes: the pioneer's oneness with nature, which enables him to become a part of everything he sees or does.

A dissolve can sometimes have the effect of **dramatic foreshadowing** if the filmmaker prepares the audience for subsequent events by hinting at their outcome earlier. In *King and Country* (1964), a skull mired in mud dissolves into the face of a soldier playing a harmonica. The dissolve prefigures the fate of the soldier, who later dies in the mud, his voice silenced by a pistol shot in the mouth.

Dissolves can also recapitulate. At the end of *The Last Picture Show* (1971), Sonny (Timothy Bottoms) returns to the house of Ruth Popper (Cloris Leachman), the coach's wife, with whom he has been having an affair. The movie house has closed its doors forever; Sam the Lion and Billy are dead; Duane is on his way to Korea. All that remain are Ruth and the dreary Texas town where the tumbleweed rolls down the main street. As Sonny and Ruth look at each other, their eyes forge the only bond that can unite them — loneliness. At that moment, Sonny and Ruth dissolve into the town and the vast Texas flatlands. There is no difference between a young man without prospects, a middle-aged woman without hope, and a town without a future. Their destinies have become one.

At the end of *Colorado Territory* (1949), Raoul Walsh's western remake of his earlier success, *High Sierra* (1941), the hands of Wes (Joel McCrea) and Colorado (Virginia Mayo), touching in death, dissolve into a shot of a ringing bell. The dissolve does not so much connect two images as it connects two events that the lovers' hands and the bell represent. Earlier in the film, Wes had hidden some stolen money in an abandoned church. After the deaths of Wes and Colorado, a priest discovers the money and uses it to restore the church bell, telling the villagers it was the gift of two lovers who passed by.

The Form Dissolve. A filmmaker can merge two images with the same shape or contours through a **form dissolve.** Often, a form dissolve is merely easy on the eyes. For example, in *Jane Eyre* the figure of a ballerina on top of a music box dissolves into a little girl dressed in the same costume. A form dissolve can also be directly related to the plot. In Hitchcock's *The Wrong Man*, a jazz musician is falsely accused of committing a holdup. As the musician (Henry Fonda) prays in front of a picture of Jesus Christ, the scene gradually changes to that of a man walking down a dark street. Then the man's head merges with the musician's. The man whose head fits into the musician's is the real criminal. The dissolve shows how easy it is to mistake the innocent for the guilty; it is just a matter of superimposing one face upon another.

The decision to cut or dissolve, or do both, is the filmmaker's choice. In his sequel to *The Godfather* — *The Godfather, Part II* (1974) — Francis Ford

The killing of Don Ciccio in Francis Ford Coppola's *The Godfather, Part II* (1974). *(Courtesy Paramount Pictures)*

Coppola chose to interweave the lives of Vito Corleone (Robert De Niro) and his son Michael (Al Pacino) by restricting each of them to a particular time period (1901–1925 for Vito, 1955–1959 for Michael). The film shifts back and forth from past to present. The shift occurs for the first time as Michael is putting his son to bed. Slowly, the scene dissolves to Vito in 1917, as he puts Michael's brother, Sonny, to bed. When Coppola wants to contrast Michael's frenetic lifestyle with his father's more leisurely one, he uses a cut. More often, however, Coppola dissolves from present to past, and vice versa. For example, when Michael learns that his wife Kay has had a miscarriage, later revealed to have been an abortion, Coppola dissolves to a shot of Vito, hovering over Michael's older brother, Fredo, who is ill with pneumonia. Coppola ends the flashback with the young Michael on Vito's lap, but then cuts to a car making its way along a wintry road and proceeding through the imposing entrance of Michael's Lake Tahoe home. The cut ushers us into a present so loveless that Kay does not even look up from her sewing to greet her husband. Rarely has a filmmaker alternated between dissolves and cuts as creatively as Coppola does.

The Wipe.　In the 1970s and 1980s, television news programs often used a line traveling vertically across the scene to switch from one news item to another. That traveling line is a **wipe,** and in the movies of the 1930s and 1940s the wipe was the most stylish of the transitions. Since the screen is rectangular, the wipe can move vertically, horizontally, or diagonally; it can create a theatrical effect by rising or falling like a drop curtain.

Sometimes wipes complement each other: one shot ends with a wipe that travels from left to right; the next with a wipe that moves across the screen from right to left. The best example of complementary wipes can be found in the opening of *The Petty Girl* (1950).

More fluid than a cut and faster than a dissolve, the wipe is ideal for presenting a series of events in quick succession. Wipes are often used in the opening sequences of Frank Capra's Columbia films of the 1930s, notably in the opening sequences of *It Happened One Night*, *Mr. Deeds Goes to Town* (1936), and *Mr. Smith Goes to Washington*. In the handwriting sequence in *Mr. Smith Goes to Washington*, for example, one expert after another testifies to the authenticity of Jeff Smith's signature. After each expert speaks, Capra simply wipes him off the screen, thereby showing the inanity of the investigation.

Rouben Mamoulian's excellent use of the wipe is apparent in *Dr. Jekyll and Mr. Hyde* (1932). After Jekyll (Fredric March) becomes Hyde, he goes off into the night, deserting Muriel Carew (Rose Hobart), his fiancée, who expects him at her dinner party. A wipe opens like a fan, dividing the screen diagonally: on the left is the departing Jekyll; on the right, the party in progress. When Jekyll leaves the Carew estate, Mamoulian wipes him out of the frame, which expands to disclose the dinner guests and the worried Muriel. At that point, the frame divides diagonally again: on the right is Ivy (Miriam Hopkins), the woman Hyde will kill, sipping champagne; on the left is Muriel, the woman Jekyll yearns to marry. The wipe acts as a parallel cut, informing us that while Muriel was at her party, Ivy was at home. But the split screen also represents the protagonist's ideal woman, who is similarly halved. It is only fitting that for a double man (Jekyll/Hyde) there should be a double woman (Ivy/Muriel).

When Muriel's father, furious at Jekyll's absence, cries, "Muriel, you will have nothing more to do with that man," a wipe begins to move him from the left of the screen to the center, revealing the man himself. However, it is not Jekyll but Hyde whom we see. The wipe is an ironic commentary on the father's outburst; clearly, he did not mean that Muriel should have nothing to do with Hyde (whom he cannot know) but with Jekyll. At this point, however, Jekyll is Hyde.

Some writers compare the wipe to a windshield wiper, and there are times when it can assume that form. Hitchcock uses the wipe in *Psycho*; as Marion drives in the rain, the sign for the Bates Motel materializes on her windshield.

The Iris. Mount Rushmore, as seen through a telescope in *North by Northwest*, appears inside a circle in the middle of the darkened screen. This is a **masking shot,** or, to be more accurate, an **iris shot,** in which everything is blacked out except what is to be seen telescopically. Depending on the form in which the director wants the audience to see an image, the frame can also be altered to simulate other shapes, such as the view from a keyhole, through binoculars, or out a submarine periscope.

The director can also choose to iris in or iris out. **Irising in** consists of opening up the darkened frame with a circle of light that keeps expanding until the picture fills the frame. **Irising out** is the opposite; it is as if darkness were seeping into the frame from all sides, forcing the diminishing picture into some part of the frame until it becomes a speck and disappears.

A director can dolly in or out of a scene or zoom in or out of one; but there is nothing quite like an iris to open the frame. In *The Birth of a Nation*, Griffith used the iris breathtakingly in Sherman's march to the sea. The frame opens from the upper-left-hand corner to reveal a mother and her children on a hill; at first we do not know why they are huddled in fear, but as the frame opens we see Sherman's soldiers in the valley below. In *Intolerance*, Griffith gradually disclosed the splendor of Babylon by expanding the frame, starting at the lower-right-hand corner.

The iris is especially effective in death scenes. Irising out can suggest death because of the way in which darkness creeps into the frame, reducing the size of the image to a pinpoint and then annihilating it. Orson Welles chose the iris to symbolize both the death of Wilbur Minafer and the end of the horse-and-buggy era in *The Magnificent Ambersons* (1942). A horseless carriage moves in long shot across the snow. The passengers sing merrily, but their song is in sharp contrast to the landscape, which is dominated by a dead tree with wiry branches. As the motor buggy moves out of the frame, Welles irises out until it disappears in the darkness of a fade. One would have expected him to iris out of one scene and into another, but the shot that follows the fade is of a black wreath on the door of the Amberson house. The iris and the fade imply finality in different ways—the iris gradually and poetically; the fade, irrevocably.

The flashbacks in George Stevens's *Penny Serenade* (1941) are also unified by irising. Julie (Irene Dunne) recalls incidents from her marriage by playing old records of songs that had meaning for her and her husband. Each flashback begins with a close-up of the center of the record, which then opens up, irislike, to reveal the scene.

Irising is still being practiced, although not as regularly as it was in Griffith's day or during the 1930s and the 1940s. However, we do find irising on certain television programs and in movies where techniques of the past function as period touches. When George Roy Hill irises out on the two con men at the close of *The Sting* (1973), it gives the ending a deliberately old-fashioned look. Similarly, the irising in Peter Bogdanovich's *Nickelodeon* lends an air of authenticity to the film, which is set in the early days of the movie industry.

A frame enlargement of an iris shot from *The Birth of a Nation*. In an iris shot, the image appears within a circle on an otherwise dark screen. *(Courtesy MOMA/FSA and Epoch Producing Corp.)*

Contemporary filmmakers such as Steven Spielberg, Francis Ford Coppola, Woody Allen, and Martin Scorsese, who have immersed themselves in the films of the past, understandably draw on the techniques that have occupied film history and proven to be effective in the past. Brian De Palma chose a fade as a sign of demarcation at the beginning of *Dressed to Kill* (1980) when he fades to white after Kate's sexual fantasy. Steven Spielberg fades to black in *Empire of the Sun* to indicate that the first part of the action is over. In Francis Ford Coppola's *Peggy Sue Got Married* (1986), a wipe takes Peggy Sue (Kathleen Turner) from high school, where she is talking with a male student, to her bedroom, where she is talking with her girlfriends. Two iris shots appear in Scorsese's *The Age of Innocence*—one of May's unusual engagement ring; the other of Newland and the countess at the opera, either to suggest intimacy by placing them within a circle of privacy or to imply that they may have come within the range of some gossip's opera glasses. Wipes and irises abound in the *Star Wars* films, which evoke the old movie serials in which such devices were common. Here they have the double function of evoking nostalgia and promoting the narrative.

The Golden Bowl (2001), an adaptation of Henry James's novel, ends with an iris shot for a specific reason. The film, set at the turn of the twentieth century, concludes with a newsreel showing the return of an American millionaire and his English wife (Nick Nolte and Uma Thurman) to the United States. Since early newsreels often closed by irising out on an image, director James Ivory did likewise to provide an air of authenticity as well as to suggest that the couple's reputation as patrons of the arts has made them newsworthy. As more film disciples go on to become filmmakers, their work will reflect what they have learned and what they have seen.

Assembling the Shots

When Alfred Hitchcock said that a film must be edited, he meant that the shots that make up the movie must be assembled and arranged in such a way that the action proceeds in a logical and coherent manner. **Editing** involves selecting and arranging the shots based on the following considerations: their place within the narrative, their contribution to the mood of a particular scene or to the film as a whole, their enhancement of the film's rhythm, their elucidation of the film's deeper meaning, and their fulfillment of the filmmaker's purpose.

The most common form of editing in the narrative film is **continuity editing,** which entails assembling shots so that they follow each other smoothly and without interruption, as opposed to the piecemeal way in which a movie is filmed. Movies are generally shot out of sequence, with location filming usually done before soundstage filming, and scenes involving actors with other commitments shot when the actors are available. Filmgoers do not care which scenes were shot first or that the climax in the Grand Canyon was shot on the second day of shooting because the weather happened to be ideal. Continuity editing preserves the illusion of an ongoing narrative.

Continuity editing is only one option a filmmaker might choose. Another might be montage.

Eisenstein's Theory of Montage

While montage is sometimes used as a synonym for editing (e.g., American montage sequence), it had deeper implications for the great Russian filmmaker Sergei Eisenstein. Eisenstein believed that shots should not so much connect as collide, and that the viewer should be affected by their collision. Unlike continuity editing, which is supposed to be unobtrusive, montage calls attention to itself. If a man postures like a peacock, cut from the man to the peacock; if he is figuratively a horse's ass, pair him with a real one. If the purpose of a scene is to show people being killed like animals, cut from workers being massacred to an ox being slaughtered. This is the kind of montage that Eisenstein practiced.

Eisensteinian montage is based on contrast and conflict, which can exist both within the film as a whole and within a particular shot or scene. In the Odessa Steps massacre in Eisenstein's *Potemkin*, a body lies diagonally across the steps; the Cossacks cast shadows that fall menacingly at oblique angles to the steps; the steps form three contrasting planes, with the Cossacks at the top firing at a woman on a landing, behind which lies a trail of bodies.

Eisenstein discovered how ideas could arise from the contrast and conflict of images. Without creating an actual series of cause and effect, he opened *Potemkin* with a shot of breaking waves and followed this image of turbulence with shots of men sleeping in hammocks that formed a shroudlike tangle, mess tables swinging back and forth, meat crawling with maggots—each image jarring us, disquieting us, but ultimately preparing us for the sailors' revolt.

Eisenstein's influence was enormous, but not always beneficial. Instead of producing an artistic effect, the collision of images sometimes produces only pretentiousness. There is an embarrassing scene in Mamoulian's otherwise impressive *Dr. Jekyll and Mr. Hyde* when Jekyll, exulting over his impending marriage to Muriel, shouts, "If music be the food of love, play on!," as he sits down at the organ and pounds away. Five shots appear in rapid succession, commenting on his rapture: a lighted candelabra, an illuminated art object, a smiling statue, the butler's beaming countenance, and a blazing hearth. Jekyll's rapture is evident from the way he plays the organ; the accompanying montage is superfluous.

To Eisenstein, montage meant the visual conflict of images. In European countries, it means editing: selecting and arranging the shots that will form the scenes and sequences of a film. In England, the same process is called editing, or cutting, but with a slight difference: "editing" means the step-by-step assembling of the shots in the cutting room, while "montage" refers to the process considered as a whole. A further complication is that during the 1930s and 1940s American films employed American montage, which, as we have already seen, is a convenient way of collapsing time. Although this form of montage, in which time is telescoped through a blend of dissolves, wipes, and superimposures, is not in vogue today, in its time it was highly effective and was regarded as sufficiently important to warrant screen credit for the montage editor. Slavko Vorkapich was especially adept at montage (*Mr. Deeds Goes to Town, Mr. Smith Goes to Washington*); Don Siegel began in montage at Warner Bros. before going on to become a well-known director (*Invasion of the Body Snatchers*, 1956; *Dirty Harry*, 1971; *Escape from Alcatraz*, 1979; and so on).

Continuity Editing

While montage may seem to be intellectually more exciting than continuity editing, it would be a mistake to dismiss continuity editing as merely the sequential arrangement of shots. Continuity editing is based on other editing principles that affect a film's rhythm, time, space, tone, and theme.

Rhythm.   No great film is rhythmically uniform. Some shots remain on the screen longer than others; some sequences move more rapidly than others. One sequence may be uncommonly slow, while another may be unusually fast. The best filmmakers vary speed, movement, and pace, knowing that long strips of roll film produce a slower rhythm, short strips a more rapid rhythm. The process itself is not the issue here, the effects are, as one can see in the first two sequences of *Citizen Kane*, "The Death of Kane" and "News on the March."

    Citizen Kane begins with a series of dreamlike dissolves culminating in a shot of a lighted window that suddenly goes dark. A mouth utters "Rosebud!" through a veil of falling snow, and a glass paperweight with a snow-covered house inside it smashes without making a sound. A nurse enters a room and folds a dead man's arms across his chest. The mood of the first part of "The Death of Kane" is slow and languid. As the camera draws closer to the window, the rhythm accelerates. Snow falls to the sound of crystal-pure music, evoking Kane's Colorado boyhood. After the paperweight breaks and the nurse enters, the rhythm decelerates, and the mood becomes solemn as she places Kane's arms on his chest. Without warning, a voice bellows, "News on the march!," as a newsreel of Kane's life unfolds. In the second scene the pace is frenetic; fifty years of a man's life are compressed into a few minutes. The pace builds inexorably until the "News on the March" is over and the camera sputters out, as if in exhaustion.

Time.   Parallel cutting makes it possible for two concurrent actions to be depicted on the screen without one being completed before the other begins—the filmmaker simply cuts back and forth between them. Most novelists would never narrate two simultaneous episodes by completing the first before going on to the second; the novelist would bring the first to a certain point and, leaving the reader in suspense, proceed to the second. The novelist would then gradually add to each episode until the episodes are

From "The Death of Kane" in *Citizen Kane*

Frame enlargement of the glass paperweight that falls from Kane's hand. The lighted window of Kane's bedroom goes dark. Suddenly snow begins to fall; it is the artificial snow in the glass paperweight that falls from Kane's hand as he utters his last word, "Rosebud!" *(Courtesy MOMA/FSA)*

resolved either separately or jointly. D. W. Griffith understood this principle when he made *The Lonely Villa* (1909), in which he cut back and forth between a mother and her daughters being terrorized by thieves who have broken into their home, and the father en route to rescue them. The action is resolved by the last-minute rescue.

Space.   Film's ability to alter our perception of space is well known. A filmmaker can combine a shot of a tractor trailer that has jackknifed on Route 81 outside Scranton, Pennsylvania, with a shot of a girl who has just gotten off the Cyclone at Coney Island, looking appropriately dazed. The combination could lead one to conclude that the girl witnessed the jackknifing, even though one event occurred in Pennsylvania and the other took place in New York.

D. W. Griffith's *Intolerance* is a four-plot film about injustice as seen in four different periods: the early twentieth century, the age of Cyrus the Great in the sixth century B.C.E., the time of Christ, and the Saint Bartholomew's Day massacre of the Huguenots in 1572. Although the film depicts events in four different parts of the world, everything converges at the climax. By alternating between shots of Christ on his way to Calvary, the Mountain Girl on her chariot to warn Cyrus, a modern-day race against the clock to save the life of an innocent man, and Prosper the Huguenot rushing through the streets of sixteenth-century Paris to rescue his beloved,

As the nurse enters Kane's room, her image is refracted through a piece of the shattered paperweight. *(Courtesy MOMA/FSA)*

Griffith makes it seem that everything is occurring not only at the same time but also in the same general area. The parallel cutting has affected our sense of time and space, as well as reflecting the film's theme: the existence of intolerance at all times and in all places.

Tone.   Just as tempo should vary in a film, so too should tone, which is primarily light, shade, and color. Again, *Citizen Kane* is an excellent example. The first sequence, "The Death of Kane," is dark and eerie. The second sequence, "News on the March," is the exact opposite.

When Francis Ford Coppola contrasts the lives of the Corleones in *The Godfather, Part II*, Vito's world, New York's Little Italy, is warm and inviting; Michael's is dark and forbidding.

Theme.   Juxtaposing contrasting shots can deepen a film's theme. As we have seen, there is a cut in *Slaves* from the manacled feet of slaves to the galloping hooves of horses. Whether the horses are in the same vicinity as the slaves is irrelevant; the point of the cut is the contrast between the enslaved and the free. In *A Doll's House* (1973), there is a cut from Nora's upper-middle-class home to Krogstad's hovel; seeing how Krogstad lives makes it easier to understand his blackmailing Nora.

The Role of the Editor

Since it is a common fallacy that films are made in the editing room, students often have difficulty distinguishing between the editor's role and the filmmaker's. We have seen that editing involves selecting and arranging the shots in a particular order. But who does the arranging—the editor or the filmmaker?

Let us use an analogy from student life. After you have written an essay or a term paper, you submit it to your instructor. Before submitting it, you have edited it: removed superfluous words, substituted the right words for the wrong ones, corrected spelling and grammar. Still, your essay may not be perfect; you have been too close to it to catch all the mistakes. Since your instructor did not write it, he or she can be more objective. You may have sentences, or even paragraphs, that should be transposed. What you thought was an introduction might work better if you made it your conclusion. Perhaps you did not prune the paper of all its excesses; your instructor will note that. A good instructor can take what you have submitted and, by making the proper corrections and suggestions, show you how it can be improved. Your instructor did not write the paper, yet he or she has made it better by doing something for it that you have not done.

An editor performs a similar task: he or she takes what has been shot and improves on it. The ideal film editor is the director's alter ego, carrying out what the director would do if he or she had the time to be all things to the film. Thus, an editor may select the shots or decide which portion of a shot should be used. An editor can give an action scene its distinctive rhythm by alternating tempo and varying directional movement. If a sequence needs greater momentum, an editor can cut it in such a way that it acquires this feature. If a scene is especially violent, an editor can cut it so rapidly that the movie will receive a PG-13 instead of an R rating. If shot A shows the pursuers moving left to right, shot B must show the pursued fleeing left to right; otherwise, it would look as if they collided. If a character exits shot A from the left, the character must enter shot B from the right.

Because all films require some form of editing, the importance of editors has often been exaggerated, and their role sometimes equated with that of directors. Lee Bobker compares editors with painters, working in isolation to create the movie's pace, mood, and rhythm. Yet, despite Bobker's respect for the editor's function, he is forced to admit that it is a subservient one: "The editor should always enjoy a wide creative latitude, but he should never fall prey to the illusion that he is creating a new film from scratch. His primary purpose is to bring to completion an artistic work already in progress."[1]

In the first edition of *The Technique of Film Editing*, Karel Reisz dubbed the editor "the interpreter of the small details rather than the prime creator of the continuity."[2] For the second edition, Professor Thorold Dickinson provided an introduction to the second part of the book in which he stated that "the modern editor is the executant for the film-maker and no longer his equal on any self-respecting film."[3]

Most good editors would agree. The best answer to the question "What is film editing?" was given by the British editor Anthony Gibbs: "Film editing is putting into dramatic form the basic filmed material given to the editor by the director."[4] However, just as there are average, good, and great directors, there are average, good, and great editors. Gibbs would call a good editor someone who can achieve "the total interpretation of the director's and the writer's intentions," and a great editor someone who is capable of "taking their intentions even farther, showing them a dimension to their project which even they may not have imagined to be there."[5]

True greatness is rare in any profession; thus, great editors are probably at a premium. It is not unlikely that an editor capable of bringing to the surface what the filmmaker did not even know was there would go on to become a director. The motto of Edward Dmytryk, who began his career as an editor and then went on to direct some fifty films between 1935 and 1975, is relevant: "Substance first—then form."[6] Director Sidney Lumet goes even further: "No movie editor has ever put anything up on the screen that hadn't been shot."[7] The filmmaker must provide the substance if the editor is to provide the form.

Alfred Hitchcock always provided the substance, as the first part of the key sequence in *Notorious* demonstrates. The effectiveness of the sequence came from the editing; but editor Theron Warth could not have achieved such effectiveness if Hitchcock had not first determined the form of the sequence by providing Warth with twelve shots that he could assemble.

Hitchcock had an imaginative approach to the scene; he knew that whatever he shot had to be edited in such a way that the audience would wonder whether or not Alicia could detach the key; and if she did, what next? The way the sequence is edited reflects the way Hitchcock wanted the viewer to experience the removal of the key:

1. Putting on her earrings, Alicia enters the frame in an LS that ends with an MS as she looks to her left.
2. She was looking in the direction of the bathroom, where we see the shadow of her husband Sebastian (MS).
3. Alicia seems to be gazing at something (CU).
4. The camera tracks up to the object of her gaze: the key ring in CU on the dressing table.
5. Alicia approaches the dressing table and glances toward the bathroom (LS).
6. Sebastian's shadow is still visible (MS).
7. Back to Alicia at the dressing table.
8. She glances again at the bathroom (CU).
9. She removes the key (CU).
10. Repeat of shot 8.
11. Sebastian comes out of the bathroom as
12. Alicia goes back to the bedroom (LS).

To paraphrase Sidney Lumet, Hitchcock provided the material; the editor gave it form. By providing Warth with a mix of close-ups, long shots, and medium shots, Hitchcock enabled him to give the scene a definite rhythm that it would not have had if the twelve shots had been reduced to Alicia's noticing the key ring and removing the correct key as her husband comes out of the bathroom.

Mise-en-Scène

You may have been told in an English class never to use a foreign word or phrase when an English one would suffice. The rule is a good one, but it is not always possible to follow. Some terms have become so much a part of our critical vocabulary that, although they derive from other languages, they crystallize a complex idea in a single word or phrase. If that word or phrase is properly understood, discussion can proceed without further explanation. Such a phrase is one that film critics use: *mise-en-scène*. *Mise-en-scène* is a French phrase used to describe the staging of a play. Often a playbill will read "Staged by" rather than "Directed by" because, in effect, the director has brought a written text to the stage, giving it the visualization it needs to go beyond being words on paper.

In film, mise-en-scène has a similar meaning: the "staging" of a movie, using the same attention to detail that is lavished on a theatrical production, so that the filmmaker, like the stage director, can realize his or her vision of the material. Some film scholars have restricted the phrase to the arrangement of the visual elements within a shot or a sequence such as camera movement, the placement of the characters in relation to each other, the set, lighting, and so forth. But there is general agreement that, just as a stage director must decide how to give life to a written text, a film director must do the same. Both cases involve a script and its realization, whether it is called a dramatization or a visualization.

Mise-en-scène is really a form of **framing,** a term that is easily understood by anyone who has either studied painting or has actually painted. Framing is the act, and sometimes the art, of composing a shot, reflecting decisions similar to those painters make about how their canvas will ultimately look. The filmmaker's canvas is the **frame,** the strip of celluloid on which the image is captured. Like a painter, the filmmaker must arrange the details of the frame in terms of the visual or dramatic points being made, or the ideas being expressed.

There is a shot in *Road to Perdition* (2002) in which a hit man is loading his gun in a room in which there is a picture of the Sacred Heart of Jesus and the Virgin Mary. Director Sam Mendes could have panned over from the gun to the picture, but instead he included both in the same frame to make a visual comment on the disparity between the hit man's profession and the religion in which he had been raised—a religion founded on the Ten Commandments, the fifth of which is "Thou shalt not kill."

In *Gangs of New York*, there is a shot showing Irish immigrants no sooner arriving in New York on one ship than they are boarding another to be transported south to fight for the Union in the Civil War. While they are boarding the ship that will eventually bring them to the battlefields of the South, a coffin is being lowered onto a dock that is already lined with coffins. By including the boarding of the ship and the lowering of the coffin in the same shot, Scorsese is suggesting the potential fate of the men who are off to fight for a cause they barely understand, if at all.

In *The Hours*, Leonard and Virginia Woolf have left London for the suburbs on the advice of a doctor, who believed Virginia's mental state would improve in a rural environment. Yearning for city life, Virginia leaves their house, heading for the train station, where she buys a ticket to London. When Leonard discovers her at the station, he confronts her on the platform. Director Stephen Daldry frames Leonard and Virginia at opposite ends of the platform, as if they were two opposing forces. All that is between them is empty space, broken only by a bench. Daldry could easily have had Virginia sitting on the bench, as Leonard approached; he could also have had Leonard sit down beside her and explain why she must return to their temporary home. Instead, Daldry chose to isolate the characters at opposite ends of the frame to convey the existing tension.

Shots can be framed graphically in terms of horizontal, vertical, and diagonal lines; they can be framed geometrically or iconographically; in deep or shallow focus; from a high or a low angle; in a frame that has been masked or doubled. A shot can last a second or run ten minutes. Each choice a director makes results in mise-en-scène that creates a unique effect. Although there are no ironclad rules of framing, certain principles are widely followed.

In **tight framing,** the subject appears to be confined within the horizontal and vertical borders of the frame, so that there is not even a hint of offscreen space. Tight framing gives a feeling of oppression. To create an atmosphere of fatalism, Edgar G. Ulmer chose tight framing for several shots of Roberts (Tom Neal) in *Detour* (1946). When Roberts's face is trapped within the frame, destiny seems to be closing in on him.

Whatever is to be emphasized in a shot should occupy a position of prominence, but not necessarily in the center of the frame. The frame can be slightly asymmetrical. An image placed dead center can give viewers the feeling they are looking at a static representation stamped on the frame. A filmmaker might want to compose a shot so that the image is closer to one side of the frame than the other, making it possible to incorporate other visual detail. In Neil LaBute's *Possession* (2002), two academics, played by Gwyneth Paltrow and Aaron Eckhart, have reached an impasse in their relationship. To convey the distance between them, LaBute places Paltrow at the left of the frame, with Eckhart behind her at the water's edge — his back to the camera. Isolating a character at the extremity of the frame is also useful if a disorienting or unusual effect is sought. For example, in *Detour*, when

Tight framing in *Detour* (1946). The camera tracks in for a close-up of Roberts (Tom Neal), who looks imprisoned within the frame. *(Frame enlargement courtesy John Belton)*

Roberts discovers that Vera (Ann Savage) has accidentally strangled herself with a telephone cord, her body is seen at the right of the frame, the head hanging above the bed.

Vertical and horizontal compositions denote solidarity, while diagonals and oblique compositions denote tension. In *Potemkin*, the masts of the ships, the raised arms of the sailors, and the waving arms of the people suggest a solidarity that is destroyed when the Cossacks appear at the top of the Odessa Steps. Their shadows falling on the steps create a diagonal that breaks the unity.

A **canted shot** (also known as a Dutch-angle shot) results in an oblique composition in which the frame looks lopsided. Edgar G. Ulmer uses canted shots in *Bluebeard* (1944) to emphasize the mental state of the mad puppeteer; the canted shots in *The Third Man* (1949) imply a world in which things are askew. In the violent argument between the title character and her mother in *Carrie* (1976), the frame looks as if it will tip over. When an IRA hostage speaks wistfully of his "special friendship" with a hairdresser in *The Crying Game* (1992), director Neil Jordan chooses a canted shot, which should cause us to wonder why the frame is tipped. Is Jordan suggesting that the relationship is not entirely conventional? Eventually we discover that this is the case: the hairdresser is a transvestite.

Sometimes vertical framing is intentionally ironic. In *Address Unknown* (1944), Griselle (K. T. Stevens) flees from a mob that has discovered she is Jewish. She hopes to find refuge in the home of a family friend. Framed by trees, she looks hopefully into the distance where the friend lives. Ordinarily such a composition, with its strong verticals, would imply hope. However, Griselle is a Jew in Nazi Germany, and the man she assumes is a friend has become a Nazi.

Vertical bars across the face, on the other hand, have another connotation: mystery, imprisonment, exclusion. When Griselle, in *Address Unknown*, finally arrives at the friend's house and stands before the gate, the composition recalls the earlier one in which she was framed by trees. Here, however, the gate is a barrier, and even though she reaches it she does not

The Conflict of Lines in the
Odessa Steps Sequence of
Potemkin

TOP RIGHT: The shadows cast by the
Cossacks create ominous diagonals on
the steps in *Potemkin* (1925). *(Courtesy
MOMA/FSA and Janus Films)*

BOTTOM RIGHT: The juxtaposition
of strong verticals (the soldiers' legs)
and stable horizontals (steps) with
broken lines (sprawled bodies and
hands raised in supplication) suggests
the dominance of the Cossacks and
the helplessness of the people in
*Potemkin. (Courtesy MOMA/FSA and
Janus Films)*

gain access to the house. The use of verticals in this different composition, as bars across the face, suggests exclusion: prevented from entering, Griselle is killed by the Gestapo.

Other types of geometrical compositions can be symbolic as well as visually interesting. In Jungian psychology, the circle is a symbol of wholeness, suggesting unity and commonality. Such is the case in *Sahara* (1943) when Sergeant Joe Gunn (Humphrey Bogart) passes a cup of water around to his thirsty men, who stand in a circle. If a composition involves three characters, triangular arrangements can make a statement about their relationship, as is the case in François Truffaut's *Jules and Jim* (1961), in which two men share the affections of the same woman.

Sometimes a filmmaker chooses to frame a shot so that it consciously evokes a famous painting, or a character is meant to represent a famous person from another era. This is called **iconography** and should be as unobtrusive as possible. If the filmmaker is imitating a painting or a sculpture, the composition should look natural even though it is a replica of, or an homage to, a work of art. The beggars' banquet in Luis Buñuel's *Viridiana* (1961) is an obvious parody of Leonardo da Vinci's *The Last Supper*, made even more so by the use of the "Hallelujah Chorus" as background music. A less blatant

Canted Shots

A canted shot of Orson Welles as Harry Lime in *The Third Man* (1949). *(Courtesy MOMA/FSA)*

parody of *The Last Supper* occurs in Robert Altman's *M*A*S*H* (1970) when the medics stage a literal last supper for the dentist who plans to commit suicide because he thinks he is impotent.

Narrative logic and symbolic implications can determine the angle at which the subject is viewed. As we have seen, if a character is looking out of a hotel window onto the street below, the shot that follows must be a high-angle one. Similarly, if a character is on the ground looking up at someone, the person at whom the character is looking must be photographed at a low angle, with the camera shooting upward. Since subjects photographed from a high angle look small and those photographed from a low angle look large, high-angle shots can imply inferiority, defeat, or

Deceptive and Debarring Verticals

TOP RIGHT: Griselle (K. T. Stevens) in *Address Unknown* (1944) is framed between two trees, expecting to be saved from the mob that is pursuing her. Here the verticals are a support, but only a temporary one. *(Courtesy Sony Pictures Entertainment)*

BOTTOM RIGHT: Griselle before the gate leading to the home of a family friend who will not receive her *(Address Unknown). (Courtesy Sony Pictures Entertainment)*

oppression; low-angle shots, power, dominance, superiority. Susan Alexander Kane is often photographed at a high angle in *Citizen Kane*, because she is dominated by her husband, who is often photographed from a low angle.

If the filmmaker decides that in a particular shot, foreground, middle ground, and background should be equally visible, the shot will have a **deep focus**. In *Citizen Kane*, Orson Welles used deep focus for several reasons: to

Triangular Compositions in *Jules and Jim* (1961) showing Catherine (Jeanne Moreau), Jules (Oscar Werner), and Jim (Henri Serre), who become a *Ménage á trois*.

TOP LEFT: The *ménage* running. *(Courtesy MOMA/FSA and Janus Films)*

BOTTOM LEFT: The *ménage* shot from below. *(Courtesy MOMA/FSA and Janus Films)*

convey a greater sense of depth, to minimize the need to cut from one shot to another, and to bring out meanings that might otherwise not be apparent. The classic deep-focus shot in *Kane* shows Mary Kane making arrangements with a banker who is to raise her son as a gentleman because she and her husband cannot. The positions of the mother in the foreground, the banker and father in the middle ground, and the son in the background, seen through the window blissfully playing in the snow, say infinitely more about the way young Kane's life is being signed away without his knowledge than if the action had been broken down into four separate shots of mother, father, banker, and son.

Sometimes **shallow focus**—when the foreground is more distinct than the background—is preferred. At other times, the background must remain indistinct until the time for it to be clear. In such a case, the filmmaker will pull focus: first, the background will be a blur and the foreground sharp; then the background will be sharp and the foreground blurry. This technique, known as **rack focus,** is one way of concealing a character's identity until the filmmaker is ready to reveal it. In *Time After Time* (1979) someone is behind the heroine, but the person's face is a blur. Then the face comes into focus, and we realize that it is Jack the Ripper's. Likewise, after a massacre in

A different triangular composition from *Citizen Kane* (1941), showing Kane (center) flanked by Thatcher (left) and Bernstein (right) as he is about to relinquish control of his enterprises after the crash of 1929. The position of Kane at the apex of the triangle makes him both the focus of attention and an object of defeat, since he is dwarfed by the more prominent figures of Thatcher and Bernstein. *(Courtesy MOMA/FSA)*

the rain in *Road to Perdition* (2002), John Rooney (Paul Newman) stands amid the bodies, as a figure seems to be moving toward him. At first, the figure is nothing more than a blur, until director Sam Mendes brings it into focus. It is the avenger, Michael Sullivan (Tom Hanks), ready to take his revenge on Rooney, whom he holds responsible for the deaths of his wife and younger son.

Focus may be deliberately erratic, with the image going in and out of focus, as might happen if a character is hallucinating, disoriented, or drunk. In *Detour*, when Roberts realizes that Vera has accidentally strangled herself, objects go in and out of focus as he looks around the room in a state of shock.

Narrative logic and symbolic value also dictate when a frame should be **masked**—that is, when its shape should be altered. If a character is peering through a pair of binoculars, a telescope, a microscope, or a keyhole, the next shot should assume the appropriate configuration. There are times in *The Truman Show* (1998) when we seem to be looking through a camera lens. Actually, we are, since Truman Burbank's (Jim Carrey) life is being televised, although he has yet to realize it.

The setting itself can offer a kind of masked frame. If a character is positioned in a doorway, the result is a frame-within-a-frame, or double framing. Double framing may reveal something about the character so framed.

Iconographic Framing

TOP LEFT: *The Last Supper* parody in *Viridiana* (1961). *(Courtesy MOMA/FSA and Janus Films)*

BOTTOM LEFT: Another *Last Supper* parody in *M*A*S*H* (1970). *(Courtesy Margaret Herrick Library of the Academy of Motion Picture Arts and Sciences)*

John Ford often uses the frame-within-the-frame, especially in *The Searchers*. When Ethan (John Wayne), who will always be a loner and a searcher, returns with Debbie, the object of his search, he remains in the doorway while the others go inside the house.

Because doorways and archways resemble the proscenium arch of a theater, they have a dramatic effect. In John Ford's *The Quiet Man* (1952), Mary Kate (Maureen O'Hara) is framed in the doorway as Sean (John Wayne) pulls her toward him. In William Wyler's *The Little Foxes* (1941), the Hubbards do their plotting in the archway of the drawing room, thus seeming like the stage villains they were in Lillian Hellman's play.

A **long take**—a shot that lasts more than a minute—can also be framed. Recall the definition of a shot: a single run of the camera. Although the average shot lasts between ten and twenty seconds, the traditional roll film camera could accommodate ten minutes' worth of film. The **Steadicam,** however, has changed that. With a Steadicam, which came into use in the 1970s, the camera is attached to a body harness worn by the cameraperson, enabling him or her to achieve the fluidity of a mobile camera without the jerkiness that often results from a handheld camera. It is not only ideal for moving shots, because it reduces the need for complex camera setups, but it also allows for a single take that runs as long as a typical movie.

When Russian filmmaker Alexander Sokurov decided to make *Russian Ark* (2003)—in which a tour of St. Petersburg's great art museum, the Hermitage, would also be a meditation on history with actors impersonating real

James Stewart (left) confronting the two murderers (John Dall and Farley Granger, right) with the means they used to kill their innocent friend in Alfred Hitchcock's *Rope* (1948), an 80-minute film in eight approximately 10-minute takes. *(Courtesy MCA Universal)*

and fictitious characters—he decided to shoot it in one unbroken take that ended up lasting 96 minutes. Sokurov's decision posed an enormous challenge to Steadicam operator Tilman Büttner, who had a special dolly built so he could occasionally rest on it for a few seconds at a time.[8] *Russian Ark* was a thrilling experience, but it is hard to imagine many filmmakers following Sokurov's lead. Even before the advent of the Steadicam, films containing ambitious long takes were extremely demanding.

Alfred Hitchcock's *Rope* (1948) consisted of eight takes, each running about ten minutes, the maximum length of film on a roll camera. If a mistake such as a flubbed line or camera mishap occurred during a take, Hitchcock would have the cast and crew start over.

Rope was based on Patrick Hamilton's play about two young men who strangle a prep school acquaintance because they consider themselves superior beings, able to commit an act for which the ordinary person would be punished (little knowing that the same fate awaits them). Convinced that theirs is the perfect crime, they celebrate by inviting the victim's fiancée, father, and sister-in-law, along with an ex-classmate and their former headmaster, to a buffet, with the trunk containing their victim's body serving as a table.

To create the semblance of a play, the action was continuous. Since the entire action took place in the murderers' New York apartment, the walls of

Robert De Niro as mafioso Jimmy Conway in Martin Scorsese's *GoodFellas* (1990). *(Courtesy Warner Bros.)*

the set had to separate and rise up, so the camera could come through on a dolly, moving from one room to another.

Hitchcock uses one traditional cut—at the beginning. After the credits, the camera tracks up to an apartment window. There is a scream, followed by a cut to the living room where the men have just strangled their friend. At that point, the first of eight long takes begins. The two men, Brandon (John Dall) and Philip (Farley Granger), place his body in the trunk, standing by it while they talk. Lighting a cigarette, Brandon walks over to the bay window, opening the blinds to reveal a view of the New York skyline. Still, no cut. Philip and Brandon discuss the murder. The camera has now pulled back, so that the men are framed in long shot as Brandon boasts of their having committed the "perfect crime." The camera then moves closer to the pair, resulting in a medium shot that captures the tension between them—Philip being as nervous as Brandon is calm. Even when Philip wants some champagne, Hitchcock does not cut, although the champagne is in the kitchen refrigerator. Instead, the camera tracks the pair as they proceed from the living room through the dining room and into the kitchen, talking all the while. Returning to the dining room, Brandon begins lighting the candles on the table that had been set up for the buffet. Suddenly, he decides to celebrate the occasion by using the trunk instead of the table. At that moment, Hitchcock has Brandon with his back to the camera, so that he could end the take by fading out on the back of Brandon's jacket.

Arguably the most famous long take in American film is the credits sequence in Orson Welles's *Touch of Evil* (1958), which lasts almost three minutes. A time bomb is in the trunk of a car. Two people get into the car and proceed down the street of a Mexican border town, past Mr. and Mrs. Vargas (Charlton Heston and Janet Leigh). The car pulls up to the booth. The driver is known to the customs officer. The woman with him complains about a "ticking noise," but the customs officer does not take her seriously. The car crosses the border, continues a short distance, and then explodes into flames. Welles chose to make the credits sequence of *Touch of Evil* a long take and framed it accordingly, creating an atmosphere of restlessness with a camera that is continually moving.

Another classic long take occurs in Martin Scorsese's *GoodFellas* as Henry Hill (Ray Liotta) and Karen (Lorraine Bracco) enter the Copacabana nightclub through the kitchen. The camera follows them as they move up a flight of stairs to the reservations line, where, despite the line, they are immediately escorted to a table. Scorsese then pans to the next table and over to the bandstand, where the comedian Henny Youngman is set to perform. The long take, lasting well over a minute, has been carefully framed to capture the unbroken rhythm of an action in one uninterrupted shot.

Guided by a script that requires a scene to be filmed in a particular way and by aesthetic considerations that will enhance the script and enrich the narrative, the filmmaker makes his or her decisions. These decisions, however, should not be accepted on faith. Knowing the many choices a filmmaker has—from the angle of the camera, to the composition of a shot, to the arrangement of a sequence—allows the viewer to ask whether the filmmaker's decisions were the right ones.

NOTES

1. Lee R. Bobker, with Louise Marinis, *Making Movies: From Script to Screen* (New York: Harcourt Brace Jovanovich, 1973), 209.
2. Karel Reisz and Gavin Miller, *The Technique of Film Editing* (New York: Focal Press, 1968), 84.
3. Ibid., 277.
4. "Film Editors Forum," *Film Comment* 13 (March–April 1977): 24.
5. Ibid.
6. Edward Dmytryk, *On Film Editing: An Introduction to the Art of Film Construction* (Boston: Focal Press, 1984), 145.
7. Sidney Lumet, *Making Movies* (New York: Vintage, 1996), 148.
8. Louis Menashe, "Filming Sokurov's *Russian Ark*: An Interview with Tilman Büttner," *Cineaste* 18, no. 3 (Summer 2003): 23.

CHAPTER 4

Enhancing the Image

Color, Lighting, and Visual Effects

Filmmakers can create certain moods throughout their movies by working with color, lighting, and visual effects. Even before the advent of color film, all three were important tools that helped filmmakers communicate emotions and information visually.

Coloring the Image

Truly creative filmmakers use color for more than mere embellishment; they use it to direct the eye to what the script is saying verbally but cannot say visually; they use color to suggest, characterize, and forge symbolic connections. One should always remember that it is only since the late 1960s that color has been the norm. Yet, even when black and white was the norm, filmmakers could work within the parameters of monochrome and achieve something akin to color. An astute filmgoer should be able to identify when color is decorative and when it is functional, and when monochrome is perfunctory and when it is motivated.

The Black-and-White Film

Film theorist Rudolph Arnheim has argued that color is accidental to film and that audiences can accept the absence of color in black-and-white movies. The history of film proves that a movie photographed in black and white can render all of the important plot details without loss of verisimilitude. Just as sound films cannot be considered superior to silent films simply because the dialogue can be heard, color films cannot be considered superior to black-and-white because all the colors can be seen. Nor are black-and-white films that include references to color less effective because the color cannot be seen; the color can be imagined. In William Wyler's *Jezebel* (1938), a black-and-white film, Julie (Bette Davis) arrives at a ball in a red dress that she has been forbidden to wear. The dress photographs as nonwhite, and white was the color Julie was expected to wear. Julie's act of rebellion is as effective today, when color films are the norm, as it was in 1938, when color films were the exception.

In *The Merry Widow* (1934), Ernst Lubitsch uses black-and-white photography to produce a color scheme that even the most advanced form of color technology would find hard to rival. Since the film is based on a Viennese operetta, everything looks as if it came from a confectionery. It is impossible not to think of chocolate, icing, and whipped cream when watching the film: the widow's mansion looks like a tiered wedding cake; her boudoir is like a pastry shell; the walls of her boudoir are creamy and incandescent. When the widow wears a black negligee, the dramatic contrast of her attire and the appointments of her boudoir satisfy whatever craving for color a viewer might have.

In the 1930s and 1940s, Paramount's films were renowned for their "white look," which was partly the creation of art director Hans Dreier, who helped to forge the studio's visual style. Middle-class bedrooms gave off a glow, telephones were opalescent, and walls and staircases gleamed like burnished ivory. Paramount seemed to revel in whiteness, from satin sheets to that indisputable touch of class, the white telephone. The suite in the luxury hotel that we see in Mitchell Leisen's *Easy Living* (1937) is a typical example of Paramount's white look. The suite is so luminous that it looks as if it had been decorated by a silversmith.

Black-and-white films can even achieve color symbolism. In *Twelve O'Clock High* (1949), Gregory Peck plays an Air Force general whose inflexibility results in a nervous breakdown. He tolerates no deviation from the rules—he might even be described as someone who thinks in "black and white." When the general breaks down, the blackness of his hair and his leather jacket and the stark whiteness of his face set against a translucent gray background imply that the gray area in human affairs that lies between the extremes of black and white is something the general had relegated to the background. It was his inability to perceive shades of difference that led to his breakdown.

The creative use of black and white in *The Merry Widow* (1934). *(Courtesy MOMA/FSA)*

The black-and-white *Citizen Kane* is rich in color symbolism. Throughout the film, white is an ambivalent symbol. It suggests innocence as well as the loss of innocence; it is the color of the real snow that Kane knew as a boy in Colorado and the color of the artificial snow in the glass paperweight he keeps as a memento of that happy time. White is also a symbol of freedom; when Susan leaves Kane, a white cockatoo screeches and flies away. But white also evokes sterility and death. Xanadu, Kane's palatial home, is adorned with useless statues and white marble; the nurse who enters Kane's room at the moment of his death wears a white uniform. The symbolic values of white can be rendered so artfully by black and white that color is not missed.

Certain contemporary directors have chosen to film in black and white, even when it was possible, and perhaps even easier, to work in color. A dreary Texas town still has color, no matter how drab it seems. However, a filmmaker might think that drabness would be better rendered in black and white than in color. If such a filmmaker decides to use monochrome, as Peter Bogdanovich did in *The Last Picture Show*, the question is not whether he should have used color but whether he achieved what he wanted by using black and white. Set in the early 1950s, *The Last Picture Show* depicts life in a small Texas town, where the only escape from a boring existence is the local movie theater. Since Bogdanovich wanted not only to capture the look of a dying town but also to give the town and the film a 1950s look, he decided on black and white.

The Color Film

Color film has become the preferred format since the late 1960s. Color may be more natural to us than monochrome, yet realism and color are not synonymous. In fact, in *The Wizard of Oz* (1939), color is used to represent the world of the imagination, as distinct from the real world. To illustrate the disparity between the real and the imagined, the Kansas scenes (reality) were photographed in sepia and the Oz scenes (fantasy) in color. Thus, to say that a color film is more "realistic" than one in black and white is to give color a power it does not possess: namely, the power to determine how lifelike an image is.

Oliver Stone's *Natural Born Killers* (1994), one of the most violent movies ever made, alternates between color and black and white. Stone deliberately disorients audiences accustomed to color by forcing them to see two different worlds: in one, blood is red; in the other, it is black. To a generation that grew up with color television and color film, violence in monochrome may seem too remote to be real. The sight of blood-splattered walls in black and white has a distancing effect: dark splotches on a white surface are not blood; in fact, they look like something created by a young artist infatuated with abstract expressionism. To a generation that grew up with black-and-white photography and film, violence in color may seem painterly, with red being just another color on the artist's palette. Regardless, blood has been spilled; whether it is blood drained of color or blood oozing red is irrelevant.

Color can be used for an effect, even in a largely black-and-white film. When Steven Spielberg decided to make the film version of Thomas Keneally's *Schindler's List* (1993), he was at a point in his career where he could make it in whatever way he chose. Spielberg chose black and white for virtually the entire film, believing that no movie about the Holocaust, the darkest event in twentieth-century history, could be made in any other way. Still, there is color at the beginning as the Sabbath candles are lit. The color, however, is short-lived; one of the candles melts, leaving darkness where there once was light. On two other occasions—each involving a young girl in a reddish coat—there is a trace of color in an otherwise black-and-white shot. The girl, Genia, is hardly even a character, but Spielberg uses her as a symbol of the six million Holocaust victims, some of whom are not even known by name. The first time we see Genia, the color of her coat stands out against the stark monochrome. When we first see Genia, she is alive; later, her body, identified only by the color of her coat, is seen on top of a pile of corpses. Full color returns with the epilogue in the Jerusalem cemetery where Oskar Schindler is buried, as we see some of the Jews whom Schindler succeeded in saving.

A filmmaker's decision to use or not to use color affects the film's visual style. Alfred Hitchcock's *Rope* was both an experiment in using long takes and his first color film. For this kind of movie, most directors in 1948 would have chosen black and white, which would have been warranted by the plot about two young men who deliberately kill a classmate. Black and white would also have been cheaper. Hitchcock, however, chose color. The credits appear against a shot of a quiet New York street. The only hint that there is something amiss is the bold red lettering of the title, *Rope,* which seems to have been splashed onto the screen. The combination of the title and the upscale neighborhood highlights the distinction between the subject matter, which is murder for thrills, and the setting in an elegantly furnished apartment with a superb view.

From 1948 to 1960, Hitchcock alternated between color and black and white. *Under Capricorn* (1949) was in color, while *Stage Fright* (1950), *Strangers on a Train* (1951), and *I Confess* (1953) were not. *Dial M for Murder* (1954), *Rear Window* (1954), *The Trouble with Harry* (1955), *To Catch a Thief* (1955), and the remake of *The Man Who Knew Too Much* (1956) were all in color, but *The Wrong Man* (1957) was not. *Vertigo* (1958) and *North by Northwest* (1959) were in color, but not *Psycho* (1960). The reasons were both personal and pragmatic. Hitchcock obviously thought that color would do more justice to Grace Kelly (who costarred in three of his films, *Dial M for Murder, Rear Window,* and *To Catch a Thief*) than black and white, although, ironically, Kelly received an Academy Award for her performance in a black-and-white film, *The Country Girl* (1954). *The Wrong Man* was based on the true story of a musician who was mistaken for a thief and wrongly incarcerated. Hitchcock planned the film as a grim semidocumentary with the kind of detachment ordinarily found in black-and-white newsreels. Although Hitchcock was still under contract to Paramount when he decided to make *Psycho,* the studio had no faith in the project; Hitchcock was forced to shoot the movie at Universal, where his television series, *Alfred Hitchcock Presents,* was filmed. If, visually, *Psycho* recalls Hitchcock's television series, it is because he used the crew from the show.

Vertigo represents Hitchcock's most creative use of color and illustrates the ways in which filmmakers have taken advantage of color to represent themes and moods. In the film, Scottie (James Stewart), a retired police detective, is hired by Gavin Elster to trail Elster's wife, Madeleine. The plot is incredibly complicated: the Madeleine whom Scottie is following is not Elster's wife but an impostor Elster has hired to establish an alibi after he does away with his real wife. Scottie becomes obsessed with the bogus Madeleine (Kim Novak), whose colors are red and green. Madeleine is mesmerized by a portrait of her great-grandmother wearing a red stone necklace. When Scottie sees Madeleine, it is in a San Francisco restaurant with striking red wallpaper; she is wearing a black gown with a green stole. She also drives a green Jaguar. Hitchcock exploits the symbolism of color: red here represents danger, passion, and also death; green symbolizes life, growth, and particularly rebirth. Elster's Madeleine does indeed die, but Scottie's Madeleine does not. She appears to have been reborn in the person of a young woman by the name of Judy (also played by Novak), whom Scottie encounters on

Vertigo's (1958) tragic climax in the bell tower after Scottie (James Stewart) discovers that Judy (Kim Novak) is not what she seems to be. *(Courtesy MOMA/FSA)*

a street in San Francisco. Thinking that she would be free to lead her own life after participating in Elster's masquerade (and never believing she would see Scottie again), Judy, the bogus Madeleine, finds herself as attracted to Scottie as he is to her.

Madeleine may have died, but her colors have not. When Scottie first sees Judy, she is wearing a green dress. Judy lives at a hotel, where at night a neon sign gives off a greenish glow. Gradually, Scottie makes Judy over until she looks as much like Madeleine as possible. Scottie learns the truth only when Judy puts on a red stone necklace, which apparently Elster had given her when she was pretending to be Madeleine. Significantly, the moment of truth occurs in the redwood forest, the scene of *Vertigo's* tragic climax.

The creative use of color can serve a variety of different purposes. Just look at how a single color—red—functioned in the hands of five separate filmmakers.

Although the heroine of Hitchcock's *Marnie* has suppressed all memory of a murder she committed as a child, the guilt persists in the form of an intense aversion to red. Instinctively, she removes red gladioli from a vase and replaces them with white mums. A drop of red ink on her white blouse sends her rushing to the washroom; the red polka dots on a jockey's uniform petrify her. Not until the end of the film do we learn that Marnie's aversion to red is the result of her having struck a sailor with a poker to protect her prostitute mother from possible harm.

The title character in Federico Fellini's *Juliet of the Spirits* (1965) is a wife whose fantasies are dominated by erotic reds. When we first see Juliet, she is trying on a red wig; then she sets the table with red candles. When she visits a clairvoyant, she wears a red scarf. Yet red is not her color; it is the color of the women of her fantasies. At the end of the film, Juliet reverts to white, the color that typifies the kind of person she is.

In *Carrie* (1976), the title character is a high school senior with telekinetic powers. Her mother is a religious fanatic, and both have reddish hair. When Carrie menstruates for the first time, she thinks she is bleeding to death. Her naïveté makes her an object of derision to her classmates, who humiliate her publicly at the senior prom by dropping a bucket of pig's blood on her. The blood reddens Carrie's pink dress, and Carrie literally sees red. Her revenge, as one might suspect, is appropriately bloody.

Red also predominates in Nicholas Ray's *Rebel Without a Cause* (1956), the film that gave James Dean his first starring role. Despite the title, the three main characters—Jim (Dean), Judy (Natalie Wood), and Plato (Sal Mineo)—who bond together have a reason to rebel: parental indifference. In Jim's case, it was a weak father and a domineering mother; in Judy's, an affectionless father; in Plato's, the absence of a father, which caused him to seek a surrogate in Jim. Their bond is highlighted by the rebel's color, red. In *Rebel Without a Cause*, the credits are in red; when Judy is first seen, she is wearing a red coat and bright-red lipstick. Despite his meekness and emotional instability, Plato even tries to play the rebel by wearing red socks. Jim dons a red windbreaker during the "chickie run," a dangerous coming-of-age ritual in which teenage males prove their manhood by driving their cars to the edge of a bluff. When Plato is killed, Jim uses the windbreaker as a shroud, placing it on his friend to suggest that at least Plato died a rebel.

American Beauty exploits the ambivalence of the color red. The film features one of the most dysfunctional families ever to appear on the screen: Lester Burnham (Kevin Spacey), a husband and father, who fantasizes about seducing his daughter's friend Angela (Mena Suvari); Lester's wife, Carolyn (Annette Benning), who tries to hide the rot within her household by planting American Beauty roses in her picture-book yard; and their daughter, Jane (Thora Birch), who is so repelled by her father that she would like to see him killed. Then there is the family next door: a homophobic retired Marine colonel; his wife, whose anguish is so intense that she barely speaks; and their voyeuristic son, who deals drugs and delights in videotaping the Burnhams, especially Jane. Red imagery begins with the title in red lettering against a background that looks like a home movie.

In *American Beauty*, red symbolizes vitality and passion on the one hand, and death on the other. When Lester sees Angela at a basketball game, he envisions her unzipping her cheerleader's uniform, as red rose petals pour out of it. Later, he imagines Angela lounging in a tub of rose petals, waiting for him to bathe her. The bloodletting at the end comes as no surprise; Jane's

Lester's (Kevin Spacey) fantasy of Angela (Mena Suvari) in her rose petal bath in *American Beauty* (1999). *(Courtesy MOMA/FSA)*

wish that her father be killed and Lester's voice-over prologue announcing that he would be dead within the year prepare us for the climax, which occurs in the Burnham kitchen. A vase filled with red roses is on the counter. Lester is seated at the kitchen table, as a gun appears against his head. A shot is fired, and blood spills across the table and onto the floor.

American Beauty represents a deliberate choice of color to complement the narrative: a wife can make American Beauty roses bloom gloriously in her yard by using eggshells and Miracle-Gro, but she cannot work a similar miracle inside the house. There is a crucial scene in the film when Ricky (Wes Bentley), the colonel's son, shows Jane what he considers to be the most beautiful sight he has ever filmed: a white bag blown across a gravelly pavement strewn with dead leaves and then against a red brick wall, rising and falling in the wind. To Ricky, the combination of the bag, the wind, and the leaves resulted in art, causing him to exclaim, "Sometimes there's so much beauty in the world I feel like I can't take it." Ricky has recorded random beauty; he was in the right place at the right time, with the right elements in place to provide him with the image. It was different when the director, Sam Mendes, and his production designer, Naomi Shohan, made artistic choices as to how red would be used in the film. Ricky couldn't change the color of the wall; a filmmaker, however, can change anything because he or she controls the entire palette.

Filmmakers choose which colors on their palettes to use to best communicate the message and mood of their films. In *The Hours* (2002), this purpose is served by the colors blue and brown.

***The Visual Style of* The Hours.** A film's visual style is determined by a number of choices—for example, a color scheme, with certain colors recurring in various shades or combinations. *The Hours* consists of three interrelated narratives, each set in a different year, although they seem to be taking place simultaneously. In 1923, Virginia Woolf is trying to write the novel that became *Mrs. Dalloway*; in 1951, a Los Angeles homemaker, Laura

Brown, is trying to read it; and in 2001, a New York book editor, Clarissa Vaughan, whose ex-lover calls her Mrs. Dalloway after Woolf's character, is preoccupied with the arrangements for a party just as is Clarissa Dalloway, her fictional counterpart.

The film deals with death and rebirth—specifically, two suicides and a near-suicide followed by a decision to adopt a radically different lifestyle. Virginia Woolf, the only historical figure in the film, took her own life on March 28, 1941; Clarissa Vaughan's ex-lover, Richard, an AIDS-ravaged poet, does the same in 2001; and in 1951, Laura Brown decides against suicide but realizes that to maintain her sanity, she must leave her family, knowing that whatever lies ahead is preferable to the empty life she is leading.

The predominant colors in *The Hours* are brown and blue in various shades (tan, rust, beige, blue-gray), with occasional suggestions of green. The film opens with a 1941 prologue as Virginia Woolf (Nicole Kidman) prepares to commit suicide. She leaves her home, proceeding along a wooded path that bears traces of the greening effects of spring, and arriving at a river, whose waters are muddied. Virginia Woolf herself is a study in brown: brown hair, brown shoes, and a plaid coat that, in the sunlight, takes on a brownish hue. She walks from the brown earth at the river's edge into the water, accomplishing what she had set out to do, as we know from the suicide notes that were left behind. The notes were written on blue stationery—one for her husband Leonard; the other for her sister Vanessa. Brown and blue, the colors of earth and sky, are not antithetical. Brown can connote birth and growth, as with the soil from which crops spring. It is also associated with death in the context of internment or when one is said to have "gone to earth." Blue is also ambivalent; it can mean working class (blue collar) or aristocratic (blue blood), comforting ("heaven's color," as poet William Morris called it) or alarming (blue baby). "The blues" as a noun is synonymous with melancholy. The lyrics to Irving Berlin's "Blue Skies" seem positive ("Never saw the sun shining so bright/Never saw things going so right"), yet the plaintive melody undercuts the optimism of the lyrics. Even a blue sky can bring on "the blues." That Virginia Woolf bade farewell to her husband and sister on blue stationery before wading into a muddy river only means that she saw no difference between the turn her life had taken and the means she chose to remedy it. She chose blue paper for her written farewell, brown water for her actual one.

In the 1923 section, we see Virginia's bedroom, suffused with beige light. When her nephews and niece discover a dead bird, Virginia seems to identify with it. She lies down on the ground beside it, grass and earth providing her with a temporary resting place that eighteen years later would become the brown waters of the river Ouse.

In the 2001 narrative, Richard (Ed Harris) wears a blue cap and robe. His skin is an unhealthy grayish brown. AIDS has also affected his mind; like Virginia Woolf, he hears voices, and like her, he too will take his life. Clarissa

Vaughan (Meryl Streep), who is planning a party for Richard, is less like Mrs. Woolf and more like her character, Clarissa Dalloway. Clarissa Vaughan's bedroom is bluish white; when she visits Richard, their colors match. She is wearing a suede jacket, a blue turtleneck, and a light blue scarf.

The 1951 narrative begins as a brown-and-white car pulls into a drive-way. A man gets out of the car and enters the house with a bouquet of yellow roses. We are in the home of Dan and Laura Brown (Julianne Moore), whose surname from Michael Cunningham's novel may have influenced the choice of one of the film's signature colors. Brown predominates throughout the house. However, brown is not Laura's sole color. Although she is a brunette, with a hairstyle similar to Virginia Woolf's, her color initially is blue. She even decorates her husband's birthday cake with a blue border. Once she decides to commit suicide, she switches to brown; but when she chooses life on her own terms, which means leaving her family after the birth of her second child, she returns to blue for her husband's birthday party. By linking color with character, mood, and setting, director Stephen Daldry, in conjunction with his director of photography, costume designer, and production designer, has integrated three lives, making it seem as if there was only one life, shared by three women.

Colorization.   Colorization is the use of a computer-aided process to apply color to black-and-white movies. Colorization requires the film to be analyzed shot by shot and scene by scene so that the colorization is consistent. The colors of the opening frames must be determined first by consulting sketches, memos, and set designs if they are available. Once the colors for the opening frames are selected, a computer applies the same colors throughout, varying the hues in terms of the lighting pattern in the original. Still, there is no guarantee that a color sketch provided for a black-and-white film would be valid if the studio had decided to shoot the film in color. Thus, the claim that a colorized version of a black-and-white film would have proved satisfactory if the filmmaker had had the opportunity to shoot it in color is false. The foes of colorization—and there have been many, including James Stewart, Burt Lancaster, Woody Allen, Frank Capra, and Martin Ritt—contend that colorization vitiates the principle of creative choice, which is essential to art.

Unfortunately, a number of classic black-and-white films have been colorized, including *The Big Sleep* (1946), *It's a Wonderful Life* (1946), *Miracle on 34th Street* (1947), *Sands of Iwo Jima* (1949), and *The Blackboard Jungle* (1955). When a studio chose to film a movie in black and white rather than in color, that choice entailed several factors, the chief one being, no doubt, the cost. During Hollywood's golden age, there was no aesthetic policy that dictated what kinds of movies should be made in black and white as opposed to color. One cannot say, for example, that color is more suited to westerns than black and white, since some of John Ford's classic westerns were photographed in black and white: *Stagecoach* (1939), *My Darling Clementine* (1946), *Fort Apache* (1948), *Wagonmaster* (1950), *The Man Who Shot Liberty Valance* (1962). Nor was color considered mandatory for musicals; the great musicals of the 1930s, notably those starring Fred Astaire and Ginger Rogers, were in black and white. Color was expensive and was not lavished on every film, only on those the studio deemed important enough to warrant it or on those that needed color to realize fully their dramatic potential. *Gone with the Wind* (1939) was intended to be in color; another film set in the South and released the previous year, *Jezebel*, was not.

When the decision is made to shoot a film in color, everything—costumes, lighting, makeup, settings—is planned and executed in terms of that choice. That choice, however, was to shoot the film in a color process such as Technicolor, Trucolor, Warnercolor, and so on. Colorization is not a color process; it is a computer-aided process that, in the absence of any guiding intelligence, allows a computer to make the choices that should be the prerogative of the filmmaker. Colorizing a film simply to appeal to viewers accustomed to watching movies in color is like hand-painting the classic black-and-white photographs of artists like Walker Evans and Diane Arbus.

Lighting the Image

Lighting has a direct bearing on the way an image is perceived. Light and darkness appear differently in a film than in real life, where, for example, darkness may simply signal the beginning of evening. In a film, darkness in the form of shadowy surfaces, low illumination, or unlit passageways can suggest mystery or danger. A film cannot always rely on available light—the light that already exists in the chosen location, indoor or outdoor. More common is the three-point model.

The classic Hollywood film is an example of **three-point lighting**—key, fill, and back lights used in combination to light the subject. These are not the only lights; still, three-point lighting is a standard lighting scheme that, if understood properly, explains how lighting can affect one's perception of a character or a setting.

The **key light,** the principal source of illumination, leaves shadows if it is used alone. For this reason, another light is necessary to fill in the areas the key light has left unlit and to soften the shadows it has cast: the **fill light,** an auxiliary light that is softer and less intense, is placed opposite the key light on the other side of the camera. But even a combination of the key and fill lights is not sufficient if a sense of depth is desired. Hence, a **back light,** placed above and behind the subject, is required. The back light alone would merely produce a silhouette. But in combination with the key and fill lights, the back light separates the subject from its environment, thereby creating a feeling of depth.

High-key lighting in *Meet Me in St. Louis* (1944). *(Courtesy MOMA/FSA)*

In terms of effect, lighting can be categorized as high-key and low-key. A low-contrast ratio of key and fill light will result in an image of almost uniform brightness, or what is called **high-key lighting,** the kind used in musicals and comedies and for scenes of tranquillity and peace. Conversely, a **high-contrast** ratio of key and fill light will result in **low-key lighting** and create a shadowy effect and a nighttime aura. This was the signature lighting of film noir, a type of melodrama where passions run high in urban settings that are grimy and often fogbound and where streets are dark, mean, and continually rain-slick. Directors of horror films and melodramas prefer low-key lighting for its shadows and its strong contrast of light and darkness.

Low-key lighting in *Crossfire* (1947). *(Courtesy WCFTR)*

In addition to these two general categories of lighting, there are five other types, distinguished by the angle from which the light source illuminates the subject: front, back, top, side, and bottom. *Front lighting* has a softening effect that makes whatever we are viewing seem more attractive than it actually is. Front lighting of the face creates an ageless look, but it also robs the face of character. Back lighting, as we have seen, adds depth and can bring out subtleties of design and pattern in the background. When a character is backlit, as Esther (Barbra Streisand) is when she sings "Evergreen" at the end of *A Star Is Born* (1976), a halo-like aura is produced that gives an ethereal quality. Similarly, **top lighting** creates an atmosphere of youthfulness or spirituality, as is the case in *The Song of Bernadette*, where it emphasizes Bernadette's saintliness. **Side lighting** leaves the subject half in light, half in shadow; thus, it can denote a split personality, a morally ambiguous character, or a femme fatale. Greta Garbo and Marlene Dietrich were often photographed in this fashion. **Bottom lighting** gives the subject a sinister air; it was the kind of lighting D. W. Griffith employed in *Dream Street* (1921) to bring out the villainy of Sway Wan.

In a black-and-white film, the interplay of light and darkness can produce visual symbolism. Throughout *Citizen Kane*, Thompson, the reporter

A publicity still of actress Claudette Colbert, front lit and back lit. *(Private Collection)*

trying to decipher the meaning of Kane's dying word ("Rosebud!"), is always seen in shadow. He is literally in the dark, and remains in that state throughout the film. Just as darkness can denote ignorance, so light can intimate knowledge. When Thompson enters the Thatcher Memorial Library to read the memoirs of Kane's guardian, shafts of light illuminate the mausoleum-like room. Perhaps the memoirs will explain the meaning of "Rosebud." But the light is deceptive, and Thompson leaves the library as much in the dark as ever.

Thompson is not the only character who suffers from ignorance. Although Thompson is ignorant of the meaning of "Rosebud," Kane is ignorant of himself. When Kane delivers his Declaration of Principles, promising to be a "fighting and tireless champion" of the people, his face is in darkness. Kane does not know that he will never live up to his declaration, and the lighting states as much.

Lighting is also used effectively in Preston Sturges's *Sullivan's Travels* (1941). In that film, some black parishioners invite the white prisoners of a local chain gang to their church to watch a movie. When we see the prisoners making their way to the church, they are in darkness; for a moment, they look like black men. The lighting establishes a bond between the black congregation and the prisoners; it also reinforces the film's theme that moviegoing is a form of brotherhood that erases all distinctions, including racial ones. Movies are the great leveler; in the dark, everyone is equal.

Back lighting in *Sunset Boulevard* (1950). The back light is coming from a projector during the screening of a silent film starring Norma Desmond (Gloria Swanson), who, in the middle of it, stands up and with arm raised vows to return to the screen. *(Courtesy WCFTR. Copyright ©* *1949, Paramount Pictures Corporation. All rights reserved.)*

Special Effects/Visual Effects (SFX, VFX)

Special effects are an integral part of many films. They have existed for as long as there have been movies. We can go back to the time of Georges Méliès in the early 1900s, who delighted audiences by showing characters vanish in a puff of smoke or by having one object or person turn into another. Méliès used such effects for their ability to astound and amaze, as well as for their storytelling potential; the effects in *A Trip to the Moon* are actually part of the plot. Even though we know how Méliès achieved his effects, we still marvel at the result. The transformations were accomplished through **stop-motion photography,** in which one frame at a time is exposed, allowing adjustments to be made between frames and producing the illusion that one object has turned into another or has disappeared.

Today, "special effects" are so much a part of moviemaking that they no longer even seem special. **Visual effects** is now the more common term. Unless effects, whether they are called special or visual, are integrated with the narrative, they are the equivalent of spectacle. In the *Poetics*, Aristotle

Kong with Fay Wray in one hand as he dispenses with a pterodactyl with the other in *King Kong* (1933), a marvel of special effects. *(Courtesy MOMA/FSA)*

described spectacle as any theatrical effect appealing more to the eye than to the mind and considered it to be the least important element of drama. Visual effects tend to call attention to themselves, regardless of the form they take. However, when effects advance the plot, moving it along like dialogue, we notice them, but within the context of the film. The best filmmakers know that visual effects need to be part of the narrative.

Today, anyone interested in learning how certain effects are achieved in a film can often log on to the film's Web site, watch the "making of" features included on DVD, or read *American Cinematographer* and the *ICG Magazine*, the publication of the International Cinematographers Guild. However, knowing about the technology that produced the effects alone will not help you determine whether the effects have been designed simply to dazzle the viewer or whether they function as narrative strategies that advance the plot and give it momentum.

Audiences seeing *King Kong* upon its release in 1933 marveled at how lifelike Kong was, even though they knew he wasn't real. That there were six eighteen-inch models of Kong, along with a twenty-foot model with a crane-operated arm, was unknown at the time; nor did moviegoers realize that the then very daring scene of Kong pulling off pieces of Ann's (Fay Wray) tattered dress and sniffing them was miniature rear projection, in which a scaled set is placed in front of a screen on which live action is projected. According to *King Kong's* codirector, Merrian C. Cooper, "a movie was first taken of [Wray] alone while invisible wires pulled off her clothes. Then the miniature Kong was placed on a set built on a waist-high platform . . . on which miniature trees, ferns and plaster of Paris rocks had been arranged. In back of this the movie of Fay Wray was projected and Kong's movements made to correspond with it."[1] The scene does not call attention to itself because it is integral to Kong's humanization as he makes the transition from beast to lover and finally protector. Clearly, Kong is perplexed by the strange creature he holds in his hand; he is also mildly aroused by her. If generations of moviegoers have thought of Kong as human, even to the point of weeping at his death, it is because of the special effects genius of Cooper and Willis O'Brien.

When Rouben Mamoulian decided that in his production of *Dr. Jekyll and Mr. Hyde* Henry Jekyll would turn into Mr. Hyde on-screen, the transformation was accomplished by dissolving a series of shots of Fredric March (Jekyll) in various stages of makeup. Jekyll's decision to take the transforming potion occurs immediately after he has encountered the prostitute Ivy (Miriam Hopkins). Mamoulian slowly dissolves a shot of Ivy's bare leg dangling over a shot of Jekyll and his friend walking along a dark London street. Knowing that he could never enjoy Ivy's favors as the respectable Dr. Jekyll, he prepares the potion that turns him into Mr. Hyde. Although the transformation may look like special effects, it was based on Mamoulian's decision to combine the arousal of Jekyll's passions with the only way they can be satisfied: by Jekyll's becoming his other self. Mamoulian also decided to accompany the transformation with a montage of images swirling across the screen, suggesting what was going through Jekyll's mind while the potion was taking effect.

Computers have totally changed the creation of special effects. Digital technology has made it possible for filmmakers to achieve effects that would have been impossible in the 1930s. Compare *Dr. Jekyll and Mr. Hyde* with the film *The Hollow Man* (2000), in which Kevin Bacon disappears piecemeal; or, rather, his digital equivalent does. No number of dissolving shots could have achieved such a transmogrification. What we are witnessing, however, is the triumph of technology, not great moviemaking. Despite its impressive effects, it is hard to imagine *The Hollow Man* ever achieving the classic status of *Dr. Jekyll and Mr. Hyde*.

The visual effects in *Forrest Gump* worked well and added to the story. Although the movie was made in 1994, Forrest interacts with Presidents Kennedy, Johnson, and Nixon, and with John Lennon of the Beatles. Through synthetic image reproduction, the filmmaker could show the fictional character in conversation with historical figures whose images had been obtained from a film archive or some other outside source. It was an effective, and novel, way to show how Forrest, who gave every indication of being a loser, eventually triumphs by going from obscurity to fame—a familiar version of the American dream. Although *Forrest Gump* employed innovative effects, it did not rely on them to bring in audiences.

There will always be effects-driven movies. *The Matrix* trilogy (1999, 2003), for example, which imagines a computer-controlled world, could never have been made without them, nor could *X-Men* (2000), based on Marvel Comics characters. The visual effects in *X-Men* were integral to the plot. Audiences do not turn out for a movie about mutants whose powers are narrated but never shown. Similarly, there was no way the storm in *The Perfect Storm* (2000)—in which, among other awesome sights, a helicopter falls into the water—could have been created except digitally. Audiences expecting a "perfect storm" were not disappointed. When visual effects become the prime reason for seeing a movie, the danger is that audiences will find it difficult to care about the characters or the plot, since both have become the servants of technology. It is like a play that is so elaborately produced that all one remembers are the sets and costumes.

Certainly there have been times when digital effects were able not only to cut down on production costs but also to save the production. When Oliver Reed died during the shooting of *Gladiator* (2000), his image was digitized into the scenes for which his character was needed so the film could be completed. For *The Hours*, Nicole Kidman had to wear a prosthetic nose to make her resemble Virginia Woolf, although the resemblance was minimal. However, the prosthesis looked obvious, so it was digitally enhanced to appear natural.

Digital technology has changed the way that filmmakers can create visual effects, but technology alone will not improve the quality of film art. As T. S. Eliot wrote in "Tradition and the Individual Talent": "Art never improves, but . . . the material of art is never quite the same." One cannot say, for example, that *Citizen Kane* is a greater film than *The Birth of a Nation*, only that Orson Welles had more technology at his disposal than did D. W. Griffith. Yet each produced a masterpiece, working with the available technology. Today's filmmakers have more available technology than ever before, but whether they will create a treasury of classics depends on their attention to all the details in their films. Innovation is preferable to stagnation, but visual effects can only be a means to an end. Filmmakers should try to subordinate the visual effects to the story they want to tell, making them only one part of the mise-en-scène.

NOTE

1. As quoted in John Bronson, *Movie Magic: The Story of Special Effects in Cinema* (New York: New American Library, 1976), 159.

CHAPTER 5

Film Genres

So far we have been talking about techniques, using examples from such films as *My Darling Clementine*, *Detour*, and *Psycho*. While these films illustrate certain principles of moviemaking, they also illustrate certain types of films. Each of these films represents a particular genre: *Clementine*, the western; *Detour*, film noir; and *Psycho*, the horror film. While this chapter will explore several different genres, remember that very few films can be described with a single label.

When English professors speak of a **genre,** they mean a literary form with certain conventions and patterns that, through repetition, have become so familiar that readers expect similar elements in works of the same type. In Periclean Athens and Elizabethan England, the two great ages of tragedy, audiences attending a performance of *Oedipus the King* or *Hamlet* were not witnessing a completely new dramatic form. Audiences were familiar with plays in which characters pursue goals that lead to their death or downfall. They also understood the tragic progression from ignorance to knowledge and from prosperity to catastrophe.

The conventions of tragedy, including protagonists with tragic flaws, fatal mistakes, and reversals of fortune, appear in all tragedies; they do not, however, always appear in the same way. The Elizabethan tragic heroes, for example, exercise free will to a greater degree than did their Greek counterparts. Modern tragedy, on the other hand, seems to be deterministic, with characters such as Blanche DuBois of Tennessee Williams's *A Streetcar Named Desire* and Willy Loman of Arthur Miller's *Death of a Salesman* destroyed by forces over which they have no control. Yet *Death of a Salesman* is as much a tragedy as *Oedipus* or *Hamlet*, even though it may not be written in verse and the protagonist may not be of royal descent. The same basic elements that make *Hamlet* a tragedy also make *Salesman* one.

Some tragedies blur into melodrama, which also features flawed characters who make tragic mistakes. But in melodrama the characters represent the extremes of good and evil, chance seems more important than causality, and the action turns violent or grotesque for theatrical or shock effect. Like most distinctions, the tragedy-melodrama one is theoretical. Some of the greatest tragedies contain melodramatic elements. Shakespeare avoids stereotypical characters in *Macbeth*, but he is not averse to including such melodramatic touches as witches, apparitions, the onstage murder of a child, a sleepwalking scene, and an ending that calls for Macbeth's head to be displayed on a pole. *Macbeth* is undeniably a tragedy, but it has its moments of sensationalism. Genres can intermingle in literature, and it is no different in film.

Genres are not monolithic. Although tragedy is clearly a genre, there are various kinds of tragedy: Greek, Elizabethan, French neoclassical, historical, modern. Similarly, there are various kinds of comedy: slapstick, bedroom farce, romantic comedy, drawing-room comedy, and Chekhovian comedy, which blends pathos and humor in a unique way. As a genre, mystery fiction can be subdivided into crime fiction, soft-boiled or hard-boiled detective fiction, gothic fiction, espionage fiction, and the police procedural.

It is not easy, therefore, to pigeonhole a work of literature. Film genres are equally complex. Although some literary genres reappear in film, not all do. Comedy is itself a genre in literature, but not in film, where genres tend to be more specific. Film genres—compared with, say, literary genres—are unique. Literary genres represent a hierarchy created by critics, while film genres represent the studios' response to the marketplace. By the sixteenth century, a hierarchy of literary forms had been established, beginning with the lowly pastoral and culminating in the lofty epic. While this particular hierarchy no longer exists, the mentality behind it does. There are still literary scholars who rank poetry above fiction and drama below it; there are others who would relegate the essay to the category of expository or informal prose and deny it literary status. In film, there is no hierarchy of genres; there are only types of movies that succeed and types that do not; for example, traditionally, sports films do not succeed, while horror films do. Furthermore, genres that succeed in one era may not succeed in another unless they can adapt to the changing times.

Finally, while the best examples of a film genre may be pure—for example, *Stagecoach* is pure western, *Bringing Up Baby* (1938) is pure screwball,

Meet Me in St. Louis (1944) is pure musical—there are also films that cross genres. Genre mixing occurs for various reasons, one being commercial: if whodunits, westerns, and comedies are successful, why not a western whodunit like Raoul Walsh's *Pursued* (1947) or a comedy whodunit like Woody Allen's *Manhattan Murder Mystery* (1993)? A comic western like *Blazing Saddles* (1974) or *Wild Wild West* (1999)? A comic horror film like *Young Frankenstein* (1974)? The end of the world is no laughing matter, but director Stanley Kubrick must have thought it could be when he made *Dr. Strangelove, or: How I Learned to Stop Worrying and Love the Bomb* (1964). Mitchell Leisen's *Easy Living* is a screwball comedy that is implicitly critical of those who enjoyed "easy living" during the Great Depression and thus takes on overtones of the social-consciousness film.

Musicals are not always "feel good" entertainment; in fact, they can incorporate elements from other genres. Some musicals end unhappily—for example, *Tonight and Every Night* (1944), *A Star Is Born* (the 1954 and 1975 versions), and Martin Scorsese's *New York, New York* (1977). Other musicals include plot elements usually associated with thrillers—such as abduction and an avalanche in *Seven Brides for Seven Brothers* (1954). Thus, one genre can take on the plot devices of another, while still remaining what it originally was. *Seven Brides for Seven Brothers* will always be a musical, despite its forays into feminism, with a bride who brings order and civility to a macho household; melodrama, with the brothers' abduction of young women as potential brides; and an armed conflict common to westerns. It can even be called a musical western, since it is set in the Oregon Territory in 1850.

The point is not to come up with a definitive classification of a particular movie; categorizing a movie is not like categorizing a biological species. Nominally, *Pursued* is a western and *Dr. Strangelove* is science fiction. Genre-blending gives each a distinctive quality, so that one ends up saying, "Yes, *Pursued* is a western, but it also reminds me of a detective story"; "Yes, *Dr. Strangelove* is science fiction, but it's scary and hilarious at the same time"; and "Yes, *Blazing Saddles* is a western, but in the traditional western nobody passes gas—at least not on the screen." Rather, the point is to see how various kinds of movies have survived over the years by repeating, varying, or altering their conventions.

The Musical

The musical is a good genre with which to begin because its plot conventions are relatively simple. It is axiomatic that, in a musical, emotions are expressed, and the plot is advanced, through song and dance. Although this may seem self-evident, there are moviegoers who find musicals unrealistic. Historically, there has been some justification for this view: the lack of integration of song and action in many musicals results in a film in which the plot is constantly being interrupted for a production number. For example, in *Lady Be Good* (1941), there is no motivation for Eleanor Powell's tap dance except that Powell was a superb tap dancer whose fans expected her to dance.

Ideally, Eleanor Powell's tap dance should have been a natural outgrowth of the action, not a diversion. However, the seamless blending of song and narrative is rare in film musicals. Indeed, the early movie musicals were not fully integrated, because the musical sequences could easily be rearranged without seriously altering the plot. In the musicals of the 1930s, the plots were thin; what is memorable about such musicals are the chic dancing of Fred Astaire and Ginger Rogers and the production numbers in which the chorus forms intricate geometric patterns. We may have vivid memories of Astaire and Rogers dancing the carioca in *Flying Down to Rio* (1933), but few of us can reconstruct the plot.

Sometimes a context has to be provided for a song so it can fit into the film; otherwise it would be simply a diversion or an embellishment. All the songs in *Holiday Inn* (1942) were composed by Irving Berlin. *Holiday Inn* is chiefly remembered as the movie in which Bing Crosby introduced Berlin's "White Christmas," a perennial favorite. The context in which he sings it is another matter. On Christmas Day, Linda Mason (Marjorie Reynolds) shows up at Jim Hardy's (Crosby) Connecticut inn, looking for a job as a performer. Job-hunting on Christmas requires a suspension of disbelief in itself. Hardy auditions Linda by having her join him in the song "White Christmas," which includes the lyrics "I'm dreaming of a white Christmas/Just like the ones I used to know." The lyrics imply that the singer's ideal Christmas has not yet materialized. In *Holiday Inn*, there is so much snow on the ground that Linda arrives at the inn in a sleigh. Furthermore, the introduction, which is rarely sung and explains why the "I" is "dreaming of a white Christmas," had to be omitted because the "I" of the song is an Easterner in Los Angeles, yearning for a traditional Christmas. Although "White Christmas" is the song with which Bing Crosby is most identified, it becomes just another musical number in *Holiday Inn*. If it had been a less-than-white Christmas, the song would have been better motivated and considerably more poignant.

Whether the first integrated movie musical was *On the Town* (1949) or *Singin' in the Rain* (1952) is a matter of debate. *On the Town* was based on a 1944 Broadway musical that was itself superbly integrated, with music by Leonard Bernstein and a book by Betty Comden and Adolph Green. *Singin' in the Rain*, which was neither a Broadway show nor a play set to music, is something of a rarity: an original screenplay, also by Comden and Green, with songs that flow out of the action. Although the film is remembered for the title song, danced in the rain by Gene Kelly, the sequence is related to the plot: the boy is so in love with the girl that he dances for joy despite the elements.

Seven Brides for Seven Brothers is a good illustration of an integrated musical. Adam Pontipee (Howard Keel), the oldest of seven unmarried brothers, decides to marry. Sauntering into town one day, he observes the women as they pass by, voicing his thoughts in the first musical number, "Bless Your Beautiful Hide." The language is typical of a male chauvinist. In a nonmusical, instead of a song, Adam's thoughts might have been expressed in voice-over. When Adam sees Millie (Jane Powell), it is attraction (if not yet love) at first sight. On their wedding day, Millie expresses her joy in the second number, "Wonderful, Wonderful Day," which reflects her mood, as well as her romantic—as opposed to Adam's pragmatic—nature.

When Millie realizes that Adam expects her to play housekeeper to his rowdy brothers, she banishes him from her bedroom on what was to have been their wedding night. Disgruntled but obedient, Adam prepares to sleep in a tree, as Millie appears at the bedroom window. In "When You're In Love," Millie describes the kind of woman she is, after which she allows Adam to enter the bedroom through the window, having taught him the first of several lessons.

After domesticating Adam, Millie starts on his brothers. In "Goin' Co'tin," she instructs them in the etiquette of courtship, so they can take part in a barn raising that is both a social occasion and an opportunity to meet young women. *Seven Brides for Seven Brothers* is best remembered for the barn raising sequence, brilliantly choreographed by Michael Kidd. The barn raising begins with a dance, in which the males of the community, who fancy themselves gentlemen, compete with the brothers, who have just learned how "gentlemen" behave. The dance evolves into a contest, and ends in a fiasco.

Their hopes dashed, the brothers pine for mates in "Lonesome Polecat," but having been exposed to the company of women for the first time, the brothers are unwilling to admit defeat. In the song "Sobbin' Women," Adam tells them about the abduction of the Sabine women, citing as his source Plutarch's *Lives*, one of Millie's favorite books. The brothers decide to pursue the same course and claim their prospective brides. Millie takes the women into the house, banishing the brothers to the barn, while Adam, sensing he has done wrong, retires to a mountain cabin. Millie and her wards bond together, as the young women, who had already met the brothers at the dance, express their yearnings for them, no longer considering them kidnappers. Millie, meanwhile, announces her pregnancy, which becomes the occasion for "June Bride," in which the women envision their own marriages. The plot peg—the avalanche that has sealed off the town from the brothers' farm—is discarded with the arrival of spring, and with it, the birth of Millie and Adam's daughter. Spring has also brought the women out of the house, each linking up with the brother of her choice in "Spring, Spring, Spring," which celebrates nature's awakening.

There is no way the musical numbers can be rearranged; each is placed where it is because it advances the plot. For example, it would have made no sense if the film began with Millie's singing "Wonderful, Wonderful Day," since the day in question is her wedding day.

If we remember that genres are not simple, we can better appreciate the diversity of the movie musical, which can assume various forms.

The musical revue features musical numbers in movies that are the equivalent of variety shows and are either plotless, as with *Paramount on Parade* (1930), or embellished with a story line, like *The Big Broadcast* movies of 1932, 1936, 1937, and 1938. Revues were popular with New York theatergoers from the 1920s through the mid-1950s, and their structure—sketches interspersed with song and dance—did not lend itself easily to film. Yet that did not stop studios from trying. Paramount Pictures was the first to make films that showcased their stars' talents with nothing more than a narrative thread that stitched the various numbers together. Other studios followed suit, and the movie revue continued during World War II—and shortly thereafter—with such films as United Artists' *Stage Door Canteen* (1943), Warner Bros.'s *Thank Your Lucky Stars* (1943) and *Hollywood Canteen* (1944), Universal's *Follow the Boys* (1944), and MGM's *Ziegfeld Follies* (1946). A star like Bette Davis, known almost exclusively for drama, had a chance to perform a number that she could never have done in any other format: namely, one of the era's best-known songs, "They're Either Too Young or Too Old," from *Thank Your Lucky Stars.*

These 1940s movie revues were originals that owed nothing to Broadway. In fact, Broadway revues were rarely turned into movies because they were too sophisticated and topical. An exception was *New Faces of 1952*, which was given a wisp of a plot to keep it from becoming a series of skits. But even the tenuous plot could not keep *New Faces* from resembling a photographed stage show.

Movie operettas, on the other hand, have often been adaptations of stage operettas; for example, *Naughty Marietta* (1935), *Bittersweet* (1940), *The Student Prince* (1954), and *The Vagabond King* (1956). Occasionally there is an operetta-like film such as Billy Wilder's *The Emperor Waltz* (1948) with a fairy-tale plot shored up by music, or *The Umbrellas of Cherbourg* (1964), in which everything, including the dialogue, is sung. Operettas, however, are rarely written for the screen.

Comedies with music are another form of musical. One of Paramount's most successful series was the Road movies of the 1940s and early 1950s, featuring Bing Crosby, Bob Hope, and Dorothy Lamour in zany adventures that took them across the world, as in *Road to Singapore* (1940), *Road to Morocco* (1942), and *Road to Utopia* (1945). Since all three performers could sing, musical numbers were added, most having no relation to the plot, which itself had no relation to reality. Many of the so-called Elvis Presley musicals were really comedies and, in a few cases, dramas with music.

Neither a dramatic musical nor a musical drama, the drama with music is rarer than the comedy with music because it provides a true fusion of music and a serious story. In George Cukor's *A Star Is Born* (1954), a musical version of the 1937 nonmusical film about the price of Hollywood fame, the basic plot remained intact: a fading male star marries a newcomer, whose career skyrockets while his plummets. This remake, with Judy Garland and James Mason, includes some excellent musical numbers, all of which fit neatly into the action. The third version of *A Star Is Born* (1975) also had no choice but to feature music, but of a different sort: rock, because the main characters were now rock stars.

The show-business musical, sometimes called the backstage musical, chronicles the joys and heartaches of show business. The backstage musical has five common plot pegs: the overnight sensation, breaking up the act, writing the song, the crucial song, and career versus marriage.

The overnight sensation is the "unknown" who substitutes for the star and achieves instant stardom. The best-known overnight sensation is Peggy Sawyer (Ruby Keeler), the understudy in *42nd Street* (1933), who is told by her director (Warner Baxter): "Sawyer, you're going out a youngster, but you've got to come back a star." She did, and a Hollywood cliché was born. The "Born in a Trunk" sequence in the 1954 *A Star Is Born* is both a parody of, and a touching tribute to, the overnight-sensation movie.

The breakup theme usually gets under way when one member of an act is hired for a Broadway show but the other isn't. In *The Jolson Story* (1946), Steve Martin (William Demarest) stays in vaudeville while his protégé, Al Jolson (Larry Parks), goes on to become a star. A family act breaks up when the children go their separate ways in *There's No Business Like Show Business* (1954); a husband-and-wife team in *The Barkleys of Broadway* (1949), when the wife decides to do serious drama instead of musical comedy; a marriage, in *The Jolson Story*, when a husband prefers an adoring audience to his wife.

Several backstage musicals revolve around pairing the right lyrics with the right melody. This kind of movie assumes that the audience knows the actual lyrics and will therefore be amused by all the difficulties the lyricists are having: the songwriters working out the lyrics to "Lady Be Good" in *Lady Be Good*; the lyricist trying to find the "three little words" for the title song in *Three Little Words* (1950).

Some musicals feature a crucial song heard so often that it becomes inseparable from the plot, as in "You'll Never Know" in *Hello Frisco, Hello* (1943). Sometimes the crucial song is sung either incorrectly or at the wrong tempo until the singer is forced to sing it correctly. In *Coney Island* (1943), Betty Grable ruins "Cuddle Up a Little Closer" with her exaggerated gestures until George Montgomery handcuffs her, thereby forcing her to tone down her delivery and sing the song as a ballad.

The backstage musical often climaxes in a big production number that illustrates another convention of the genre. The production number supposedly takes place in a Broadway theater, although these numbers were actually filmed on Hollywood soundstages because no theater had facilities that were comparable to Hollywood's.

No Broadway theater could ever have accommodated the winding ramp down which Rita Hayworth rushes in *Cover Girl* or the gigantic platform on which Frank Sinatra sings "Ol' Man River" at the end of *Till the Clouds Roll By* (1946). A movie musical that is an adaptation of a stage musical clearly shows the difference between a soundstage and a theater stage. Vincente Minnelli's movie version of Lerner and Loewe's *Brigadoon* (1954) was shot entirely on an MGM soundstage. In both the stage and screen versions, the lovers walk through the heather on the hill as they sing the duet "The Heather on the Hill." No stage designer could have created such spectacular heather, nor could there ever have been as much of it on the stage as there is in the movie.

A dance musical is one in which dance is a means of furthering the action as well as expressing the characters' emotional and psychological states, as is the case in *The Red Shoes* (1948). A film featuring only dancing, like Gene Kelly's *Invitation to the Dance* (1956), is a rarity; it will attract ballet lovers but few others. Even *The Red Shoes*, arguably the best film about ballet ever made, has a memorable plot. More common is the song and dance musical, which has a discernible plot, unlike, say, the play *Cats*, which has none at all.

While every conceivable kind of dance has been featured in movie musicals, the courting dance is the most familiar. Its effectiveness depends on star chemistry. In the Fred Astaire–Ginger Rogers musicals, the chemistry is complementary. Astaire courted an aloof Rogers, who gradually responded as he encircled her, wooing her with every step. Their dancing was the epitome of Art Deco, stylized and sleek. When Astaire danced with Rita Hayworth in *You Were Never Lovelier* (1942) and later with the long-legged Cyd Charisse in *The Band Wagon* (1953) and *Silk Stockings* (1957), the dancing became more erotic, since Astaire had more sensuous partners. When Gene Kelly and Rita Hayworth danced to the music of "Long Ago and Far Away" in *Cover Girl*, their dancing took on elements of yearning, as if each were looking for the dream lover suggested by the lyrics "I dreamed a dream one day."

One of the best examples of the courting dance occurs in *The King and I* (1956). In the 1860s, Anna, a Welshwoman (Deborah Kerr), has come to Siam (today's Thailand) to teach the king's children. Although Anna and the king have their share of differences, both cultural and ideological, they gradually come to respect each other. After a formal ball, at which the king observed the way Western men and women dance, he asks Anna to show him the same steps. At first, Anna is coy, behaving very much like the proverbial schoolmarm. But when the king reminds Anna that a man always puts his arm around the woman's waist — and Anna admits he is right — the unspoken affection they feel for each other erupts in the celebrated "Shall We Dance" sequence, as they polka around the room.

Gene Kelly, who combined athleti-
cism with a ballet dancer's gracefulness, and Rita Hayworth in *Cover Girl*
(1944). *(Courtesy Sony Pictures Entertainment and MOMA/FSA)*

The two great exponents of the dance musical, Fred Astaire and Gene
Kelly, had diametrically opposed styles. Astaire was cool and aristocratic;
he was born for top hat, white tie, and tails. On the other hand, Kelly, who
once played ice hockey and taught gymnastics, was more athletic. Yet Kelly
could work aspects of ballet into his dancing, which was something Astaire
couldn't do. Astaire, for example, could never tap-dance on roller skates as
Kelly did so brilliantly in *It's Always Fair Weather* (1955). Although each performer represented a different style, together they epitomized the golden
age of the Hollywood musical.

Whether or not the traditional musical will return to its glory days is
debatable. When the studio system, based on the principle of tailoring the
script to the star, ended in the 1960s, actors were no longer groomed
for certain types of films. Judy Garland, Rita Hayworth, and Betty Grable
became stars in the 1940s because their respective studios (MGM, Columbia, and Twentieth Century-Fox) put them in films that revealed their special talents. Since Garland, Hayworth, and Grable could sing and dance, they
were cast in musicals that allowed them to do both. Esther Williams was a
passable singer but a superb swimmer, whose talents were highlighted in water
ballets. Ann Miller's specialty was tap, not the easiest form of dance to work
into a plot. But that rarely mattered in an Ann Miller musical. In *On the Town*,
Miller, playing an anthropologist, started tapping away in New York's Museum of Natural History—an action that, under ordinary circumstances,
would have had her removed from the building.

Genres never die, but they do reinvent themselves, emerging in other
forms. The films *Moulin Rouge* (2001) and *Chicago* (2002) demonstrate this.
Moulin Rouge has little in common with the traditional musical, which features long takes. *Moulin Rouge* has the rapid cutting of a music video. Neither are there any complete musical numbers in *Moulin Rouge*. Instead, there
are snippets of such well-known songs as "Diamonds Are a Girl's Best
Friend" and "The Sound of Music," both of which derive from movie musicals of the past—*Gentlemen Prefer Blondes* (1953) and *The Sound of Music*

Fred Astaire (in his signature clothes) and Ginger Rogers, the musical film's most popular dancing team, in *Swing Time* (1936), with a score by Jerome Kern. *(Courtesy MOMA/FSA)*

(1966). If anything, *Moulin Rouge* represents the postmodern musical, in which the movie's setting, in this case Paris in 1899, is not reflected in the music, which is drawn from various time periods.

When *Chicago* opened on Broadway in 1976, it was advertised as a "musical vaudeville" based on a 1920s play, later made into the movie *Roxie Hart* (1942). *Chicago* is about a woman who murders her lover and briefly becomes a celebrity—until another, who has committed a more sensational crime, arrives on the scene. The 1996 Broadway revival enjoyed a much longer run

The courtesan (Nicole Kidman) and the writer (Ewan McGregor) in Baz Luhrmann's *Moulin Rouge* (2001), a radical departure from the traditional movie musical. *(Courtesy Twentieth Century-Fox)*

than the original because it tapped into the public's fascination with, and skepticism about, alleged perpetrators of crime who manage to be acquitted, despite the overwhelming amount of evidence pointing to their guilt—the O. J. Simpson case being a prime example. Unlike the 1976 and 1996 Broadway productions of *Chicago*, which featured trained dancers in the leading roles of Roxie Hart and Velma Kelly, the 2002 movie version starred Renée Zellweger, a fine actress with minimal singing and dancing ability, and Catherine Zeta–Jones, an actress who had been a dancer.

In a traditional movie musical, such as *Seven Brides for Seven Brothers*, there were long shots of the dance sequences, so that it was obvious doubles were not used. In *Chicago*, Zellweger's lack of musical experience required occasional long shots in which she did not so much dance as move sinuously. Since traditional movie musicals are a rarity today, the kind of dancing that was once commonplace on the screen is limited to the stage musical. One has only to compare *Seven Brides for Seven Brothers* with *Chicago* to see the difference.

The most popular type of contemporary musical seems to be the animated musical, which has an interesting history. The first full-length animated feature, *Snow White and the Seven Dwarfs* (1937), was also a musical

Adam Pontipee (Howard Keel), temporarily banished from the bedroom by his wife, Millie (Jane Powell), in *Seven Brides for Seven Brothers* (1954). *(Courtesy MGM and Movie Star News)*

that introduced such perennial favorites as "Whistle While You Work" and "Some Day My Prince Will Come." The team of Alan Menken (music) and Howard Ashman (lyrics) must be credited with the revival of interest in the animated musical. Their collaboration has resulted in *The Little Mermaid* (1988), and later *Beauty and the Beast* (1991), which captivated the public in a way that no other animated film had since *Snow White* and was the first animated feature to receive an Academy Award nomination for best picture. Generally considered to be the quintessential animated musical, *Beauty and the Beast* is not only a tightly constructed narrative; it is also an integrated musical. The musical numbers bear directly on the action. For example, the title song is sung by the enchanted teapot, Mrs. Potts (the voice of Angela Lansbury), to her favorite cup, Chip. The song, motivated by the desire of the maternal Mrs. Potts to explain an important fact of life to Chip, explains how two dissimilar people could be attracted to each other—particularly a beautiful woman to a grotesque—and expresses the film's eternal theme: "Tale as old as time/Song as old as rhyme." It could almost be used to describe the musical genre itself.

The Western

The American western is more complex than might be assumed by the over-worked and often misleading distinction between the black-hatted villain and the white-clothed hero. In fact, many westerns totally disregard that color code. In *My Darling Clementine*, the true villain, Old Man Clanton (Walter Brennan), dresses in black, but so does Doc Holliday (Victor Mature), who is far from evil. In Fred Zinnemann's *High Noon*, the good marshal (Gary Cooper) wears a black hat; so does the hero Ethan (John Wayne) in *The Searchers*.

As James Kitses has demonstrated in his study of the western, *Horizons West*,[1] the western is not so much a matter of good versus evil as one of wilderness versus civilization. Within these extremes are three others: the individual versus the community, nature versus culture, and West versus East. The tension between the wilderness and civilization is evident in *Clementine* when the civilizing institutions of the church and the school begin to encroach on the frontier, bringing order and stability into lives that have neither. As the film shows, the frontier is changing: the one-street town of Tombstone sports a barbershop where a haircut is capped by a spray of cologne; a church is being dedicated; an actor gives a reading of Shakespeare; Clementine (Cathy Downs) becomes Tombstone's first teacher.

In the western, opposites continually confront each other: freedom/responsibility, self-concern/commitment, ignorance/education, the desert/the garden. The western hero is a loner, often fiercely independent. If he is to develop as a person, he must assume a sense of responsibility—for example, by marrying or by serving the community as peace officer, educator, or wagon-train leader. Nor can retirement stand in his way if he is needed, as Captain Brittles (John Wayne) is needed in John Ford's *She Wore a Yellow Ribbon* (1949).

Initially, the western hero avoids marriage because it is an institution that curtails freedom. Thus the hero can be comfortable only with a woman who is his alter ego or his complement. If the hero has a criminal past, he may be drawn to a social outcast, as Ringo (John Wayne) is to the prostitute Dallas (Claire Trevor) in *Stagecoach* or as Link (Gary Cooper) is to Billie (Julie London) in Anthony Mann's *Man of the West* (1958). If he is an upright man, like Wyatt Earp (Henry Fonda) in *Clementine*, he will be attracted to a virtuous woman.

The frontier encourages a survival instinct that is so strong it can cause a community to abandon its lawman, as the townspeople do in *High Noon* when they refuse to come to the aid of their marshal. The frontier is also parochial: easterners are regarded with suspicion because they bring with them education and knowledge of the law. In *The Man Who Shot Liberty Valance*, an eastern lawyer is an object of ridicule; in Anthony Mann's *The Man from Laramie* (1955), a frontier woman dismisses her rival as "a piece of

John Wayne as the black-hatted but hardly villainous Ethan in *The Searchers* (1956). *(Courtesy MOMA/FSA and Warner Bros., Inc.)*

fluff from the East." The East, however, is necessary to the West; it can bring the garden to the desert in the form of irrigation. In *Liberty Valance*, the cactus rose is all that can bloom in the desert until the arrival of irrigation — the result of legislation initiated by an eastern lawyer, who was dismissed as a "dude."

Still, there are those who cannot adapt to the wilderness-turned-garden: outlaws, uncompromising individualists, romantic idealists. For the unassimilated, there are two choices: flight or a return to the wilderness. In *Stagecoach*, Ringo and Dallas are "saved from the blessings of civilization," as one of the characters observes — they head for Mexico, taking the individualism of the frontier with them. In *The Searchers*, Ethan spends five years trying to find Debbie, who, as a child, had been abducted by Comanches. When he brings her back at the end, he stands in the doorway momentarily as the others enter the house. Ethan does not enter, because home and community are not meant for him; instead, he returns to the wilderness like the gods of myth, who descend to earth to help humankind and leave when their job is done.

In *Beyond Formula: American Film Genres* (1976), author Stanley Solomon offers a single explanation for the plots, characters, and locales of the western: the landscape, which determines not only setting but also the kinds of people who would be attracted to it and the kinds of situations they would encounter there.[2] Because the West is rugged, only the hardy can survive there. But even they need protection from unscrupulous bankers, cattle barons, crooked lawyers, and land speculators. Hence, they need the cavalry, lawmen, crusading newspaper editors, honest lawyers, fearless clergymen — the traditional heroes of the western.

The landscape explains a certain sameness of setting: plains, valleys, mesas, deserts, ranches, trading posts, forts, and towns with a single street that features a combination saloon, gambling house, and brothel and, if civilization has made any incursions, a barbershop and a newspaper office. It also accounts for modes of travel — stagecoach, horseback, wagon train, rail — and helps to explain recurring plot devices and rituals. The western plot often revolves around a quest or a journey: a search for a loved one in *The Searchers*, or for a loved one's killers in *The Bravados* (1957) and *Last Train from Gun Hill* (1956). It can also include a trek across inhospitable terrain: the trip through Apache territory in *Stagecoach*, the cattle drive in Howard Hawks's *Red River* (1948), the Mormons' journey across the mountains in John Ford's *Wagon Master*.

Those embarking on the quest or making the journey are a varied lot, usually a mix of individualists and traditionalists, the educated and uneducated, moral people and amoral ones, romantics and realists. The passengers in *Stagecoach* are representative: the loner hero with a criminal past, the prostitute, the good woman, the drunken doctor, a southern gambler, a whiskey salesman, an embezzling banker, a kindly lawman, and a driver with a Mexican wife. Other films broadened the list to include homesteaders, cavalry officers, miners, trappers, prospectors, geezers, bullies, and matriarchal and patriarchal figures. As the genre matured, unusual variations on traditional character types were introduced: the sheriff turned bounty hunter in Anthony Mann's *The Tin Star* (1956); bilingual and trilingual Indians in *Fort Apache* and *She Wore a Yellow Ribbon*; the white men who marry Indian women in *Broken Arrow* (1950) and *Broken Lance* (1954); and the loner heroine in Nicholas Ray's *Johnny Guitar* (1954).

Despite its realistic nature, the western is also ritualistic. Certain acts are invested with a ceremonial quality, as if they were being performed according to a rite or a liturgy. Such rituals include gunplay, confrontations, modes of dressing, returns, departures, and burials. In a western, one does not just reach for a gun and shoot; one draws from the hip, with style. The gun is more than a weapon; it is an extension of one's personality. Sometimes a character removes it slowly from the holster with a cool gracefulness; at other times, the character whips it out and fires it by thumbing or fanning. A character might even fire two guns, standing defiantly with legs apart and holding the guns at different angles. The gun is also an icon — an image that inspires awe — to be held as one might hold a talisman or a sacred object.

In a western, clothes make the character. The virtuous woman is dressed primly and simply, covered up to her neck. The prostitute is usually dressed provocatively, in an off-the-shoulder blouse or a low-cut gown. In symbolic

Alan Ladd in his white buckskins in *Shane* (1953). *(Courtesy MOMA/FSA and Paramount Pictures)*

westerns like *Shane* and *The Searchers*, the hero's dress is so striking that it gives him the aura of a medieval knight or an epic warrior. Shane, who materializes like a god descended to earth to aid a homesteader and his family, wears white buckskins that set him apart from the others. Ethan in *The Searchers* makes his first appearance wearing a black neckerchief and a Confederate cloak, and carrying a saber. His rifle is in a fringed buckskin cover that resembles an aegis. His dress, a vestige of his Civil War days, marks him as an anachronism in postbellum Texas, but it also gives him heroic stature.

Ever since the first western, E. S. Porter's *The Great Train Robbery* (1903), the shoot-out has been a dramatic, sometimes operatic, event. In *The Great Train Robbery*, when one of the outlaws is shot he does a ballet-like twirl, firing his gun as he falls. Sam Peckinpah's westerns continue the tradition of choreographed death, often in slow motion, that adds a macabre quality to the bloody climax. Perhaps the most operatic death occurs in King Vidor's *Duel in the Sun* (1947), in which Pearl and Lewt (Jennifer Jones and Gregory Peck) are firing away at each other when suddenly they realize they are in love; thereupon Pearl crawls up rocks and boulders to die, blood-splattered, in Lewt's arms.

Most shoot-outs, though less bizarre, are still theatrical. Even those that seem to be conventional usually have a theatrical touch: Doc Holliday's handkerchief fluttering in the wind after he has been killed at the O. K. Corral in *Clementine*, McCabe's solitary death in the snow in Robert Altman's *McCabe and Mrs. Miller* (1971). Sometimes the shoot-out takes the form of a long walk:

the hero walks down a street that the townspeople have cleared or deserted, to confront the villain or the villain's gang, as in *High Noon*. A variation on the shoot-out is the climax of *Red River*, when Tom Dunson (John Wayne) strides down a street intending to challenge his surrogate son, Matt (Montgomery Clift), only to discover that Matt has too much respect for him to retaliate.

Homecomings, departures, and burials in the western are also acts of ritual. The homecoming is often a *nostos*, a return in the epic sense, like Odysseus's return in *The Odyssey*. When Ethan returns from the Civil War at the beginning of *The Searchers*, it is as a hero; he walks toward his brother's house as if he were in a one-person processional, with each member of the family looking at him with awe. When Wyatt Earp takes leave of Clementine, and Shane of Marion, each behaves like a knight bidding farewell to his lady. In John Ford's cavalry films, the cavalry does not merely leave the fort; it troops out in the grand manner to the music of "The Girl I Left behind Me" or "She Wore a Yellow Ribbon." Burials are strikingly framed, with the mourners set against the horizon as if they were figures in a painting. Occasionally a touch of pathos is added. In *Shane*, the dead man's dog stretches out a paw to touch his master's casket as it is lowered into the ground; in *She Wore a Yellow Ribbon*, a woman uses part of her red petticoat to make a flag for an officer's burial.

The western, then, is far from a gathering of the good, the bad, and the ugly; it is a complex genre that, in its own way, records the history of America.

Throughout the 1960s, the Vietnam War polarized the nation as no other conflict had. However, except for *The Green Berets* (1968), which glorified America's involvement in Vietnam, filmmakers tended to avoid the war in the late sixties and early seventies. Yet the war was not entirely absent from the screen; the western performed a double function: it became a metaphor for an ugly war as well as a mirror of an America that the civil rights movement had made more sensitive to the portrayal of minorities. The two functions were related: Vietnam was perceived as a war that discriminated against minority males who were unable to attend college—thereby qualifying for a deferment—and ended up being drafted.

If the West became less mythic in the 1970s, and the movie western more violent, part of the reason was the documentation of the atrocities American troops had committed in Vietnam. The 1968 My Lai massacre inspired *Soldier Blue* (1970) and *Ulzana's Raid* (1972), which contained some of the most graphic violence seen in a western—but nothing compared with what had happened in Southeast Asia.

By the 1990s, the Vietnam western had run its course, leaving in its wake a demythologized West that could no longer be considered a metaphor for an ideal America. John Ford's mythic West had become too closely associated with John Wayne—who was still an icon but was also a symbol of the gung-ho patriots who supported the war—to inspire filmmakers to imitate it. If the West is now a microcosm of anything, it is of America as it was (and perhaps still is), not of an America that could have been. In the absence of myth, there is antimyth and revisionism. The myths are either inverted or the historical events that inspired them are reexamined in an attempt to provide a less fanciful depiction of "what really happened" or "what it was really like." Revisionism, which challenges received interpretations, is hardly new. John Ford had been experimenting with revisionism since the late 1940s with *Fort Apache*, as he gradually altered the way Native Americans had been portrayed on the screen, even to the point of presenting their point of view in *The Searchers* and *Cheyenne Autumn* (1964). Unfortunately, Ford's revisionism, which included, for one thing, Apaches speaking Spanish instead of the gibberish often used to suggest authenticity, may have been too subtle to register the impact it should have had. While other westerns such as *Broken Arrow* and *Apache* (1954) also tried to correct the negative image of Native Americans that Hollywood had fostered, they came at a time when television was usurping the role that movies once played in influencing the public's attitude toward everything from sex to race.

It was in the early 1970s that American filmmakers began looking at the Old West more closely, questioning the way it had been portrayed. The American Indian, in the past the perpetrator of violence, was now the victim. *Little Big Man* (1970) challenged the legend of the heroic George Custer and his last stand at Little Big Horn; far from being the romantic figure Errol Flynn played in Raoul Walsh's *They Died with Their Boots On* (1941), the Custer of *Little Big Man* was almost deranged, and the American Indians were the victims of his madness. The revisionist western was already established when *Dances with Wolves* (1990) appeared; *Dances with Wolves* marked the culmination of two decades of revisionism, which succeeded in reversing the familiar character types of the American Indian and the civilized white man. The film's popularity also suggests that audiences are now less inclined to think of good and evil in terms of race and ethnicity.

Antimyth is similar to revisionism: the original myth, along with its plots and character types, is either parodied or turned inside out. Two westerns in which Clint Eastwood starred and which he directed are clearly antimythic: *Pale Rider* (1985) and, particularly, *Unforgiven* (1992). Eastwood came to prominence in the westerns of Italian director Sergio Leone, who, despite his professed love of the American western, also loved to portray violence as graphically, and, at times, operatically, as the times allowed. Instead of heroes, there were antiheroes. No longer was the protagonist a man with a violent past that he would like to put behind him, like the Ringo Kid, Shane, and Ethan Edwards; he *was* that past. The protagonist was now the dark side of the hero that was only hinted at in films like *Shane* and *The Searchers*. Leone's antiheroes are nameless men who appear out of nowhere, looking like prophets of doom; who kill off their rivals, go off with the gold or ransom money, and clean up the town, leaving a trail of bodies behind them—not just the villain's corpse, as Shane did. *Pale Rider* is, in fact, almost

An ex-gunslinger (Clint Eastwood) and his friend (Morgan Freeman) off to collect a reward in *Unforgiven* (1992), one of the finest examples of the antimythic western. *(Courtesy MOMA/FSA)*

a parody of *Shane*, with gold miners replacing the homesteaders and the Shane figure transformed into the Preacher (Clint Eastwood), who, like the Pale Rider in the Apocalypse, brings death with him.

Because of its ambivalence and its avoidance of obvious parallels with other films, Eastwood's *Unforgiven* is perhaps the finest example of the antimythic western. The traditional character types and themes of the classic western have been inverted, so that instead of a hero, there is a hero-as-villain—the other villains having no redeeming qualities. The hero-villain has at least two: the desire to reform and lead a decent life, and a code of retribution that is the flip side of the code of honor. William Munny (Eastwood), an ex-gunslinger who remains faithful to the memory of his dead wife, wants nothing more than to raise his two children in peace. However, the prospect of a $1,000 reward for killing the men who disfigured a prostitute prompts him to return to his old life. No western, not even an antimythic one, ever opened like *Unforgiven*—with a woman's face being slashed. And no western ever used contemporary vulgarisms and obscenities in such profusion, as if the language of R-rated movies had become the language of the Old West.

In the classic western, there were gunfighters who tried to forget their past but whose "eye for an eye" philosophy required them to avenge the cold-blooded murder of a friend (*Shane*); and gunfighters goaded into killing by glory-seeking kids who scoff at the idea of a reformed killer (*The Gunfighter*, 1950). There have been bounty hunters before (*The Naked Spur*, 1953) and even bounty hunter–sheriffs (*The Tin Star*). In the traditional western, the protagonist embarks on some kind of journey—a quest, search, cattle drive, or rescue operation—often accompanied by an old friend (*Red River*) or saddled with a bipolar opposite (*The Searchers* and *Two Rode Together*, 1961). Sometimes there is a boy or a young man who either learns from the reformed gunfighter (*Shane*) or represents the kind of reckless youth the gunfighter once was (*The Gunfighter*). Finally, there is a sheriff who can be anything from a tough law-enforcement officer (*My Darling Clementine*) to a sympathetic fellow human being who bends the law for those whom society has misjudged (*Stagecoach*). All these types—the ex-gunfighter, the old friend, the callow youth, and the sheriff—appear in *Unforgiven*, but in a completely inverted way.

In the traditional western, the ex-gunfighter might come to the aid of a farmer (*Shane*), but he is not a farmer himself. In *Unforgiven*, Munny is an unsuccessful pig farmer. In the traditional western, the sidekick is white; in the multicultural 1980s and 1990s, the partner's color is irrelevant. Thus there was nothing unusual about Munny's old friend Ned Logan (Morgan Freeman) being an African American with a Native American wife. Munny learns about the reward money from the Sheffield Kid, who, despite his youth, boasts of having killed five men, when the truth is that he is nearly blind and has yet to kill anyone. No sheriff in the traditional western was ever nicknamed Little Bill (Gene Hackman), a character in *Unforgiven* whose real name is Bill Daggett and who uses a goon squad to keep law and order in the town of Big Whiskey. Occasionally the upholder of the law is a villain (the federal judge in *The Man from Colorado*, 1948; the marshal in *Pale Rider*), but there has never been a more sadistic one than Daggett, who derives great pleasure from kicking and flogging lawbreakers, or those he assumes to be such. When Munny becomes Ned's avenger, he does not wear buckskins like Shane but drab brown. Nor is he the avenging angel; he is the angel of death, who leaves a saloon floor littered with corpses, including the sheriff's, before he heads back to his farm.

Except for a few shots, notably the opening and closing scenes of the Munny homestead at sunset, this is a dark world, epitomized by the color of Eastwood's face, which is not so much tan as brown, with his clothes looking much the same.

By inverting the past, *Unforgiven* brings the Old West into the present, suggesting perhaps that there is not that much difference between them. However, the success of *Unforgiven*, which won Oscars for best picture and best director (Eastwood), did not spark a revival of interest in the western among moviegoers. Subsequent westerns proved far less popular, even though they starred well-known actors. Examples include Kevin Costner in *Wyatt Earp* (1994), Robert Duvall and Gene Hackman in *Geronimo: An American Legend* (1993), and Sharon Stone in *The Quick and the Dead* (1995). Perhaps the only way the western can regain its pride of place is with iconic actors like Eastwood starring in movies that speak as much to the present as they do to the past, encouraging viewers to rethink their own era as well as the one portrayed in the film, even if it means turning the conventions of the classic western upside down—something Kevin Costner did not do in *Open Range* (2003), in which he served as both director and costar with Robert Duvall. Except for the violence, which led to an R rating, *Open Range* recycles plot devices, motifs, and character types from the traditional western: conflict between the cattle barons and the newcomers, the gunfight, the loner, an older male as mentor, the Eastern types, and the parting of the hero from a woman. Although well made, *Open Range* is more of a textbook for the study of the classic American western than a questioning of its codes and conventions. Eastwood took chances and succeeded, while Costner played it safe and came up short.

The Crime Film

Filmmakers have always been intrigued by the gangster and the criminal. The gangster era coincided with the beginning of Hollywood's golden age in the late 1920s, thereby providing screenwriters with fresh plot material. The plots often came straight from the headlines—and with Al Capone, Bonnie Parker and Clyde Barrow, John Dillinger, and "Lucky" Luciano making headlines, there was no dearth of subject matter. Filmmakers weren't the only ones who were attracted to criminals—the public was also. Gangsters were colorful figures amid the bleak Great Depression, doing what moviegoers couldn't do, even if they wished to. Gangsters didn't so much break the law as flout it. But they flouted it in accordance with the American success scenario. They practiced their own form of upward mobility, beginning with holdups and graduating to bank heists. They started as lackeys and ended up as heads of syndicates. As they advanced, they acquired the trappings of success—overcoats, fedoras, and dark or pinstriped suits. But, most of all, gangsters exercised their freedom, the quality Americans prize most dearly. Unrestrained by conventional mores, they gloried in their independence, achieving an emancipation that moviegoers might envy but could never experience because the price was too high.

Thus, the crime film portrays gangsters and criminals with a combination of fascination and compassion, stopping just short of exoneration. As the Production Code insisted, crime could not pay; but this stricture didn't stop Hollywood from giving gangsters a sinister charisma and making their lives high drama until the last few minutes when it came time for retribution. And even then, the gangster died in a grand manner, whether in the street or on a sidewalk, the surface of which was always elegantly black, as if specially prepared for those who revealed their dark side.

In addition to being gunned down in the streets, as in Howard Hawks's *Scarface* (1932), and on sidewalks, as in *He Ran All the Way* (1951),

Stylized death in the classic crime film as seen in *The Public Enemy* (1931). *(Courtesy WCFTR)*

gangsters often met their end on steps and cliffs, symbolizing their fall from power. In Raoul Walsh's *The Roaring Twenties* (1939), Eddie Bartlett (James Cagney) dies on the steps of a church, cradled in the arms of his mistress. When a police officer asks Eddie's identity, his mistress replies, "He used to be a big shot." Roy Earle (Humphrey Bogart) in *High Sierra* plunges from the top of a cliff. His death is a literal fall from the heights, as opposed to the figurative fall in classical tragedy. Sometimes when a criminal and his beloved die, one body is draped over the other, as in Robert Siodmak's *Criss Cross* (1949). Sometimes physical union is impossible; at the end of Arthur Penn's *Bonnie and Clyde* (1967), Bonnie's (Faye Dunaway) body is hanging out of a bullet-ridden car, while Clyde's (Warren Beatty) lies a few feet away on the ground.

Like the western, the crime film has inspired theatrical death scenes. Two of the best occur in James Cagney films. In Michael Curtiz's *Angels with Dirty Faces* (1938), Rocky Sullivan (Cagney) agrees to feign cowardice in an effort to discourage the teenagers who idolize him from turning to a life of crime. Walking cockily to the electric chair, Rocky pretends to be terror stricken and begs hysterically for his life. In Raoul Walsh's *White Heat* (1949), Cody Jarett (Cagney) dies amid an apocalyptic explosion of chemical tanks, yelling, "Top of the world, Ma!" Cody Jarett made it to the top, only to go up in flames.

Warren Beatty and Faye Dunaway as the title characters of Arthur Penn's *Bonnie and Clyde* (1967). *(Courtesy Warner Bros.)*

The crime film has other features in common with the western. In both, the gun is an icon. Just as the gun in the western can be a reflection of the user's personality, the gun in the crime film can be a projection of the user's neurosis or sexuality. Cody Jarett brandishes a gun as a child would who fancies himself an adult. Jarett's behavior is understandable: he has a relationship with his mother that is so oedipal that he sits on her lap. In *Bonnie and Clyde*, the gun is sexual. For the impotent Clyde, it is a substitute for potency; for Bonnie, it is the equivalent of a sexual thrill.

The crime film unfolds within a world of back rooms, bars, diners, sleek cars, mean streets, sleazy hotel rooms, speakeasies, nightclubs, tenements, gaudy apartments, and mausoleum-like homes. Unlike the western, which allows loners—even if they have been on the wrong side of the law—to find a mate and live happily ever after, the crime film cannot. Gangsters sometimes find their true love, only to die in the loved one's arms.

The classic American crime film depended for its effectiveness on performers who were themselves icons: James Cagney, Humphrey Bogart, Edward G. Robinson, John Garfield. With actors who were able to ignite a human spark in characters that could be otherwise flat or unlikable, the gangster and the criminal become both lower and higher versions of ourselves. They are our dark side, doing what we would never dare, and yet achieving the American dream of success, wealth, and fame. While we are glad we are not them, at the same time we cannot help but envy their daring because, as one film scholar has noted, the gangster is "the archetypal

American dreamer whose actions and behavior involve a living out of the dream common to most everyone who exists in the particular configurations and contradictions of American society, a dream in conflict with the society."[3]

The crime film has its own kind of diversity. There are films in which criminals act alone, as in *He Walked by Night* (1948), or as a team, as in *Gun Crazy* (1949) and *Bonnie and Clyde*, as well as those in which they become part of a mob, such as *Little Caesar*, *The Roaring Twenties*, and *The St. Valentine's Day Massacre* (1967). The Mafia movie is a special case. The best example is *The Godfather* trilogy, which was preceded by *Black Hand* (1950) and the underrated *The Brotherhood* (1968). The classic Mafia film operates according to a number of conventions, such as the code of silence (*omertà*), which, if broken, results in death; respect for elders; observance of territorial rights; and a top-down chain of command ranging from the Don or head of the crime family to his *consigliere* (counselor, usually a lawyer), capo (captain) and "soldiers" in charge of maintaining discipline among the mafiosi as well as outsiders who threaten what the Mafia euphemistically calls *la cosa nostra*—"our thing." The secondary cast of characters includes corrupt police officers, Mafia wives, and the righteous who cannot be bought.

Although the crime film has never shied away from violence, it has become bloodier since the 1930s and 1940s. The contemporary screen is much freer than it was in the past; no longer is the "crime does not pay" mandate enforced. Oliver Stone's *Natural Born Killers* was widely criticized for its violence; Mickey and Mallory (Woody Harrelson and Juliette Lewis) are "natural born killers" who create bloodbaths, but always spare one eyewitness who can add to the ongoing saga of Mickey and Mallory. Oliver Stone is a serious moviemaker, who does not portray violence for its own sake. He is implicitly criticizing the tabloid media for capitalizing on our fascination with violence by giving Mickey and Mallory the kind of coverage that should be reserved for those who improve society, not those who threaten it.

The fact that Mickey and Mallory become media figures—as have American gangsters, Mafia figures, criminals, and murder suspects—suggests that the public can't get enough of types they would never want to encounter in real life, only on the screen. It is therefore not surprising that, of the one hundred films that the American Film Institute (AFI) judged the best of those made during the first one hundred years of the American cinema (1896–1996), crime plays a major role in many of them. In the order in which the AFI has ranked them, these films are *The Godfather* (#3), *Psycho* (#18), *Chinatown* (#19), *The Maltese Falcon* (#23), *Bonnie and Clyde* (#27), *The Godfather, Part II* (#32), *Double Indemnity* (#38), *Rear Window* (#42), *A Clockwork Orange* (#46), *Taxi Driver* (#47), *Silence of the Lambs* (#65), *The French Connection* (#70), *GoodFellas* (#94), and *Pulp Fiction* (#95).

Woody Harrelson and Juliette Lewis as the title characters of Oliver Stone's *Natural Born Killers* (1994). *(Courtesy Warner Bros.)*

Mafia father and son: Marlon Brando (right) as Don Vito Corleone and Al Pacino as his son Michael, a godfather-in-the-making, in Francis Ford Coppola's *The Godfather* (1972). *(Courtesy AMPAS and Paramount Pictures)*

Film Noir

Film noir does not have a concrete definition, yet its characteristics are among the most recognizable of any genre. Literally, the term means "dark film"—film that is both dark in its look, with the look of nighttime rather than daylight, and dark in the sense of revealing the dark side of humankind and society. In film noir, the interplay of light and dark is accomplished by high-contrast photography and low-key lighting, which create a monolinear

The Noir Night (above) and the Noir Corpse (Page 139) in *Mildred Pierce* (1945).

Wally (Jack Carson) and Mildred Pierce (Joan Crawford) on the pier. *(Courtesy WCFTR)*

world of white and black. Street lamps shed circles of light on glistening black pavements, wet from rain; neon signs illuminate dark skies; blondes wear black gowns decorated with silver stripes; the hoods of dark cars look glazed by the moonlight. Murders are committed in darkness or in shadow, but during the struggle a table lamp is often knocked over, so that when the body is discovered the victim's face is illuminated by the overturned lamp. Sunlight coming through Venetian blinds in late afternoon forms rows of horizontal shadows on living room walls.

While film noir has its roots in hard-boiled detective fiction, it can take the form of either a private-eye story or a crime film without a private eye. Note, however, that neither a private-eye film nor a crime film is necessarily film noir. *Murder, My Sweet* is a private-eye film that is also a classic film noir; *Meet Nero Wolfe* (1936) is just a private-eye movie. *Criss Cross* and Joseph H. Lewis's *Gun Crazy* are crime films and film noir; *Angels with Dirty Faces* and *The Roaring Twenties* are just crime films.

The world of film noir is one of paranoia and entrapment, of forces bearing down on the individual that are too overwhelming to resist. Tight framing encloses characters within a universe from which there is no escape.

Slow tracking shots create a mood of uncertainty; long backward tracks suggest continuous movement, pursuit, life on the run. Canted shots imply a world gone haywire. That world is often enshrouded in fog that is not so much real as symbolic of a universe whose workings are impenetrable and whose design, if there is any, can never be known.

The stock characters of film noir—private detectives, insurance salesmen, prostitutes, murderous housewives, two-time losers, ex-convicts, and gamblers—are essentially reducible to two: a man and a woman caught up in a chain of circumstances from which only the death of one—or both—can extricate them. In classic noir, the femme fatale is a siren who draws the male into a murder plot—often the murder of her husband (*Double Indemnity*); involves him in a murder she has committed, as in *The Strange Love of Martha Ivers* (1946), or in which she has played a role, as in *Dead Reckoning* (1947); or lures him away from his middle-class world into the criminal demimonde, as in *The Woman in the Window* (1944), *Scarlet Street* (1945), *Nora Prentiss* (1947), *Pitfall* (1948), and *The File on Thelma Jordan* (1949). Occasionally, the femme fatale fails to elicit the hero's support in the murder scheme, as in *Human Desire* (1954); in Fritz Lang's *The Big Heat* (1953) she even discards her persona midway and comes over to the hero's side—but too late.

In noir, the femme fatale can be killed by her lover (*Double Indemnity*), ex-lover (*Criss Cross*), or husband (Orson Welles's *The Lady from Shanghai*, 1948; *Murder, My Sweet*). Her death can even be an accident (*Detour, The Postman Always Rings Twice*, 1946); still, the male must pay despite his complete (*Detour*) or partial innocence. If the male gets away with murdering the femme fatale, he still pays: Chris (Edward G. Robinson) in *Scarlet Street* never stops hearing the sound of Kitty's (Joan Bennett) voice.

The male can either follow the femme fatale to his—or their—fate or free himself from her snares. In either case the end is violent, sometimes dramatically so. While O'Hara (Orson Welles) does free himself from Elsa Bannister (Rita Hayworth) in Welles's *The Lady from Shanghai*, Elsa dies in a hall of mirrors where she shoots it out with her husband as their images, reflected in the mirrors, shatter with the glass. Mirrors and other reflectors are a favorite prop of film noir because the characters are often mirror images of each other. Before he fires at Elsa, O'Hara, appropriately, tells her that in killing her, he is killing himself.

Sometimes the climax of a film noir is a *Liebestod* (love-death). Common to film noir is the theme of *l'amour fatal* (fatal love)—love generated by a combination of passion and infatuation that takes a perverse turn, causing one lover to kill or attempt to kill the other. At the end of *Double Indemnity*, Phyllis fires at Neff, wounding him; then, suddenly regretting what she has done, she moves toward him. Neff takes her in his arms and embraces her while at the same time firing a bullet into her heart from her own gun.

Film noir plots are convoluted, reflecting the intricacies of fate. Voice-over narration and **flashbacks** are common; in *The Locket* (1946) there are

Wally discovering Monty Berrigan's (Zachary Scott) body in *Mildred Pierce* (1945). Note the overturned lamp, a typical noir prop in a typical noir framing. *(Courtesy WCFTR)*

flashbacks within flashbacks. Chance—in the sense of a character's being in the wrong place at the wrong time—is more significant in film noir than in most other genres. In *Gun Crazy*, a young man, whose fascination with guns landed him in reform school, wanders into a carnival featuring a female sharpshooter; the chance encounter changes both their lives, as they become bank robbers in the tradition of Bonnie and Clyde and end up dying in a foggy swamp. In *Detour*, Roberts (Tom Neal), hitchhiking from New York to Los Angeles, is picked up by a man with a heart condition who dies en route. Thinking the man's death will be misconstrued as murder, Roberts adopts the dead man's identity. He later makes the mistake of picking up a woman who knew the dead man and who therefore knows that he is not the owner of the car. The woman, Vera (Ann Savage), makes Roberts her prisoner and dies in a manner that is bizarre even by film noir standards. Drunk, Vera grabs the phone, rushes into the bedroom, and locks the door behind her. Falling on the bed, she becomes entangled in the telephone cord, which is coiled around her neck. Outside, Roberts pulls at the part of the cord that is under the door, not knowing the rest of it is around

The hall of mirrors in *The Lady from Shanghai* (1948). *(Courtesy MOMA/FSA and Columbia Pictures)*

Vera's neck. When he finally breaks the door open and bursts into the bedroom, we see the reflection of the prostrate Vera in the mirror. This is Roberts's second brush with fate; he is now a two-time loser.

Unlike the western, whose popularity is intermittent, film noir has never gone out of fashion because its stylistic elements are applicable to a wide range of plots: the whodunit, the man/woman in hiding, the old dark house, the cover-up, the murderous couple, the murderous lover, and so on. The familiar husband/wife/wife's or husband's lover plot admits of several possibilities: wife and lover plot to kill husband in the tradition of *Double Indemnity*, *The Postman Always Rings Twice*, and *Body Heat* (1981); husband's lover terrorizes husband's household until wife takes action and kills her (*Fatal Attraction*, 1989); husband kills wife's lover (*Unfaithful*, 2002; *The Man Who Wasn't There*, 2001); husband and lover conspire to drive wife to commit suicide (Douglas Sirk's *Sleep, My Love*, 1948); wife's lover kills husband, planning to marry her for the money she will inherit (*The Prowler*, 1951); husband's lover is killed because she knows too much (*Mulholland Falls*, 1996). An interesting variation on the noir trio occurs in *The Grifters* (1990), in which the three are a mother, her son, and the son's lover, who is as amoral as the mother.

While purists may argue that true film noir is black and white, the same high contrast can be obtained by creating a color scheme where black and white predominate. It was not unintentional that in *Body Heat* and *The Grifters*, the *femmes noires* (Kathleen Turner and Anjelica Huston, respectively) wore white, which looked striking against a dark background. Curtis Hanson's *L.A. Confidential* (1997) creates a noirish picture of Los Angeles of the 1950s. This "city of angels" is more of a modern Inferno, with its ever-widening circles of sins and sinners. All the elements of film noir appear in the movie: the unsuspecting male; the *femme noire* (blonde, as is often the case, but not the predator she often is); the usual assortment of villains, including those in high places; frame-ups and cover-ups; dark streets lit only by neon; cheap motels; a coffee shop that becomes the scene of a homicide; and the climactic shoot-out that leaves its usual share of corpses. Hanson's palette captures every hue Los Angeles noir can offer, ranging from the decadently bright to the ominously dark, with the tacky and the garish in between.

When Joel and Ethan Coen decided to pay homage to film noir in *The Man Who Wasn't There*, they chose black-and-white to replicate the style of 1940s noir. Once they realized they could not achieve the noir look that way, the brothers opted for color stock that was printed in black and white. Because the color negative had to be converted into black and white, *The Man Who Wasn't There* has a more extreme — you might even say more mannered — look than the usual film noir. The barber, Ed Crane (Billy Bob Thornton), has hair with a silvery glaze, and his pallid complexion often has a shadowy finish. The few out-of-doors scenes have a brightness bordering on glare. The barbershop is awash with white (the barbers' uniforms, Ed's face, the porcelain sink, the light through the windows). The Cranes' bathroom has the same strange glow as the fatal motel bathroom in *Psycho*.

The Coens have also observed such noir conventions as silhouetted figures, dimly lit corridors, the inevitable cigarette (lit and unlit), bars and hotel rooms with minimal illumination, the familiar overturned lamp after a murder, and restaurants where the only light seems to come from the Exit sign and the low-wattage lamps on the tables. Although circles of light are common in noir, there is one unusual composition in *Man*, in which two shafts of light stream through a prison window, forming the sides of a cone whose base is reflected on the floor. The extent to which a viewer appreciates the brothers' efforts to replicate 1940s noir depends upon how well acquainted he or she is with the genre. If a viewer's knowledge of noir is minimal, the film can still be enjoyed as a thriller with a twist at the end.

Combat Film

The appeal of the American combat film, or war movie, often depends on the particular war, the public's attitude toward it, and the way the war is portrayed. The American Revolution may have given birth to the United States of America, but one would never know it from the unenthusiastic reception to *Revolution* (1985) and *The Patriot* (2000), even though the films starred Al Pacino and Mel Gibson, respectively. The musical *1776*, which dramatized the events leading up to the signing of the Declaration of Independence, was a huge hit on Broadway in the late 1960s; the 1972 movie version, which could not conceal its stage origins, is hardly anyone's idea of a real movie musical. The Revolution and the Declaration of Independence are matters Americans appear to take for granted.

The same holds true of the Civil War—at least as far as movies are concerned. The Civil War seems to attract audiences only when it is treated as an epic: Civil War = epic = *The Birth of a Nation* and *Gone with the Wind*, both of which run over three hours without addressing the "peculiar institution" that led to the conflict: slavery. Instead, each film seems to lament a way of life that has "gone with the wind." While contemporary filmmakers have dealt with slavery—Steven Spielberg in *Amistad* (1998); Jonathan Demme in *Beloved* (1999)—neither movie registered a major impact. The small screen has had more success with the subject; *Roots* (1977) is one of the most popular miniseries in television history, and Ken Burns's classic Public Television series *The Civil War* (1990) drew a huge audience.

World War I, which produced some of the greatest antiwar poetry ever written, also occasioned two of the finest American antiwar movies ever made, Lewis Milestone's *All Quiet on the Western Front* (1930) and Stanley Kubrick's *Paths of Glory* (1957). But perhaps because "the war to end all wars" proved to be such a disastrous experience for the Americans who fought in it, as well as becoming the prelude to a far worse conflict, World War I has never been an attractive proposition for moviemakers; it is difficult to muster much enthusiasm for a conflict that left so many maimed, disfigured, and embittered.

It was quite different during World War II, the great age of the American combat film. No sooner had a significant event occurred than there was a movie about it: the London blitz inspired *Mrs. Miniver* (1942) and *Journey for Margaret* (1943); the December 7, 1941, attack on Pearl Harbor led to *Remember Pearl Harbor* (1942); Guadalcanal resulted in *Guadalcanal Diary* (1943); the fall of France and Norway to the Nazis inspired *Arise, My Love* (1940) and *Edge of Darkness* (1943), respectively; and so forth. Even after the war ended in 1945, filmmakers continued to mine its potential. World War II had been declared the "good war," not because it was good (no war can claim to be that) but because it represented a concerted effort to defeat the forces of fascism.

The best World War II films did not attract audiences by relying on combat scenes, whether staged at the studio or inserted from newsreels. Screenwriters had to devise a plot that would deal with emotions and relationships that made the film more of a movie than a history lesson. Thus they drew upon such themes as male bonding, the loss of a spouse or family member, the importance of faith in time of crisis, heroism in the face of

Robert Taylor firing away at the enemy in *Bataan* (1943), a typical World War II combat film. *(Private collection)*

death, the last-ditch stand against the enemy, two men in love with the same woman, the fate of women in war, cowardice versus courage, a raw recruit's coming of age, and so forth.

Like the musical and the western, the American combat film has had a spotty history. While it thrived in the 1940s and, occasionally, during the next two decades, much depended on the war in question. The Korean War (1950–1953), or "police action" as it was called, resulted in some harrowing films—for example, Sam Fuller's *The Steel Helmet* (1951) and *Fixed Bayonets* (1951), which were unappreciated in their time because Korea was not a "good" war. Vietnam, which is difficult to date in terms of America's involvement, was a far more unpopular war. Vietnam was not something American audiences wanted to confront until well after it had ended in 1975 with the fall of Saigon. Then, such films as *Platoon* (1986), *Full Metal Jacket* (1987), and *Casualties of War* (1989)—the last being the best of the lot —emphasized the horrors of the Vietnam War, which could have been the horrors of any war. Had it not been for the Southeast Asia setting, *Casualties of War* could have taken place wherever men, denied their "rest and relaxation," decide to abduct a woman to satisfy their needs, as if they were owed sexual gratification for serving their country. *The Deer Hunter* (1978) and *Apocalypse Now* (1979), even though they dealt with Vietnam, told audiences little about the war or the reasons for America's involvement in it. Rather, these films emphasized such universal themes as friendships and relationships altered and even shattered by war (*The Deer Hunter*) and the mental deterioration caused by war (*Apocalypse Now*). At the end of *Apocalypse Now*, whether or not we know the source was Joseph Conrad's *Heart of Darkness*, we might still find ourselves echoing Kurtz's dying words from Conrad's novel: "The horror! The horror!"

The phenomenal success of Steven Spielberg's *Saving Private Ryan* (1998) proves that the combat film can still attract audiences. The opening sequence, the Normandy invasion of June 6, 1944, is presented in such

Women in war: *Cry Havoc* (1943), an unusual World War II film with an all-female cast. *(Private collection)*

harrowing detail—with limbs being blown off and entrails spilling forth—that previous re-creations of D-Day seem like dress rehearsals. However, once the landing is over, *Saving Private Ryan* takes on the features of a 1940s World War II movie, complete with such familiar characters as the bereaved mother, the surviving son who becomes the object of a rescue operation, the compassionate captain, the treacherous Nazi, the nostalgia addict, and the intellectual who comes of age by killing one of the enemy.

While the Normandy invasion formed the prologue of *Saving Private Ryan*, the attack on Pearl Harbor became the centerpiece of *Pearl Harbor*. Yet the movie itself is little more than another variation on the "two men in love with the same woman" plot, a staple of the World War II film—as in, for example, *Thunder Birds* (1942), *Aerial Gunner* (1943), *Crash Dive* (1943), *Bombardier* (1943), and the best of the lot, John Ford's *They Were Expendable* (1945). The World War II movie provides the template; any screenwriter interested in the subject has only to impose that template on the story he or she wants to tell.

Future combat films will have to do more than restage battles to find an audience. Like the early Vietnam movies, contemporary films must compete with television. Cable news channels provide the kind of immediate war coverage with which film cannot compete despite its vast arsenal of visual effects. These channels did not exist in the 1940s, when the studios fitted World War II with a plot and called the result a "movie." For purists, who simply wanted the facts without the dramatization, there was the newsreel.

No doubt there will be movies about the 2003 Iraq war and its aftermath. Such films, however, will need a plot—and an unusual one—to attract audiences that have witnessed the conflict on television. The drama will not come from the battles, but from those caught up in them. The plot peg could be a rescue operation, an attempt to recover stolen art, the consequences of cultural misunderstanding, an interracial romance, and so on. Then, too, there is the matter of taking sides. The World War II film operated on the assumption that the Allies were the heroes; the Nazis and Japanese militarists, the villains. Moviegoers no longer automatically accept such simplistic dichotomies. Filmmakers must find a middle ground, one that, ideally, is lacking in propaganda.

Three Kings (1999), set at the end of the 1991 Gulf War, is an excellent example of an intelligent combat film. The title characters are American soldiers who are less concerned about the plight of the Iraqis than they are about finding the location of the gold that had been taken from Kuwait—not to return it, but to keep it for themselves. The Americans will change, but their transformation will come when they learn how the Iraqis feel about the United States and their bitterness toward President George H. W. Bush for failing to help them overthrow Saddam Hussein. This is not really a film about heroes and villains, but about human beings, who are often all *too* human. But unlike, say, *Guadalcanal Diary*, it is no flag waver. The combat film, like so many genres, evolves with the times.

Comedies

Like tragedy, comedy has its own conventions: mistaken identity, lovers' quarrels and reconciliations, marital mix-ups, the deflation of the pompous, trickery, deception, and masquerade. It also has its own gallery of stock characters, such as irate fathers, errant husbands, clever servants, fops, foundlings, and amorous wives, all of whom speak in maxims, non sequiturs, puns, double entendres, and malapropisms—the traditional sources of verbal humor.

Although film comedy draws on the same sources of humor as stage comedy, it has several genres peculiar unto themselves.

Screwball Comedy

Because of its witty and sophisticated dialogue, **screwball comedy** has overtones of romantic comedy and drawing-room comedy, so named because it is often set in an elegant living room, with fashionably dressed characters and dialogue brimming with wit. But screwball comedy also contains elements of farce and slapstick that are alien to the comedy of the drawing room: a food riot in an Automat in *Easy Living*, a leopard on the loose in Howard Hawks's *Bringing Up Baby*, destruction of property for comic effect in the shooting spree in Preston Sturges's *The Palm Beach Story* (1942).

Like film noir, screwball is better described than defined. One or both of the leading characters is a screwball—an oddball whose unconventional nature is responsible for the equally unconventional situations in which the characters find themselves. In *It Happened One Night*, an heiress rebels against her father; ends up hitchhiking with a reporter, masquerading as his wife; and finally discards the masquerade for marriage. In *Easy Living*, a young working woman is riding on the top deck of a double-decker bus at the very moment an irate husband hurls his wife's sable coat from the roof of their apartment house. The coat lands on the young woman, who is then mistaken for the husband's mistress and ensconced in a luxury hotel. She later falls in love with a worker at an Automat who turns out to be the son of the man who threw the coat off the roof. A socialite and a paleontologist become involved with a leopard that responds to the song "I Can't Give You Anything but Love, Baby" in *Bringing Up Baby*. In *The Awful Truth* (1937), a couple in the process of divorcing vie for custody of their dog and then try to sabotage each other's prospects for remarriage.

The hero in screwball is usually a professional: a reporter in *It Happened One Night* and *Nothing Sacred* (1937); an editor in Howard Hawks's *His Girl Friday* (1940); a herpetologist in *The Lady Eve*; a film director in *Sullivan's Travels*; a professor in Howard Hawks's *Ball of Fire* (1941). The heroine can be a socialite, as in *It Happened One Night*, *Bringing Up Baby*, and *My Man Godfrey* (1936); a Cinderella figure (*Easy Living*); a reporter (*His Girl Friday*), or a gold digger (Mitchell Leisen's *Midnight*, 1939; *The Palm Beach Story*). Rarely are hero and heroine from the same social class. Sometimes the heroine is from the higher class (*It Happened One Night*, *My Man Godfrey*); at other times the hero is (*The Lady Eve*, *Easy Living*). In any event, class barriers never stand in the way of a happy ending.

One distinguishing feature of screwball comedy is sharp, fast, witty dialogue. One character picks up on what another says to put the other down and score a point. In *Sullivan's Travels*, Sullivan (Joel McCrea) is trying to convince a studio executive of the importance of making social-consciousness films. When he is told that one such film failed in Pittsburgh, he scoffs, "What do they know in Pittsburgh?" "They know what they like," the executive replies. "If they knew what they liked, they wouldn't live in Pittsburgh" is Sullivan's capping retort.

Screwball comedy delights in non sequiturs. In an attempt to fend off Susan's (Katharine Hepburn) advances in *Bringing Up Baby*, Henry (Cary Grant) informs her that he is engaged to be married. Susan replies with screwball logic: "Then she [his fiancée] won't mind waiting. If I was engaged to be married to you, I wouldn't mind waiting. I'd wait forever."

Clark Gable as a reporter and Claudette Colbert as a runaway heiress in *It Happened One Night* (1934). *(Courtesy Sony Pictures Entertainment and MOMA/FSA)*

Cary Grant and Rosalind Russell, the editor and his star reporter, in Howard Hawks's classic screwball comedy *His Girl Friday* (1940). *(Courtesy Columbia Pictures)*

Double entendre, too, is common in screwball. Since the Production Code frowned on suggestiveness in dialogue and situations, writers encoded the dialogue with double meanings, expecting that at least some members of the audience would choose the right meaning; most did. In *The Palm Beach Story*, a millionaire tells the fortune-hunting heroine that he admires women who can cook. "You should taste my popovers," she says playfully. "I'd love to," he replies. Somewhat more subtle but also more suggestive is

Cinderella (Jean Arthur) in the Automat in the classic screwball comedy *Easy Living* (1937). *(Copyright by Paramount Pictures. Courtesy MCA Publishing Rights, a Division of MCA, Inc.)*

a character's slip of the tongue about a boys' magazine in *Easy Living*; instead of calling it by its correct name, *The Boy's Constant Companion*, the character keeps calling it *The Boy's Constant Reminder*.

Like film noir, screwball comedy will never become extinct. Audiences are always ready for a "meet cute." *French Kiss* (1995) reverses the classic screwball situation, in which the bride-to-be bolts from the altar because she cannot say "I do." In *French Kiss*, the prospective bridegroom (Timothy Hutton) phones his fiancée (Meg Ryan) from Paris to inform her that he has found someone else. En route to Paris to reclaim him, Ryan finds herself seated next to a Frenchman (Kevin Kline), who happens to be a thief. In screwball, a profession, no matter how shady it might be, has never been known to stand in the way of romance.

One of the better contemporary screwball comedies is *While You Were Sleeping* (1994), in which a subway employee (Sandra Bullock) comes to the aid of a handsome passenger (Peter Gallagher) when he is mugged on the platform. When the passenger becomes comatose, his family assumes that the employee is his fiancée. The subway employee is not meant to marry the passenger, although she does become part of the family. In screwball, true love is the only constant, and it rarely occurs at first sight; everything else is a variable.

Performers like Tom Hanks, Richard Gere, Meg Ryan, Sandra Bullock, and Julia Roberts have the right combination of breeziness and style to handle battle-of-the-sexes dialogue without becoming shrill. The best screwball is really romantic comedy with irrepressibly wacky but articulate men and women instead of gawky adolescents. But, like adolescents, they have the same need for love—except that, as adults and professionals, they cannot show it as openly. That one of 1999's most successful films was *The Runaway Bride*, a title inspired by the title of Elizabeth Kendall's critical study of the same name about the romantic comedies of the 1930s, is a tribute to screwball's abiding appeal.

Farce

While screwball comedy is indigenous to film, farce is not. Farce is sometimes referred to as low comedy, an unfortunate term for a venerable art form that over the centuries has brought pleasure to countless audiences. Farce abounds in improbable situations: men dress up as women and join an all-female band in *Some Like It Hot* (1959); a prime minister makes his entrance by sliding down a fire pole in *Duck Soup* (1933); a college president appears at a faculty meeting shaving in *Horse Feathers* (1932). However, in farce the pace is so brisk, and the laughter so incessant, that no one bothers to question, for example, what kind of college would hire a wisecracking comic as president.

Some of the greatest comedies written for the stage contain farcical elements. The Greek playwrights, for example, did not think farce was beneath them. Aristophanes' *Lysistrata*, in which the women of Athens resolve to abstain from sex until war is outlawed, has some outrageously funny scenes. Men enter, visibly excited in costumes that included a phallus as well as padding for the stomach and buttocks; one of the women pretends she is pregnant by placing a helmet under her dress. Aristophanes' comedies contain farcical situations, but the plays themselves are not pure farce, since they deal with serious issues, such as war, education, politics, utopianism, and the state of the theater.

Farce was even more natural to the Romans. Roman comedy evolved out of farcical skits with such stock characters as the foolish father, the amorous son, the swindler, the glutton, the cheating wife, and the cuckolded husband. These early farces, which were often quite bawdy, gave birth to comedy, which never abandoned its origins. The Roman playwright Plautus wrote several farces, including the *Menaechmi* (the basis of Shakespeare's *Comedy of Errors*), about long-lost twins with the same name; and *Casina*, in which a male slave disguises himself as a woman to prevent the heroine from being married to someone she does not love, only to end up married to one of her suitors. Naturally, everything is resolved happily. The movie version of the Broadway musical *A Funny Thing Happened on the Way to the Forum* (1966), an interweaving of Plautus's stock characters and plot devices set to music by Stephen Sondheim, comes close to illustrating the nature of classical farce.

Mistaken identity, disguise, and deception are staples of farce. Cross-dressing is almost as old as the theater itself. As we have already seen, Plautus used it in *Casina*, which was written somewhere around 200 B.C.E. However, the play that immediately comes to mind is *Charley's Aunt*, which was filmed three times (1925, 1930, 1941) and became the basis of the 1948 Broadway musical *Where's Charley?*, which was also made into a movie in 1952. The comic potential of drag has never been exhausted, as is evidenced by the highly successful *Tootsie* (1982) and *Mrs. Doubtfire* (1993). Nor is the cross-dresser always a male. Perhaps no other film has gone so far as Blake Edwards's *Victor/Victoria* (1982) in terms of gender-bending. Here, Victoria (Julie Andrews) disguises herself as a man (Victor), who is then hired as a female impersonator. Thus, a woman pretends to be a man impersonating a woman. That Victoria succeeds in making herself desirable to both sexes proves that, without human folly, comedy could not exist.

The same holds true of *Some Like It Hot*, in which two musicians (Jack Lemmon and Tony Curtis), who have witnessed a gangland slaying, go into hiding by masquerading as women. Lemmon is so convincing that he attracts a millionaire who proposes marriage. But the masquerade has also affected Lemmon, who seriously considers the proposal. Cross-dressing is also at the heart of *Tootsie*, in which an actor (Dustin Hoffman), unable to get decent roles as a male, disguises himself as a woman and becomes a soap opera queen. *Tootsie* is unusual in that it begins with a farcical situation (the consequences of cross-dressing, some of which are hilarious) and then turns serious as the cross-dresser realizes the indignities that women often experience at the hands of men. Like any device, cross-dressing can be treated lightly or seriously. After *Boys Don't Cry* (1999), in which a young woman's attempt to pass as a male results in tragedy, the subject can no longer be considered the exclusive preserve of comedy. Everything depends on the writer's approach to the subject and the filmmaker's vision of the script. The abandoning of a child can result in a classic tragedy like Sophocles' *Oedipus the King* or a classic comedy like Oscar Wilde's *The Importance of Being Earnest*.

Sight gags are often an element of farce. However well crafted a film farce may be, there are moments when the absurd and the incongruous take over. On such occasions, logic is thrown to the winds, and the only question is not how such scenes fit into the plot (they often don't) but how well they do what they are supposed to do—namely, provoke laughter. The Marx Brothers film, *A Night in Casablanca* (1946), opens with the silent brother Harpo propping himself against a wall next to a building. A suspicious police officer comes along and asks, sarcastically, if he is trying to hold up the

Musicians in drag (Tony Curtis, left, on saxophone; Jack Lemmon on bass fiddle) in *Some Like It Hot* (1959). *(Courtesy the Margaret Herrick Library of the Academy of Motion Picture Arts and Sciences)*

building. Harpo nods yes. The officer tells him to move on, and, as he does, the building collapses. In an earlier Marx Brothers film, *A Night at the Opera* (1935), people start piling into the stateroom of an ocean liner, despite the fact that there is room for only one occupant. The scene reaches the height of absurdity when an engineer, his assistant, a manicurist, a cleaning woman, and stewards arrive, as if there were no limit to the number of people the room could hold. A similar scene occurs in *Some Like It Hot* in the upper berth of a sleeping car. Farce can—and does—involve elements of slapstick, a name that derives from the paddle that comic actors once used to hit one another. The impact caused such a loud noise that it automatically got a laugh, even if what was happening onstage wasn't especially funny.

Sight gags, however, are one thing; structure, another. Naturally, there are sight gags in the best of farces, but the plots are quite intricate. In pure slapstick, any semblance of a plot disappears in an eruption of crude humor, abusiveness, bodily contortions, and generally immature behavior. The result truly deserves to be called low comedy. The Three Stooges shorts are a prime example of pure slapstick; in fact, some of their antics (eye-poking and head-bashing) looked so realistic that, when the shorts were first aired on television, the networks warned children not to imitate what they saw.

It is important to distinguish between films that are pure slapstick and those that are true farce. The former—for example, *Dumb & Dumber* (1994) —appeal to audiences that judge a movie by the number of belly laughs it provides, regardless of how they were achieved; the latter, such as *A Night at the Opera* and *Some Like It Hot*, to audiences who laugh at humor in context, not just at sight gags and one-liners that could be inserted into any movie and get the same response. Great farceurs like W. C. Fields and the Marx Brothers knew that laughs had to be earned. A comedy with the Marx Brothers or W. C. Fields is not simply a series of sight gags or tired vaudeville routines. Much of the humor is verbal and is intended for viewers who appreciate wit and wordplay.

In the Marx Brothers comedy *A Day at the Races* (1937), Groucho, the best known of the brothers, performs a number for which he will always be remembered, "Lydia the Tattooed Lady," in which he extols Lydia's illustrated body, noting that "when her robe is unfurled / She will show you the world." Groucho was never tasteless, only suggestive. He relied on puns and metaphors rather than on bluntness. In *Monkey Business* (1931), after commiserating with Thelma Todd about all the "dirty breaks" she has received, Groucho then puns on the word "breaks," claiming that he will "clean and tighten [her] brakes," which will require her to stay in the garage all night. In *My Little Chickadee* (1940), Fields, as con man Cuthbert J. Twillie, refers to Mae West's "hot house cognomen" because her character's name is Flowerbelle. *My Little Chickadee* also contains an interesting variation on the bed trick, an old comic device in which one bed partner is substituted for another. In Shakespeare's *Measure for Measure*, Angelo, thinking he will be spending the night with Isabella, really spends it with Mariana, who has taken Isabella's place. In *My Little Chickadee*, Flowerbelle substitutes a goat for herself. Twillie does not realize that he is snuggling up to an animal, even though the odor is not particularly enticing, until the goat bolts out of the bed.

Farce is a true genre, but gross-out comedy like *There's Something About Mary* (1998), *American Pie* (1999), *Me, Myself and Irene* (2000), and *Jackass* (2002) is, if anything, a subgenre, rather like a second-level heading in an outline. Early gross-out, such as *National Lampoon's Animal House* (1978) and *Porky's* (1981), seems wholesome compared with the above. *Animal House* portrayed campus fraternities as breeding places for bad manners and boorish behavior, and *Porky's* (along with its two sequels) suggested that there were high school males who could end up like the fraternity brothers in *Animal House*. These movies, however, were more vulgar than offensive. But as the 1990s came to an end, America was bombarded with detailed news of President William Jefferson Clinton's liaison with a White House intern and couldn't help but become desensitized to vulgarity.

Not coincidentally, gross-out became more audacious, on the principle that anyone and anything is good for a laugh. It is not even a question of taste, since gross-out filmmakers admit they have none; they aim for easy laughs, which, if they resonate widely enough, will be heard at box offices throughout the world. In gross-out, nothing is sacred: dogs, cows, hamsters, minorities, senior citizens, the disabled. In classic farce, if a scene is to culminate in a burst of laughter, the audience must be prepared for it—perhaps by

Two comic icons, W. C. Fields and Mae West, in *My Little Chickadee* (1940). *(Courtesy MOMA/FSA)*

a scene or a series of scenes leading up to it. The goat incident in *My Little Chickadee* makes sense because, earlier, Flowerbelle had tricked Twillie into a "marriage" that he is anxious to consummate but she is not. Hence, the goat substitute. In gross-out, the buildup is unnecessary, since what matters is the laugh. In *There's Something About Mary* the audience experiences a parade of "gross" scenes such as a man getting his genitals caught in the zipper of his fly. Some may defend gross-out on the grounds that it observes the "offend and mend" rule of comedy: shatter taboos, shock the prudish, and transcend the boundaries of good taste—but at the end turn kind-hearted, so that what appeared to be grossness will seem like good dirty fun. Until gross-out joins the canon of comedy, there is still more to explore in the crazy-quilt world of the Marx Brothers and W. C. Fields.

Satire

Like practically every literary genre, satire goes back to the ancients, who thought of it as a way of poking fun at human folly. The subjects of classical satire ranged from hypocrites, upstarts, and social climbers to untalented writers, gluttons, and overdeveloped athletes—in short, those lacking in self-knowledge. Literary satire has a long and venerable tradition, with outstanding examples in verse (the *Satires* of Horace and Juvenal, Pope's *Dunciad*), prose (Erasmus's *In Praise of Folly*), prose fiction (Swift's *Gulliver's Travels*, Waugh's *The Loved One*), and theater (the satires on the movie industry, *Beggar on Horseback* by Marc Connelly and George S. Kaufman, and David Mamet's *Speed-the-Plow*).

Wag the Dog (1997) is pure satire, centering around an attempt to divert attention from a presidential scandal by staging a war with Albania, even if it means using fake newsreel footage to fool the public. The ideal audience for *Wag the Dog* would be one familiar with the President Clinton–Monica Lewinsky affair, not to mention conditions in the former Yugoslavia, where Albanians were victims of ethnic cleansing. However, future audiences, to whom the Clinton-Lewinsky affair is a memory and Albania is the name of a country in eastern Europe, will still be able to understand how fabrication can become fact when the right combination of a president, a producer, and a staff conspire to create history.

Most movie satire is not as topical or as outrageous as *Wag the Dog* or *The Player* (1992), which offers such a jaundiced view of Hollywood that it should cause the fainthearted to think twice before entering the business. Generally speaking, Hollywood has been willing to kid itself, but in moderation. For example, *Singin' in the Rain* pokes fun at silent stars with atrocious voices who had to face the advent of sound; *The Big Picture* (1989) makes it abundantly clear that a major in Film Studies is no preparation for the world of corporate Hollywood; and *The Freshman* (1990) mocks the esoteric jargon that academics use in their film classes.

Whether film satire will grow into a genre with as many classics to its name as screwball comedy or the musical remains to be seen. The most that can be said is that human folly has always found a place on the screen, where it has sometimes been treated gently, sometimes scathingly. To its credit, the movie industry has never exempted itself from the company of fools who labor for our enjoyment and edification.

The Reflexive Film

Reflexive literature calls attention to itself as literature: a reader, for example, may sense that the novel he or she is reading is really about the art of the novel or the act of writing a novel, and is not just a work of prose fiction. Literary critics use the term **intertextuality** to describe texts that draw on other texts—mentioning them by name, alluding to them, commenting on them, or imitating them. Authors who draw on the works of others hope their readers are familiar with their sources; or, if readers are not, that at least they understand that what they are reading is more than the mere telling of a story. The ideal audience for Michael Cunningham's novel, *The Hours*, and the 2002 film version, would be someone familiar with

Virginia Woolf's *Mrs. Dalloway*, which inspired it. Yet the movie versions of both *Mrs. Dalloway* and *The Hours* can be enjoyed on their own terms by those who have never read Woolf's or Cunningham's novels. The same is true of any work based on another: it should be able to stand on its own merits. We should not judge Eugene O'Neill's trilogy, *Mourning Becomes Electra*, in terms of Aeschylus's *Oresteia*, on which it was based. Naturally, audiences or readers familiar with both works would note the parallels and differences. Regardless, *Mourning Becomes Electra* is an effective piece of theatre that can be appreciated and understood by those who have never even heard of Aeschylus, much less the *Oresteia*.

The same is true of film. Steven Spielberg must have expected some moviegoers to get his references to *Pinocchio* (1940), especially the Blue Fairy, in *A.I. Artificial Intelligence* (2001). However, *Pinocchio* is not a prerequisite for *A.I.* Knowing *Pinocchio* might deepen our appreciation of *A.I.*, but it should not affect our evaluation of Spielberg's film as an original work.

In discussing films, we generally use the term **reflexivity,** rather than intertextuality, but the idea is the same. The root meaning of *reflect* is "throw back"; the reflexive film "throws back" a reflection of itself—it is something more than just a movie, but rather is a movie that has something to say about the medium of film. There are varying degrees of reflexivity.

Certain reflexive films suggest something about the nature of film. Woody Allen's *The Purple Rose of Cairo* (1985) explores the consequences of mistaking the illusion of the screen for the reality of life. During a movie, which has the same title, a character steps off the screen and into the audience, leaving the other characters stranded in mid-plot. The other characters then become autonomous, refusing to continue with the plot until he returns. The character's adventures in the real world point up the difference between life and art: one cannot live art, only life.

There are also films that refer to specific films, directly or indirectly. These are sometimes called "movie movies" because of their allusions to other movies that sometimes take the form of visual quotations. Just as a student writing a term paper might decide to quote an author verbatim instead of paraphrasing the author's ideas, a filmmaker might choose to "quote" another film by providing a clip from it, as Peter Bogdanovich does in *The Last Picture Show* by including the final moments of Howard Hawks's *Red River*. It is true that one can enjoy *The Last Picture Show* for its plot alone; however, anyone who is knowledgeable about film will have a deeper appreciation of Bogdanovich's movie. "The last picture show" of the title is *Red River*, which serves two purposes: it allows the movie theater to close with a bang rather than a whimper and it is a metaphor for the film itself. In *Red River*, the John Wayne character befriends a fatherless boy (Montgomery Clift), with whom he develops a close relationship. In *The Last Picture Show*, Sam the Lion (Ben Johnson) befriends two boys who might as well be fatherless. With its references to *Red River*, *The Last Picture Show* establishes

Montgomery Clift about to remove an arrow from Joanne Dru's shoulder in *Red River* (1948), "the last picture show" in *The Last Picture Show* (1971). *(Private collection)*

itself as a film that, at least on one level, is about America's film heritage, reflecting not only the way generations of Americans behaved but also the way generations of filmmakers portrayed America.

In Vincente Minnelli's *Two Weeks in Another Town* (1962), Kirk Douglas plays a failed actor-turned-director, shooting a film in Rome. For a scene requiring the actor-director to watch one of his earlier films, Minnelli chose *The Bad and the Beautiful* (1952), in which Douglas played an unscrupulous movie producer. In terms of plot, it's a director looking at himself when he was an actor; reflexively, it is Kirk Douglas in one Minnelli movie looking at Kirk Douglas in another.

Anyone old enough to have seen the movie serials of the 1940s, particularly *Nyoka and the Lost Tablets of Hippocrates* (1942) and the anti-Nazi movies of that period, would know that both were the inspiration for Steven Spielberg's *Raiders of the Lost Ark* (1981). Nora Ephron's *You've Got Mail* (1998) is a remake of Ernst Lubitsch's *The Shop Around the Corner* (1940). Those familiar with the original will pick up on the name of the children's bookstore in *You've Got Mail*: The Shop Around the Corner.

Lars Von Trier's *Dancer in the Dark* (2000) contains a scene in which Selma (the Icelandic pop singer Björk) and Kathy (Catherine Deneuve) are sitting in a theater watching the Warner Bros. musical *42nd Street*. Selma, who is suffering from a congenital eye disease that will lead to blindness, is unable to perform in a community theater production of *The Sound of Music*. Nevertheless, she needs the "sound" of music—the melody, rhythm, and, above all, the liberating effect. Nowhere is that freedom more evident than in the movie musical, where characters break into song and dance even on crowded streets. As a respite from the tedium of her factory job, Selma imagines herself and the other employees dancing to the rhythms produced by the machines.

The title of Pedro Almodóvar's *All About My Mother* (1999) suggests Joseph L. Mankiewicz's *All About Eve*. In fact, Almodóvar's film opens with Manuela (Cecilia Roth), a single parent, and her son, an aspiring writer and movie buff, watching a Spanish-dubbed version of *All About Eve* on television in their Madrid apartment. The film has reached the point at which Margo Channing (Bette Davis) is inveighing against the "coyotes," the fans who pursue her for her autograph. To celebrate her son's birthday, Manuela takes him to a local production of Tennessee Williams's *A Streetcar Named Desire*, which also functions as an intertext. Eager to get the autograph of the actress who plays Blanche DuBois, the boy pounds on the window of her taxi, only to be ignored. Rushing after the cab, he is hit by a car and dies. Unable to forget what happened, Manuela leaves for Barcelona, where she discovers that the actress whose autograph her son wanted is appearing in another production of *Streetcar*. In *All About Eve*, the aspiring actress Eve Harrington ingratiates herself with Margo, eventually becoming her understudy and even going on for her. Similarly, Manuela "pulls an Eve Harrington"; after becoming the actress's personal assistant, she finds an opportunity to play the role of Blanche's sister, Stella, by taking unfair advantage of a cast member who has a drug problem. Manuela, however, is far less manipulative than Eve. Her reason for becoming part of the *Streetcar* company is that the play provides the only link she has with her dead son. *All About My Mother* is a film that works on many levels, one of which is the intertextual.

Some reflexive films evoke other films. This type differs from the previous one the way an echo differs from a sound. There are some films that have clearly been influenced by other films and reveal their debt through visual quotations—not necessarily by incorporating actual shots from the film, as was the case with the *Red River* clip in *The Last Picture Show*. The much admired assembly-line sequence in Chaplin's *Modern Times* (1936), in which mechanization comes in for some sharp satire, was not original; it was derived from an earlier French film, René Clair's *À nous la liberté* (1931). Hitchcock's *Saboteur* inspired the climax of *The House on Carroll Street* (1988)—not atop the Statue of Liberty, as Hitchcock had done, but at another American landmark, Grand Central Station. The result, however, was the same: the villain plunges to his death from a high place.

When Martin Scorsese decided to remake *Cape Fear* (1991), he knew that he would be inviting comparison with the 1962 original, in which

Robert Mitchum played Max, an ex-convict who terrorizes the family of the judge who convicted him. Since one of Scorsese's favorite actors, Robert De Niro, would be playing Max, Scorsese incorporated elements of another Mitchum characterization, Harry Powell, the murderous preacher Mitchum played in *The Night of the Hunter* (1955), and had De Niro play Max as a sadist who is also a Bible-spouting religious fanatic. Thus, Scorsese fashioned a character that brings to mind two of Mitchum's best-known roles; still, Scorsese's Max is neither Mitchum's Max nor Mitchum's Powell but merely evokes them.

Under this category comes the *hommage* (French for "tribute"), a film that literally "pays homage" to another filmmaker or genre, either in whole or in part. Rarely is an entire film an *hommage*, in the sense of replicating the original the way Gus Van Sant's 1998 remake of Hitchcock's *Psycho* did. Generally, the acknowledgment is in the form of a shot or a sequence that recalls another film. For example, Spielberg is a great admirer of Hitchcock. *Close Encounters of the Third Kind* acknowledges the climactic scene in *North by Northwest* when Cary Grant is trying to prevent Eva Marie Saint from sliding off Mount Rushmore. In the Spielberg film, it is Melinda Dillon who does the same for Richard Dreyfuss in the Devil's Tower sequence. *Young Frankenstein* and *Dead Men Don't Wear Plaid* (1982) are, respectively, more than just spoofs of horror and film noir. They display a fondness for these genres that results in a special kind of parody: parody "rooted in affection," as *Lord of the Flies* author William Golding describes a work that harks back to another work, or several other works.

Todd Haynes's *Far from Heaven* (2002) is an *hommage* to director Douglas Sirk's romantic melodramas of the 1950s, particularly *All That Heaven Allows* (1955). Sirk, unappreciated in his day and regarded as just a maker of women's films, is now acknowledged as a major director who portrayed hypocrisy and prejudice within a visually appealing setting that contrasted sharply with the subject matter. Both *All That Heaven Allows* and *Far from Heaven* are set in Connecticut suburbs. The credits for *All That Heaven Allows* begin with a high shot of a town square in autumn. The camera pans right to left across the square and over to a quiet street with white houses. This is a town where women drive blue station wagons, and where class consciousness prevails. Thus, when the relationship between a widow (Jane Wyman) and her gardener (Rock Hudson) turns serious, the very fact that the widow would consort with someone of a lower class—much less a younger man—scandalizes the community.

Far from Heaven also starts with a high shot of an autumnal scene. Haynes's camera, however, does not pan but seems to crane down from the red leaves to the street below, eventually providing a full view of the downtown area before the credits end. The plot also involves a growing attraction between Cathy (Julianne Moore) and Raymond, her gardener (Dennis Haysbert). However, Cathy is married with children, and Raymond is

The widow (Jane Wyman) and the gardener (Rock Hudson) in Douglas Sirk's *All That Heaven Allows* (1955). *(Courtesy MCA Universal)*

African American. The time is the dawn of the civil rights era—fall 1956 to spring 1957, as we learn from a desk calendar and a movie marquee with such titles as *Miracle in the Rain* (1956), *Hilda Crane* (1956), and *The Three Faces of Eve* (1957). Thus there is no hope for an interracial couple in a community that is both class- and race-conscious. In fact, there is no hope for Cathy, whose husband is gay, as she discovers when she finds him in a compromising position with another man.

Knowing that Sirk's favorite colors were blue (for bedrooms, particularly), green, and red, Haynes used them in various shades throughout the film. The credits are in aquamarine; Cathy drives an aquamarine and white car. She favors blue, green, and red apparel. Buildings and alleyways are bathed in bluish moonlight, and a steak house even has a blue neon sign. The gardener's colors are of the earth (brown, red), as they were in *All That Heaven Allows*. Like Sirk, Haynes framed his narrative within a visually lush setting that emphasized the disparity between the film's *mise-en-scène* and the subject matter: a marriage based on deception, social and racial prejudice, and a mature relationship that never had a chance to develop.

The credits of Joel and Ethan Coen's *O Brother, Where Art Thou?* (2000) claim the film is based on Homer's *Odyssey*. George Clooney's character is

The wife (Julianne Moore) and the gardener (Dennis Haysbert) in *Far from Heaven* (2002), Todd Haynes's *hommage* to *All That Heaven Allows*. *(Courtesy Focus Features)*

Fugitives from a chain gang (left to right, John Turturro, Tim Blake Nelson, and George Clooney) in the Coen brothers' production of *O Brother, Where Art Thou?* (2000), partly inspired by *Sullivan's Travels*. *(Courtesy Touchstone Pictures and Universal)*

named Everett Ulysses McGill, and John Goodman plays a Cylopean figure with one eye. There are sirens, a Penelope figure (Holly Hunter), and a host of other Homeric counterparts. However, the film's real inspiration is Preston Sturges's *Sullivan's Travels*, in which a Hollywood director, John L. Sullivan, known for his comedies, wants to "go serious" and make a social-consciousness movie based on a fictitious proletarian novel, *O Brother, Where Art Thou?* Refusing to listen to studio executives and even his own butler, Sullivan embarks on an odyssey to learn about deprivation firsthand and eventually ends up in a chain gang because he has failed to heed his butler's warning that attempts by the "morbid rich" to learn about poverty can be "extremely dangerous." The Coens' film, which recounts the odyssey of three fugitives from a chain gang, is an *hommage* to Sturges's film as well as an attempt to imbue screwball comedy with a sense of humanity, as Sturges had done in *Sullivan's Travels*.

Another Coen brothers film, *The Man Who Wasn't There*, is, as we have seen, a faithful recreation of 1940s film noir; it is also an *hommage* to the genre and to classic 1940s Hollywood cinema. In this film, Ed Crane, a mild-mannered barber, blackmails "Big Dave," his wife's employer (and lover) to get $10,000 to invest in a dry cleaning enterprise proposed to him by a con man, Creighton Tolliver. When Dave discovers that Ed is the blackmailer, he

The director (Joel McCrea, left) and the actress (Veronica Lake) experiencing the Great Depression firsthand so the director can prepare himself to shoot *O Brother, Where Art Thou?* (which he never does) in Preston Sturges's *Sullivan's Travels* (1941). *(Courtesy Paramount Pictures and Movie Star News)*

Billy Bob Thornton as the barber Ed Crane in the Coen brothers' production *The Man Who Wasn't There* (2001), inspired by the film versions of two James Cain novels, *Double Indemnity* (1944) and *The Postman Always Rings Twice* (1946). *(Courtesy USA Films)*

Phyllis Dietrichson (Barbara Stanwyck) and Walter Neff (Fred MacMurray) making the murder of Phyllis's husband seem like an accident in Billy Wilder's *Double Indemnity* (1944). *(Courtesy Paramount Pictures)*

turns violent, causing Ed to kill him in self-defense. When Ed's wife Doris is accused of Dave's murder, Ed remains silent, hoping that the fast-talking trial lawyer, Freddie Riedenschneider (Tony Shalhoub), can get her acquitted. (The lawyer's last name derives from another classic noir, John Huston's *The Asphalt Jungle*, 1950, in which Sam Jaffe played a criminal by the name of "Doc" Riedenschneider.) When Doris hangs herself in prison, her suicide is considered proof of her guilt.

The film's point of departure is *Double Indemnity*, both James M. Cain's novel and Billy Wilder's 1944 film. In the novel, the femme fatale's name is Phyllis Nirdlinger, which, as has been noted, Wilder changed to Phyllis Dietrichson. In *Man*, Nirdlinger's is the name of a department store where Doris works; a medical examiner, known only as Dietrichson, informs Ed that Doris was in her third trimester of pregnancy when she committed suicide.

Cain's novel, written in the first person, is actually Walter Huff's confession of murder, as the reader discovers at the beginning of Chapter 14—the final chapters being an addendum before he and Phyllis take "the big swim" by slipping off a ship's rail into the water where a shark awaits them. In the film, the Huff character, now called Walter Neff, makes his confession into a dictaphone, as opposed to the novel, in which he wrote it out. *Man* is also a first-person film, beginning with a line in the hard-boiled tradition: "Yeah, I worked in a barber shop." Although Ed Crane is clearly the narrator, we learn at the end that what we have been watching is the visual

Frank (John Garfield) and Cora (Lana Turner), the murderous pair in *The Postman Always Rings Twice* (1946). *(Courtesy MGM)*

equivalent of a piece that Ed is being paid five cents a word to write for a magazine, while he is on death row.

The Coens were also influenced by another first-person Cain novel, *The Postman Always Rings Twice*, which became a noir classic when it was filmed in 1946. While voice-over was used in *Double Indemnity* for a confession of murder, in *Postman* it serves a different function: Frank Chambers's (John Garfield) attempt to piece together the various events that brought him to death row for a murder he did not commit. The triangle again consists of a wife, Cora Smith (Lana Turner); her husband Nick (Cecil Kellaway); and her lover, Frank. Again, wife and lover conspire to murder husband, with the lover delivering the deathblow. After the murderous pair is acquitted, Cora is killed in a car accident; Frank, however, is accused of murdering her and is sentenced to die in the electric chair.

In *The Man Who Wasn't There*, Ed Crane also dies in the electric chair for a murder he did not commit. And like Frank Chambers in Cain's novel, he is also writing out his story in prison. Whether or not it is coincidental that Nick Smith had a $10,000 life insurance policy and that Ed needs $10,000 to invest in the dry cleaning operation is hard to say. However, since the Coens have drawn so heavily on Cain's two novellas as well as their film versions, one suspects $10,000 was not an arbitrary figure.

The Man Who Wasn't There embodies the visual and narrative conventions of 1940s noir and hard-boiled detective fiction. Still, the film has an originality of its own. Like many artists, the Coens re-create the past within the present, giving it a freshness as well as a timelessness. They would have agreed with Ezra Pound's advice to poets: "Be influenced by as many great artists as you can, but have the decency either to acknowledge the debt outright or try to conceal it." When names like "Nirdlinger" and "Dietrichson" are used in a film, or traditional plot devices are given a new slant, the debt is certainly acknowledged.

Reflexive films about the filmmaking process include a behind-the-scenes look at the movie world and those who work in it. *Nickelodeon* is historically accurate in its portrayal of silent-film making; *Sweet Liberty* and Vincente Minnelli's *Two Weeks in Another Town* are valid depictions of contemporary on-location filming. Although *The Perils of Pauline* (1947) is loosely based on the life of silent serial queen Pearl White, the movie is quite accurate about the chaotic conditions under which silent films were often made.

In *Hollywood Ending* (2002), Woody Allen plays another hypochondriac à la *Hannah and Her Sisters*—this time a film director trying to make a comeback and suddenly finding himself blind, even though the brain tumor he thought he had proves to be nonexistent. Still convinced he is blind, the director shoots the movie, which the American critics savage because it is incomprehensible. Just when his career seems to be over, the French declare the film a masterpiece, and the director is invited to work in Paris. Allen's fondness for Paris was evident in *Everyone Says I Love You* (1996), which evoked the city's magic. In *Hollywood Ending*, Allen is gently spoofing the way the French lionize what Americans dismiss as trivial or inconsequential. For example, Americans regard Jerry Lewis as a slapstick comic, but the French view him as the heir to the great clowns of the silent era. It was the French who gave the name of "film noir" to the B-movies that came out of Hollywood in the 1940s, giving stature to, among other directors, Edgar G. Ulmer, whose *Detour* is now regarded as a noir masterpiece, even though the *New York Times* never thought it was worth reviewing. Finally, if the French regard Woody Allen as more of an intellectual than Americans do, it may be because they can see beneath the comic and satiric veneer into the writer-director's deeper concerns with commitment and responsibility.

"What price Hollywood" films demythologize the industry by stripping away the glamour and exposing the grim reality beneath the painted surface. All three versions of *A Star Is Born*, even though the third is about the rock scene, show the extent to which stars are replaced in the pantheon. *Sunset Boulevard* dramatizes a silent star's descent into madness because she cannot adjust to a Hollywood that is not the one she remembers. Vincente Minnelli's *The Bad and the Beautiful* and Robert Altman's *The Player* reveal the awesome power that movie executives have over writers; *The Player*, a darkly satiric look at corporate Hollywood, goes so far as to have an executive kill a writer.

There is always the danger that a reflexive film will become so obscure in its allusions and quotations that it will appeal only to film buffs. No one enjoys being trapped in a conversation that's so specialized only experts can participate in it. The films mentioned in this section can be appreciated by anyone, regardless of one's knowledge of movies or lack of it. On the other hand, a film like Godard's *Detective* (1985), which expects the viewer to be familiar with all of the incongruities of the private-eye movie that Godard renders even more incongruous, is a parody of reflexivity; by its elitism, it alienates moviegoers who can accept the incongruous but not the incomprehensible.

The Woman's Film

Woman's film is an accepted term in film criticism as well as a legitimate film genre. The woman's film became a genre for two main reasons: Hollywood's early attempts to woo female audiences, and the emergence of female stars whose personalities elevated them to the level of icons.

Female audiences were always special to the industry, either because it was assumed that women had more time for moviegoing than men did or that women were more inclined to be movie fans than men were. Whatever the reasoning, in the early days of film some nickelodeon owners attempted to attract middle-class women to their theaters by offering them free admission for pre-noon shows. Others, less generous, allowed women in for half price. Theater owners used a different tactic in the 1930s and 1940s: they sponsored "dish nights." Once or twice a week, a free piece of dishware was included in the ticket price and, in the course of time, a complete set of dishes could be acquired. Because women made up such an important—and, during World War II, major—segment of the audience, Hollywood responded by giving them their own genre, with such stars as Bette Davis, Joan Crawford, and Barbara Stanwyck—actresses who became so inseparable from their personae that one often speaks of a "Bette Davis movie" or a "Joan Crawford movie."

Bette Davis and Joan Crawford played women who were the equal and, at times, the superior of men. In Michael Curtiz's *Mildred Pierce* (1945), Mildred (Joan Crawford) goes from being a housewife to owning a restaurant chain; in *The Corn Is Green* (1945), Miss Moffat (Bette Davis) establishes a school for Welsh coal miners and sends her prize student to Oxford.

In a woman's film, the plot revolves around the woman, and her only limitations are those imposed by her mortality. Even when faced with death, the woman dies nobly. In *Dark Victory*, Judith Traherne (Bette Davis), dying of a brain tumor, not only manages to conceal her imminent death from her husband; she also chooses to die alone. In *No Sad Songs for Me* (1950), a wife faces terminal illness with a spirit of resignation that puts her husband to shame.

The woman's film of the 1930s and 1940s promoted self-sacrifice. When a daughter decides to marry above her class, her mother disappears

Bette Davis as Judith Traherne and George Brent as Dr. Steele in *Dark Victory* (1939), a major woman's film. *(Courtesy Movie Star News)*

from her life but reappears to watch the wedding ceremony through the window, in King Vidor's *Stella Dallas* (1937). Women struggled to provide a better life for their children in *Mildred Pierce* or were willing to raise a friend's illegitimate child in *The Great Lie* (1941). Forced to give up an illegitimate child of her own in *The Old Maid* (1939), she must stand by, watching the child address someone else as "mother."

While women suffered nobly in many films of the 1930s and 1940s, they were also depicted as being able to succeed in male-dominated professions. The woman's film of the period portrayed women in a variety of occupations: lawyers, copywriters, reporters, actors, surgeons, nurses. By the 1960s, there was nothing unusual about a successful woman lawyer or entrepreneur. Terminal illnesses had become standard television fare and were no longer special. The cancer victim had become the cancer patient, and resignation to the inevitable was no longer the noble gesture it was in *Dark Victory* but, rather, the final stage of a process that begins with denial and ends with acceptance.

The portrayal of women on the screen has changed through the years. In the classic woman's film, women did not so much have friends as confidantes, who were either supportive sisters or wisecracking sidekicks. Genuine friendship between women was rare on the screen; women who seemed to be friends were actually rivals, as in *Old Acquaintance* (1943). It was not until *Julia* (1977) that American audiences saw a true friendship between women depicted on the screen. The title character (Vanessa Redgrave) and her friend

Lily (Jane Fonda, playing Lillian Hellman) are not at odds with each other; they complement each other. Thus, the politically committed Julia inspires the apolitical Lily to take a stand against the spread of fascism that is soon to bring about World War II.

When Barbara Stanwyck in *My Reputation* (1946) played a young widow who refused to wear black as a sign of mourning, she scandalized her friends. In Martin Scorsese's *Alice Doesn't Live Here Anymore* (1975), Ellen Burstyn plays a widow who would no more wear black than she would mourn in silence. Instead, she takes her son on the road in an attempt to resume her singing career, but eventually has to work in a diner. The point is that each of these women, although they belong to different eras, exercised the same kind of independence; one defied her mother and refused to have her dresses dyed black (*My Reputation*); the other defied convention and took off with her son in search of work (*Alice*). Contemporary filmmakers may have more freedom to employ explicit language, nudity, and overt sexuality, but it is not entirely correct to say that current films portray women more realistically than did those of the past. On the other hand, had the Production Code not inhibited filmmakers, the dialogue of the films of the 1940s and 1950s would have been far less subtle, and the portrayal of sexuality more direct.

It is important to remember that the women depicted on the screen during Hollywood's golden age were often strong-willed, but various factors, including the Production Code, audience expectations, and a general suspicion of women who succeed in male-dominated professions, necessitated either a last-minute conversion to marriage — always regarded as more satisfying than a career — or some sign of imperfection on the woman's part.

Rosalind Russell was known for her career women, who were always elegantly dressed, witty, and the equal of any male. Yet, in movie after movie, she ended up preferring marriage to a career. In *Tell It to the Judge* (1949), Russell played the title character, a federal judge nominee who is in every way the intellectual superior of her ex-husband. However, the script called for Russell not only to remarry him but also to forsake the judgeship. When her grandfather announces that her appointment has been approved and that her job is in Washington, Russell replies, "Tell them I'm off to my job as a wife." To her credit, Russell tossed the line off as if she didn't believe it — and hoped the audience agreed with her.

MGM's *Woman of the Year* (1942), the first pairing of Spencer Tracy and Katharine Hepburn, was to end with Tess Harding (Hepburn) telling her husband, Sam Craig (Tracy), that she wishes to be known as Tess Harding Craig, not as Mrs. Sam Craig. This should have posed no problem, except that MGM thought audiences would leave thinking that Tess had scored a victory over Sam. Instead, a scene was added in which Tess tried to make breakfast for Sam and proved to be totally incompetent in the kitchen. Her inability to brew coffee was apparently a cardinal sin, despite her awesome intelligence

Rosalind Russell, the quintessential career woman of the 1940s, in *A Woman of Distinction* (1950). *(Courtesy Sony Pictures Entertainment)*

and fluency in various languages. MGM insisted on some sign of Tess's vulnerability; unfortunately, the kitchen scene—which Hepburn has admitted she hated—marred what might have been a truly feminist film.

Still, there were films in the 1930s and 1940s in which women defied convention—but they paid the price for it, which was often death. *Back Street* (both the 1932 and 1941 versions) portrayed a woman who accepted her role as mistress, even sailing to Europe with her married lover (but always boarding the ship after he and his family had done so). However, the prevailing mentality—that the wages of sin is death—meant that both husband and mistress died at the end.

In 1968, an event occurred that affected all of the genres, but especially the woman's film: the introduction of movie ratings. The changeover really began in the 1950s, when filmmakers, motivated by the need to offer audiences something other than what was available on television, started challenging the Production Code. Thus, language and subject matter that were once forbidden found their way to the screen. By the early 1960s, another taboo subject, homosexuality, was clearly implied—though not depicted—in *Suddenly, Last Summer* (1959) and *The Children's Hour* (1962). As a result, the Production Code proved to be obsolete and was replaced by a rating system, which originally gave films designations of G (general audiences), M (mature audiences), R (restricted to viewers over sixteen, unless accompanied by parent or guardian), and X (under sixteen not admitted). As film content became more explicit, the designations changed, eventually becoming G, PG (parental guidance), PG-13 (parental guidance for children under thirteen),

R (restricted for anyone under seventeen unless accompanied by an adult), and the rare NC-17 (no children, only seventeen and older).

These changes, combined with the attack on female stereotypes mounted by women's groups, allowed filmmakers to explore a theme in the woman's film that had been treated superficially in the past: female bonding. The traditional woman's film never denied the possibility of close relationships between women; however, the notion of women bonding like the title characters played by Paul Newman and Robert Redford in *Butch Cassidy and the Sundance Kid* (1969) was unthinkable in the 1935–1960 period. Women could be friends or rivals. If two women were friends, at least one of them would marry, as in *These Three* (1936); if they were rivals, they would resolve their differences, realizing that they might have to spend the rest of their lives together, as in *Old Acquaintance*. But in *Julia*, Lily and Julia are the closest of friends but not rivals; they differ only in the degree of their social commitment. Prior to the ratings, if there was the slightest chance of a woman's having a relationship with another man after her husband left her, she would never forgo it to open an art gallery; but that is exactly what happens in *An Unmarried Woman* (1978). In 1946, the year after World War II ended and Hollywood turned its attention to the problems of returning veterans, no studio would have considered a film about a married woman who falls in love with a paraplegic veteran. But Vietnam was not World War II, and a situation that was unthinkable in 1946 worked some thirty years later in *Coming Home* (1978).

Although the woman's film has undergone many changes since a woman was expected to give up her career for marriage or give up her lover to preserve the integrity of the family name (always the man's family), it is not entirely accurate to say that women are no longer depicted as victims; rather, women are at least allowed to retaliate against their victimizers. In *Thelma and Louise* (1991), a female-bonding film in which the women become fugitives from justice, Louise (Susan Sarandon) comes upon her friend Thelma (Geena Davis) as she is about to be raped. Louise might have spared the rapist's life if he were repentant, but when he becomes verbally abusive she shoots him. Thelma and Louise thus become women on the run. Pursued by the police, they take a suicidal drive over the Grand Canyon; the car heads into space, the frame freezes, and Thelma and Louise move out of time into eternity (or, at least, myth). The ending recalls *Butch Cassidy and the Sundance Kid*, in which the pair, outnumbered and about to be killed, also freeze into a composition that is slowly drained of color until it becomes monochrome. If men can bond, turn outlaw, and freeze into myth, why not women?

At present, there seem to be two kinds of woman's films: the terminal illness and the woman-as-free-spirit kind. Although women have been dying from cancer on the screen since *Dark Victory*, men had been spared that particular death until *My Life* (1993), which showed that a man (Michael Keaton in a brilliant but, unfortunately, unheralded performance) could succumb to the disease as well. Still, *My Life* did not usher in a spate of male terminal-illness movies. That is still the domain of the woman's film, particularly now that the "disease of the month" movie has run its course on television, and cancer has become just another plot peg.

In *Terms of Endearment* (1983), the cancer victim is a young mother (Debra Winger); in *Stepmom* (1998) and *One True Thing* (1998), the mothers are older (Susan Sarandon and Meryl Streep, respectively), but the subject matter is the same. Then there is the freewheeling mother personified by Shirley MacLaine in *Postcards from the Edge*—the postmodern Auntie Mame, who upstages her daughter (Meryl Streep) whenever she can; and the madcap mother—the kind that would think nothing of taking off for Los Angeles with her daughter to make her into a movie star, even if it means leaving family and friends behind (Susan Sarandon in *Anywhere but Here*, 1999). Winger, Sarandon, and Streep are gifted actresses, but cancer victims and flighty mothers are only two of the many kinds of women the screen has to offer. Even during the patriarchal studio system, there was a greater range of roles.

The chief obstacle to the woman's film is presently the dearth of decent scripts for middle-aged women. In Patricia Arquette's documentary, *Searching for Debra Winger* (2002), a number of women actors, including Winger herself, are all in agreement about two of the major problems they continually face: the preponderance of male film executives whose first condition for casting a woman in a role is how desirable she appears as a potential sex partner—a point they never make explicitly but indirectly by the way they size her up during an interview or an audition; and the lack of good roles for women over forty, compared with the much larger selection for men of the same age—and older.

The woman's film will never die out, but it will never regain the popularity it once had until producers and screenwriters realize there can be as much drama in a movie about a middle-aged woman as there is in a movie about a younger one; that cancer is neither a woman's disease nor the only cause of death for female characters of a certain age; and that there are many more kinds of mothers than those who hog the spotlight from their children and subordinate their children's interests to their own. Above all, writers attempting to create an "Auntie Mame" mom should remember that Auntie Mame, as played definitively by Rosalind Russell in the 1958 movie of that name, was never a mother.

The Documentary

The Kid Stays in the Picture (2002), a documentary on the life of movie producer Robert Evans based on Evans's own memoir of the same name, opens with a title: "There are three sides to every story—your side, my side, and the truth. And nobody is lying. Memories shared serve each differently." In the

Poetics, Aristotle distinguished between history and tragedy, or imaginative literature in general, such as fiction and, by extension, film. History, he claimed, portrays the particular—what was; tragedy portrays the universal—what should be. Historians tell the truth in their way; playwrights and filmmakers in theirs. One way in which filmmakers attempt to do so is through the **documentary.**

It is customary to distinguish between the fiction and the nonfiction film; the former is the traditional narrative or story film, which, even if based on a historical event as with *Pearl Harbor* or *Gangs of New York*, is still very much a "movie" in the traditional sense. The second type, the nonfiction film, is virtually synonymous with the documentary, which is generally assumed to be more "truthful" than the fiction film. As opposed to *looking* real, it is assumed to *be* "real." We have learned to expect the truth, or as much of it as is available, from a documentary. This expectation, however, can also be a tool for filmmakers. *The Blair Witch Project* is a mock documentary, or mockumentary, that used the conventions of the documentary and succeeded in convincing many viewers that it was the footage of three student filmmakers who disappeared in the Maryland woods while trying to solve the mystery of the so-called Blair Witch. Even in an authentic documentary, "truth" is a relative term.

To expect complete truth—unedited, unscripted, unembellished—in a documentary is to expect it to conform to life. The documentary is an art, or at least it can be. However, we live life. We do not live art; we experience it. At a 1927 symposium on the Russian documentary, the poet-playwright Surgey Tretyakov said, "There is an arbitrary element in any film. The 'treatment' of the material already shows the side chosen by the director."[4] He argued that there is distortion and falsification even in a film that purports to capture real life, however minimal that distortion might be. A filmmaker wanting to capture the 5:00 P.M. rush hour scene on a typical New York subway platform would have no problem depicting the throngs ready to enter the arriving trains. However, unless we see some faces or hear some comments, we are simply witnessing a crush of people. Even if the filmmaker managed to get a few sound bites from a couple of passengers, there would be others who would be neither heard nor seen. The filmmaker obviously had to make certain choices.

Choice is a common word in the arts; one actor, for example, will compliment another on his or her choices in a particular scene, meaning that the actor decided to deliver a line in one way rather than in another. In the arts, "choice" does not mean something you have decided to do, but something you have decided to do after eliminating other possibilities.

Documentary filmmakers also make choices, in the sense of deciding what they want to omit, as opposed to what they want to include. No matter how objective a documentary purports to be, the footage must still be edited. And it is in the editing that objectivity breaks down, as the filmmaker begins making his or her selections — deleting some shots, arranging others in a particular order for reasons of contrast, dramatic effectiveness, or ideology. The more passionate a documentary filmmaker is about his or her subject, the less likelihood there is of a thoroughly impartial film.

One of the earliest documentary filmmakers added a special effect to make the film more dramatic. In 1898, Albert E. Smith filmed Theodore Roosevelt charging up San Juan Hill in Puerto Rico during the Spanish-American War. Disappointed by the static quality of what had been filmed, Smith decided to enliven the scene by simulating explosions, using cigarette and cigar smoke. Since the sound era was twenty years away, all Smith needed was an image, and the audience was none the wiser for the deception.[5]

Sometimes, when filmmakers want to contrast their subject (for example, present-day London) with the same subject at an earlier time (say, London during the Blitz in 1940), they will draw on the resources of a film archive to interweave previously shot footage with their own. Although the viewer will be seeing contemporary London juxtaposed with images of London during World War II, there is no falsification, even with the then/now comparisons. Still, a choice was made to use World War II London for comparison rather than, say, London in the "swinging sixties." And even if the documentary's purpose was to contrast London at two different times, the filmmaker would still have had to choose the archival footage as well as the contemporary sites to be featured.

Some documentary filmmakers use staged action, employing actors, professional or otherwise, to dramatize events for which archival footage does not exist. This is common with programs on the History Channel that deal with periods, such as ancient Rome or the American Revolution, for which there is obviously no filmed material. Thus, professional actors will reenact a battle or impersonate well-known figures like Julius Caesar or George Washington. Such documentaries, therefore, should be judged on how accurately the person or the event has been portrayed.

If a documentary filmmaker has a political agenda, it is bound to be reflected in the film. Ernest Hemingway, who wrote the script for Joris Ivens's classic documentary *The Spanish Earth* (1937), took the side of the Spanish Loyalists during the Spanish Civil War, as did Ivens, who was more of a radical than Hemingway. The Loyalists were fighting to keep Spain a republic (albeit a socialist one); the Nationalists, to keep Spain from falling into the hands of what they considered to be the radical left.

Like Homer's *Iliad*, whose subject is the wrath of Achilles, not the entire Trojan War, *The Spanish Earth* seems to deal with a relatively minor event: the irrigating of a Spanish village so that food can be grown for the defenders of the Spanish republic. At the end, Ivens moves back and forth between shots of the upturned earth and those of the war-scarred streets of Madrid; and between water flowing through ditches and tanks moving across the road. Since Ivens assumes that his audience is familiar with the roots of the conflict, he neither provides background information nor offers a simplistic Loyalists (Yes), Nationalists (No) approach. Ivens does not deny that there is a Nationalist point of view, nor does he argue for the Loyalists. His politics are reflected in the images, which in themselves are neutral. Life (water) is contrasted with death (tanks); country (the village) with city (Madrid). The combination of images leads the viewer to conclude that the Loyalists are fighting to preserve a way of life exemplified by a village where people live and work together in harmony. By moving from one event (the irrigation of a village) to another (the war itself), Ivens achieves a balance that would have eluded most left-wing ideologues.

We might compare *The Spanish Earth* with Frank Capra's *Prelude to War* (1942), a Cliffs Notes kind of account of the events leading up to World War II. Capra's documentary is also constructed along traditional lines, beginning and ending with two globes—one bright, one dark, symbolizing the free and enslaved worlds, respectively. Filled with sermonizing, *Prelude to War* is so concerned with oversimplification that it presents Italian fascism, Nazism, and Japanese imperialism as identical forms of tyranny. We are told which world is the best, as if anyone with sense would prefer the world of darkness to the one of light.

Some documentaries have found favor with mass audiences because they assume the form of the fiction film. When *Spellbound* (2002) begins, it looks like a typical Hollywood movie: the screen splits into eight vertical panels, each with an image of a finalist in the Scripps Howard National Spelling Bee. *Spellbound* has an air of authenticity about it; there is no voice-over narration to prejudice or manipulate viewers. Information such as participants' names and hometowns is given in title form at the bottom of the screen. The film itself follows the conventional beginning-middle-end structure, with each contestant given his or her share of the narrative. Naturally, director Jeffrey Blitz has made choices; some parents receive more screen time than others, and contestants are introduced in a deliberate order.

Spellbound unfolds like a well-plotted thriller; suspense builds up steadily to the denouement, when one of the finalists will emerge as winner. Director Blitz has admitted that the structure of *Spellbound* was influenced by *And Then There Were None* (1945), the movie version of Agatha Christie's *Ten Little Indians*, in which ten people are invited to a mansion on an island for a weekend, during which one murder after another occurs until there are—not really none, thanks to a clever screenplay. Blitz has no agenda except to dramatize the National Spelling Bee by involving the viewer in the lives and aspirations of eight students from a cross section of obscure towns and large cities. He has succeeded in making a film in which there are no stars, not even the winner; or rather, there are eight stars, and a supporting cast of parents, friends, siblings, and former winners. If the film is making a point, it is that the children of immigrants know the meaning of achievement in a special way; and that the ability to spell the most difficult words in the English language should not be dismissed as rote learning. Such mastery requires a knowledge of roots and derivatives, sensitivity to sound and pronunciation, and, often, an educated guess. Significantly, the winner is the daughter of Indian immigrants; and the winning word is *logorrhea* (often defined as "diarrhea of the mouth"), from which *Spellbound* does not suffer.

Andrew Jarecki's *Capturing the Friedmans* (2002) attracted audiences that would not ordinarily turn out for a documentary, partly because of the sensational subject matter—the alleged sexual abuse of children by a Long Island father and his son; but also because the case itself left so many questions unanswered—questions that audiences might have hoped the film would resolve. *Capturing the Friedmans* hints at closure—but not the kind that we usually get. In other words, we get facts, but not necessarily answers.

Capturing the Friedmans opens with "Be Yourself" on the soundtrack, suggesting that the song may be the key to the film—that everything we see will be real. Yet the film itself is a clever blend of the Friedmans' home movies and videos, interspersed with testimonies from various people, including one abuse victim, his face covered, who graphically describes the sex games the students played in the computer classes that Arnold Friedman conducted in his home; the former student also implicated Arnold's son, Jesse. However, another student, willing to appear on camera, dismisses the allegations as unfounded.

At the end of the film, Jarecki leaves the audience with a handful of facts, which are confirmed by some of the interviewees but denied by others. The viewer knows that Arnold admitted he was attracted to boys at an early age and collected child pornography, a cache of which the police discovered in his home. According to Jesse's lawyer, Jesse confessed that his father had sexually abused him; Jesse, however, denies having made such a statement. Arnold eventually pleaded guilty, believing (so it seems) that his confession would spare his son. However, with his father admitting his guilt, Jesse had no other choice but to plead guilty as well. While in prison, Arnold committed suicide. Prior to Arnold's death, his wife divorced him and subsequently remarried. Jesse served thirteen years in prison. In the 2004 DVD version of *Capturing the Friedmans*, Jarecki adds new material that raises further questions about the charges against Arnold Friedman and his son.

The film ends with shots of Arnold's three boys as children, looking and behaving like typical kids. Jarecki may be suggesting a connection between a child's loss of innocence and a father's exploitation of that innocence. Or he may simply want us to reflect on what happens to children who look so normal on home video and grow up to be quite the opposite.

Documentary filmmakers may have a higher regard for truth than fiction film colleagues, yet they, too, can create a version (usually their own) of it by drawing on the same techniques that moviemakers use, such as juxtaposing events that are unrelated in time and place to make them seem similar or simultaneous, and omitting opposing views in order to achieve a unified vision. Some have even gone further and included scenes from feature films for contrast or transition, employing classical narrative construction (beginning-middle-end) to allow the documentary to unfold as if it were a movie. If the end result is art, the lie has been transformed into truth.

"History has many cunning passages, contrived corridors," T. S. Eliot wrote. Ever since movies began, filmmakers have been exploring these passages and corridors that epic poets, dramatists, and novelists had discovered earlier. But because the passages are "cunning" and the corridors "contrived," filmmakers, including makers of documentaries, must not fall victim to the belief that their version of the truth is the only one; it is only another one.

The Horror Film

The classic horror film involves a metamorphosis: an individual is transformed into an animal, insect, semihuman (e.g., werewolf), antihuman (e.g., somnambule, ghoul, zombie, or vampire), antiself (Dr. Jekyll), shrunken self (homunculus) — or, as in the Frankenstein tradition, a synthetic creation is turned into a living creature. The inanimate can also be an object of transformation: a house can change from a habitation for humans to a habitation for ghosts, as in *The Uninvited* (1944); it can even acquire an evil personality that affects those who live there, as in *Burnt Offerings* (1976), *The Haunting* (1963, remade in 1999), and *The Amityville Horror* (1979). The same principle applies to the hotel in Stanley Kubrick's *The Shining* (1980).

The prototypical horror film is *The Cabinet of Dr. Caligari* (1919), whose visual style, pruned of exaggerations, became a standard for the genre. Visually, *Caligari* is expressionistic; its asymmetrical and bizarre settings suggest a world out of joint, a world not so much of our dreams as our nightmares. Chimneys look as if they will topple over, windows are shaped like diamonds, walls seem on the verge of caving in. The American horror film uses a less extreme form of expressionism; the high-contrast photography of the German-made *Caligari*, in which there are no grays but only black and white, was not entirely discarded by American filmmakers but made less pronounced through low-key lighting that allowed for the interplay of light and shadow.

Caligari also features two plot devices that have become conventions of the horror film: the team of the mad doctor and his subhuman accomplice (whose most familiar successors were Dr. Frankenstein and his hunchback assistant in James Whale's *Frankenstein*, 1931); and the creature's desire for a mate. In *Caligari*, the doctor's accomplice may be a somnambule, but he is not impervious to the heroine's charms; nor are the Wolf Man and Dracula unaffected by the presence of beautiful women. Embalming does

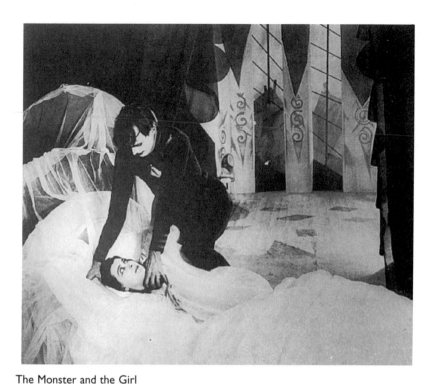

The Monster and the Girl

Caesare the somnambule and Jane in *The Cabinet of Dr. Caligari* (1919). *(Courtesy MOMA/FSA)*

not stop the mummy from searching for his beloved Princess Ananka, even if she happens to be in the United States (*The Mummy's Curse*, 1946). A synthetic creature like Frankenstein's monster needs a bride: when his bride rejects him (James Whale's *Bride of Frankenstein*, 1935), he retaliates by destroying the laboratory in which he was created. The monster's attraction to women is easily explained: the creature is the personification of the id, or libido, which is virtually all that is left after the transformation. The creature's libido may even be more active because it is no longer under the control of reason.

The basic types of horror films—ghost, creature, dual-personality, and mad scientist—had been established in the 1930s and 1940s along with the conventions of low-key lighting, shadowy surfaces, dissolve transformations, cellar laboratories with overflowing test tubes, fogbound woods, and Gothic mansions.

The ghost story is transformation in reverse, with the ghosts taking on human qualities. The ghosts may be benign or vengeful; both types are

Larry Talbot (Lon Chaney, Jr.), whose transformation does not diminish his interest in the heroine in *The Wolf Man* (1941). *(Copyright by Universal Pictures, a Division of Universal City Studios, Inc. Courtesy MCA Publishing Rights, a Division of MCA, Inc.)*

featured in *The Uninvited*. If they are not at rest, they work through the living until they are vindicated—like the mother's ghost in *Lady in White* (1988), which cannot be reunited with her daughter in the hereafter until the daughter's murderer is apprehended. The ghost story is a perennial favorite with moviegoers; not coincidentally, one of 1999's most successful films was *The Sixth Sense*, a highly intelligent example of the genre that, like most such films, has a plot twist that many moviegoers took as a surprise ending, although it had been anticipated from the beginning when a psychiatrist (Bruce Willis) is shot by his ex-patient. *The Sixth Sense* purports to be about the psychiatrist's attempt to help a nine-year-old boy (Haley Joel Osment), who can actually see ghosts, to adjust to his special sense—although it has an otherworldly aspect as well that is best appreciated at the end.

Another unconventional ghost story is *The Others*, set on an estate in Normandy that seems straight out of a gothic novel: fog-enshrouded woods, a family plot, dead leaves swirling around gravestones, and a house that seems more bedeviled than haunted. The house's sole occupants, or so it seems, are a mother, her two children, a housekeeper, the housekeeper's husband, and their daughter. Soon, there appear to be "others," who turn out to be the legal occupants of the house. *The Others* builds up to a climactic revelation that gives new meaning to "purgatory"—the state, according to Catholic teaching (and the mother is clearly a Catholic), where the souls must remain until they have been cleansed of their sins.

In the 1930s and 1940s, while the musical and the western were photographed in either monochrome or color, the horror film was shot almost exclusively in black and white. In the 1950s, the use of color began with *House of Wax* (1953) and *Phantom of the Rue Morgue* (1954), but it was the British-made *Curse of Frankenstein* (1957), the first of Hammer Films' horror series, that set the trend toward the color horror film.

Although color and horror are not incompatible, as Roman Polanski's *Rosemary's Baby* (1968) and *Carrie* prove, color cannot capture the shadowy world of the unconscious as well as black and white, which is also more conducive to horror by suggestion. Color is suited to gore, the hallmark of the latest kind of horror film: the slasher film. Like every addition to a genre, the slasher film is not without precedent; its parent is *Psycho*, a genuine horror film with a subtle transformation. The oedipal Norman Bates becomes so closely identified with his mother that he assumes her personality, even to the extent of dressing in her clothes and murdering in her name. Significantly, Norman does not die at the end of *Psycho*; and as the years passed and *Psycho* became a classic, the need for sequels arose—*Psycho II* (1983), *Psycho III* (1986), *Psycho IV* (1990). As long as there is an audience for horror, there will be a *Psycho* of some sort, although it is hard to imagine any of them surpassing or even equaling Hitchcock's, as Gus Van Sant's 1998 remake proved.

The *Psycho* sequels illustrate a time-honored tradition in horror: the monster ceases to exist when the series or the cycle does. Even though it seems obvious that, at the end of *Frankenstein*, the monster dies in the fire that destroys the mill, he is discovered in the cellar at the beginning of *Bride of Frankenstein*. And even though the monster clearly perishes again in the inferno at the end of *Bride of Frankenstein*, he is resurrected for *Son of Frankenstein* (1939) four years later, and he is paired with the Wolf Man in *Frankenstein Meets the Wolf Man* (1943) four years after he was revived by Frankenstein's son.

The same principle applies in the slasher film, the most popular being *Friday the 13th* (1980), which spawned nine sequels. Far more original is *Halloween* (1978), which introduced a plot device that *Friday the 13th* and similar films, such as *Terror Train* (1979) and *Prom Night* (1980), imitated: a prologue depicting an earlier murder that bears heavily on the plot.

Like other horror cycles, the *Friday the 13th* spin-offs work from the premise of the undying monster. In *Friday the 13th*, two teenage camp counselors are killed because they were making love when they should have been rescuing the drowning Jason. The killer is Jason's mother, who is also killed at the end. The sequels feature Jason himself, who emerges from the mud to continue his mother's work.

In addition to the obligatory prologue, the slasher film practices its own form of voyeurism: subjective camera. The camera is often stationed outside a window, representing the point of view of someone looking in; it tilts up to a bedroom, as if someone were spying. The slasher film also uses off-center compositions and framing that exclude the killer, leaving only the victim in the frame. While the slasher film may be a lesser form of horror, its use of subjective camera is a feature worth noting.

The slasher film, however, does not have a monopoly on subjective camera, a technique that has been used in movies as dissimilar as *The Grapes of Wrath* and *Marnie*. Whether or not the slasher film can be considered a genre or merely a subgenre of horror, as the doomsday film is a subgenre of science fiction, is problematic. Those who favor genre status argue that director Wes Craven (*Nightmare on Elm Street*, 1984) in his *Scream* trilogy— *Scream* (1995), *Scream 2* (1997), and *Scream 3* (2000)—codified the conventions of the slasher film, thereby suggesting that it constitutes a genre of its own. Just as film noir and the musical have certain features that distinguish them as genres, so does the slasher film: voyeuristic camera, terrorized teens, the psychopathic phone caller, quick cuts punctuated by ominous sounds, sex as a prelude to death, eerie music with an echolike quality, the sudden appearances of a character at a window or doorway, the "everybody's a suspect" philosophy, a murder that occurred prior to the main action, the climactic bloodbath, the dead mother whose sins are visited upon her children, and the undying monster figure in the form of the killer(s), who, even after they have apparently expired, get up on their feet for one last charge.

What distinguishes the Craven trilogy from slasher films like *Halloween* and *Prom Night*, which occasioned four sequels, is its self-consciousness: not only do the films reflect Craven's knowledge of the slasher conventions, but the characters' knowledge of them as well. The teens in *Scream* appear to have seen every horror movie ever made. There are references to such films as *Nightmare on Elm Street*, *The Exorcist* (1973), *Psycho*, *The Silence of the Lambs* (1991), and *Prom Night*, to mention only a few. The first victim (Drew Barrymore) is terrorized by a phone stalker who interrogates her by asking, among other questions, the identity of the killer in *Friday the 13th*. *Frankenstein* is on the screen in the local video store; in the knife-wielding finale, *Halloween* is on television. The teenage lovers, Billy Loomis and Sidney Prescott (Skeet Ulrich and Neve Campbell), characterize their relationship in terms of movie ratings (R, PG-13); later Loomis tells Sidney that life's "one great big movie, but you can't pick your genre." Loomis's knowledge, it turns out, is not restricted to movies; he knows a great deal about Sidney's mother, who was brutally raped and murdered a year earlier. But, as horror buff Randy Meeks (Jamie Kennedy) notes, in slasher films everyone's a suspect, and "sex is death"—particularly R-rated sex.

Just as *Scream* is conscious of being a slasher film, in which the characters are living out a slasher scenario and in some cases know it, *Scream 3* is conscious of being the last installment of a trilogy. In *Scream 2*, the events depicted in *Scream* become the basis of a best-seller, "The Woodsboro Murders"; the book is made into a movie called "Stab," which becomes so popular that it spawns a trilogy of its own. *Scream 3* is about the making of "Stab 3," which, like *Scream 3*, is the last of a trilogy. By the end of *Scream 3* we realize that we have seen what would have been "Stab 3," if such a movie had ever been made. One of the *Scream 3* characters even states the three requirements of the finale: firing at the killer's heart is ineffective, since his bullet-riddled body will continue to lurch forward; anybody can die, including those we would prefer to live; and finally, "the past will come back to bite you in the ass."

Craven's trilogy makes it easy to identify some of the characteristics of the slasher film, which in turn allows us to better understand the popular genre to which it belongs: the horror film.

The Science-Fiction Film

"There is no clearly recognized border between SF [science fiction] and such genres as fantasy and horror," a science-fiction expert notes.[6] Such a statement is not surprising, since, as we have seen, genres often overlap or share conventions. While the western and the crime film portray both sides of the law, the designations are different: bandits in one, criminals in the other; sheriffs in one, police officers in the other. Futuristic themes, fantasy, time travel, and the invasion motif are common to science fiction. However, what one critic would call horror, another might term science fiction. In *Science Fiction in the Cinema*, John Baxter categorizes *The Birds* as science fiction even though it is neither futuristic nor a fantasy. *The Birds* does, however, deal with an invasion—not of Martians but of killer birds. The invasion suggests science fiction; the transformation motif with benign creatures turning malevolent, horror. Another anomaly is *Frequency* (2000), a variation on the time-warp film, with elements of the supernatural thriller and the tearjerker, set in two time periods, 1969 and 1999. In 1969, a firefighter (Dennis Quaid) perishes in a fire; in 1999, his son (James Caviezel), while playing around with his father's ham radio set, discovers that he can communicate with his father, thus altering destiny.

The Birds and Frequency are hard to classify, but some films are easy to identify as science fiction. Utopian, fantasy, and doomsday films, as well as those about space travel and warring planets, are rarely mistaken for anything else.

Nonhumans, often extraterrestrials, play a major role in science fiction; they are also a diverse lot and even differ in their attitude toward humans. While some extraterrestrials seek the destruction of the planet, as they did in *War of the Worlds* (1953), not all are treacherous. Some bring warnings to help humankind, as in *The Day the Earth Stood Still* (1951); others, to enlighten humans about the nature of aliens in the hope of bridging the gap between "us" and "them," as in *Close Encounters of the Third Kind*; still others have come to use Earth's resources for their own purposes, as in *This Island Earth* (1955). The aliens in *It Came from Outer Space* (1953) mean no harm; they merely wish to repair their spaceship.

The creatures themselves can represent various life-forms: plant life in *The Thing* (1951); aquatic life in *The Creature from the Black Lagoon* (1954) and *Revenge of the Creature* (1955); a protoplasmic mass in *The Blob* (1958); birds in *The Giant Claw* (1957); and insects such as spiders in *Tarantula* (1955), grasshoppers in *Beginning of the End* (1957), and ants in *Them!* (1954).

Roy Neary (Richard Dreyfuss) encountering otherness in Steven Spielberg's *Close Encounters of the Third Kind* (1977).

In his book *Seeing Is Believing*, Peter Biskind argues that science fiction can be classified by its political extremes of right and left.[7] In conservative science fiction, science, the federal government, and the military appear as forces for good: science succeeds in destroying the alien in *It Came from Beneath the Sea* (1955) and *The Thing*. Liberal science fiction either depicts science, the federal government, and the military as ineffectual or criticizes their methods. In *I Married a Monster from Outer Space* (1958), salvation comes not from the government but from a dog. In conservative science fiction, aliens have no redeeming features. In liberal science fiction, they are portrayed sympathetically. In *The Seven Year Itch*, The Girl (Marilyn Monroe) remarks on how moved she was by *The Creature from the Black Lagoon*. In *Close Encounters of the Third Kind*, the government, learning that an alien spacecraft will be arriving in the vicinity of Devil's Tower in Wyoming, concocts an elaborate scam to evacuate the area, thereby causing enormous hardships to the residents. It is the Machiavellian principle of the end justifying the means: find out what the aliens are up to, even if it means deceiving the public. The possibility that the aliens are coming in peace is never even considered.

Both *Pleasantville* (1998) and *X-Men* are blatantly liberal. In the former, David (Tobey McGuire) expects to stay home and watch a marathon rerun of an old black-and-white TV sitcom, "Pleasantville." His sister Jennifer (Reese Witherspoon) wants to watch another program. When the TV remote breaks during their argument, a repairman materializes on the screen to offer them a new remote, which transports them to Pleasantville itself—a (literally) black-and-white community, in which color is a sign of individuality and is therefore suspect. Eventually, as the brother and sister introduce more emancipated ways of thinking, those who embrace the new philosophy find color entering not only their lives but also themselves, as their faces become suffused with it. Naturally, there are those who feel that color is subversive, but eventually the liberal spirit wins out, and Pleasantville becomes a more "colorful" place.[8]

The mutants in *X-Men*, gifted men and women who by their very nature are "different," find their civil rights threatened by an ultraconservative, racist senator. The battle lines are drawn, with the evil Magneto (Ian McKellen) willing to resort to violence to block the legislation, and the benign Xavier (Patrick Stewart) preferring nonviolent resistance, which does not preclude a display of the mutants' powers. The senator is forced to relent, and Xavier's philosophy, which reflects that of Dr. Martin Luther King Jr., prevails.

Such creatures as are found in *X-Men* abound in both horror and science fiction films; how are they to be distinguished from each other? The most basic way is to determine the roles of science (including technology), time (past/present/future), and experimentation (individual, local, global) in the film.

While neither horror nor science fiction mirrors the real world, science fiction tries to convince us that it does by dealing within the boundaries of factual science. Horror tends to skip over the specifics. In *Bride of Frankenstein*, we never know how Dr. Pretorious shrinks humans to the size of miniatures. In *Dr. Cyclops* (1940), on the other hand, we know that the physicist creates his homunculi by subjecting humans to atomic radiation. Because science is the film's point of departure, we tend to think of *Dr. Cyclops* as science fiction.

Science fiction can either reflect the present or evoke the future. The futuristic film is easily recognized; the future portrayed in such films is usually unsettling, as in *Things to Come* (1936), if not nightmarish, as in Fritz Lang's *Metropolis* (1926). The time travel film, in which travelers move either backwards or forwards in time, is a special case; one can easily argue that unless science is actually involved (e.g., the construction of a time machine in *The Time Machine*, 1960), fantasy is the more accurate term. In *Berkeley Square* (1933), Peter Standish (Leslie Howard) is transported to his favorite era, the eighteenth century. Standish had an easy time of it: he just stepped into a painting.

Science fiction's approach to the present can be quite subtle. In the 1950s, science-fiction movies capitalized on two of America's major fears: flying saucers and the atomic bomb. The possibility of extraterrestrial life resulted in one of the era's best science-fiction movies, Don Siegel's *Invasion of the Body*

Science fiction as mythology in *Return of the Jedi* (1983): the confrontation of Good and Evil, Luke Skywalker (Mark Hamill) and Darth Vader (David Prowse). *(Courtesy Lucasfilms, Ltd.)*

Snatchers, in which aliens descend on a California town and take possession of the inhabitants by an ingenious method of transformation: pods are placed under their beds, absorbing the inhabitants' personalities and leaving them as parodies of human beings. The film's implications were far-reaching: aliens threatened the race with a unique form of extinction—the extinction of the human personality. The threat to civilization posed by the atomic bomb triggered a host of science-fiction movies that imagined the results of atomic detonations: mutants in the form of giant ants, creatures dislodged from the ocean depths, humans turned into steel.

In the 1950s, a villain that was a computer would have made sense to only a few. By 1968, the name of HAL, the dispassionate computer of Stanley Kubrick's *2001: A Space Odyssey*, had entered the movie vocabulary, joining such unforgettable names as *Casablanca*'s Rick Blaine and *Gone with the Wind*'s Rhett Butler.

In the 1970s, the science-fiction movie took an interesting turn. The threat of the atomic bomb had mushroomed into the fear of nuclear destruction. Since, as T. S. Eliot observed, "humankind cannot bear very much reality," George Lucas in *Star Wars* (1977) amalgamated science fiction—which was never a pure genre to begin with—not with horror but with adventure. The result was not mindless escapism but a return to myth in its earliest stage: fairy tale or dream narrative with stock characters rather than individuals— heroes, princesses, villains, half-humans, nonhumans, animal-like humans, and humanlike animals—that we have met many times before in our dreams. In the original *Star Wars* trilogy, the characters include the pure-hearted Luke Skywalker, the virginal Princess Leia, the evil Darth Vader, the 900-year-old Yoda, the patriarchal Obi-Wan Kenobi, Chewbacca the Wookie, the treacherous Jabba the Hut, the porcine Gamorrean guards, the reptilian Admiral Ackbar, and a lovable pair of robots, C-3PO and R2-D2.

Equally important are the contributions of Steven Spielberg to the genre. While Lucas added adventure and an uncritical form of myth to science fiction, Spielberg humanized the genre. *Close Encounters of the Third Kind* portrays real people—a man, a woman, and a child—whose response to aliens reflects the film's philosophy. The child and the childlike characters in the film do not fear the aliens. Spielberg is advocating tearing down the wall that divides one group from another, one race from another, and humans from extraterrestrials. The aliens bring love; thus, one can learn from them. The humans who return to Earth at the end of *Close Encounters* have been changed for the better. Likewise, in Spielberg's *E.T.: The Extra-Terrestrial* (1982), a human—again, a child—learns from an alien.

Similarly, the aliens in Spielberg's *A.I. Artificial Intelligence* (2001) make it possible for David, a robot child (Haley Joel Osment), to be reunited with his mother, if only for one day. In Spielberg's *Minority Report* (2002), a futuristic film set in 2054, the murder rate has dropped 90 percent in Washington, D.C., because an organization called Precrime draws on the prescience of three "precognitives" ("precogs"), unique beings who can foresee a murder before it occurs. The precogs are similar to Spielberg's aliens, since they are "other" in every sense, including appearance. When two of the precogs foresee a murder that the head of Precrime (Tom Cruise) is supposed to commit, the third (Samantha Morton) makes it possible for him to prove his innocence and expose the founder of Precrime as a murderer.

All the films in this section are characteristic of science fiction. However, like any label, science fiction is a fluid term that can apply to various kinds of films, including futuristic, doomsday, "mad" scientist, and extraterrestrial movies.

Understanding Genre

There are two important facts to remember about genres:

Genres never die. A genre may go out of fashion for a while or reconstitute itself. When it reappears, it may look like a totally new creation, when it is really "old wine in a new bottle." All that has happened is that the film reflects both the conventions of the genre and the mores—that is, the language, values, and morality—of its own age. In 1937, the very idea of using strong language in a screwball comedy like *Easy Living* was unthinkable; in 1999, the screwball comedy *Notting Hill* was classified PG-13 for language. Yet each film observed the conventions of screwball, as well as being a product of the times.

Genres can no more be pigeonholed than can human beings. We are all classified in one way or another, maybe by race, gender, ethnicity, age, marital status, sexual orientation, or religion. This does not mean that human beings do not transcend the limits of classification. It is that way with films. Unless it can be determined that a particular film belongs to one, and only one, genre, it is best to say that while a film may typify a particular genre, it contains elements of others. Similarly, we can say that someone is a male or female with qualities that go beyond those traditionally ascribed to that gender. The most interesting actors, for example, are impossible to categorize in terms as limited as gender. Obviously Meryl Streep is female, and Jack Nicholson is male. Yet each seems to possess his or her own specific set of qualities (a "Streep," a "Nicholson"). Such actors—and there are many—combine elements traditionally called "male" and "female." To say that Katharine Hepburn is female is to state the obvious; to say that her performance style is defined not by her sex ("female") but by her own brand of personality (a "Hepburn") is to say that it is possible to speak of a "Hepburn movie," a "Hepburn role," or a "Hepburn-like performance."

Genres work the same way. Think of a film genre as a handle that enables you to get a grasp on a particular kind of movie. Once you understand the various genres, you can see how a film belongs more properly to one than to another yet still has features of the other—or maybe several others. Ford, for example, manufactures several kinds of cars. Nominally, an Escort is a Ford. Specifically, it is a Ford Escort. Practically, it is just an Escort. *Some Like It Hot* is primarily farce; it also belongs to a subgenre of farce, drag comedy. It can also be considered as screwball, but with music thrown in; and let's not forget romantic comedy, which it is as well. But what is *Some Like It Hot* essentially? A classic farce. Remember that *farce* comes from the Latin word for "stuffing." And a good many elements from other genres can be folded into a farce, as they can into any kind of film.

NOTES

1. James Kitses, *Horizons West* (Bloomington: Indiana University Press, 1969), 8–27.
2. Stanley J. Solomon, *Beyond Formula: American Film Genres* (New York: Harcourt Brace Jovanovich, 1976), 12–15.
3. Jack Shadoian, *Dreams and Dead Ends: The American Gangster/Crime Film,* 2nd ed. (New York: Oxford University Press, 2003), 4.
4. Lewis Jacobs, ed., *The Documentary Tradition*, 2nd ed. (New York: Norton, 1979), 29.
5. Erik Barnouw, *Documentary: A History of the Non-Fiction Film* (New York: Oxford University Press, 1983), 23.
6. William Johnson, "Journey into Science Fiction," in *Focus on the Science Fiction Film*, ed. William Johnson (Englewood Cliffs, N.J.: Prentice-Hall, 1972), 1.
7. Peter Biskind, *Seeing Is Believing: How Hollywood Taught Us to Stop Worrying and Love the Fifties* (New York: Pantheon Books, 1983), 102–159.
8. I owe this observation to Robert Sprich, Professor of English, Bentley College.

CHAPTER 6

Film Subtext

How often have you read a story or seen a film that you felt was not entirely what it seemed to be about? Many first-year college students read "The Widow of Ephesus," a tale from Petronius's *Satyricon*, written in the first century C.E. In this frequently anthologized story, a woman is so shattered by her husband's death that she cannot beat her breast or tear her hair, the ancient rites of mourning. Instead, accompanied by her maid, she retires to the underground tomb where the body lies. A soldier, patrolling a crucifixion site nearby to prevent the bodies from being taken down from the crosses, notices her presence, enters the tomb, quotes Virgil, and finally wins her over. When a corpse disappears from one of the crosses, the soldier fears that his negligence will cost him his job. But after three consecutive nights of lovemaking, the widow of Ephesus offers him her husband's body as a fair exchange.

What was just summarized is the story's plot, which consists of a situation (a widow in mourning), a complication (the soldier's appearance), and a resolution (the substitution of the husband's body for a criminal's). However, a classic tale like "The Widow of Ephesus" cannot be reduced to its story line. In every narrative worth studying, whether it's a work of fiction or a work of film, there is a **subtext,** a complex structure beneath the narrative consisting of the various associations the narrative evokes in us. In other words, there is a surface meaning and a deeper meaning. "The Widow of Ephesus" has a surface wit that cannot mask the underlying cynicism. The surface meaning is that love conquers all; the deeper, or subtextual, meaning is that love conquers lovers, generating such passion in them that they think nothing of sleeping three nights in a row next to a corpse. Film also has a subtext, or what might be called an **infranarrative.** Whether we realize it or not, film has a dual nature. There is the film projected *on* the screen and the film projected *from* the screen; in other words, the film is both the result of the collaboration between a director, a writer, a cast, and a crew, and a text that viewers experience in their own way. The situation is analogous to a novel that has just been published; prior to publication it was revised and edited. Now it awaits readers. The text is there, but readers, reviewers, and scholars must find their own way into it. When they do, they will be entering the infranarrative and will experience the text more deeply, finding levels of meaning in symbols, image patterns, and references to other works that must be discovered through sensitive reading.

Film infranarrative, or subtext, is the result of the various associations we make during the film, comparable to the symbolic or metaphorical level in literature. In a literature class, a professor may say that Dante's *Inferno* is, *literally*, about a man's descent through the nine circles of hell; *symbolically*, about a man who's trying to put his life in order by envisioning what awaits him in the hereafter. Another professor may argue that although Robert Frost's "Stopping by Woods on a Snowy Evening" seems to be a poem about a man stopping to observe the snow-covered woods, it is actually about a man contemplating death on the longest night of the year.

Naturally, the narrative and infranarrative, or text and subtext, are not two separate entities. There is, after all, only one film. Think of them, rather, as two concentric circles, the infranarrative being *within* the narrative. But, just as English teachers distinguish between form and content, and philosophers between matter and form, we do the same with the two narratives. Beneath the first narrative, which is the plot as the ordered arrangement of the incidents, is the second narrative, which is the associations, conscious and otherwise, that arise from the plot's visualization. The former can be summarized as one would a novel or a play; the latter, however, has no place in a synopsis. Asked for a plot synopsis of *Psycho*, for example, one would never say it is about an Oedipus complex gone haywire, sexual repression, voyeurism, transvestitism, schizophrenia, and necrophilia, although these are all part of the film's subtext. But saying that *Psycho* is about such matters implies that certain associations must have been made between what we saw on the movie screen. What we saw was a film about a woman who absconds with a $40,000 bank deposit and ends up in a motel, where she is murdered by a young man who can kill only by dressing as his mother. What we experienced, consciously or otherwise, was a film about a man so obsessed by the spirit of his dead mother that he dresses like her and kills women of whom his mother would have disapproved; a film that showed us an indentation in the mother's bed, suggesting that her corpse had occasionally been placed there; and a film in which the son's identification with his mother is so complete that, finally, he believes he has become his mother. *Psycho* may also remind us of a famous story about necrophilia, William Faulkner's "A Rose for Emily." It might even remind us of certain Greek myths in which sons murder their mothers—Alcmaeon killing his mother, Eriphyle; Orestes killing his mother, Clytemnestra, and her former lover (now her husband) Aegisthus. Or it might recall a novella like Stevenson's *Dr. Jekyll and Mr. Hyde*, in which the respectable Henry Jekyll is incapable of doing what his evil alter ego, Mr. Hyde, can. By making certain associations between *Psycho*, mythic figures, and literary characters, we have gone beneath the film's surface into its infranarrative.

Such associations can be mythic, visual/iconic, intellectual, or musical; they can even exist in some combination within the same film.

Mythic Associations

To understand how myth becomes part of a film's subtext, we must reconsider the meaning of myth. In the popular mind, *myth* is synonymous with *falsehood*. In literary and film criticism, however, it has another meaning altogether. William York Tindall defined myth as "a dreamlike narrative in which the individual's central concerns are united with society, time, and the universe."[1] Erich Fromm called myth "a message from ourselves to ourselves."[2] The film critic Parker Tyler regarded myth as "a free, unharnessed fiction, a basic prototypic pattern capable of many variations and distortions, even though it remains imaginative truth."[3] Lillian Feder's definition is the most detailed: "Myth is a narrative structure of two basic areas of unconscious experience which, of course, are related. First, it expresses instinctual drives and the repressed wishes, fears, and conflicts that they motivate. These appear in the themes of myth. Second, myth also conveys the remnants within the individual consciousness of the early stage of phylogenetic development in which the plots were created. This characteristic is evident mainly in its plots."[4] In other words, myth is a form of racial history—a narrative distillation of the wishes and fears both of ourselves and of the human race.

Common to all four definitions are the following:

1. Myth is a narrative, and as such obeys the rules of narrative (for example, the beginning-middle-end structure).

2. Myth also operates on an unconscious level, presenting us with characters (questers, the enchanted and the enchanter, ogres, scapegoats, monsters, talking animals, apparitions), themes (the homeward journey, the quest, ancestral curses, revenge, patricide,

matricide), and settings (caves, wastelands, subterranean rivers, enchanted islands, flat-topped mountains, ominous castles, desolate moors, lost worlds) that we recognize without having experienced them because they tap into our collective memory and recall early stages in the development of humankind, as well as events that occurred during those stages and that are now regarded as stories.

3. The themes of myth are universal: the return of the hero, the desire for forbidden knowledge, the quest for identity, coming of age, rebellion against tyranny. No single age has a monopoly on such themes. Thus myth transcends time and place.

4. Myths are ultimate truths about life and death, fate and nature, gods and humans. For this reason, they can never be false, even though the characters they portray may not have existed. Myths also endure long after the civilizations that produce them have vanished because they crystallize, in narrative form, unchanging patterns of human behavior. There will always be rebels like Antigone and Prometheus, homeward-bound voyagers like Odysseus, vengeance seekers like Medea, those who pursue reason and favor Apollo over Dionysus, and those who favor emotional release at the expense of reason and prefer Dionysus to Apollo.

Film is receptive to myth for two reasons. First, film and myth can speak the same language—picture language. Long before myths were written down, they were transmitted orally through epics, and visually through artwork on walls, vases, bowls, and wine vessels. Thus, from the outset myth was oral and visual; and so was film, for even during the silent period there was always some form of sound, as we have seen. Another reason film and myth are so compatible is that both are intimately associated with dreams. Parker Tyler coined a phrase for film: "the daylight dream." It is not coincidental that Hollywood has been dubbed "the dream factory." We dream individually, of course; but we also dream collectively. The stuff of our dreams is the stuff of fairy tales, legends, and romances. Such dream material belongs to the human race, and thus our dreams make us one with humankind. The psychologist Carl Jung compared the dream to a screen on which the history of humankind is projected; the same can be said of the movie screen. When mythic figures appear on the screen, they strike a responsive chord because they are familiar: we have encountered them before—if not in actual myths or fairy tales, then in our dreams.

Film has a dream level to which we respond the way we respond to myths: we respond instinctively, never questioning their origins or even their existence. Making a mythic association involves remembering a pattern of experience that is universal. Sometimes we can determine the specific myth: *King Kong* evokes Beauty and the Beast; *The Blue Angel* (1930), in which a respected teacher is destroyed by a seductive singer, recalls myths about such temptresses as Circe, Calypso, and the Lorelei. More often, you will not be able to isolate the specific myth but only mythic types such as the quester, the convert, the foundling, the exile, the knight-errant, the blessed damsel, the earth mother, the lost child, the eternal child, the alien, the shadow self (doppelgänger), or the liberator; or mythic themes such as the descent to the underworld; the quest for the grail, sword, ring, or chalice; the journey into the unknown; the homeward journey; the birth of the hero; the life force versus the force of reason; wilderness versus civilization; and the like. The following films provide a few examples of the different ways filmmakers use mythic associations to tell their stories.

The Transformation Myth in Jacques Tourneur's Cat People (1942)

The transformation myth is one of the most common myths, as anyone who has ever read Ovid's *Metamorphoses* knows: Daphne is transformed into a laurel tree, Philomela into a nightingale, Chiron the centaur into the constellation Sagittarius, Niobe into stone, and so on. There are also instances of mythological figures, such as Proteus and the sea nymph Thetis, who are capable of changing form. In *Cat People*, Irena (Simone Simon), the ill-starred descendant of a Serbian cat cult, is doomed to revert to a panther whenever her passions are aroused; the reason could be anything from jealousy to sexual desire—not so much on her part as on the male's.

The script, as might be expected in a 1942 film, skirts the issue of Irena's frigidity; instead, we assume that Irena, who bears the curse of her ancestors, the cat women, is unable to consummate her marriage because she is afraid of turning into a panther and killing her husband. Rather, she insists on a relationship based on friendship; her husband tries to understand but eventually turns a female coworker, Alice, who recommends a psychiatrist, Dr. Judd. The psychiatrist is so intrigued by Irena that he tries to seduce her, not realizing that a man's touch can release the panther in her. The panther emerges and attacks Judd, who mortally wounds Irena with his sword cane.

The narrative seems to be a Freudian reworking of a transformation myth. But the infranarrative points to something far deeper: a woman who wants a man only as a friend, not as a lover; who cannot bear a man's touch; who, after taking on animal form, pursues Alice, now her rival, unseen through Central Park and later to a health club, where—also unseen—she terrorizes Alice while she is swimming. Discerning audiences now regard *Cat People* as more than just another horror movie: some see elements of lesbianism in the way Irena stalks Alice; others see Irena as a mother goddess to whom men are meant to be subservient; still others view her as a woman who yearns in vain for a healthy relationship with a man—a

Irena (Simone Simon) and her husband in name only (Kent Smith) in *Cat People* (1942). *(Courtesy MOMA/FSA)*

woman who, when she commits an act of violence, must cleanse herself by taking a hot bath. For a movie that was not taken seriously in its time, *Cat People* now enjoys critical acclaim.

The Savior Myth in George Stevens's Shane (1953)

Every critic who has written about *Shane* has sensed a mythic subtext in this film about an ex-gunfighter who aids a family of homesteaders, eventually jeopardizing his own life to avenge the death of one of their neighbors. In *Shane*, there appear to be at least three mythic levels.

Shane as a Christ Figure. *Shane* begins with the credits, with Alan Ladd as Shane entering on horseback from the left to the "Shane theme," a melody that suggests cantering horses and deer drinking peacefully from a stream against a background of snow-decked mountains. Shane is descending into a valley; he is not moving horizontally across the frame like a gunfighter, although he will later change both speed and direction during his ride of vengeance. For the moment he is moving *downward*—in symbolic terms, he might be said to be lowering himself—as he descends into the lives of the Starretts, the family of homesteaders.

Shane can be seen as a Christ figure. Just as Christ descended from heaven and humbled himself by assuming human nature, so Shane descends into the valley, temporarily putting aside his divinity to serve humanity. Shane's resemblance to Christ has been noted by the critic Donald Richie:

> Shane . . . came from nowhere and he is going nowhere—like the vagrant Jett Rink in *Giant*, like the hitchhiking George Eastman [in Stevens's *A Place in the Sun*], like Jesus Christ. . . . His difference from the romantic hero is that he—like Christ himself—rather than merely feeling that he ought to do something to express his inner values and to affect the world, actually does something about it.[5]

Shane's past is as enigmatic as Christ's. Christ's life before he began his public ministry at thirty is a mystery. And so is Shane's; he simply appears one day, looking like a god in white buckskins. As part of his ritual incarnation, he sheds his divine trappings and dresses in the clothes of mortals—blue denim and dark trousers. But he will not retain that outfit forever. Before he avenges the death of Torrey (Elisha Cook, Jr.), he changes back into his buckskins, becoming a god once more.

Jesus Christ preached meekness: "If someone strike thee on the right cheek, turn to him the other also" (Matthew 5:39). Shane displays his meekness when Chris (Ben Johnson) challenges his manhood after Shane orders a bottle of soda pop for young Joey Starrett. Chris offers Shane a "man's drink" by spilling a jigger of whiskey on his shirt. At that moment, Shane does not retaliate; but later, when he returns to the saloon, he reciprocates by buying Chris a drink and disposing of its contents in the same way. In the ensuing brawl, the abandon with which Shane swings his fists suggests a wrathful god not unlike the Christ who overturned the tables of the moneychangers as he drove them out of the Temple of Jerusalem. Meekness and righteous anger are not incompatible.

Shane's message is for the chosen. It is for the homesteaders, not for the cattle ranchers. Sometimes, as history has proved, the chosen must take up arms. Thus, Shane teaches young Joey how to shoot. When Marion Starrett (Jean Arthur) finds Shane teaching her son how to handle a gun, Shane's explanation is simple: "A gun is as good or bad as the man using it." Joey, who has a male child's notion of manhood (men do not flinch when turpentine is applied to an open wound, and they settle disagreements with their fists), is given a rare opportunity to see his theory put to the test when he watches Shane kill Wilson (Jack Palance), the gunfighter. Shane leaves Joey with the command to grow up "strong and straight." Now Shane is no longer a man but a god delivering one of his commandments before he disappears from view.

Shane as Apollo-Hercules. One writer has called Shane "the frontier Christ, coming down from a Western Olympus."[6] This description characterizes Shane as part Christ, part Greek deity.

In Greek mythology, Zeus punished Apollo for killing one of his sons by forcing him to spend a year of servitude in the household of Admetus, the king of Thessaly. Admetus respected Apollo's godhead, and in gratitude Apollo allowed him the privilege of living beyond his allotted time, provided he could find someone to die for him. Unable to find a volunteer, Admetus turned to his wife, Alcestis, who agreed. During the funeral, Hercules stopped off at the palace on one of his labors, learned what had happened, wrestled with Death, and restored, so the legend goes, Alcestis to her husband.

Although Shane's golden hair is a good metaphor for Apollo's radiance, Shane is as much a Hercules as he is an Apollo. His power of endurance is

Shane's farewell to Joey in *Shane*. Shane leaves Joey (Brandon de Wilde) with the command to grow up "strong and straight," as he departs, presumably to aid another family of homesteaders. *(Courtesy Paramount Pictures)*

Herculean; in one scene a stubborn tree trunk is uprooted, a task that required Shane's perseverance as well as Starrett's brawn. Two themes are common to both *Shane* and the Greek myth: a god's bondage in a mortal's household in expiation for a crime, and a god's saving a mortal's life. As we have seen, Shane's life is a mystery, yet from the way he draws when little Joey Starrett clicks the trigger of his unloaded rifle, he seems to be an ex-gunslinger. That he humbles himself through voluntary servitude suggests that he is atoning for his past.

Just as Apollo served the family of Admetus, Shane serves the Starretts; just as Hercules restored Alcestis to her husband, Shane restores Starrett to his wife. Instead of allowing Starrett to kill Wilson and lose his own life in the bargain, Shane knocks him unconscious and goes in his place, thus increasing Starrett's life span and saving him for Marion and Joey.

Shane as Knight-Errant. According to André Bazin, the subtext also encourages us to think of Shane as a "knight errant in search of his grail," pursuing the ideals of courtly love in the American West.[7] While it is Starrett whom Shane aids, it is Marion whom he serves. But in the tradition of courtly love the knight not only served the lady but also tried to emulate her gentleness and thus offset his rough ways. Physically, there is a great re-semblance between Shane and Marion. Both have golden hair, blue eyes, and a diminutiveness that suggests a gentle heart, not a natural failing. It is significant that Shane chooses to wear blue, one of the lady's favorite colors. However, the medieval knight was a living paradox; the lady he honored as the embodiment of natural perfection was frequently the unsatisfied married woman he took to his bed.

Here the analogies cease; the closest Shane comes to Marion is to dance the Varsouviana and to shake her hand in a farewell gesture. Yet *Shane* is a magnificently subtle film. When Marion is tucking Joey into bed, we hear his voice from behind the closed door: "Mother, I just love Shane." Good-nights are exchanged; Marion enters her bedroom, and Shane retires to the barn. "Good night, Shane," Joey calls, but there is no answer. A declaration of love has taken place, shared by mother and son, but in different ways. Marion's graceful entrance into the bedroom is neither slinking nor erotic but willowy and feminine. She may be retiring to her husband's bed, but she is clearly thinking of Shane. The mythic hero has many faces. Three of Shane's have been described here.

The War of the Worlds in the Wachowski Brothers' The Matrix Trilogy (1999, 2003)

On the surface, the Matrix movies seem like nothing more than high-tech science fiction with dazzling special effects; mythically, they illustrate the agon, or clash between the forces of good and evil. The good would preserve human life as we know it; the evil would reduce humans to the equivalents of batteries energized by artificial-intelligence machines within the Matrix, an elaborate computer simulation that understands only virtual reality.

The Matrix is the equivalent of the evil planet Mongo in *Flash Gordon* (1936); if the Matrix could take on human form, it might look like Darth Vader of *Star Wars* or the characters in Richard Wagner's opera cycle *The Ring of the Nibelungs*, who lust after the ring, knowing that whoever possesses it can wield unlimited power. What makes *The Matrix* different from other good versus evil movies is the plot twist: the conflict takes place in a world of programmed reality, where a handful of humans, holding on to their humanity, resist becoming slaves of the Matrix. Mythically, *The Matrix* evokes other battles that have been waged in antiworlds, myth's equivalent of virtual reality. The Greeks, for example, believed that before there was human life on earth there was warfare in the heavens: the Titans' rebellion against the tyrannical Uranus (Sky), led by Uranus's son Cronos, who had to castrate his father so that life could continue; the revolt of the Olympians, led by Cronus's son Zeus, against the Titans, resulting in the enlightened rule of the

Virtual combat in *The Matrix* (1999). *(Courtesy the Margaret Herrick Library of the Academy of Motion Picture Arts and Sciences)*

Olympians. Even then, there was rebellion: Prometheus disobeyed Zeus and gave the gift of fire to humankind; Eris (Discord), though a minor deity, was powerful enough to precipitate a war between Greece and Troy by causing three goddesses to vie for a golden apple.

The Book of Revelation speaks of another heavenly battle — one between the angels, led by the archangel Michael, and those headed by Lucifer, who was expelled from heaven and became Satan. According to Dante, Satan inhabits this world, at the bottom of a conical cavity caused by his fall from heaven and known as hell.

The writers of *The Matrix* must have had biblical sources in mind when they were creating the script, which, however complicated, is merely a reworking of old ideas. Morpheus's (Laurence Fishburne) name suggests the Greek god of sleep, who is also the sender of dreams. The name is apt, since in the inverted world of the Matrix, reality and illusion are reversed. In the first Matrix film, Morpheus, eager to overthrow the Matrix, contacts a computer hacker (Keanu Reeves), who goes by the code name of Neo, which is Greek for "new." It is as if Neo had been sent a reality dream: he thinks he is living in 1999 rather than the year 2199 — 1999 being nothing but a virtual construct of the Matrix. Morpheus, who is looking for a messiah, suspects that it might be Neo. First, Neo must be brought before the Oracle (Gloria Foster) to determine if he is the One who is destined to destroy the power of the Matrix.

Ritual initiation by a woman is common in myth. In Homer's *Odyssey*, Circe instructs Odysseus in what he must do to visit the abode of the dead. In Virgil's *Aeneid*, the Sibyl does the same for Aeneas before he makes his descent to the underworld. However, the initiator can do only so much for the hero, who then must face the unknown himself. Similarly, in *The Matrix* the Oracle's knowledge is incomplete; this has always been the case with oracles, whose prophecies must be decoded. Neo is a savior on the order of Prometheus. He is the New Prometheus, bringing the gift of selfhood to a world of computerized conformity.

The success of *The Matrix* was due, in part, to its arrival in the wake of a series of purchases that resulted in the creation of new media empires. In the 1980s and 1990s, it seemed that the conglomerates had gone on a buying spree. Rupert Murdoch's News Corporation purchased the Twentieth Century-Fox Corporation (1985); Sony, Columbia Pictures (1989); Time, Inc., Warner Communications (1989), becoming Time Warner; Seagram, MCA, the parent company of Universal Pictures (1995); Disney, ABC (1995); and Viacom, Paramount Communications (1994) and then CBS (1999). These purchases raised fears that the flow of information would be dominated by a handful of giant conglomerates controlling access to the print and electronic media as well as the Internet. In the Matrix films, the villain, Mr. Smith of the multiple selves, wears dark suits, black ties, and white shirts, looking as if he (and his clones) would be at home in corporate America. As the world became more computer-governed and computer-dependent, there was the additional fear of hackers causing computer viruses, breaking into systems, and wreaking havoc with communication. *The Net* (1995) showed how a woman could be robbed of her identity by the removal of every possible means of identification.

The Matrix films go deeper than a fear of corporate control or even mechanization; the agents of the Matrix deny the existence of free will— a view that, if universally accepted, would allow the system to absorb humankind, thus bringing an end to life as we know it. Unfortunately, the second film in the trilogy, *The Matrix Reloaded* (2003), while intellectually more challenging than the first, is less accessible; in fact, those who had never seen the original might find it hard to understand. There is no prologue to summarize what had gone before; instead, we are plunged into the war between good and evil: between Zion, the last human outpost on Earth, and the Matrix.

Although *The Matrix Reloaded* may alienate viewers who just want visual effects without digressions on free will and cause-effect, the film makes it clear that the Wachowski brothers know their mythology. Zion, the promised land, is an underground city, since everything above the earth has been taken over by the Matrix. Zion's name fits in with the film's inverted world order, where humans, who should be living above ground, are now living below it. This Zion is not a place of peace and harmony; it is more like Homer's Mount Olympus, where the gods and goddesses are often at odds with each other, sometimes disobeying Zeus's commands and sulking when they have no other choice but to concede.

Some of the Zionists' names pose a problem for those seeking mythological equivalents for all the characters. For example, "Niobe" was chosen to evoke mythology, not because there is any relationship between Niobe of the film and the mother in classical mythology who witnessed the tragic death of her fourteen children because she boasted that she had borne more offspring than the goddess Leto. Similarly, Morpheus's ship is named "Nebuchadnezzar" after the Babylonian king, with whom there is no connection in the film. "Merovingian," the name of an agent of the Matrix, comes from the royal Merovingian dynasty in the Middle Ages. The character Persephone is named after the goddess of the underworld in Greek mythology. "What's in a name?" one might ask. Something, in the case of Neo and Morpheus; less so in the case of the Oracle, who may not be what she seems; and nothing in the case of the Merovingian, Persephone, and Niobe. And what is to be made of Neo's nemesis, Mr. Smith, who bears one of the most common of Anglo-Saxon surnames? Perhaps Smith can be seen as a typical corporate climber, and his ability to replicate himself implies that his kind is indestructible.

Like the epic hero on a quest, Neo must seek out the Key Maker for the key to the Source, the creator of the Matrix. In the final scene, Neo comes face to face with the Source, who undermines Neo's belief that he is the savior of humanity by explaining that five other would-be messiahs have preceded him — the Matrix being in its sixth format, like the latest version of Windows; and that this is the sixth confrontation between Zion and the Matrix. The Source also suggests that this was all the work of the Oracle, which does not surprise Neo, who wondered earlier if the Oracle were in league with the Matrix. In the old movie serials, when the train was heading toward the heroine tied to the tracks, CONTINUED NEXT WEEK appeared on the screen. "TO BE CONTINUED" signals the end of *The Matrix Reloaded*.

The Matrix Revolutions (2003), the last film of the trilogy, introduces a new motif: a subway connecting the worlds of Zion and the Matrix with a conductor (the Trainman), reminiscent of Charon, the ferryman in classical mythology, who transported the dead across the river Styx. A bridge — or some way of spanning, and thereby entering, two antithetical worlds — is common in myth, because of humankind's perennial need to believe that the other world exists and is accessible. Using a stone for a pillow, Jacob (Genesis 28:10–15) dreamed of a ladder stretching from earth to heaven. When he awoke, he memorialized the place, designating it the gate of heaven and giving it the name of Bethel. The other world is also locatable. In Homer's *Odyssey*, Odysseus was told to sail to the land of the Cimmerians, somewhere in the Black Sea region, where the sun never shines. In Virgil's *Aeneid*, the entrance to Hades is a cave in southern Italy. Often there is an actual bridge. In Persian mythology, the souls traverse a bridge bringing them to the other world. The souls in medieval folklore do the same, except that crossing is more perilous, since below is a river of boiling pitch. In the

Inferno, Dante descends into a conical cavity at the earth's center, proceeding through nine circles of decreasing size.

The worlds of Zion and the Matrix are therefore bridgeable, suggesting perhaps some kind of rapprochement or at least an armistice. Since *The Matrix Revolutions* lacks the kind of closure expected in a trilogy, we are left with the possibility that these two worlds, seemingly antithetical, differ only in their perception of reality and are just a subway ride away. The concluding film does not answer the question as to whether two such diametrically opposite worlds can coexist. Regardless, by tapping into our collective unconscious, the Wachowski brothers posed some serious questions about a world where machines have become more valuable than people.

Visual/Iconic Associations

Sometimes we make associations on a visual level; for example, some performers, such as Katharine Hepburn, John Wayne, Bette Davis, James Dean, Marilyn Monroe, and Sean Connery, have such strong screen personas that we make little distinction between them and the characters they play. Whether John Wayne was playing the Ringo Kid in *Stagecoach* or Rooster Cogburn in *True Grit* (1969), he was always John Wayne. Any movie in which he starred became a "John Wayne movie," and his fans turned out for it; it could have been a romantic film like *The Quiet Man*, a World War II movie like *Sands of Iwo Jima* (1949), or a western like *The Searchers*. For John Wayne buffs, it hardly mattered that each of these films revealed a different aspect of the John Wayne persona. John Wayne was an icon.

In medieval art, an icon is a pictorial representation of a religious subject invested with a spiritual aura that makes it worthy of veneration. An icon of the Virgin Mary, for example, is not just a picture of a woman but of a special woman, the mother of Jesus Christ. An icon therefore has a dual nature: it depicts not just a person but a person who stands out from the ordinary, as indicated by a halo, a nimbus, or a gilded background.

Humphrey Bogart as Screen Icon in Raoul Walsh's High Sierra (1941)

Bogart is a true screen icon, inseparable from the cool, unemotional types he played — characters who seemed totally indifferent to the plight of humanity. "I stick my neck out for no man," Rick, perhaps his most famous character, says in *Casablanca*. Yet when Rick's help is needed, as it is by two Bulgarian refugees in the film, he comes to their aid but is embarrassed

Two screen icons, Katharine Hepburn and John Wayne, who had such distinctive personas that they personalized their films, becoming inseparable from the characters they played. (*Private Collection*)

when they show gratitude. Bogart's screen persona was forged with his first starring role, Roy Earle in *High Sierra* (1941). Bogart might never have appeared in the film, which made him a star, if George Raft, who was originally slated for the lead, had not refused to be in a movie in which he had to die. Raft, however, could never have suggested the inward drive for freedom that propels Earle to the summit from which he falls. *High Sierra* is a film about existential freedom — that freedom to which a human being is

The Actual and Intended Stars of
High Sierra (1941)

TOP LEFT: Humphrey Bogart, who
played Roy Earle in the film. *(Courtesy
Collector's Book Store)*

BOTTOM LEFT: George Raft, who was
slated for the part of Roy Earle but refused to be in a movie where he had
to die. *(Courtesy Collector's Book Store)*

condemned, as Jean-Paul Sartre would say. It is not surprising that Bogart
became an existential cult hero. Throughout his career, he projected the
image of a man living in the present, striving for freedom, and performing
meaningful actions to achieve it—financing an operation for a girl with a
club foot in *High Sierra*; relinquishing the woman he loves to her freedom-
fighter husband, who can do more for the world than he can, in *Casablanca*;
leading a detachment through the desert like Moses in *Sahara* (1943); refusing to allow his love for the woman responsible for his best friend's death to
stand in the way of justice in *Dead Reckoning* (1947); and defending an un-
derprivileged youth when no other lawyer would in *Knock on Any Door*
(1949).

At the end of *High Sierra*, Earle lies dead at the foot of a mountain;
when Marie (Ida Lupino), the woman who stood by him, asks Healy what

it means when a man "crashes out," Healy replies that it means he is "free." "Free," Marie says as she walks triumphantly into the frame, knowing that Earle has won his freedom—and his essence—in death. The existential implications of "crash out" would have eluded a mediocre actor like George Raft. Bogart understood them and embodied them in his performance, thus giving the film its existential character. Even Bogart's face was extraordinary and fittingly existential. It was not a neighborhood face, nor was it especially handsome. It was a face that knew the mixed blessings of life; a face that did not slacken with age but grew tauter, the eyes retreating into their sockets until by the end of his career they had settled into omniscience.

Not every actor becomes an icon like Humphrey Bogart; screen icons are, in fact, rare. There are talented actors who never become icons because they cannot be pigeonholed. Nicole Kidman, for example, does not make "Nicole Kidman films." Rather, she has created a gallery of characters ranging from a Henry James heroine in *The Portrait of a Lady* (1996) and a consumptive courtesan in *Moulin Rouge* to the historical Virginia Woolf in *The Hours* and an uneducated janitor in *The Human Stain* (2003). Each of her films is so different from the others that it is impossible to single out one and call it "a Nicole Kidman film."

Visual associations are similar to iconic associations. We make visual associations when (1) we equate an actor's physical appearance with our image of the way a historical figure might have looked (for example, an actor playing a Christ figure and looking the way Christ is traditionally represented, or an actor playing a rebel in a manner consistent with the popular image of the rebel); and (2) we relate an actor's performance style to that of another actor, who is not in the film but whose presence is clearly felt. For example, Sean Penn recalls Marlon Brando in his uncanny way of inhabiting a character so that we feel we are experiencing life rather than art, although what we are experiencing is the art of acting. Brad Pitt, Val Kilmer, and Jason Patric recall the brooding intensity of James Dean in the three films he made; *East of Eden* (1955), *Rebel Without a Cause* (1955), and *Giant* (1956). Clint Eastwood is a "John Wayne" type of actor. Like Wayne, Eastwood has a laconic, uninflected way of speaking, avoiding cadence or a definite speech rhythm; like Wayne, he also projects the image of the loner —helpful under the right circumstances, vengeful in others.

Al Pacino as Christ Figure in Sidney Lumet's Serpico (1973)

When *Serpico* premiered in 1973, several critics noted a resemblance between Al Pacino, who interpreted the title role magnificently, and pop-art pictures of Jesus Christ. The *New York Times* critic, Vincent Canby, also compared Pacino with Saint Francis of Assisi. All sensed that there was more to Pacino's Serpico than just great acting; behind his Serpico they saw either a

Al Pacino as Frank Serpico (*Serpico*, 1973), one of the few visually acceptable Christ figures in film. *(Courtesy Paramount Pictures)*

god-man doomed to suffer for his love of humanity or a saint who resisted the attempts of the religious establishment to interfere with his mission.

It was not merely Al Pacino's beard, his mesmeric eyes, or his uncontrollable rage at corruption that caused critics to think of Jesus Christ. Certain details of Serpico's life recalled similar details in Christ's; Serpico was a cop who found his apostolate on the streets and who underwent the traditional scapegoat cycle of harassment, betrayal, and desertion. Thus, the text, or Serpico, is coordinated with the subtext, or Christ, and both come together in the person of the star who is Pacino. Such coinciding of actor and historical figure does not occur in every movie with a police officer hero. The identification of Christ with Serpico was present in Pacino's performance in a way that it was not in the performances of Stacy Keach in *The New Centurions* (1972), Robert Duvall in *Colors* (1988), or Morgan Freeman in *Seven* (1995), all of which were hero-cop movies.

Jack Nicholson as Free Spirit and Louise Fletcher as Boss Lady in Miloš Forman's One Flew over the Cuckoo's Nest (1975)

The impression made by an actor's performance is based on many factors, including such seemingly irrelevant details as hairstyle and wardrobe. Yet it is through such details that filmmakers realize their intentions; it is also through such details that we see in the characters what directors want us to see.

Hairstyle as a Visual Association

Nurse Ratched (Louise Fletcher) and Randle McMurphy (Jack Nicholson) in *One Flew over the Cuckoo's Nest* (1975). Louise Fletcher's hairstyle is a throwback to the 1940s. *(Courtesy Fantasy Films)*

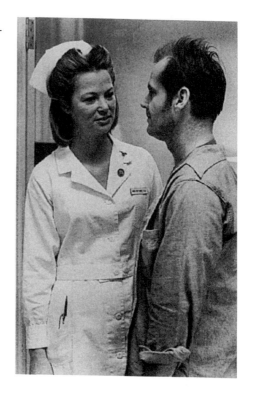

As the director of *One Flew over the Cuckoo's Nest*, Miloš Forman was faced with the task of making a movie out of a cult book of the 1960s. During the last few years of that decade, Ken Kesey's novel seemed a tragically accurate mirror of America. The animosity between Randle P. McMurphy and Big Nurse paralleled similar confrontations between the pacifist and the draft board, the militant Students for a Democratic Society and the police, and the student activists and the campus administration.

In 1975, however, the Vietnam War was a painful memory, the draft had been suspended, and campuses were quiet. To make the film meaningful, Forman had to deemphasize all the political overtones the novel had acquired in the 1960s. The film's text emphasized the humanism and comedy of Kesey's novel; the subtext transformed the conflict between McMurphy (Jack Nicholson) and Nurse Ratched (Louise Fletcher) into a battle between man and woman. Forman capitalized on Nicholson's exposed and often vulnerable masculinity, but he also saw more in it than locker-room bravado. There is an impishness about Nicholson; at times he seems to be putting us on, challenging us to make the hackneyed connection between a man's small stature and his ego. Little details about Nicholson's portrayal of McMurphy suggest the imp: the cap pulled down over the ears, the hornlike tuft of hair that gives the impression of a satyr, the eyes that dart from one direction to another, as if they, too, were free spirits.

Although the time of the film is the 1960s, Louise Fletcher's hairstyle came out of another era. Forman had her wear her hair the way women did in "lady executive" movies of the 1940s, which were typified by such movies as Mitchell Leisen's *Take a Letter, Darling* (1942) and Alexander Hall's *They All Kissed the Bride* (1942). These films, however, were harmless screwball comedies featuring women as executives and men as their subordinates. *Cuckoo's Nest* is hardly screwball comedy, and Nurse Ratched, by her hairstyle and manner, is a savage parody of the female executive of the 1940s.

Barbara Stanwyck as Marlene Dietrich in Billy Wilder's Double Indemnity (1944)

The name of the femme fatale in James Cain's novel *Double Indemnity* is Phyllis Nirdlinger. When Billy Wilder was working on the screenplay for the film version, which he also directed, he changed the character's last name to Dietrichson. He wanted audiences to think not of Marlene Dietrich herself but of Dietrich's persona, the embodiment of the extremes of desire and danger, passion and aloofness, and femininity and masculinity. Wilder even had Barbara Stanwyck, whom he cast in the role, wear a blond wig. Stanwyck is alternately seductive and passionless, ruthless and repentant. "I'm rotten to the heart," she admits just before her ex-lover shoots her—after she has shot him. Thus, throughout the film one senses something about Stanwyck that suggests Dietrich; behind Stanwyck's Phyllis lurks Dietrich's persona.

Intellectual Associations

When we make a mythic association, we are reminded of universal patterns that are true of all human beings at all times. When we make an iconic or visual association, we perceive a likeness between an actor's persona and the character, between the actor and the kind of film in which he or she customarily appears, or between one actor's persona and another's. When we make an intellectual association, we relate the film as a whole—not just one aspect of it—to history, to another medium such as literature or opera, to another film, or even to an earlier version of itself.

When we relate a film to history, we look at how faithfully the film reflects its time period. Was Rome during Nero's reign the way Cecil B. De Mille depicted it in *The Sign of the Cross* (1933)? DeMille packaged sex and religion so attractively that historical accuracy was secondary to mass entertainment. There was indeed an emperor by the name of Nero (Charles Laughton), who had a mistress Poppea (Claudette Colbert); it is also true

Fred MacMurray and Marlene Dietrich in *The Lady Is Willing* (1942). *(Courtesy Columbia Pictures)*

Barbara Stanwyck as Marlene Dietrich

Fred MacMurray and Barbara Stanwyck in *Double Indemnity* (1944). Wilder changed the name of Stanwyck's character to Dietrichson and had the actress wear a blond wig to evoke the Dietrich persona. *(Copyright © by Paramount Pictures. Courtesy MCA Publishing Rights, a Division of MCA, Inc.)*

that under Nero the persecution of Christians became a form of entertainment for jaded Romans, who enjoyed seeing members of the outlawed religion torn apart by lions in the Coliseum. But the crux of the plot—the love of a Roman general for a Christian woman that is so strong that he embraces her religion and shares her fate—is pure melodrama. In *The Sign of the Cross*, history is only the background for a DeMille spectacle.

In June 1941, less than two years after World War II broke out in Europe, the Nazis attacked Russia. Suddenly, Russia, a Communist country—anti-capitalist, anti-religious, and anti-democratic—became an ally—but only for the duration of the war. To celebrate this dubious alliance, Warner Bros. put *Mission to Moscow* (1943) into production. The film glorified the former Soviet Union, ignoring such vital matters as the show trials of the so-called enemies of the state and widespread famine in the Ukraine. *Mission to Moscow* also justified the Soviet Union's invasion of Finland as a request from the Soviet government to maintain a presence in Finland to ward off the Nazis. Even in 1943 the film's accuracy was questioned, although at the time there was no groundswell of support for the opposing view. Today, the film is seen as nothing more than propaganda designed to welcome a new ally in the fight against fascism while downplaying the ally's totalitarianism.

Historical accuracy is only one way of looking at a film that is supposedly based on fact. A film can also suggest an era without re-creating that era.

History by Suggestion

Frequently overlooked is history's evocative power, its ability to function as a backdrop for the action without advertising its presence. It is rather like a stage set that subtly captures the mood and theme of the play without competing with the text. *The Day of the Locust* (1975), John Schlesinger's film version of Nathanael West's blatantly anti-Hollywood novel of the same name, seems to be more about the superficiality of Tinseltown than it is about history. Yet the action takes place on the eve of World War II, as we see from the headlines of a newspaper that blows down Hollywood Boulevard on the eve of a movie premiere. The master of ceremonies at the premiere is a Hitler look-alike, and the fans behave like the ones that would turn out for a Nazi rally. They are all oblivious to the world at large, which, in 1939, appeared to be on the verge of destruction; all that matters is catching a glimpse of the stars as they sweep into the theater.

The premiere is portrayed as a sacred ritual that cannot be profaned. When Adore, a child actor, hurls a stone at Homer (Donald Sutherland), Homer retaliates by stomping him to death. Adore's fame-obsessed mother had turned her son into a grotesque by letting his hair grow long and curly like Shirley Temple's. And as if shoulder-length hair weren't enough, she also had it dyed platinum. Because Homer has polluted the holy rite of the Hollywood premiere by killing a male Shirley Temple, the fans turn on him, doing to him what he did to Adore. The film does not equate Homer with Hitler's scapegoats who ended up in death camps. Nor does it equate the frenzied fans with Germans who shouted their support for Hitler at torchlit rallies. *The Day of the Locust* only suggests that their reactions have something in common: destroyers of the dream—whether it is a dream of

The ritualized killing of Homer (Donald Sutherland) in *The Day of the Locust* (1975). *(Courtesy MOMA/FSA and Paramount Pictures)*

Hollywood as a Mount Olympus, with gods and goddesses, or the dream of a world inhabited only by Aryans—must be exterminated.

A film, therefore, may be set in a particular era but evoke that era only indirectly. Such a film does not declare itself "historical" in the sense of dramatizing an actual event, as when, for example, *Tora! Tora! Tora!* re-created the Japanese attack on Pearl Harbor. Yet to appreciate a film such as *The Day of the Locust*, one has to know history; unlike the historical film, the background information is not in the dialogue but in the visuals.

A knowledge of history also deepens our appreciation of the screwball comedies of the 1930s, even though such films were intended to take viewers' minds off the Great Depression. The breeziness and happy endings led people to believe that one of the era's most popular songs, "Happy Days Are Here Again," was not all that far-fetched. *It Happened One Night* delighted moviegoers by showing a society woman being put in her place by a middle-class man who didn't even wear an undershirt. Yet the film convinced audiences that the two could live happily ever after, even though they belonged to different social classes.

Mitchell Leisen's *Easy Living*, another classic screwball comedy, was released in 1937—a year in which there were 4,720 strikes in America, the bloodiest being the one against Republic Steel in Chicago, where eighteen

Cinderella in sable (Jean Arthur) is exposed to the grim realities of the Great Depression in the Automat sequence of *Easy Living* (1937). *(Copyright © by Paramount Pictures. Courtesy MCA Publishing Rights, a Division of MCA, Inc.)*

people were killed and more than ninety were wounded. However, an America of labor unrest and unemployment, where the average yearly wage was $1,348, was far removed from the America of *Easy Living*, where an irate husband thought nothing of throwing his wife's $58,000 sable coat from the roof of their Fifth Avenue apartment. The movie is best remembered for the Automat sequence in which Mary Smith (Jean Arthur), wearing the coat that literally fell on her, is sitting alone, eating a beef pie. Although there are no longer any Automats in New York, they were once popular eating places as well as tourist attractions. Automats were coin-operated cafeterias. The selections were inside small windowlike compartments that would spring open when the correct change was deposited in the slot. In *Easy Living*, when a mishap causes all the glass lids to pop open, the customers rush to get the free food. Mary, however, keeps eating, oblivious to the chaos around her. In the context of the film, the sight of people sliding around on a food-spattered floor is uproarious; in the context of Depression America, it is disturbing. When the camera captures the sable-clad Mary eating in the foreground, with the masses fighting in the background, it does more than record a comic free-for-all. By highlighting the extremes of affluence and poverty, the Automat sequence defines the Great Depression as a time of fur coats for the fortunate and cloth coats, or none at all, for everyone else.

Film History by Suggestion

Bernardo Bertolucci's *Last Tango in Paris* (1972) is ostensibly about a woman caught between two men, one of whom debases her while the other idealizes her. Bertolucci used this narrative structure to work out a theory of film that he illustrates with references to movies of the past. Thus, when Pauline Kael reviewed *Last Tango*, and alluded to the film's constant "feedback," she

Léaud as Tom, the TV director, in *Last Tango in Paris* (1972), with Maria Schneider. Even as Tom, Léaud typified the casual, naturalistic form of acting that the New Wave directors encouraged. *(Courtesy United Artists)*

meant that much in the film—the performances as well as the imagery—recalled other films.

"Movies are a past we share, and, whether we recognize them or not, the copious associations are at work in the film and we feel them," Kael observed.[8] As we have already seen, the way a movie is cast can create certain associations between the actor and his or her role. In *Last Tango*, Marlon Brando plays Paul, an American in Paris, who meets Jeanne (Maria Schneider) when both of them show up to look at the same apartment; Jean-Pierre Léaud is Tom, the TV director and movie lover who is using Jeanne for a television film. Brando and Léaud are not ordinary actors. Each epitomizes a style of acting and a type of film that revolutionized the cinema. Brando will always be synonymous with the Method, an approach to acting that requires the performer to draw on past experiences, emotions, and memories for a particular role. Brando was the definitive Method actor of the 1950s—brooding, introspective, often inarticulate. Léaud typified the New Wave—that extraordinary burst of creativity that started in France in the late 1950s, when directors like François Truffaut and Jean-Luc Godard rejected literary scripts for shooting scripts and improvisation; filmed in the streets rather than in studios; demanded naturalistic acting instead of old-fashioned emoting; and quoted liberally from the movies of the past.

Just as Brando and Léaud represent two different eras of filmmaking, the characters they portray represent two different ways of life. Paul isolates himself in the apartment, where he works out his sexual aggression on Jeanne; Tom roams the streets of Paris, scouting for locations for his movie. Jeanne is trapped not just between two men but between their worlds: Paul's closed world of the apartment and Tom's open world of the city. Yet filmmakers are in the same predicament: do they remain within the closed world of the studio set (the past) as their predecessors did, or do they venture outside, where an entire city can be their soundstage (the present)?

What Kael calls "feedback" is not limited to the eras Brando and Léaud evoke. Bertolucci used *Last Tango* as a vehicle for his ideas on film in the same way that Paul and Tom were using Jeanne for their respective purposes. Thus Bertolucci invokes movies of the past that have some bearing on his own film. When Jeanne and Tom are on a barge, there is a life preserver with "L'Atalante" inscribed on it. *L'Atalante* is the title of Jean Vigo's classic film (1934), and the barge scene in *Last Tango* pays homage to Vigo's exquisite production, in which a young bride leaves her barge-captain husband to experience the excitement of Paris, only to return to the secure world of the barge at the end. However, Bertolucci is also replying to Vigo's optimism: Vigo's bride can be reunited with her husband, but once Paul and Jeanne leave the apartment no reunion is possible.

Last Tango is like a course in film history. The scene in which Paul looks out on the roofs of Paris before he dies recalls René Clair's *Sous les toits de Paris* (Under the Roofs of Paris) (1931), which the director made when he was thirty, the same age Bertolucci was when he made *Last Tango*. When Jeanne shoots Paul, the scene is a part not only of *Last Tango* but of the many Hollywood movies, including *The Letter* (1940), *Double Indemnity*, and *Sunset Boulevard*, in which a woman pulls a revolver and pumps her lover full of bullets. *Last Tango* purports to be about male-female relationships, but subtextually it is about the relationship between filmmakers and their art.

With its mix of animation and live action, Robert Zemeckis's *Who Framed Roger Rabbit* (1988), set in 1947, seems to have a double subtext: the animated cartoons of the 1930s and 1940s and the private-eye films of the 1940s. While *Roger Rabbit* has been enjoyed by children who have never seen a private-eye movie and who know cartoons only from television, it speaks most directly to those who have a knowledge of film history. The dancing hippos bring back memories of Walt Disney's *Fantasia* (1940); Roger's sexy wife, Jessica, with her red tresses and low-cut gown, recalls Rita Hayworth in *Gilda* (1946); Eddie Valiant (Bob Hoskins), the private eye hired to trail Jessica, whose infidelity is causing Roger to forget his lines, is a seedier version of the 1940s private detectives Sam Spade and Philip Marlowe.

However, the plot of *Roger Rabbit*—a detective's discovery of a scheme that would, if executed, change the face of Los Angeles—is not to be found in any cartoon or 1940s detective movie, but in one particular film, Roman Polanski's *Chinatown*, the true subtext of *Roger Rabbit*. In *Chinatown*, the private investigator J. J. Gittes (Jack Nicholson) uncovers a shady land deal involving Noah Cross (John Huston), who is buying up property in the San Fernando Valley, where a projected reservoir will turn the area into choice real estate. In *Roger Rabbit*, Eddie Valiant discovers that Judge Doom (Christopher Lloyd) plans to transform Los Angeles from a city that relies on trolley cars for transportation into a city of freeways. To do so, he must destroy Toontown, the enclave in which the cartoon characters live. If he succeeds, he will be destroying a venerable film tradition: the animated cartoon and the characters, like Bugs Bunny, Donald Duck, and Porky Pig, who are part of it.

Judge Doom's plan is thwarted through the combined efforts of Eddie and the Toons. The actual history of Los Angeles and Hollywood, however, has proved otherwise. Thus moviegoers who remember a time when theaters featured a cartoon, two movies, a newsreel, and a chapter of a serial find *Roger Rabbit* bittersweet: the film conjures up a Hollywood of another time and place—to many, perhaps a better time and place.

Remaking the Original: The Shop Around the Corner (MGM, 1940), In the Good Old Summertime (MGM, 1949), You've Got Mail (WARNER BROS., 1998)

The Shop Around the Corner was freely adapted from Nikolaus "Miklaus" Laszlo's play *Parfumerie*. Although the play is virtually unknown, it has inspired three films and a Broadway musical. The plot is an unusual variation of the battle of the sexes. Ordinarily, in this kind of movie each tries to beat the other at his or her game, until both realize that the game they have been playing is the game of love. As we have seen, the "battle of the sexes" was a staple of screwball comedy. However, the usual screwball characters do not appear in *The Shop Around the Corner*, a romantic comedy with an unusual twist: the man and woman are pen pals who communicate anonymously, falling in love through their letters, although in real life they thoroughly dislike each other.

The *Shop Around the Corner* was directed by the German-born director Ernst Lubitsch, whose genius resulted in a phrase that is still used today: "the Lubitsch touch." The touch that Lubitsch brought to romantic comedy is like the touch a master chef brings to a dish that is truly unique, although the ingredients that went into it were common knowledge. Other directors made romantic comedies, but Lubitsch stamped them with his personal signature. When sex was involved, he was slyly discreet, leaving everything to the imagination. Lubitsch knew the difference between a wink and a leer. In *Trouble in Paradise* (1932), one scene ends with the bedroom door closing on two lovers; in the next, each awakens in his or her own room. Lubitsch delighted in posing the "Did they or didn't they?" question. Just when you think they did, the camera implies otherwise. Sex, like life, was a game to be played with wit and discretion. It was passion by suggestion, not depiction.

In *The Shop Around the Corner*, in which sex is virtually nonexistent, the touch consisted in presenting the battle of the sexes as playacting, until the players reach the stage when they can approach each other without having to hide behind a mask—specifically, the mask of anonymity that "lonely hearts" correspondence offers. Most of the action in *The Shop Around the Corner* is set in a gift shop in Budapest, Hungary, where Alfred Kralik, the head clerk (James Stewart), and a new hire, Klara (Margaret Sullavan), take an immediate dislike to each other, not knowing that they have been

James Stewart and Margaret Sullavan as the pen pals in *The Shop Around the Corner* (1940). *(Courtesy MOMA/FSA)*

Judy Garland and Van Johnson as the same in the musical remake, *In the Good Old Summertime* (1949). *(Courtesy MOMA/FSA)*

Tom Hanks and Meg Ryan as yet another pair of anonymous correspondents, this time online, in *You've Got Mail* (1998). *(Courtesy MOMA/FSA)*

corresponding. What they have in common is their romantic idealism: they write to each other as "dear friend," expressing their deepest thoughts about love—not as passion but as the shared enjoyment of the pleasure that comes from common interests such as art and literature. Lubitsch, however, is suggesting that the correspondence school of romance is a form of immaturity, allowing writers to reveal themselves at their best and thus avoid the frankness that comes from face-to-face communication.

We wait for the moment when Alfred and Klara will reveal their identities. They plan to meet at a café, where Klara will be at a table with a copy of Tolstoy's *Anna Karenina* and a red carnation. Although Alfred has been fired that day, he keeps the appointment. To his dismay, he discovers that his "dear friend" is none other than Klara; still, he approaches her table. Klara, assuming that "dear friend" might get the wrong impression if another man is sitting with her, treats Alfred so shabbily, even calling him "insignificant," that he leaves without telling her who he is. The action culminates on Christmas Eve, and in a happy ending. Alfred, newly rehired, and Klara are alone in the shop, getting ready to face Christmas Eve alone. Alfred then recites a passage from one of his letters to Klara, which she immediately recognizes. As the snow falls gently outside the shop, their embrace makes it evident that neither of them will be spending Christmas alone.

Within less than a decade, MGM remade *The Shop Around the Corner* as a musical for Judy Garland and Van Johnson called *In the Good Old Summertime*. It is not surprising that the studio decided to turn the old Laszlo play, which seemed like the perfect text for an operetta, into a musical. Garland and Johnson were still popular stars, although neither was at her or his peak. Garland could still belt out a song, however, and was given several opportunities to do so.

Summertime is set in Chicago, in the early years of the twentieth century. The characters of Klara and Alfred become Veronica (Garland) and Andrew (Johnson). The shop is now a music store. The pen pals meet as Andrew is racing out of the post office with his "dear friend" letter, colliding with "dear friend" herself, causing Veronica's hair to come undone, her hat to get crushed, her parasol to collapse, and her skirt to come off. With such an introduction, Veronica can hardly be expected to feel kindly toward Andrew after she joins the sales staff.

There are a few new plot points involving a female violinist and a priceless Stradivarius, but these are superficial, not radical, changes. Since the owner of the music store is now single and can be paired off with an older employee, there is no wife to seduce, as there was in the original. If there is no seducer, there is no suicide attempt, as there was in *Shop* when the owner learned that his wife was cheating on him with one of his own employees. The restaurant rendezvous, however, is a replica of the original. A colleague peers through the window, informing Andrew that his "dear friend" is at a table with a red carnation and a book (a copy of Elizabeth Barrett Browning's poetry). When Andrew approaches Veronica's table, she—like Klara—behaves so abominably that he leaves without telling her who he is. The ending also follows the original. Andrew and Veronica are alone in the store on Christmas Eve when Andrew finally decides to reveal his identity by quoting from one of his letters. Since the remake is entitled *In the Good Old Summertime*, there is a dissolve from a Christmas tree in the store window to a summer scene, with Andrew, Veronica, and their three-year-old daughter, played by Garland's own three-year-old daughter, Liza Minnelli, in her film debut.

Between *In the Good Old Summertime* and the next *Shop Around the Corner* remake, the same plot became the basis of a stage musical, *She Loves Me* (1964), which is extremely close to the original. Although it wasn't a huge hit, *She Loves Me* had a major New York revival in the 1990s. The original cast album is still in print, and Jerry Bock's score is highly regarded by lovers of musical theater. *She Loves Me* made it clear that *The Shop Around the Corner* is perfect operetta material, especially with its old-world setting and Christmastime ambience.

In the 1990s, Nora Ephron gave new life to *The Shop Around the Corner*; the result was *You've Got Mail*. Ephron adhered to the same story line, updating the method of correspondence—the main characters now communicate via e-mail—and adding the familiar 1990s scenario of a neighborhood business threatened by the arrival of a megastore. The cyberspace communicators, Joe Fox III (Tom Hanks) and Kathleen Kennedy (Meg Ryan), are business rivals—and know it. She owns a children's bookstore called the Shop Around the Corner, which is clearly an *hommage* to the Lubitsch film. Joe's family runs a bookstore chain on the order of Barnes & Noble, which is opening a branch literally around the corner from her shop. To remain true to the spirit of the original, *You've Got Mail* makes use of anonymous correspondence, an urban ambience, and a moment of truth.

Although Joe and Kathleen meet in an online chat room instead of through the personals columns, they still address each other as "dear friend." Anonymity is preserved through meaningful code names: hers is "shopgirl," which is accurate in view of her store's name; his is "Brinkley," his dog's name, and also the means by which he reveals his identity.

Shop and *Summertime* were filmed on MGM soundstages and both have a quaint picture-postcard look. *Mail*, on the other hand, seems more authentic because most of it was filmed on location, specifically on New York's Upper West Side. What Ephron succeeded in capturing was not just the look of the Upper West Side for those who had never been there but also the lifestyle, rhythm, and ambience of a multiethnic, liberal community where intellectuals and young professionals work and live within walking distance of specialty stores and trendy restaurants. Since Kathleen is an independent bookseller and Joe is part of a conglomerate, they inhabit two different worlds, each of which is shown. Hers is very much like the one in *Shop*, where each worker had his or her distinctive personality. Joe's milieu is a corporate stereotype filled with martinis, yachts, and gleeful descriptions of the latest rival to go out of business. It is a world devoid of warmth and feeling, signified by the elaborate but impersonal Fox bookstore, with its coffee bar, deep leather chairs for reading, and uninformed sales staff.

In *Shop, Summertime,* and *Mail,* the male character is the first to learn his correspondent's identity. *Mail* repeats the obligatory rendezvous scene—Kathleen waits for Joe at a restaurant with a book (here, Jane Austen's *Pride and Prejudice*) and a rose. When Joe's colleague looks through the window, as happened in both *Shop* and *Summertime,* and informs Joe that his date is Kathleen, Joe is at first reluctant to enter, but eventually does. And just as Klara's behavior alienated Alfred, and Veronica's Andrew, Kathleen's alienates Joe.

In all the versions it is the male who ends the masquerade. The compassion that Alfred feels for Klara, and Andrew for Veronica, is that of a man for a woman he loves but from whom he has kept the truth. Joe's case is more complex because of Ephron's script, in which Kathleen is forced to close her bookstore. While Joe's philosophy has always been "It's not personal, just business," his feeling for Kathleen becomes personal, starting with sympathy and slowly changing to love. Ephron seems to have preferred the ending of *Summertime* to *Shop,* bringing the film to a close when nature is in bloom, not when it is dying. Unlike *Shop,* which ends on Christmas Eve, *Mail* starts at holiday time and ends in early summer. Joe and Kathleen plan to meet in Riverside Park. Kathleen arrives first; then Joe, with his dog. Joe, rather than quoting from one of his letters, reveals his identity by using his code name when he calls his dog: "Brinkley!"

You've Got Mail, in addition to being a well-acted film, makes intelligent use of the conventions and plot techniques of the romantic comedies of the 1930s and 1940s. "I've seen this before," we often say of a particular movie; quite possibly we have. Twentieth Century-Fox constantly remade its musicals: to see *Wabash Avenue* (1950) is to see *Coney Island* (1943). *Three Blind Mice* (1938) was set to music and became *Moon over Miami* (1941), which was remade as *Three Little Girls in Blue* (1946) and later as *How to Marry a Millionaire* (1953). Often, time and place were changed, but the basic plot remained the same: Raoul Walsh's *Colorado Territory* (1949) was *High Sierra* in a western setting; *I Died a Thousand Times* (1953) was *High Sierra* again, with Jack Palance in the Humphrey Bogart role and the same name, Roy Earle. *High Society* (1956) was George Cukor's *The Philadelphia Story* (1940) with a Cole Porter score; *Against All Odds* (1984) was not only a remake of Jacques Tourneur's *Out of the Past* (1947) but also featured one of the stars from the original, Jane Greer. *The Preacher's Wife* (1996) was *The Bishop's Wife* (1947) from an African American perspective. The classic *Detour* (1946), which starred Tom Neal, was remade as a less-than-classic movie of the same name in 1992; it starred Neal's son, Tom Neal, Jr., and proved that unless filmmakers can enhance, surpass, or at least equal the original—by clarifying ambiguities or bringing out details that were only hinted at initially — they would be best advised to stay with less familiar material.

Musical Associations

Music has two main functions in a film: it either advances or enhances the narrative. When it advances the narrative, it is a plot device and is not subtextual. In Mitchell Leisen's *Lady in the Dark* (1944), a childhood song the heroine tries to remember is the key to her neurosis. In *Coney Island* and the remake, *Wabash Avenue*, a singer (Betty Grable in both films), who is belting out a tender ballad, has to be taught how to sing it properly. We have already seen how in many musicals, working out the melody or the lyrics to a song was the significant moment in the film. There are also songs that drift in and out of the characters' lives, becoming *their* song and playing at appropriately dramatic moments; the classic example is "As Time Goes By" in *Casablanca*. Some movies have a classical score, usually a ballet or an opera, that catapults an unknown to stardom, as in *The Red Shoes* (1948), or notoriety, as in the synthetic opera Salammbô in *Citizen Kane*. Sometimes a piece of music forms the film's climax, achieving an effect that words cannot: "Remember My Forgotten Man" in *Gold Diggers of 1933* (1933); George Gershwin's Concerto in F in *Rhapsody in Blue* (1945); and the title ballet in Vincente Minnelli's *An American in Paris* (1951).

In Stanley Kubrick's final film, *Eyes Wide Shut* (1999), there is a reference to a musical work, not a note of which is heard, but which is doubly important to the plot: the name of the work is both the password to an orgy and the standard for comparing a marriage characterized by sexual fantasy and possible infidelity with one based on love and devotion. Bill Harford (Tom Cruise) is curious about a world other than his own—that of a respectable doctor with a wife and daughter. When a college acquaintance describes a masquerade party where anything goes, Harford is so curious as to ask for the password, which happens to be "Fidelio." *Fidelio* is the name of Beethoven's only opera, about a faithful wife, Leonora, who disguises herself as a young man named Fidelio, hoping to rescue her husband Florestan, a political prisoner, from the dungeon where he is being held. Kubrick expects those familiar with the opera to compare the selfless love of Leonora for Florestan with the self-absorbed Harfords, each of whom is looking for a sexual adventure, real or imaginary.

Eyes Wide Shut is atypical because *"Fidelio"* is a verbal reference, not an aural one. Generally, Kubrick, known for his careful choice of music, wants us to hear his selections and perhaps even forge associations with the films. Anyone familiar with *2001: A Space Odyssey* might find it hard to hear Richard Strauss's *Also Sprach Zarathustra* without thinking of that film; it is also difficult to hear "We'll Meet Again" without recalling the final moments of *Dr. Strangelove*, as World War III gets underway and the bombs start falling.

Thus music can also be functional as subtext, when it deepens the narrative by bringing it to another level of interpretation. Consider, for example, a musical phrase that is repeatedly associated with a character, a mood, or a situation. Such a recurring musical phrase is a **leitmotif.** When a leitmotif identifies a character, it becomes the character's musical signature. Heard in conjunction with the appearance of a character, or the representation of an idea, the leitmotif is inseparable from the individual with whom it is associated or the idea it underscores. It also enjoys a kind of autonomy. A leitmotif can confirm a declaration of love, but it can also recur when the lovers are quarreling or parting, mocking what it had previously celebrated. As part of the character, a leitmotif can remind the audience of what the character is feeling at a particular moment. In Hitchcock's *I Confess* (1952), when Ruth (Anne Baxter) tells her husband she does not love him, we hear the leitmotif that is associated with the man she really loves.

The leitmotif expresses aspects of the character that lie beyond the capacity of language. The nursery tune that opens the 1942 version of *Cat People* is the first indication that the movie is not an ordinary horror film. It is fitting that such a singsong motif should be Irena's signature, for she is emotionally a child.

The leitmotif also concretizes abstract themes. Power is an abstraction, yet Bernard Herrmann, who composed the music for *Citizen Kane*, called one of the leitmotifs of the film "power." As a musical phrase, "power" is no longer abstract because we hear it. The power motif is heard for the first time as the camera ascends the gate of Xanadu, taking us into the pleasure dome and then to Kane's deathbed. But it is a synesthetic experience: we see, feel, and hear power. We watch its calculatingly slow rise, feel the isolation it brings, and hear the grim consequences it holds for those who seek it.

There are all kinds of motifs—love motifs, death motifs, and even love-death, or *Liebestod*, motifs. At the end of *Duel in the Sun*, which has one of the lushest scores ever composed, Pearl Chavez (Jennifer Jones) crawls over sunbaked rocks to die in her lover's arms. As their blood mingles, the love motif heard when they first met seems to surge out of some chasm in the great Southwest to become their *Liebestod*.

For *The Private Life of Sherlock Holmes* (1970), Billy Wilder fashioned a love motif out of a few measures of Miklos Rozsa's Concerto for Violin and Orchestra. It is a bittersweet but dignified theme expressing a yearning that is never to be satisfied—in this case, Holmes's love for Ilse von Hofmannstahl. When Holmes receives the news of Ilse's death, the same theme is heard, no longer an expression of unfulfilled love but of love irretrievably lost.

Music is also capable of forging ethnic and national connections. In the pre–civil rights era, blacks were stereotyped both dramatically and musically. When they appeared on the screen, the original soundtrack often ceased, and a spiritual was heard, presumably because it was more fitting. Even in such a brilliant film as *The Little Foxes*, blacks were given this kind of musical treatment, which not only equated them with their music but also perpetuated the misguided image of southern blacks as passive. Music has the power to reinforce stereotypes: "The Internationale" is associated with Communists; a few gongs with the mysterious East; "Deutschland über alles" with Nazi Germany; a tarantella or "O sole mio" with Italy. Although a few references were made to Job Skeffington's (Claude Rains) being Jewish in *Mr. Skeffington*, a leitmotif vaguely based on traditional Jewish melodies affirmed it. Music can evoke certain associations, but it should be used with care so as not to create caricatures or stereotypes.

During World War II, movie music programmed its audiences to patriotism. People not only saw flag-wavers; they also heard Old Glory hymned on the soundtrack. Planes streamed across the sky to the accompaniment of "Wild Blue Yonder," which also doubled as death music for the marines who went off to be executed by the Japanese at the end of *The Purple Heart* (1944). To evoke American values, Frank Capra frequently incorporated typical American songs like "Red River Valley" and "Buffalo Gals" into his films.

Using classical music that was written centuries ago is a special case, since it is music that was not composed for a specific film. Yet the media have made extensive use of classical music. In the 1930s and 1940s, when radio was a mass medium, listeners were exposed to classical music without being aware of it. Rossini's *William Tell* Overture ushered in *The Lone Ranger*; Sibelius's "Valse Triste" introduced *I Love a Mystery*; Prokofiev's March from *Love for Three Oranges* was the theme of *The FBI in Peace and War*; the second movement of César Franck's Symphony in D Minor heralded the opening of *Quiet, Please*. Thus, associations were created between the radio programs and their introductions, which were the equivalents of musical signatures.

Movies used classical music in the same way. Even if many moviegoers could not identify Rachmaninoff's Second Piano Concerto, they knew it as background music in *Brief Encounter* (1946). In fact, for people who know the film, the concerto has such indelible associations that it never fails to evoke a dingy railroad station where two married people, on the verge of committing adultery, choose to say goodbye and never meet again.

Thus, the Rachmaninoff Second Piano Concerto took on associations of extramarital love, and it was used for that purpose in *September Affair*, where it forms the background for a story of adultery. Like any venerable device, the Rachmaninoff Second ended up being parodied; still, parody attests to its associations. In *The Seven Year Itch*, in which a husband whose wife is away for the summer imagines himself seducing the woman upstairs, Billy Wilder parodies the tradition. In a fantasy sequence, the husband fancies that he's a great pianist, sitting down at the piano and breaking into the concerto to impress his potential conquest.

Since classical music is added to a film rather than being composed for it, it may already have produced certain associations within us; the film may either reinforce those associations or change them, so that thereafter we associate the music only with the movie. Certainly, it is difficult to disassociate the Rachmaninoff Second from *Brief Encounter* and, in a totally different way, from *The Seven Year Itch*. Similarly, anyone who has seen *Shine* (1996), based on the life of the gifted but troubled pianist David Helfgott, will always associate the Rachmaninoff Third, Helfgott's signature concerto, with the film. This type of association should not be surprising, since few Lone Ranger fans can separate the *William Tell* Overture from the program.

Wagner's music occupies a peculiar place in the American film. There has always been a connection between Wagner and the Third Reich. Wagner was said to be Hitler's favorite composer; in fact, Hitler identified with Wagner's Siegfried and maintained that to understand National Socialism (Nazism) one first had to understand Wagner. To the Hollywood of the 1940s, then, Wagner was the composer of the Third Reich: it is difficult to recall a movie in which Nazism was not orchestrated with a Wagnerian motif. In *Brute Force* (1947), Munsey (Hume Cronyn), a prison captain, tortures an inmate to the Venusberg music from Wagner's Tannhäuser. Munsey performs a kind of ritual before the torture, strutting around with his chest sucked in beneath a skintight undershirt. That the captain is a homoerotic sadist is evident in the film, but Wagner's music, with its historical and erotic associations, characterizes him even further. Music unites his lust for power and his need for sex, neither of which he can achieve except through the degradation of others.

Although *Apocalypse Now* deals with America's tragic involvement in Vietnam, the film uses Wagner in much the same way it is used in *Brute Force*: as a symbol of sexual energy channeled into militarism. The "Ride of the Valkyries," from Wagner's *Die Walküre*, orchestrates the parade-of-the-helicopters sequence. Had the same music been used in a World War II movie in which bombs rained down on German cities, American audiences would have applauded; in light of the Vietnam debacle, however, "The Ride of the Valkyries" is accusatory rather than nationalistic. It is as if Coppola were accusing America of emulating Nazi Germany by invoking the spirit of Wagner to justify war.

The use of Wagner's music in *Apocalypse Now* is ironic. So is the use of Bach's in *The Silence of the Lambs*, in which Hannibal Lecter, a killer who cannibalizes his victims, has a great fondness for Bach's Goldberg Variations. Irony is not the easiest of devices to manipulate, however. It can backfire, becoming blatant, as happens in *The Night Porter* (1974) when two inmates in a Nazi concentration camp perform an act of sodomy to the music of Mozart's *The Magic Flute*. What should have been a devastating moment becomes merely appalling. Far more intelligent is Ingmar Bergman's use of Bach in *Through a Glass, Darkly* (1961) when a schizophrenic daughter discovers that her father is using her sickness as material for a novel. The nobility of the music underscores the father's ignoble intentions.

In some films, classical music constitutes the entire subtext. It is not just a question of repeating motifs but of using music — either one work or

Karin (Harriet Andersson) in *Through a Glass, Darkly* (Ingmar Bergman, 1961) when she discovers that her father is using her schizophrenia for his novel. At that moment, the haunting opening of Bach's Suite No. 2 in D Minor for violoncello is heard. *(Courtesy MOMA/FSA and Janus Films)*

several works—from beginning to end. What happens to music in Stanley Kubrick's *A Clockwork Orange* (1971) is what has happened to society. The social order gives way as thugs and disenchanted youths, leather boys and loafers become the citizens of the future. There is a corresponding degeneration of music; it becomes estranged from art, perverted, capable of producing effects that its composers never intended.

One of the most innocent songs ever written is "Singin' in the Rain," which brings to mind Gene Kelly sloshing around without missing a tap in the classic 1952 musical of the same name. It is hardly the kind of song we would associate with violence, yet in *A Clockwork Orange* Alex does a soft-shoe to it while brutalizing a writer and his wife.

Rimsky-Korsakov's *Scheherazade* is an exotic piece of music, lush and sensuous. Yet this is the music that is heard when Alex imagines himself as a Roman centurion lashing Christ on his way to Calvary. *Scheherazade* is one of the most pleasurable compositions ever written, as Alex would be the first to admit. But the pleasure we receive from it is clearly not his.

Alex is also a lover of Beethoven's Ninth Symphony, with its ringing affirmation of humanity in the last movement. He knows that such sublime music can only be the result of intense suffering. While Alex listens to it, on one occasion masturbating to it, Kubrick cuts to various shots of Christ, because Alex associates Christ with suffering and suffering with music. Therefore the sublimity of the music inspires the hearer to make others suffer. "Preposterous!" we say; or, if this is so, how can the love of music be the mark of a cultivated person? It would be better to raze the concert halls and ban recordings. But in Alex's world, where good and evil have lost their meaning as moral terms, music has no value except the one that is placed on it. In such a society, it makes no difference whether one meditates to Beethoven's music or masturbates to it. Yet Alex is not alone in misusing the classics; his elders have discovered an equally perverted use for the Beethoven Ninth. During his rehabilitation, Alex is forced to watch Nazi films while the last movement of the Ninth is played electronically.

While *A Clockwork Orange* draws on the works of several composers for its musical associations, *Moonstruck* draws on one: Puccini's opera *La Bohème*. In *La Bohème*, Mimi meets Rodolpho and within minutes they are pouring out their love in a soaring duet. In *Moonstruck*, Loretta (Cher) no sooner meets her fiancé's brother than he whisks her off to bed to the music of *La Bohème*, his favorite opera. Later, he takes her to the Metropolitan Opera House to see it. *Moonstruck* celebrates the passion that brings men and women together, using opera as a point of departure, where the characters experience such powerful emotions that they cannot express them except through song.

Pretty Woman (1990) uses another popular opera, Verdi's *La Traviata*, as a frame of reference. A wealthy entrepreneur (Richard Gere) takes a prostitute (Julia Roberts), with whom he has become involved, to a performance of *La Traviata*. Although she has never seen an opera before, she immediately identifies with the character of Violetta, who belongs to the same profession and also suffers abuse at the hands of men. The film's emotional climax is believable within an operatic context; *Pretty Woman* rewrites the tragic ending of *La Traviata* and allows two people from totally different worlds to live, we are left to assume, happily ever after.

Close Encounters of the Third Kind (1977) illustrates a highly sophisticated use of music. Roy (Richard Dreyfuss), with whom aliens are communicating telepathically, is a mystery to his wife and children. A boy at heart, Roy wants to take his family to see a revival of Disney's *Pinocchio* (1940), in which they profess to have no interest. In a Spielberg film, a movie reference should never be ignored. During the end credits, John Williams's brilliant score segues into "When You Wish upon a Star" from *Pinocchio*, placing *Close Encounters* within a special context. Roy has gotten his wish: he has become a space cadet and will enjoy the experience of interplanetary travel. But more important, like *Pinocchio*, who wanted to be a real boy rather than a puppet, Roy will remain, spiritually, a child—indifferent to time, which, like a puppeteer, controls human lives. It is significant that the humans, who had been declared missing and return at the end of the film, look the same as they did when the aliens abducted them. Roy will be leaving a world dominated by time for one in which time, as we know it, has no meaning.

A film has an outer and an inner world, a text and a subtext or, if you prefer, a narrative and an infranarrative. Beneath the text woven by the filmmaker's creativity and technology is the subtext, with its network of associations and implications that, when understood, broaden our knowledge of the film. Because what lies beneath the surface is usually more intriguing than what lies above it, one may be tempted to proceed to the subtext before the text is understood. However, just as in literature a work's symbolic level cannot be appreciated before its literal level is clear, so, too, in film the narrative must be grasped before it can be transcended. Only then are we free to seek out the associations—mythic, iconic or visual, historical, musical—that provide access to the film's inner world.

NOTES

1. W. Y. Tindall, *James Joyce* (New York: Grove Press, 1960), 102.
2. As quoted in W. Y. Tindall, *A Reader's Guide to James Joyce* (New York: Noonday Press, 1959), 129.
3. Parker Tyler, *Magic and Myth of the Movies* (New York: Simon & Schuster, 1970), xviii.
4. Lillian Feder, *Ancient Myth in Modern Poetry* (Princeton: Princeton University Press, 1971), 10–11.
5. Donald Richie, *George Stevens: An American Romantic* (New York: Museum of Modern Art, 1970), 62.
6. Michael T. Marsden, "Savior in the Saddle: The Sagebrush Testament," in *Focus on the Western*, ed. Jack Nachbar (Englewood Cliffs, N.J.: Prentice-Hall, 1974), 97.
7. André Bazin, "The Evolution of the Western," in *What Is Cinema?*, vol. 2, trans. Hugh Gray (Berkeley: University of California Press, 1971), 152.
8. Pauline Kael, "Introduction," Bernardo Bertolucci's *Last Tango in Paris: The Screenplay* (New York: Dell, 1973), 17.

CHAPTER 7

The Film Director

If film is a collaborative art, no single person should get credit for a particular movie. Yet it is standard practice to speak of "John Ford's *Stagecoach*" or "Alfred Hitchcock's *Psycho*," or to suggest that directors enjoy a preeminence that writers do not by placing their names beside their films: *Mystic River* (2003) is a "film by Clint Eastwood"; *The Missing* (2003) is "a Ron Howard film." The elevation of the director to the rank of author is an outgrowth of **auteurism,** a theory of filmmaking in which the director is considered the primary creative force behind a film.

Although auteurism is a controversial idea, it represents another way in which audiences can develop a deeper appreciation for film. No film by one director is exactly the same as another, but understanding the particular style or common themes that a director uses can give the audience a richer viewing experience.

Auteurism

When the *New York Times* lists film revivals, the director's name precedes the film's title, just as an author's name precedes the title of his or her book.

Certain film critics, like Andrew Sarris and David Denby, still designate films that way; many film historians prefer to place the director's name and release date in parentheses after the film. In the traditional main title, the director's name is the last credit, but it is also the one audiences see before the film begins—a rather subtle way of suggesting what has always been known in the industry: movies are a director's medium. Certainly, movie directors receive a unique form of recognition.

Directors are also accorded retrospectives even though others may have written the scripts of the films for which they are being honored. Then why "John Ford's *Stagecoach*" and not "screenwriter Dudley Nichols's *Stagecoach*"? The answer lies in auteurism.

The Beginnings of Auteurism

During the German occupation of France in World War II, the French were denied American movies, but upon the end of the war they rediscovered the greatness of the American cinema. The movies Americans often took for granted, the French took seriously. André Bazin wrote appreciatively of William Wyler and Orson Welles; Jean-Luc Godard saw more in the B-movies of Monogram Studios than did the American kids who saw them as the second half of double bills at their neighborhood theaters.* The rediscovery of American films by the French led to a reconsideration of the director as artist. What impressed the French was the fact that Hollywood directors could be—and frequently were—handed a screenplay, a cast, and a crew (none of which they had personally selected) and still manage to leave the stamp of their personality on the films.

In 1951 André Bazin and Jacques Doniol-Valcroze began publication of *Cahiers du cinéma*, a journal that evolved into a critical forum for young film enthusiasts such as Jean-Luc Godard, François Truffaut, Eric Rohmer, and Claude Chabrol, who expressed themselves in its pages and later went on to become directors. *Cahiers du cinéma* had the reputation of a maverick; it was often pretentious and erratic in its preference for one director over another. Still, whatever one may think of the journal and the eccentric taste of its writers, it moved directors from the background to the foreground, establishing them as creators instead of studio orderlies.

For the first three years of its existence, *Cahiers du cinéma* had no real editorial policy; in 1954 Truffaut provided it with one in his famous essay "*Une certaine tendance du cinéma français*," which attacked classic French cinema for preferring literary scripts to shooting scripts, adaptations to original

---

*Monogram made low-budget movies and "series pictures" (*The Bowery Boys, Charlie Chan, Bomba the Jungle Boy*, the *Cisco Kid*). The Monogram product was undistinguished except for an occasional melodrama like *Suspense* (1946) or *The Gangster* (1947).

screenplays, studio sets to actual locations, and a team of specialists to a single individual. Truffaut argued for "a cinema of auteurs"; and so it was that *auteur*, the French word for "author," entered the critical vocabulary of film.

Cahiers du cinéma now had a policy: *la politique des auteurs*, "the policy of authors," which has had various interpretations, the most common one being that the journal was partial to certain directors, such as Orson Welles, Alfred Hitchcock, and Jean Renoir, and indifferent to others, such as John Huston, René Clair, and René Clément. Another interpretation was that *Cahiers du cinéma*'s favored directors were infallible and incapable of making bad films. Bazin corrected this misconception in 1957, when he pointed out what should have been obvious: a great director can make a dud, and a mediocre director can occasionally make a classic. Essentially, Bazin endorsed the policy of ranking directors, although he was often disturbed by the indiscriminate taste of some of his writers. Bazin summed up his position in the equation: author + subject = work.

That equation was adopted as the critical principle of Andrew Sarris, through whom auteurism entered America. In his essay "Notes on the *Auteur* Theory in 1962,"[1] Sarris defended the ranking of directors as an extension of a policy that has always prevailed in the arts. We rank Shakespeare over Ben Jonson, Beethoven over Brahms, Mozart's *Don Giovanni* over Beethoven's *Fidelio*. It was inevitable that Sarris would establish a ranking order of his own. In his book *The American Cinema*, he divided American directors into eleven categories, including the "Pantheon," such as Charles Chaplin, John Ford, D. W. Griffith, Howard Hawks, Alfred Hitchcock, and Orson Welles; "the Far Side of Paradise," such as Robert Aldrich, Frank Capra, Samuel Fuller, and Vincente Minnelli; "Expressive Esoterica," such as Tay Garnett, Arthur Penn, and Edgar G. Ulmer; and "Less Than Meets the Eye," such as John Huston, Elia Kazan, and William Wyler. Despite the historical importance of *The American Cinema*, it is the kind of book that requires periodic revision. The current critical estimate of Huston and Wyler, for example, suggests that there is more to each of them than met Sarris's eye.

Sarris reduced the auteur theory, which is how *la politique des auteurs* came to be known in America, to three principles: (1) an auteur is technically competent; (2) an auteur has a personality that manifests itself in recurring stylistic traits that become his or her signature; and (3) an auteur's films exhibit a tension between the auteur's personality and his or her material—that is, there are aspects of an auteur's personality that will seep into the films, aspects that may not be readily discernible but may come out when a number of the auteur's films are studied and analyzed. Thus Hitchcock's ambivalence toward women, especially blondes, is not immediately evident; yet after analyzing such films as *The 39 Steps* (1935), *Saboteur*, *Psycho*, and *The Birds*, we see that while blondes held a certain fascination for him, he often subjected them to various forms of degradation—being handcuffed to a man, being slashed to death in a shower, having their faces pecked by attacking birds.

On the basis of Sarris's criteria, it is possible to consider certain directors—admittedly, few—as auteurs or surrogate authors of their films. Film is not the only medium in which auteurism is practiced, however; forms of auteurism exist in all the performing arts. A ballet lover may refer to Nureyev's *Romeo and Juliet* as opposed to another dancer's, emphasizing not Prokofiev's score but its interpreter. A theatergoer who remembers Ralph Fiennes's Hamlet is not remembering Shakespeare's play but its interpretation by a particular actor. Plays are also sometimes thought of in terms of the acting companies that produced them. Thus one theatergoer might ask another, "Did you see the Abbey's *Juno and the Paycock*?," meaning not Sean O'Casey's play but its production by Dublin's Abbey Theatre. Similarly, moviegoers might ask, "Did you ever see Mel Gibson's Hamlet?," meaning Gibson's interpretation of Hamlet in Franco Zeffirelli's 1990 film version; or they might ask, "How would you rank Kenneth Branagh's *Hamlet* (1996) in comparison with Laurence Olivier's *Hamlet* (1948)?" These moviegoers are referring to two very different things: they are talking about *Hamlet* as interpreted by two different directors, Kenneth Branagh and Laurence Olivier, both of whom also played the title character in their respective film versions.

A symphony orchestra provides another analogy. If the brass section is mediocre, if the woodwinds fail to come in on time, if the horns sound flat, the conductor shoulders the blame. Critics may berate the conductor who "led a sluggish performance of César Franck's Symphony in D Minor" or "who failed to elevate the orchestra to the heights the music demanded." When Leonard Bernstein conducted a Mahler symphony, it was no longer Mahler's symphony but Bernstein's. Bernstein took Mahler's work and attempted to realize the composer's intentions and communicate them to the orchestra. If Bernstein succeeded, he was praised; if he didn't, he was criticized. Similarly, if a director is successful at blending the elements that make up a film into an organic whole that realizes the script's intent, he or she is commended; if not, the director is criticized for being unable to achieve the necessary integration.

However, just as every conductor is not a Leonard Bernstein, every director is not an Alfred Hitchcock. Hitchcock, then, clearly fulfills the criteria of the auteur: when we designate *Psycho* as "Hitchcock's *Psycho*," we mean that Hitchcock has been successful at integrating the efforts of the writer, the cast, and the crew into a reflection of his vision of the material.

The Debate over Auteurism

Even though some film scholars agree that there is such a thing as an Alfred Hitchcock film and therefore that there are Hitchcockian elements in the films of others, many would argue against establishing auteurism as a general theory of film, on grounds that the genesis of a film is often too complex to be attributed to a single person, that some films bear the stamp of their studios more than that of any individual, and that special effects films illustrate the limitations of auteurism.

Some films are the result of a producer's rather than a director's conception. Victor Fleming is credited as the director of *Gone with the Wind* (although George Cukor and Sam Wood also had a hand in the direction), yet the film was the brainchild of the producer David O. Selznick; if anything, then, it might be called a David O. Selznick film. The disaster films *The Poseidon Adventure* (1972) and *The Towering Inferno* (1975) are associated with the producer, Irwin Allen, not with the directors, Ronald Neame and John Guillermin, respectively. Although Val Lewton never directed a single film, he left his mark on everything he produced at RKO, including *Cat People*, *I Walked with a Zombie*, *The Curse of the Cat People* (1944), and others. As a result, we think of *Cat People* primarily as a Val Lewton film and only secondarily as Jacques Tourneur's. Michael Bay may have directed *Pearl Harbor*, but the film would never have been made had it not been for producer Jerry Bruckheimer's commitment to the project.

If there is any similarity between *Poltergeist* (1982) and *E. T.*, it is because Steven Spielberg, who directed *E. T.*, coauthored and produced *Poltergeist* even though he did not direct it. Directed by Tobe Hooper, *Poltergeist* bears the Spielberg signature and is imbued with the same childlike innocence that characterizes *E. T.* If *Batteries Not Included* (1987), in which aliens come to the aid of tenants whom a greedy developer is pressuring into moving, sounds like Spielberg again, it is because the film is a Spielberg production, even though it was directed by Matthew Robbins.

Certain films, especially those made when the studios were at their peak between 1930 and 1960, bear the stamp of their studios more than that of any individual and are therefore thought of as "MGM movies" or "Warner Bros. movies." *Singin' in the Rain* is clearly an MGM musical, specifically a musical that came from Arthur Freed's production unit at MGM. If *Singin' in the Rain* is compared with other Arthur Freed productions, such as *Easter Parade* (1948), *On the Town* (1949), and *An American in Paris*, it is clear that they have something in common: the musical numbers are integrated with the action. While *Singin' in the Rain* was directed by Stanley Donen and Gene Kelly, film historians consider it an MGM musical or an Arthur Freed production, not a Donen-Kelly film.

Films that involve special effects illustrate the limitations of auteurism. When David Denby and Terrence Rafferty reviewed *Who Framed Roger Rabbit* in *New York* magazine and *The New Yorker*, respectively, each referred to "Robert Zemeckis's *Who Framed Roger Rabbit*." Yet Zemeckis was not responsible for the animation; the animation director Richard Williams and his staff were. Furthermore, the film was a cooperative venture between Disney's Touchstone Pictures and Steven Spielberg's Amblin Entertainment. Spielberg is not the kind of producer who remains aloof from a production; in fact, he had certain ideas about how the cartoon figures should look (for example, he wanted Roger's mouth to resemble Thumper's in *Bambi* [1942]). The answer to the question "Who framed Roger Rabbit?" is easy. The answer to the question "Who made *Who Framed Roger Rabbit?*" is not.

For these reasons, not every director can be considered an auteur; actually, comparatively few can. The auteurs are directors whose work is studied in film courses and who have become the subjects of books, articles, and retrospectives. These directors do not necessarily write their own scripts: Woody Allen generally does, but John Ford never did. There have also been directors who worked within the studio system and still made films that were their own. William Wyler made some of his best movies for Samuel Goldwyn, such as *Dead End* and *Wuthering Heights* (1939). Shortly before Pearl Harbor, Wyler was hired by MGM to direct *Mrs. Miniver*, which dramatized the impact of World War II on a typical British family. In one sense, *Mrs. Miniver* is an MGM film; it was made by a specific studio because the head of that studio, Louis B. Mayer, believed in the "family film." However, Wyler was able to make it a William Wyler film. Wyler always tried to encompass as much as he could in a single shot, thus minimizing cutting. *Mrs. Miniver* is filled with such shots: Kay Miniver sitting on the bed while her husband is off in the dressing room; the Minivers seated at the dinner table while their son is seen talking on the phone in the alcove; Kay standing on the bridge with the station master below her and water behind him.

Directors who are taught, written about, and honored with retrospectives and tributes have several things in common: their films repeat favorite themes in the same or different genres, they allude to their earlier films, they borrow from the films of others, and they illustrate the collaborative nature of the medium because such directors tend to work regularly with the same—or similar—talent (writer, actors, cinematographer, editor) in a succession of films.

Collaboration

A director might collaborate with a screenwriter, a cinematographer, a composer, an actor, an editor, a producer, or a studio.

Sometimes a director will have the same screenwriter for several movies; undoubtedly, those movies will have certain features in common. Joan Harrison worked on the scripts for Hitchcock's *Rebecca*, *Foreign Correspondent* (1940), *Suspicion*, and *Saboteur*, in all of which the wrong person was under suspicion. Billy Wilder and Charles Brackett coauthored the scripts for three Mitchell Leisen films: *Midnight*; *Arise, My Love*; and *Hold Back the Dawn* (1941). All three entail some form of deception.

Historically, the most famous collaboration between a director and a cinematographer was that between D. W. Griffith and Billy Bitzer. Other creative director-cinematographer collaborations have been between Erich von Stroheim and William Daniels on *Blind Husbands* (1918), *Foolish Wives*

(1921), *Greed* (1924), and *The Merry Widow* (1925); Josef von Sternberg and Lee Garmes on *Morocco* (1930), *Dishonored* (1931), and *Shanghai Express* (1932); Ingmar Bergman and Gunnar Fischer on *Smiles of a Summer Night* (1955), *The Seventh Seal*, and *Wild Strawberries*.

Examples of collaboration between a director and a composer include John Ford and Alfred Newman on *Arrowsmith* (1931), *The Hurricane* (1937), *The Grapes of Wrath*, and *How Green Was My Valley*; Federico Fellini and Nino Rota on *La strada* (1954), *La dolce vita* (1960), *8 1/2* (1963), and *Juliet of the Spirits*; Hitchcock and Bernard Herrmann on *The Wrong Man*, *Vertigo*, *Psycho*, and *Marnie*; Spielberg and John Williams on *Jaws* (1975), *Close Encounters of the Third Kind*, *Raiders of the Lost Ark*, *E.T.: The Extra-Terrestrial*, *Empire of the Sun*, *Indiana Jones and the Last Crusade*, *Jurassic Park*, *Schindler's List*, *A.I. Artificial Intelligence*, *Minority Report*, and *The Terminal* (2004).

Notable collaborations between a director and an actor or actors are John Huston and Humphrey Bogart on *The Maltese Falcon* (1941), *Across the Pacific* (1942), *Treasure of the Sierra Madre* (1948), *Key Largo* (1948), and *The African Queen* (1951); von Sternberg and Marlene Dietrich on *The Blue Angel*, *Morocco*, *Dishonored*, *Shanghai Express*, and *Blonde Venus* (1932); George Cukor and Katharine Hepburn on *A Bill of Divorcement* (1932), *Little Women* (1933), *Sylvia Scarlett* (1935), *Holiday* (1938), *The Philadelphia Story*, *Keeper of the Flame* (1943), *Adam's Rib* (1949), *Pat and Mike* (1952), and the TV movies *Love Among the Ruins* (1975) and *The Corn Is Green* (1979); Truffaut and Jean-Pierre Léaud on *The 400 Blows*, *Stolen Kisses* (1968), *Bed and Board* (1970), and *Day for Night* (1973); Bergman and Liv Ullman on *Persona* (1966), *Hour of the Wolf* (1968), *The Shame* (1968), *A Passion of Anna* (1969), *Scenes from a Marriage* (1973), and *Face to Face* (1976); Billy Wilder and Jack Lemmon on *Some Like It Hot*, *The Apartment* (1960), *Irma la Douce* (1963), *The Fortune Cookie* (1966), *Avanti!* (1972), *The Front Page* (1974), and *Buddy Buddy* (1981). John Ford had a stock company that consisted of Ward Bond, Victor McLaglen, John Wayne, Maureen O'Hara, and Ben Johnson. Woody Allen and Mia Farrow worked together on *Broadway Danny Rose* (1984), *The Purple Rose of Cairo*, *Hannah and Her Sisters*, *Radio Days*, *September* (1987), *Another Woman* (1988), *Crimes and Misdemeanors* (1989), *Shadows and Fog* (1992), and *Husbands and Wives* (1992); Martin Scorsese and Robert De Niro collaborated on *Mean Streets* (1973), *Taxi Driver, New York, New York, Raging Bull, The King of Comedy* (1983), *Good-Fellas, Cape Fear*, and *Casino* (1995).

Thelma Schoonmaker has edited a number of Martin Scorsese's films, including *Raging Bull*, *The King of Comedy*, *The Color of Money* (1986), *The Last Temptation of Christ*, *GoodFellas, The Age of Innocence, Casino, Kundun*, and *Gangs of New York*. Arthur Schmidt did the same for Robert Zemeckis in *Back to the Future* (1985), *Back to the Future Part II* (1989), *Back to the Future Part III* (1990), *Death Becomes Her* (1992), *Forrest Gump, Contact* (1997), *What Lies Beneath* (2000), and *Cast Away* (2000). Woody Allen relied heavily on editor Susan E. Morse for a number of films, including *Manhattan, Stardust*

Billy Wilder with Jack Lemmon, who appeared in six Wilder films. (*Courtesy Margaret Herrick Library of the Academy of Motion Picture Arts and Sciences*)

Memories (1980), *A Midsummer Night's Sex Comedy* (1982), *Zelig* (1983), *Broadway Danny Rose, The Purple Rose of Cairo, Hannah and Her Sisters, Radio Days, September, Another Woman, Crimes and Misdemeanors, Shadows and Fog, Husbands and Wives, Manhattan Murder Mystery, Bullets over Broadway* (1994), *Mighty Aphrodite* (1995), *Everyone Says I Love You, Deconstructing Harry* (1997), and *Celebrity* (1998). When that collaboration ended, Allen found a new editor, Alisa Lepselter, for *Sweet and Lowdown* (1999), *Small Time Crooks* (2000), *Hollywood Ending,* and *Anything Else* (2003).

The best examples of a collaboration between a director and a producer are Wyler and Samuel Goldwyn on *Dead End, Wuthering Heights, The Westerner* (1940), *The Little Foxes,* and *The Best Years of Our Lives* (1946); Jacques Tourneur, Robert Wise, and Mark Robson, who directed the films Val Lewton produced for RKO; William Dieterle and Hal B. Wallis at Paramount, who made *The Searching Wind* (1946), *The Accused, Rope of Sand* (1949), *Paid in Full* (1950), *Dark City* (1950), and *Red Mountain* (1951); and Arthur Freed, who had his own musical unit at MGM, and Vincente Minnelli, who worked together on *Meet Me in St. Louis, Yolanda and the Thief* (1945), *The Pirate* (1948), *An American in Paris, The Band Wagon, Kismet* (1955), and *Gigi* (1958). Similarly, Lawrence Gordon produced seven of Walter Hill's films, including *Hard Times* (1975), *The Driver* (1978), *The Warriors* (1979), *48 Hours* (1982), and *Brewster's Millions* (1985). Until its dissolution in 2001, the producer-director team of Jean Doumanian and Woody Allen was one of the most productive in contemporary Hollywood: *Bullets over Broadway, Mighty Aphrodite, Everyone Says I Love You, Deconstructing Harry, Celebrity, Sweet and Lowdown,* and *Small Time Crooks.*

Directors who were identified with particular studios include Frank Capra and Columbia, Ernst Lubitsch and Paramount, Preston Sturges and Paramount, Raoul Walsh and Warner Bros., and Vincente Minnelli and MGM. Paramount was synonymous with sophisticated comedy during the 1930s and 1940s, and it was such directors as Lubitsch, Sturges, and, to a lesser extent, Leisen who gave the studio that reputation. Lubitsch could do more with the closing of a bedroom door than most directors could by keeping it open. In corporate Hollywood, director-studio relationships are short-lived. Until he became a cofounder of DreamWorksSKG, Steven Spielberg enjoyed a mutually beneficial relationship with Universal, where his production company, Amblin Entertainment, was based. Spielberg's Universal films include *The Sugarland Express* (1974), *Jaws, E. T.: The Extra-Terrestrial, Raiders of the Lost Ark, Jurassic Park, Schindler's List*, and *The Lost World: Jurassic Park* (1997).

Variety

A great director need not have a wide repertoire of themes; there is a difference between a varied body of work and a varied number of themes. The same themes can recur within that body of work, repeated or modified to fit a particular type of film. Billy Wilder's films, for example, center around two major themes: deception in the forms of disguise, fraud, and masquerade; and the impact of one social or political order on another—capitalism and communism, rich and poor, youth and age. Even the scripts that he and Charles Brackett wrote before he began directing reflect these themes: the female commissar of Ernst Lubitsch's *Ninotchka* (1939), who comes in contact with capitalism and falls under its spell; the chorus girl of *Midnight*, who impersonates a countess; the female reporter of *Arise, My Love*, who rescues a man from prison by pretending to be his wife; the gigolo of *Hold Back the Dawn*, who feigns love in order to become an American citizen; the college professors of Howard Hawks's *Ball of Fire*, who find themselves learning slang from a stripper.

Then there are the films that Wilder directed himself:

The Major and the Minor (1942): A woman disguises herself as a twelve-year-old in order to purchase a train ticket at half price.

Five Graves to Cairo (1943): A British officer impersonates a lame servant in a desert hotel.

Double Indemnity (1944): An insurance agent tricks a man into signing a policy with a double-indemnity clause; the agent and the client's wife then conspire to kill her husband and collect on the policy; the agent briefly poses as her husband on board a train.

The Lost Weekend (1945): An alcoholic is continually devising ways to conceal his bottle.

The Emperor Waltz (1948): An Austrian countess meets an American phonograph salesman (a "two social orders" film).

A Foreign Affair (1948): An army captain in postwar Berlin tries to conceal his relationship with a nightclub singer from a visiting congresswoman.

Sunset Boulevard (1950): An aging silent star deludes herself into thinking that she can make a comeback as Salome; her kept man conceals his status from his girlfriend.

In *The Major and the Minor* (1942), a career woman (Ginger Rogers) disguised herself as a twelve-year-old in order to ride to her home in Iowa for half fare. (*Courtesy Margaret Herrick Library of the Academy of Motion Picture Arts and Sciences*)

The Big Carnival (*Ace in the Hole*) 1951: A reporter deceives the victim of a cave-in into believing he is the victim's friend.

Stalag 17 (1953): An informer infiltrates a POW camp.

Sabrina (1954): A rich young man courts a chauffeur's daughter (a "two orders" film).

The Seven Year Itch (1955): A summer bachelor plays at being Don Juan.

The Spirit of St. Louis (1957): An atypical Wilder film, which depicts Lindbergh's flight across the Atlantic.

Love in the Afternoon (1957): A May-December romance develops between an older man and a young woman whose father is a detective.

Witness for the Prosecution (1957): A woman tricks a noted barrister into thinking she is a cockney.

Some Like It Hot (1959): Two musicians dress up as women; a millionaire (male) falls in love with one of the disguised men.

The Apartment (1960): A woman with a checkered past masquerades as a virgin.

One, Two, Three (1961): An American Coca-Cola executive and a radical East Berliner clash ideologically.

Irma la Douce (1963): To keep a prostitute from sharing her favors with others, her lover resorts to disguise.

Audrey Hepburn as Sabrina and Humphrey Bogart as Linus in *Sabrina* (1954). (*Courtesy Paramount Pictures and MOMA/FSA*)

Kiss Me, Stupid (1964): A single female bartender impersonates a married woman; a wife allows her songwriter-husband to think his song succeeded on its own merits although it became a hit because she spent the night with a famous pop singer.

The Fortune Cookie (1966): A TV cameraman is persuaded by his brother-in-law to sue for nonexistent injuries.

The Private Life of Sherlock Holmes (1970): Deception is implicit in any treatment of Holmes.

Avanti! (1972): A married man and the daughter of his late father's mistress arrange to have a yearly rendezvous in Italy, repeating the deception their parents (his father, her mother) had practiced until their death.

The Front Page (1974): An editor will do anything to get his star reporter back, even resort to a lie that also happens to be one of the most famous curtain lines in American theater: "The son of a bitch stole my watch."

Fedora (1979): An international movie star who has been facially disfigured passes her daughter off as herself.

Buddy Buddy (1981): To prevent himself from being unmasked, a hit man attempts to save a television censor from suicide.

Variety is achieved more through genre than through theme. Wilder's theme of deception and disguise manifests itself in farce (*The Major and the Minor, Some Like It Hot, Irma la Douce*), romantic comedy (*Sabrina, Love in the Afternoon, Avanti!*), political comedy (*A Foreign Affair, One, Two, Three*), social comedy (*The Apartment, The Fortune Cookie*), social realism (*The Lost Weekend, The Big Carnival*), espionage and wartime melodrama (*Five Graves to Cairo, Stalag 17*), courtroom melodrama (*Witness for the Prosecution*), gothic melodrama (*Sunset Boulevard*), period pieces (*The Emperor Waltz, The Private Life of Sherlock Holmes*), and film noir (*Double Indemnity*).

Wilder's films are derived from several sources: *The Lost Weekend* and *Love in the Afternoon* are based on novels; *Stalag 17, Sabrina, The Seven Year Itch, Avanti!, One, Two, Three, Irma la Douce*, and *Kiss Me, Stupid* are adapted from plays; *The Emperor Waltz, Sunset Boulevard, The Big Carnival, The Apartment, The Fortune Cookie*, and *The Private Life of Sherlock Holmes* are based on original screenplays; *Buddy Buddy* is a reworking of a much better French film known in English as *A Pain in the A*— (1974).

Repetition

Great directors may use favorite themes as motifs within their movies. Thus the deception/disguise theme recurs as various motifs in Wilder's movies. He uses adultery in *Double Indemnity, The Seven Year Itch, Love in the Afternoon, The Apartment, Kiss Me, Stupid*, and *Avanti!* Insurance fraud is a motif in *Double Indemnity* and *The Fortune Cookie*. Women physically alter their appearance in *The Major and the Minor, Witness for the Prosecution*, and *Fedora*. Men physically alter their appearance in *Some Like It Hot* and *Irma la Douce*. A woman deceives the man she loves in *The Major and the Minor, The Apartment, Kiss Me, Stupid*, and *The Private Life of Sherlock Holmes*. A man deceives the woman he loves in *The Seven Year Itch, Some Like It Hot*, and *Irma la Douce*. Men deceive each other in *Five Graves to Cairo, Double Indemnity, The Lost Weekend, The Big Carnival* [*Ace in the Hole*], *The Fortune Cookie*, and *Buddy Buddy*.

In the films that use the "two orders" theme one can find similar motifs. Distinctions of class are demonstrated by the countess and the commoner in *The Emperor Waltz*, and by the commoner (female) and the privileged (male) in *Sabrina*. Distinctions of age appear between a young woman and an older man in *Sabrina, Love in the Afternoon, The Apartment*, and *Avanti!* and between a young man and an older woman in *A Foreign Affair* and *Sunset Boulevard*. Distinctions based on war take the form of allies and enemies in *Five Graves to Cairo* and *Stalag 17* and victor and vanquished in *A Foreign Affair*. Distinctions of ideology can be seen in the theme of capitalism versus communism in *One, Two, Three* and freedom versus fascism in *A Foreign Affair*.

Quotations

Directors repeat themes, character types, characters' names, or visual motifs. Sometimes the repetition is unconscious, but generally it occurs because directors assume that the audience will interpret the repetition as a sign of continuity—not as a lack of imagination. Thus, in casting John Wayne to play a character called Lieutenant Colonel Kirby Yorke in *Rio Grande*, John Ford might have hoped the audience remembered that two years earlier Wayne played Captain Kirby Yorke in *Fort Apache*.

The opening credits of Ford's *The Man Who Shot Liberty Valance* are shown on broken crosses intended to evoke the opening credits of *My Darling Clementine*, which appeared on signposts. In the sixteen years between *Clementine* and *Liberty Valance*, Ford's vision of the West had changed from romantic to realistic. The stars of *Liberty Valance*, John Wayne and James Stewart, play roles that would have been more suitable for them twenty years earlier; hence the broken crosses to suggest that time has left its mark on both the director and the stars. In *Empire of the Sun*, when a boy is reunited with his parents amid a vast throng of people, Steven Spielberg repeats a composition from a movie that he made ten years earlier, *Close Encounters of the Third Kind*, in which a man and a woman push their way through a crowd to find each other.

Hitchcock often quotes himself, but his quotes are rarely verbatim. Rowley's fall from the cathedral tower in *Foreign Correspondent* prefigures similar falls, but in different contexts, in *Saboteur*, *Vertigo*, and *North by Northwest*. The airplane wing that becomes a life raft when a plane crashes in the Atlantic in *Foreign Correspondent* yields to the real thing in *Lifeboat* (1944), a totally different kind of film that uses a more conventional form of survival at sea.

In Hitchcock's *Family Plot* (1976), when Blanche (Barbara Harris) and her boyfriend are driving in a car whose brakes give way, she grabs hold of his necktie, almost strangling him with it. Her action recalls the necktie murders in *Frenzy* (1972). Similarly, when the pair is on a deserted stretch of highway, we almost expect the crop-duster plane from *North by Northwest* to materialize and spray them with bullets. And to avoid detection when he's in a jewel thief's home, the boyfriend takes the same precautions Marnie took in Hitchcock's film of that name: he removes his shoes and tiptoes past the kitchen. In fact, we wait for him to drop a shoe, as Marnie did. These are old tricks, but they appear in new settings.

In *Witness for the Prosecution*, Billy Wilder added a flashback to show how Leonard Vole (Tyrone Power) met his wife, Christine (Marlene Dietrich), in a Hamburg nightclub at the end of World War II. Dietrich had the same profession in Wilder's *A Foreign Affair*. Wilder must have had the earlier film in mind when he decided to open up the Agatha Christie play a bit by putting in the flashback. Yet *Witness for the Prosecution* is not *A Foreign Affair*, any more than *Family Plot* is *Frenzy* or *North by Northwest*.

A Director Quotes Himself

TOP LEFT: Marlene Dietrich as Erika, a cabaret singer in post–World War II Berlin; and John Lund as her lover, Captain John Pringle, in *A Foreign Affair* (1948). (*Copyright © by Paramount Pictures. Courtesy MCA Publishing Rights, a Division of MCA, Inc.*)

BOTTOM LEFT: Marlene Dietrich as Christine, who meets her future husband, Leonard Vole (Tyrone Power), in a Hamburg nightclub at the end of World War II in *Witness for the Prosecution* (1957). Wilder added the nightclub scene, which does not appear in the Agatha Christie play, to show how the Voles met. He is clearly repeating a plot device from *A Foreign Affair*—the smoke-filled basement nightclub where Pringle came to hear Erika sing. (*Courtesy MOMA/FSA*)

Borrowings

Wilder regarded Ernst Lubitsch as the unrivaled master of subtlety. Whenever someone in a Lubitsch film closed a door, drew the curtains, or shut the blinds, one always wondered, "Did they or didn't they?" In *Double Indemnity*, the camera dollies back from Phyllis and Neff as they sit snugly on the sofa in his apartment. "We just sat there," Neff's voice is heard saying. We no more believe him than we believe the Lubitsch heroine who closes the door of her lover's bedroom and in the next shot awakens in her own.

Homage to the Odessa Steps Sequence

The Odessa Steps massacre in *Potemkin*. (*Courtesy MOMA/FSA and Janus Films*)

As a rule, great directors are not troubled by the question of originality, because they see themselves as part of a tradition. Although they respect the past, they neither worship it blindly nor lean on it for support; instead, they view it as a legacy on which they can draw. The Odessa Steps massacre in *Potemkin* left its mark on many filmmakers, including Busby Berkeley, who paid it a curious tribute in the "Lullaby of Broadway" sequence in *Gold Diggers of 1935*. Hitchcock did the same in *Foreign Correspondent*, in which an assassination was staged on the steps of an Amsterdam conference hall. Brian De Palma paid homage to the Odessa Steps sequence in his film *The Untouchables* (1987), which even includes the careening baby carriage. Most directors are flattered when viewers evidence an awareness of a borrowing or a quote; in fact, in some cases viewers are *expected* to notice the borrowings so they can appreciate the director's integration of past and present.

An Interview with Billy Wilder (1906–2002)

Billy Wilder is an ideal director for study. He directed his first film in 1942, his last in 1981. He is also a true auteur, inasmuch as he coauthored the scripts of all the films he directed. After *The Big Carnival* [*Ace in the Hole*], with a few minor exceptions, he produced his own films. Wilder has been the subject of retrospectives, doctoral dissertations, books, articles, and television tributes by the American Film Institute and the Film Society of Lincoln Center. He is a six-time Academy Award winner: twice for direction (*The Lost Weekend, The Apartment*); three times for best screenplay (*The Lost*

Hitchcock's homage to the Odessa Steps in *Foreign Correspondent* (1940). (*Courtesy MOMA/FSA*)

Weekend, Sunset Boulevard [technically for story and screenplay], *The Apartment*); and once for best picture (*The Apartment*).

D. H. Lawrence once said, "Trust the tale, not the teller." Yet the teller can have much to tell, especially one who writes, directs, and produces his or her own tales. Wilder told much during an interview on June 11, 1976:

DICK: The critics who like to minimize the director's role will say that all a director did during the Studio Years was carry out the studio's policy. They would not speak of "Billy Wilder's films" but of "Billy Wilder's Paramount period [1942–1954]." When you were at Paramount, were you conscious of turning out a Paramount product?

WILDER: Never, not even in the early days when I did not have script approval and the right of final cut. If this were true, then Lubitsch's pictures, Sturges's pictures, Mitchell Leisen's pictures, my pictures—in fact, all the pictures made during those interesting days at Paramount—would have been the same. They were not. Once Paramount and I agreed on the subject of the movie, the cast, and the budget, and once they realized I would not have censorship problems (and in those days we had to smuggle things past the censors)—once all of this was settled—I was on my own. I wrote the film the way I wanted to, I cut it the way I wanted to. Of course, I may have to give a little when a picture is sold to television and make a cut here or a cut there. But even when I was beginning and did not have the ultimate control I have now, never for a moment did I think of myself as a foreman on the Paramount lot.

You see, the auteur theory, in emphasizing the director who takes over someone else's script, has little to say about a director like myself, who writes, directs, and produces his own. Although I do not belong to the producers' guild (I do, of course, belong to the screenwriters' and directors'), I think I can evaluate the auteur theory better than most critics. Being the writer, director, and producer of a picture, naturally I am the auteur.

DICK: Then you do not accept the auteur theory?

WILDER: I accept it only up to a point. The auteur theory does not emphasize the script. I deeply believe in the script and in the director's getting the maximum out of it. A mediocre director with a great script will still come out on top, but a brilliant director with a poor script will inevitably fail.

DICK: Is it easier to become a director now than it was when you began in the industry?

WILDER: It is much easier now, because television provides you with a training ground. In the past, there was no training ground except shorts and a series like MGM's *Crime Does Not Pay*, where Fred Zinnemann got his chance. Otherwise, unless you worked on Broadway or had important connections, or unless powerful stars requested you, it was extraordinarily difficult to get a break. You might think that by becoming an assistant director you would stand a good chance of becoming a director. Yet the assistant director had the least chance of ever becoming a director. The dialogue coach, the cameraman, the actor, the actor's relatives stood a better chance of becoming directors.

Of course, all that has changed with television. With the enormous demands it makes on one's time, you can learn by being on the set long enough. And with highly trained crews at his disposal, a director can't make a total ass of himself.

Directing is not Chinese glassblowing or the art of making Inca gold statuettes. It can be learned, and it can be learned quickly if you have a flair and a style for it. It is also an exhausting profession, and one that has a finality about it. In the theater, you can rewrite a play during its tryout; in my profession you can't say "Let's reshoot the film" if you don't like it. The sets are down, the actors are in Yugoslavia, and plans have already been made for the picture's distribution.

DICK: Do you have an image in your mind of what the film will look like in its final form?

WILDER: Even though you lose yourself in the picture while you're making it, ultimately it is back to what it was when you did the script, which

Billy Wilder on the set. (*Courtesy Billy Wilder*)

is proof that the script was good and the choice of material was good. If a film doesn't work—and often it doesn't—it was because I was telling the wrong story or an uninteresting story; I was telling a story that didn't have a chance no matter how brilliantly I might do it. Maybe I chose the right story at the time, but it turned out to be the wrong time for the picture. If I write an article for a magazine, it will be published a few weeks later. The mood of the public has not changed, and there is still interest in the subject. But my picture will not see the light of day for two years, when the mood of the public may be entirely different.

DICK: Are your scripts complete when you begin shooting?

WILDER: They are complete in the sense that I know how the film will end, but I want to see how the first two acts will play before I go on to the third. They are not complete in the sense that every line has been written down. I am always open to suggestions. If a scene does not play well in rehearsal, I will change it. If an actor has a good idea, or even an electrician, I can add it. But you must first have something to add it to.

DICK: Is there any truth to the story that Shirley MacLaine and Jack Lemmon were handed their dialogue for the final scene of *The Apartment* on the last day of shooting?

WILDER: Could be. But we knew very well how it would end: the boy would get what he wanted, give it up, and get the girl. Maybe the actual words were typed the night before. But we did not improvise; I never depend upon improvisation.

DICK: Your films evidence an incredible range—romantic comedy, farce, social drama, film noir, melodrama, biography. Did you aim for such diversity?

WILDER: I know a man who always wears a dark blue suit when he goes out in the evening. It's rather boring, you know. Why not a striped suit once in a while? Sometimes I wonder if I did the wrong thing by experimenting so much. Hitchcock, whom I greatly admire, stayed with one kind of picture. When people go to a Hitchcock movie, they know what to expect. Certain directors develop a style, refine it, and never give it up; they never leave their own neighborhood. I ventured out and tested myself. But whatever kind of film I make, there is always one quality I aim for: a complete simplicity of style, a total lack of pretentiousness; there is not one phony setup in a Billy Wilder picture.

Also, making films is a matter of mood. Now I am in the mood for something a bit serious, so I will do *Fedora*, which may remind some of *Sunset Boulevard* at least in texture, but it will be quite different. [*Fedora*, the first novella in Thomas Tryon's *Crowned Heads* (1976), is about a movie star who does not seem to age.]

DICK: It's well known that you write your scripts with a collaborator, but do you ever look upon your editor as a collaborator? I ask because Doane Harrison edited several of your early films.

WILDER: Doane Harrison was an old-time cutter, going back to the time when George Stevens was a cameraman for Hal Roach. He was very close to me when I made *The Major and the Minor*; he taught me a great deal because until then I had spent my life behind the typewriter, not behind the camera. [Wilder began his career as a reporter in Vienna. It was in Berlin in the late 1920s that he turned to screenwriting.]

DICK: How did you get behind the camera?

WILDER: How I became a director is very interesting. When I was writing scripts with Charles Brackett, we were never allowed on the set when the film was being shot. First of all, directors didn't want writers on the set; and second, we were off writing another picture. I decided to assert myself because I wanted some control over my scripts. So I started to raise hell, and Paramount finally let me direct a picture. Actually, it was no big deal because at that time Paramount was turning out fifty pictures a year. They said, "Let Wilder make a picture and then he'll go back to writing." Everyone expected me to make something "fancy-schmancy." Yet I made something commercial. I brought back the most salable hunk of celluloid I could—*The Major and the Minor*.

You see, unless you control your film, you are also at the mercy of actors. It's easy for an actor to argue with a director who is weak or who isn't convinced about the script. I remember Mr. Brackett and I were working on the script for *Hold Back the Dawn*, which Mitchell Leisen was directing. We had written a very fine scene for Charles Boyer, who was playing an immigrant waiting for his visa to come through. Unkempt and unshaven, Boyer waits in a cheap Mexican hotel. Well, to show the kind of hotel it was and to suggest something about the character Boyer was playing, we included a scene where Boyer makes some cynical remarks to a cockroach climbing up the wall. I assumed the scene would be shot as we had written it. A short time later, I ran into Boyer and asked him how he liked the scene with the cockroach. He said, "We cut that scene." I was shocked. "Why was it cut?" I asked. "How can I talk to a cockroach when the cockroach can't answer?" was Boyer's reply. I was so angry I told Brackett, "If that son of a bitch ain't talking to a cockroach, he ain't talking to anybody." We hadn't finished the script yet, so we pared Boyer's remaining scenes down to the bare minimum.

DICK: Is it important for a director to be able to write?

WILDER: It is more important for a director to be able to read. Many directors do not understand the script, and they don't have the nerve to say so. But they go ahead and shoot it, regardless.

DICK: There is a great deal of confusion today about the role of the editor. Did an editor ever change the form of any of your films?

WILDER: No, I learned to shoot with utmost economy, so there is not much an editor can do. I cut the film in the camera. I do not protect myself by shooting the scene eighteen different ways: it exhausts the actors, and the words begin to lose their meaning. I will go over the rushes with the editor and we will discuss them. I may say to him, "I need an additional shot here," but that is the extent of it. The worst that can ever happen is that I must alter my film or add to it.

DICK: Yet some directors rely very heavily on their editors. Dede Allen has become a legend in her own lifetime. Some critics have even said that she bails out Arthur Penn time and time again with her editing.

WILDER: I would not say she "bailed" him out; it was more like the way Maxwell E. Perkins helped Thomas Wolfe reorganize his novels for publication. If an editor bails a director out, it is because he shot crap. Dede Allen fully deserves the billing she gets, because she makes the picture better. It is the same with Verna Fields, who cut *Jaws*. She has the knack of knowing which frames to cut and how fast to cut them.

DICK: You edited *The Front Page* in four days, yet Terrence Malick supposedly spent a year editing *Badlands*.

WILDER: That is because he shot a great deal of film; I don't. I also work with very expensive actors, so I do not have the time. In the case of *Badlands*, you have a crew of very talented beginners who do everything themselves, including moving the camera from place to place.

They can go out and shoot where they like; and by the time the sheriff comes around to ask if they have permission, they've gone. I must apply for permission and wait until I get it. If I pick up a chair on the set, I have the unions to contend with. Our approaches are totally different; it's like commedia dell'arte as opposed to the legitimate theater.

DICK: Did you go into producing because you wanted more control over your pictures?

WILDER: Yes, and also because there were so few creative producers. Look at this ad in *The Hollywood Reporter*:

Silver Streak
A Martin Ransohoff–Frank Yablans Production
An Arthur Hiller Film
A Miller–Milkis–Colin Higgins Picture

This is insane. What happens is that somebody buys a property or two people buy it, so their names must appear. If the star becomes involved in the production, then his name appears. The director says it must read "A Bill Friedkin Film" or "Bill Friedkin's Film." Then the schleppers and the hangers-on get into the act. The vanity game is enormous. Even in the theater, it's "a such-and-such production in conjunction with so-and-so." Ultimately, when it's all over, it's Josh Logan's *South Pacific*.

The true producers, like Thalberg, Selznick, and Goldwyn, would add to a picture and enrich it; they were there when you needed them for important decisions. When the picture was finished, they got the maximum exposure for it and arranged for it to be shown in the best theaters.

DICK: Since *Ace in the Hole* [*The Big Carnival*], you have produced all of your films except for *The Spirit of St. Louis*, which Leland Hayward produced, and *Witness for the Prosecution*, which Arthur Hornblow, Jr., produced. Was there any reason for your not producing these yourself?

WILDER: Leland Hayward was my agent when I first came to Hollywood, so there was no real problem with his producing my film. Arthur Hornblow produced my very first film, *The Major and the Minor*. He was also a friend of Marlene Dietrich, who wanted the part in *Witness for the Prosecution* and asked me to direct so she would be sure to get it.

DICK: How do you feel about directors like Peter Bogdanovich, who pay homage to the work of other directors?

WILDER: You know what we call Bogdanovich? "The Frank Gorshin of directors." He is so steeped in film history that it is difficult for him to find a style of his own.

DICK: Have you ever paid homage to other directors?

WILDER: If I did, it was unconscious.

DICK: What about Lubitsch? There is a Lubitsch quality about *The Emperor Waltz* and *The Private Life of Sherlock Holmes*.

WILDER: I advise everyone to stay away from Lubitsch; he cannot be imitated. I did not set out to make a Lubitsch film in either case. And incidentally, you picked two of my failures. *Holmes* didn't make a ripple. I even had to cut two episodes out of it.

DICK: It is a film that is gaining in popularity. It was recently revived as part of a Sherlock Holmes Film Festival in New York, and those who had never seen it before were quite taken with it.

WILDER: It was, I think, the lushest of the Holmesiana and truest to the period.

DICK: Most of your films employ some form of disguise or deception. Would you agree?

WILDER: Some, but not all. Not in *Double Indemnity*.

DICK: It does appear in the way Neff gets Dietrichson to sign the insurance policy.

WILDER: Yes, I see what you mean. Well, there is a lot of that in *Fedora*, I assure you.

DICK: You said before that you were not conscious of any Lubitsch influence. Were you aware of the fact that in both *Five Graves to Cairo* and *The Private Life of Sherlock Holmes* you used a parasol as part of the plot and as a symbol of femininity? In *Five Graves*, Bramble places it on Mouche's grave; in *Holmes*, Ilse uses her parasol to send messages as well as to say goodbye to Holmes.

WILDER: No, I was not conscious of *Five Graves to Cairo* when I was making *Holmes*. In *Five Graves to Cairo* the parasol was a sentimental touch; there are no flowers in Tobruk, so he brings her a parasol. In *Holmes* Ilse used it for Morse code. And a parasol is so photographable, you know. There is something exquisite about it, especially when it is opened out against the sun. I am very fond of the proper use of props, and I like to make them part of the script. In *The Apartment* I used a broken compact mirror as the means of identifying Shirley MacLaine as the girl Fred MacMurray had been bringing to Jack Lemmon's apartment.

DICK: Were you influenced by the Book of Genesis when you were writing *Ace in the Hole* [*The Big Carnival*]? I am thinking of the continual emphasis on serpents, the desert as a kind of Eden that turns into a carnival, the rescue operations that take six days.

WILDER: That is a very interesting theory. You see, personally my mind doesn't go that way. And if it did, I couldn't admit it.

DICK: Several years ago you made this statement: "We're just like the guys in Detroit, putting out cars, no matter what anyone thinks we are." This is rather strange coming from a man who is the subject of retrospectives, books, articles, and Ph.D. dissertations. Do you still believe it?

WILDER: I did not mean what people think. How do you interpret it?

DICK: That directors are assembly-line workers.

WILDER: What I meant was that it takes tremendous artistry to put something into an assembly-line product so it will not have that mass-produced look. If someone is writing a poem or composing a symphony, he is doing it himself and on his own time. In our business we are playing for enormous chips supplied by other people. They give me the chips to gamble with, and I in turn am responsible to them. In this kind of situation it takes more artistry to produce something of value —sometimes to sneak in something of value—than it does when you are given as much money as you want, with no strings attached, and told to go to Salzburg and bring back a two-hour film. If I get behind schedule or exceed my budget, or if I indulge myself, after a couple of such pictures I would be flat on my ass. I would not get a chance to work again. I must do something that is hopefully superior, hopefully innovative, and at the same time it must be profitable. I personally believe that anything worthwhile ultimately finds some kind of audience. If somebody says, "This is the goddamnedest greatest picture ever made but no one went to see it," then it is not the goddamnedest greatest picture ever made.

I assure you, I have as many sleepless nights and as many ulcers as the truest of artists. But I have an added burden. If a painter buys a canvas for a couple of dollars and does not like what he has painted on it, he can throw it away. My canvas costs $4 million; if I don't like it, it can't be thrown in the fire. It's going to be shown, reviewed, maybe even play to empty houses. In the theater the producers can decide to close a show on the road and not bring it to Broadway. I can't. I've always said that the trouble with making pictures is that we can't try out in New Haven. If a picture is bad, it will come back to haunt you on the Late-Late Show. Its stench will endure forever.

An Interview with Alan Alda

In the movie industry, when a writer becomes a director, he or she is said to have "gone hyphenate." To use movie jargon, Alan Alda has gone double hyphenate: while Billy Wilder is a writer-director, Alan Alda is an actor-writer-director. Alda's career began on Broadway, with major roles in *Purlie Victorious* (1961), *The Owl and the Pussycat* (1964), and *The Apple Tree* (1966), which won him a Tony nomination. When Hollywood beckoned, he began the second phase of his career, appearing in such films as *The Paper Lion* (1968), *The Extraordinary Seaman* (1969), *The Mephisto Waltz* (1971), *California Suite*, and *Same Time, Next Year* (both 1978). When the success of the movie *M*A*S*H* led to the television spin-off in 1972, Alda's already varied career took another direction. As Hawkeye Pierce, Alda became one of television's most popular stars, a favorite among college students, and one of America's most sought-after commencement speakers.

What contributed to M*A*S*H's longevity on television was an emphasis on human relationships that was quite different from the absurdist and often cruel humor of the film. The series underwent a transition from sitcom to human comedy, and Alda played a significant role in the change, first by writing some scripts and then by directing them. By the mid-1970s, Alan Alda was a former Broadway star turned Hollywood actor who was then acting in, writing for, and directing some of the episodes of one of the most popular programs in the history of American television.

By the end of the 1970s, Alda had experience writing for television but had not yet written for the movies. The next stage in an already thriving career was to write his first screenplay, the highly successful *Seduction of Joe Tynan* (1979). Alda didn't direct *Joe Tynan*, however. Thus there was one more height to scale: directing an original screenplay in which he would also appear. He achieved that goal with *The Four Seasons* (1981), which proved to be both a critical and a commercial success. Three other films followed, which he directed and in which he appeared: *Sweet Liberty* (1986), *A New Life* (1988), and *Betsy's Wedding* (1990).

After the less than successful *Betsy's Wedding*, with which even Alda has admitted he was unhappy, he returned to acting, appearing in both TV movies (*And the Band Played On*, 1993) and theatrical films (for example, *Mad City*, 1997; *The Object of My Affection*, 1998; and *What Women Want*, 2000). In 1991, Alda returned to the Broadway stage, starring in Neil Simon's *Jake's Women* (filmed for television in 1998 as *Neil Simon's Jake's Women*) and in 1998 in Yasmina Reza's *Art*, which proved to be enormously popular. His lifelong interest in science led to his being chosen to host the public television series *Scientific American Frontiers*, which premiered in 2003.

Although Alda no longer directs, his views on filmmaking are as valuable as Wilder's because, as an actor-writer-director, he understands the role each plays in the creation of a movie.

The following interview took place in Alan Alda's office at Martin Bregman Productions in New York on June 13, 1988:

DICK: Some writers become writer-directors, or "go hyphenate" as *The Hollywood Reporter* would say, because they want greater control over their scripts. Was that true of yourself?

ALDA: No. I think I became a director because I thought I would love directing; it turned out I did. When I started to direct, I was on M*A*S*H. I was eager to direct anything, whether I had written it or not. It would be a chance for me to work under the best conditions, where there were people who could catch me if I fell. Yet I can understand what writers go through when someone else directs their work. Unless a writer and a director are in close touch and are lucky enough to see things the same way, the result may be quite different from what the writer intended. My first *M*A*S*H* script had a very good director, yet the scenes didn't have the point I thought they should; in some cases, the actors didn't get the jokes, and I just had to sit by helplessly. It's a good idea, in general, for writers to direct their own material, and for directors to write their own material—but only if the directors can write. Unfortunately, there are a lot of directors who can't write but who keep doing it. I have great respect for the written word; that comes from having been an actor first. Since I come from the stage, I would never think of changing a word in a script. And I wouldn't do it as a director, either, unless I consulted with the writer.

DICK: You don't believe, then, that the director is the author of the film, as the auteurists do?

ALDA: I have a problem with the auteur theory; the author of the film is the author of the script. I could understand if, by the auteur theory, you mean that the director contributes something to the film. If the director tells the story successfully through the lens, he or she has contributed something the writer couldn't because the writer told the story on paper. John Wayne contributed something unique to his movies, but you don't call a John Wayne film "A Film by John Wayne." After Marshall Brickman finished directing *Simon*, he was asked if he would like it called "A Film by Marshall Brickman." He replied, "No. It's a film by Kodak."

DICK: An editor also contributes something to the film. How much latitude did you allow William Reynolds, who edited *A New Life*?

ALDA: Since we had to get the film out in a hurry, I gave Bill a lot of latitude. As I watched the rushes, I made detailed notes about preferred takes and angles, and how I saw the scenes fitting together. I didn't sit over his shoulder. Actually, I liked the idea of loosening my grip a little. I think I was able to do it on *A New Life* because I was more secure. I told Bill what my ideas were; if he had a better idea or if he felt one of mine wouldn't work, he would tell me and we would proceed from there. I find that editing is like script writing. You refine what you've written and get other ideas. All the cuts have some of my ideas and some of Bill's.

DICK: Did you allow Michael Economou the same latitude on *Sweet Liberty*?

ALDA: No, and I'm sorry I didn't. The fact that I allowed Bill Reynolds more on *A New Life* represents growth on my part. Whether you have tight reins or loose reins, it all boils down to communication. No matter to whom you are talking—the editor, the cinematographer, the actors—you have to be able to describe what you see. You just can't say to someone, "This is the script; you do it." That's not the job of the director or even the producer; that's what the studio does. The studio says, "I like that script; I like that cast. Here's the money. Go make

Alan Alda on the set of *Sweet Liberty* (1986). (*Copyright © Universal Pictures, a Division of Universal City Studios, Inc. Courtesy MCA Publishing Rights, a Division of MCA, Inc.*)

the movie." From that point on, everybody must start communicating with each other. The producer has to say to the writer or the writer-director, "Do you really need that scene? Do you think these lines are clear?" The producer does not do this to achieve the producer's vision, but the writer-director's. And the writer-director tries to get everyone else to realize the vision he or she has.

DICK: Do you have an image in your mind of how the completed film will look?

ALDA: For *Sweet Liberty* I storyboarded. There was a picture of every scene in the movie. An artist I was working with came back with a storyboard that represented the way he thought everything should look. I said, "Thank you, but that's not the point. They hired me to tell the story as I see it." A storyboard conveys a great deal of information; it's supposed to be a visualization of the script as well as an aid to all the departments involved in shooting the script. What I did was draw stick figures and discuss them with the artist so that he could draw the figures properly. Eighty percent of the film looked like the storyboard.

DICK: What about your relationship with the cinematographer?

ALDA: We would discuss what kind of lens, dolly, or crane we would use. I also had a specific shot list. That part of the job was over before I even got to the set, so we didn't have to waste half the morning wondering whether we would shoot this way or that.

DICK: Did you storyboard *A New Life* also?

ALDA: Not as much, since I didn't have an artist. I just drew stick figures.

DICK: Is storyboarding difficult if you're verbally oriented?

ALDA: No. I think in images. I usually start writing when I have a visual image. Novelists do the same, you know. John Fowles had an image of a woman at the end of a jetty, so he wrote *The French Lieutenant's Woman* to find out who she was.

DICK: Did *The Four Seasons* begin with an image?

ALDA: That film came from several sources. First there was Vivaldi's *Four Seasons*. Wouldn't it be interesting, I thought, to make a movie showing the same people on vacation in each of the four seasons? The musical form would dictate the form of the film. Then I had another image: I envisioned three couples getting out of a car. I kept seeing them getting out of the car and walking somewhere, and doing it over and over. It was like seeing a film in a loop. It haunted me. I had to find out more about those people.

DICK: In the film, the car is a very unobtrusive way of starting the film.

ALDA: Yes, in the credits sequence one couple picks up the other couples, so that by the time the actual film begins, you know who everyone is.

DICK: Did you plan to have *The Four Seasons* begin in spring and end in winter?

ALDA: It wasn't until after I had written the film that I realized the whole spring-winter progression corresponds to the four stages of friendship. There's a springtime to a friendship when nobody can do any wrong. In the glare of the summer sun, you see your friends as they are. In autumn, illusions fall away like leaves. In winter, you're "frozen" with your friends; you have to accept them as they are or find new ones who won't be a burden to you because you don't know who they are yet. I think this is what happens in the movie, but didn't understand it until I had written it.

DICK: Do you have a complete script at the time of shooting?

ALDA: Absolutely. I have to, because I haven't got time to rewrite on the set. That's why I go through about a dozen drafts and am overly particular about what I want to shoot.

DICK: When you were in the theater, you did improvisations as a member of the Second City [a Chicago-based improvisational group]. As a film director, do you improvise?

ALDA: If you mean during filming, very little. I may do a bit in scenes where several people are talking at once. In *A New Life*, I improvised a scene in which the character I play is arguing with a lawyer at a party. We did one episode on M*A*S*H that was an improvisation. It was called "The Interview" and consisted of someone interviewing the M*A*S*H unit as if for a documentary. Yet it was a highly controlled situation. We rehearsed for weeks by improvising into a tape recorder; the tape was edited by the writer, Larry Gelbart, who added some of his own jokes, and that became the script. But there were also last-minute questions that we had never heard before; that part of the episode was spot improvisation. There's a great difference between a spot improvisation and a script that has been derived from improvisation. When you're improvising, and it works, it is very hard to repeat the improvisation and get the same effect. It may take fifteen or twenty attempts for it to come to life again. If you're working from a script that came out of an improvisation, it's the same as working from any other script. Filmmakers should know that. There is a difference between improvising during rehearsal and improvising whole scenes in front of the camera. But a lot of young directors who have had little experience working with actors think that improvising is a technique that gets the actors to be more truthful. There's a danger that the values of the script will get lost in the improvisation and that nothing will replace them. Also, if the actors improvise in rehearsal, and something exciting happens, the director assumes that if the actors repeat these lines the excitement will recur. The director doesn't realize that it wasn't the lines that were exciting but the creative impulse that inspired them. The first time the impulse passes through the actor is thrilling, yet nobody knows the source of that impulse, and to rediscover it takes several more improvisations. You may or may not get it again.

Directors who feel it's the actors' fault if they improvise brilliantly during rehearsal but can't repeat what they did in front of the camera don't realize it has nothing to do with the actors; it's the way the brain works. Something mysterious might happen during an improvisation that brings the scene to life. What happens is that connections are made and impulses arise that should be explored. The actual words that are said are not nearly so important. Improvisation is useful to find out who the characters are and what their pasts have been, and I've used improvisation during rehearsals for that purpose. Once the actors understand their characters—and improvisation is one way of accomplishing this—they may be able to play the scene with more life. Improvisation also gets the actors to feel comfortable with one another and with the director.

DICK: To make them comfortable, would you change dialogue with which they are uncomfortable?

ALDA: That's a traditional way of making actors comfortable. I do it with caution, but I do it. What is important is what the script is communicating and the truth of the relationships expressed in the script. If changing a word here or there doesn't vitiate that truth, then I'm happy to. But if it wrecks the story, makes it illogical, or denies something truthful about the character, I explain to the actor that I can't. It's the director's job to keep the whole picture in mind. Every department may have a wonderful idea, but it might not fit into the whole scheme of the film. However, an actor may be uncomfortable with a line of dialogue, and after a few days of rehearsal, when the context is clear, the actor is not only comfortable with it but would kill to keep it. Improvisation and changing dialogue are only two ways to make actors feel comfortable. The most important thing is for the actors and director to eat dinner together.

DICK: Is that why food is so important in your films?

ALDA: That happens to be the way I am, the way I run my life. A lot of it is devoted to eating.

DICK: Do you believe in eating with the cast because the meal has always been a symbol of unity?

ALDA: That reason never occurred to me. I think that food is an image that comes to me a lot because I like food.

DICK: Since you've written both teleplays and screenplays, is the basic difference between them that the half-hour teleplay is in two acts, while screenplays are not divided into acts?

ALDA: Actually, a screenplay is divided into acts even though the acts may not be indicated as such in the script. Most screenwriters talk in terms of act one, act two, act three. You introduce the situation, complicate it, and resolve it. George S. Kaufman used to say that in act one you get the hero up a tree; in act two you throw stones at him; and in act three you get him down. All stories are like that. You introduce the characters in the beginning, along with their goals; then there are complications in their achieving those goals because everyone wants something different. Thus, it won't be so easy for the main character to get what he or she wants because of the obstacles thrown in the way by the other characters. It's what Aristotle in the *Poetics* called "dramatic action"—action in the sense of the characters' trying to achieve something. The resolution is the final working out of their either getting what they want or not, or getting not what they want but what they need. In that case, they experience growth, sometimes tragic growth. They may no longer be able to do what they did in the past, but they have achieved insight. This may not always be apparent in what I write because I stress relationships and internal struggles, but I'm always thinking in terms of action—dramatic action, not car chases. Someone's always trying to accomplish something, even if it's just to understand something.

It's almost impossible for the actor to act unless the character wants something. That doesn't mean the character has to want something external; it can be internal. It may be peace, tranquillity, or self-knowledge. And a director must know what that goal is. Otherwise, if it's a play, you'll just hear a lot of talking, or if it's a film, you'll see a lot of fancy shots.

The writer must give the character a goal, even if it's a limited goal, as it is in *Rocky*. Rocky only wants to go the distance; the fact that he doesn't win is unimportant. He achieved his goal: he went the distance. An actor shouldn't be allowed to go onstage or before the camera if he or she is playing a character without an objective or a goal. If the character doesn't want something, turn the lights out and save electricity. The scene will go dark anyway if the actors are only feeding each other lines so the author can get the exposition out. Shakespeare knew how to handle exposition: in the opening scene of *Othello*, we learn who Iago, Roderigo, Desdemona, and Othello are without one expository line being uttered. Everything comes out of the action. The actors have not been forced to say to themselves, "Well, we just have to say these lines so the audience will get what's going on."

DICK: You have been speaking of writing, acting, and directing as if they were part of the same process.

ALDA: They are. The actors need an objective that the writer provides and that the director achieves. It's painful for me to see writers and actors at odds with each other. The writers complain, "Those damn actors aren't saying my words right." The actors complain, "Who wrote this crap?" They both work the same way, yet they'll never know it unless they sit down and talk with each other. If actors don't speak the dialogue properly, it's probably because they don't understand it. Writers blame actors because they fail to realize an actor must go through a certain process to absorb in a few days what it may have taken the writer two years to create. Being an actor, a writer, and a director, I understand all three.

DICK: If you had to describe the role of a director to someone outside the industry, how would you do it?

ALDA: A director gives direction; it's inherent in the job title. However, it's not a good idea to direct actors down to the last little movement of their pinkie. It's not only a bad idea; it can also wreck the picture. You must find out how you can communicate your vision to each department so that everyone will give you what you want from their heart. What's the point of hiring an art director if you say, "This is what I want — nothing else." All the art director will do is draw the set you designed. You want to be able to get design ideas from the art director, but those ideas must serve *your* vision. All of this is done through communication. You must be able to describe what you see to everyone, and you should be able to compare what you see happening with what you see can happen. But you must understand the specific capabilities of each department, what each can and cannot do. Actors cannot work from results. The first mistake a director makes is to say to an actor, "Be mysterious." That's a result; mystery is what you experience when the actor is doing the scene right. The director has to find out, with the actor, what the actor is trying to accomplish in terms of the action that will make the actor appear mysterious. You have to find the cause that produces the result. Actors can play a state; they can depict a state of drunkenness, for example. But once an actor establishes that the character is drunk, the actor has to achieve something, even if it's trying not to appear drunk.

DICK: Is it possible to learn directing?

ALDA: The only way to learn anything is with a mentor who will go through the steps with you, then let you do it and go over your mistakes. It's like the way my wife and I taught our children to wash their hands. We would put all of our hands under the faucet and rub them back and forth with the soap. Then the kids got the feeling. It's the way an artist guides the hand of a pupil or the way the tennis instructor puts his or her hand over yours on the racket. But you still have to make the shots; still, it's better if you've had hands-on experience with someone who is experienced.

NOTE

1. The article appeared in *Film Culture* (Winter 1962–1963); it has been reprinted in Leo Braudy and Marshall Cohen, *Film Theory and Criticism*, 5th ed. (New York: Oxford University Press, 1999), 515–535.

CHAPTER 8

Film and Literature

"Film has nothing to do with literature," Ingmar Bergman declared.[1] Yes and no. Like so many dogmatic statements, Bergman's is not entirely true. A film can be subjected to the same criteria as a work of literature, and analyzed in terms of form, rhythm, imagery, and symbolism. A film, however, is not treated like a novel or a poem. A film's rhythm is determined by the way it is edited, not by the variation of stressed and unstressed syllables, as in poetry; or by the alternation of description and dialogue, as in fiction. In film, imagery is visual; in literature, it is verbal.

A film's form derives partly from literature, partly from the visual arts. *Literature* implies something written. A screenplay may be "literature" in the most basic sense because it is a written text, but rarely in the traditional sense of being a literary classic. On the other hand, a film can be a work of cinematic art, while the script would never pass muster as literature. In fact, while the published screenplays of Ingmar Bergman, Harold Pinter, and Woody Allen may read like literature (or, at least, like plays), they are not always reliable guides to the actual films. In Bergman's screenplay of *Through a Glass, Darkly*, Martin cuts his finger, which begins to bleed; his wife, Karin, then starts sucking the blood from the cut. The incident is described in the screenplay as, "Karin sucks the blood, looks at it, sucks again, is suddenly all enthusiasm." What happens on the screen is far less extreme: Martin cuts his finger, and Karin kisses it. When Bergman wrote the screenplay, he may have envisioned the scene differently. When he directed the scene, he apparently decided to make it less theatrical. Likewise, the film based on the screenplay may—and usually does—include scenes that were never in the screenplay.

A screenplay is like an opera libretto. While there are many great operas, there are few librettos that deserve to be studied as literature. Just as a libretto needs music, a screenplay needs visualization.

Literary Techniques

A screenplay, as the term implies, is a *play*—a play intended for the screen; thus, a screenplay contains many features of drama. A screenplay is also a form of narrative, sharing certain techniques with fiction. Like a play, a film can have a prologue and an epilogue. In film, the prologue may appear as print in an opening title or as drama in a credits or a precredits sequence. Opening title and credits/precredits sequences are, of course, peculiar to film; even so, they are prologues—in one case, a prologue involving the written word; in the other, a prologue involving visualized action.

Film also uses many techniques that are found in literature, the most notable of which are **flashback, flash-forward,** and **point-of-view.**

The Flashback

In ancient epics, the flashback was the poet's way of incorporating material into the narrative that could not be added in any other way. For example, the *Odyssey* begins ten years after the end of the Trojan War; thus, Homer describes Odysseus's postwar adventures by providing the hero with an occasion—a banquet—where he could recount them. In the *Aeneid*, Virgil, imitating Homer, also has Aeneas summarize his seven years abroad at a banquet.

The flashback has always been a favorite device of authors who prefer to start in the middle of an action or who choose to work from the present back to the past. In a film, a flashback—which can be introduced by a slow fade-out/fade-in, a dissolve, a wipe, or a quick cut—serves three basic functions: it can furnish information that is otherwise unavailable, dramatize a past event as it is being narrated because the filmmaker has decided that it must be visualized, or explain the connection between past and present when none of the characters can do so.

The first kind of flashback is the most obvious; for example, without the flashbacks in *Sorry, Wrong Number* (1948), we would never know why a husband has arranged to have his wealthy wife murdered. Tennessee Williams's one-act play *Suddenly, Last Summer* concludes with Catherine Holly's monologue about the death of her cousin Sebastian, whose flesh was devoured by the boys he had propositioned and probably debauched. When Joseph L. Mankiewicz was planning the movie version in 1959, he decided to intersperse Catherine's (Elizabeth Taylor) monologue with shots of boys begging Sebastian for food as he sat at an outdoor restaurant, the beaches that Sebastian frequented, and Catherine in a revealing white bathing suit that Sebastian made her wear to attract attention. It is an extremely complex flashback. Sometimes Catherine's face, and even her mouth, appears right of frame, as she narrates the details of her cousin's gruesome death. As Catherine does this, what she is narrating fades in behind her—her face appearing in double exposure along with the image.

Not all flashbacks are memory flashbacks. *The Godfather, Part II* is a flashback film, but not a memory film; no one in the movie is remembering the past, because no one knows enough about it. The purpose of the sequel to *The Godfather* is to integrate the lives of Vito Corleone and his son Michael. Since Vito is dead when the film begins, his story is told in flashback. *Godfather II* is an example of the impersonal flashback, which is not the result of a reminiscence, an inquest, or an investigation but, rather, of the integration of past and present under the supervision of a central intelligence, which might be called the omniscient filmmaker. Stanley Donen's *Two for the Road* (1967) is a good example of the impersonal flashback: a couple's European trip is intercut with incidents from their previous trips. Because past and present are so subtly interwoven, we never ask who is remembering—the wife (Audrey Hepburn) or the husband (Albert Finney).

Memory flashbacks, although common, can be poorly motivated. Sometimes a character no sooner says, "It seems only yesterday that . . . ," than the present fades out and the past fades in. Some of the best memory flashbacks are occasioned by an object. In *Kitty Foyle* (1940), a glass paperweight with a girl on a sled is the cue for Kitty's memories; in *Penny Serenade*, a phonograph record triggers a woman's memories of her marriage; in *Brute Force*, a woman's picture on a calendar causes four convicts to recall the women in their lives.

The Flash-Forward

A device that enjoyed popularity with filmmakers beginning in the 1960s was the flash-forward, in which some aspect of an event is shown before it occurs. The flash-forward is a distant relative of **dramatic foreshadowing,** the literary device in which one incident presages another, or some indication is given that an event is going to happen before it actually does. The true ancestor of the flash-forward is *prolepsis*, a rhetorical technique in which a speaker anticipates—and answers—an objection before it has even been raised.

Because of their anticipatory force, proleptic devices can be quite dramatic. In George Stevens's *The Greatest Story Ever Told* (1965), after Pontius Pilate delivers Jesus Christ to be crucified, an off-camera voice is heard saying, "And he suffered under Pontius Pilate." It is a compelling moment in the film: a historical event is described with a quote from the Apostles' Creed, which has not yet been written. Often a movie's main title has a foreshadowing character. During the credits for *Saboteur*, the shadow of the saboteur moves from the right of the frame into the center. Billy Wilder used the same technique in *Double Indemnity*; in that film the shadowy figure is on crutches, a prefiguration of the insurance salesman's attempt to pass himself off as the man he has just murdered, who had been using crutches because of a broken leg.

Sometimes what seems to be a flash-forward isn't one. During the course of *They Shoot Horses, Don't They?* (1969), the narrator (Michael Sarrazin) speaks directly to the camera—or is he speaking to someone we cannot see? At the end, we discover that he is speaking to a judge, explaining why he shot Gloria (Jane Fonda) at her request. Flash-forwards succeed in *Horses* because, from the audience's point of view, they exist in the future; but from the narrator's, they are part of the past. In retrospect, it becomes apparent that the entire movie was a flashback told to a judge.

A shot can have the impact of a flash-forward although it is really a comment on an earlier incident. Well after the midpoint of *The Story of Adele H.* (1975), François Truffaut inserts a shot of Adele on the Isle of Guernsey, gloriously confident as she prepares to sail for Halifax to reclaim the affections of Lieutenant Pinson. Her voice is equally self-assured: "This incredible thing—that a young girl shall walk over the sea, from the Old into the New World, to join her lover—this, I shall accomplish." Obviously this is an Adele we have not seen before, since the film begins with her arrival in Halifax. The shot is placed where it is to mark the end of Adele's fruitless quest and the beginning of her descent into madness. Had the shot appeared at the beginning, it would simply have been a prologue. Because it appears where it does, it has the force of dramatic irony: Adele did make a journey from the Old World to the New, but it was also a journey from obsession to self-inflicted degradation. At the very end of the film, Truffaut repeats the shot, this time drained of its color and looking like a faded photograph. Adele's voyage is now just an item of memorabilia.

Point of View

Like a work of literature, a film can be narrated in the first or the third person. A first-person film—one recounted by an "I" who begins speaking at the outset and continues right up to the end, as Pip does in Dickens's novel *Great Expectations* and Roquentin does in Sartre's novel *Nausea*—is rare.

What generally happens in film is that the "I" is heard at the beginning and perhaps intermittently thereafter. The semidocumentary may seem to be an exception, since it may use first-person narration throughout; however, the narrator is not a character but a disembodied voice. When the voice intrudes periodically, it acts like a fade-out, demarcating the film into narrative blocks.

Something similar happens in *Radio Days*, which is narrated by an adult who is seen only as a child. If *Radio Days* has a distinctly literary quality and seems like a filmed short story, it is because continuous first-person narrative calls attention to itself as narrative. First-person narration can present a credibility problem if the "I" relates something to which it would not have had access. Despite the excellence of *Radio Days*, even Woody Allen has difficulty explaining how a grade-school boy can know what he does.

A film need not use "I" narration to achieve a first-person effect; a film can employ subjective camera, which doubles as a character so that we are aware of both an "I" and an "eye." In slasher movies, when the camera looks in through the window from the outside, it is both an "I" (the predator) and an "eye" (the predator's eye and, by extension, ours).

Sound can also be subjective; when a character hears something, the character becomes an "I" telling "us" what he or she is thinking or hearing. In *A Streetcar Named Desire*, Blanche hears a gunshot that no one else can hear. She associates the sound with an incident that she cannot erase from her memory: her husband's suicide. *We* hear the sound because we have been given access to her consciousness.

It is important to remember that voice-over narration does not necessarily mean a first-person film. Since the voice tends to come and go, one may soon forget the narrator. Instead, film emulates first-person narrative throughout, using subjective camera and subjective sound. Third-person narration in film, however, requires omniscient camera, similar to the omniscient narrator in literature.

Omniscient Narrator. In fiction, the **omniscient narrator** tells the story in the third person, moving from place to place, time to time, and character to character, disclosing or concealing details at will.[2] The film equivalent, omniscient camera, is best seen in multiplot films or films that move back and forth in time. When the camera is omniscient, it behaves very much like an omniscient author. The camera in *Nashville* is omniscient. It leaves a freeway crack-up and moves to a hospital to look in on a country singer recovering from a breakdown. It abandons a private home for the local tavern, a nightclub for a smoker, a church for an automobile graveyard.

Omniscient narrators can be intrusive if they pass judgment on what is seen, or they can be unintrusive if they suspend judgment. The camera can do likewise, because omniscience does not mean impartiality. In *The Day of the Locust*, Homer Simpson (Donald Sutherland) sits in the backyard of his

Hollywood home. An orange drops from a bough with the sound of ripe fruit. In the yard above his, a woman looks down on this scene of other-worldly tranquility. Her face has the overripeness of rotting fruit. The camera has said nothing, but by moving from Homer to the woman it makes its own comment on Hollywood's relationship to those who bask in the glow of an endless summer and those who decompose in it.

Instead of traveling back and forth among the characters, authors can select one of them as a "center of consciousness," to use Henry James's phrase. In film, this "reflector" method works well when the script involves a character trapped by his or her fantasies or victimized by some neurosis. In *The Lost Weekend* (1945), Billy Wilder draws us into the consciousness of Don (Ray Milland), an alcoholic. We share Don's experiences even when they are portrayed objectively, as they often are. Early in the film, there is a scene in which Don attends a performance of Verdi's *La Traviata* and develops an uncontrollable urge to drink during the first-act "Drinking Song." Wilder cuts from Don to the stage, where Violetta and Alfredo are toasting each other, and back again to Don. So far, the camera has been objective: what Don sees on the stage is what everyone else in the audience sees. But not everyone in the audience is an alcoholic; thus, Wilder allows the camera to turn subjective at this point, as Don sees, superimposed against the stage, the checkroom where his raincoat is hanging, with a bottle in one of the pockets. We clearly understand his craving and the effect the "Drinking Song" has had on him.

Implied Author.   Some fiction is written so impersonally that it appears to be authorless. To some, Hemingway's "The Killers" seems to have been written by a scientist rather than a novelist. In "The Killers," Hemingway obliterated his actual self and created a second self who mediates between Ernest Hemingway and the story that bears his name. Filmmakers can likewise suppress or mask their personal feelings so that they do not interfere with the film. The use of the author's second self, the implied author, usually results in an impersonal movie because it does not encourage emotional involvement and generally does not reach a high level of emotional intensity.

Barry Lyndon is such a film. First, it is Stanley Kubrick's *Barry Lyndon*, not William Makepeace Thackeray's; not only did Kubrick produce and direct it, but he also wrote the screenplay. Kubrick remains aloof from his characters, but he does not shun them. The implied author approach is not emotional evasion; it is emotional noninvolvement. Kubrick was more interested in the characters as embodiments of their age than as human beings.

In adapting Thackeray's *Barry Lyndon* for the screen, Kubrick worked with a novel written in the nineteenth century but set in the eighteenth. For this reason, the tone had to be Victorian and the atmosphere neoclassical. Kubrick achieved an eighteenth-century air by framing scenes in the

The famous *Barry Lyndon* candlelight. All the candlelight scenes were photographed with a special Zeiss lens and entirely with natural light. *(Courtesy Warner Bros., Inc.)*

style of painters of that era — Watteau, Dayes, and Gainsborough — and by orchestrating them with selections from Bach, Handel, Vivaldi, and Mozart. He re-created a Victorian tone by using an off-camera narrator whose voice was fittingly snobbish.

Seeing *Barry Lyndon* is like viewing a painting. A great painting draws a viewer toward it; but once the viewer is face-to-face with it, he or she instinctively walks backward to see it from a distance. Kubrick uses the same technique. He begins with a close-up, then slowly zooms out. *Barry Lyndon* is like a tour of the world's great museums. The glow of candlelight is not the smoky haze it usually is in most films; specially created lenses give the candlelight in *Barry Lyndon* the look of melting gold. Light floods a window, not in neat spotlighting cones but in a burst of silver. To achieve such beauty, Kubrick had to sacrifice a certain amount of emotion. There are some films that seem to have come from the filmmaker's heart, as if he or she identified with the material in such a way that we feel a similar involvement. Admittedly, this feeling is subjective. Yet we should be able to look at a film and say, "The filmmaker has kept his or her distance, preferring to treat the material like a scientist performing an experiment"; or "The filmmaker feels so strongly about the project that the result seems personal, or perhaps even autobiographical." Within Hitchcock's body of work, such films as *Rope* and *Frenzy* feel as if they were camera created. Others such as *Notorious, North by Northwest, Vertigo* — and even *Psycho* — have a distinct feeling for the human condition, which can only be detected once the veneer has been stripped away.

Mr. Hyde (Fredric March) about to strangle Ivy (Miriam Hopkins) in Rouben Mamoulian's *Dr. Jekyll and Mr. Hyde* (1932), loosely based on Robert Louis Stevenson's novella, in which there is no Ivy. *(Courtesy Paramount Pictures)*

Film Adaptation

The distinction between film and literature becomes especially blurry when a film is an adaptation of a novel, short story, or play. The adaptation occasions the greatest amount of criticism because the original work becomes the standard against which the film version is compared; hence the often repeated charge, "Well, it wasn't the book (or the play)." There is only one answer to that charge: it wasn't meant to be. The adaptation is *a* version, not *the* version. A particular novel or play can even inspire several film versions. Which *Phantom of the Opera* is *the* version of Gaston Leroux's novel *The Phantom of the Opera* — the 1925 version, the 1943 version, or the 1962 version?

A film version will always differ from the original. Why else would a filmmaker adapt a work for the screen, and why should audiences be expected to see it if they have read the book or seen the play? The adaptation must be different — but how different? The adaptation may preserve the essence of the original, even when it alters plot details, adds or eliminates characters, or changes the conclusion so that it is the opposite of what it was in the original. On the other hand, a film can follow the original to the letter and still lack its spirit.

A filmmaker must regard a literary source as a blueprint that can either be followed closely or radically altered to conform to the filmmaker's vision. Robert Louis Stevenson's novella *Dr. Jekyll and Mr. Hyde* has been filmed many times, but not as Stevenson wrote it. A faithful adaptation would

The creature (Boris Karloff) and Maria playing a game that turns deadly in *Frankenstein* (1931). *(Courtesy MOMA/FSA)*

have resulted in a thoroughly uninteresting movie, for a variety of reasons. There are no women in the novella, which is really a study in doubles. Not only are Jekyll and Hyde doubles (Hyde being the dark side of Jekyll) but so are two other male characters, Utterson and Enfield: Utterson is a stuffy, conservative lawyer, while Enfield, a "distant kinsman," is his complete opposite—outgoing and pleasure-loving. Jekyll's house also has its double: the façade is pleasant, but the back door, which Hyde uses, is sinister-looking. The last third of the novel consists of two documents—Dr. Lanyon's eye-witness account of the transforming power of the potion Jekyll concocted to turn himself into Hyde, and Jekyll's own "statement of the case," in which he explains the reasons for his experiments to separate humankind's two natures.

In Rouben Mamoulian's 1932 film version, the best of the lot, Utterson and Enfield are replaced by two women: Jekyll's fiancée, Muriel, and Hyde's mistress, Ivy. Jekyll's valet, Poole, is retained; Carew, one of Hyde's victims in the novel, becomes Muriel's father. The addition of the women allowed Mamoulian and his writers to create a sexual subtext: Jekyll's desire to explore his sexuality, which he cannot do as a respectable physician but can as the disreputable Hyde. Significantly, Jekyll takes the potion after befriending the prostitute Ivy—the image of her leg dangling over the side of the bed lingering in his memory, as the prolonged superimposition of the leg indicates. Faithful to the spirit? Definitely, since it reflects Jekyll's obsession with duality, his experiments to separate the two natures, and the consequences of his folly, which he even admits.

Mary Shelley's *Frankenstein* has also served as the basis of a number of films, the best being James Whale's *Frankenstein* (1931), which has hardly anything to do with the work on which, according to the credits, it was based. All that was retained was Frankenstein's creation of the monster, which, visually, is the high point of the film. However, there is one incident in the film that is as horrifying as the episode in the novel when the monster strangles Frankenstein's brother, William. In the film, the monster comes upon a child, Maria, who, unlike William, shows no fear of him. Maria invites the monster to join her as she throws flowers into the lake. Watching them float, the monster thinks that Maria might float, too, and drops her into the lake. The horror of the scene is not just that Maria drowns but that the monster realizes the enormity of what he has done, and cannot save her. Faithful to the spirit or the letter? Neither. Still, James Whale's *Frankenstein* is an acknowledged masterpiece, as is the sequel, *Bride of Frankenstein*, in which Mary Shelley appears as a character in the prologue (played by Elsa Lanchester, who doubles, uncredited, as the bride), giving us the impression that the monster, who supposedly died at the end of the 1931 movie, didn't really die and is ready for a mate — meaning that Universal Pictures was ready for a sequel and needed an explanation for audiences that were familiar with the earlier film.

In the 1990s, actor–director Kenneth Branagh decided to make a movie that was, more or less, faithful to the novel. He therefore called his version *Mary Shelley's Frankenstein* (1994), which featured himself as Frankenstein and Robert De Niro as the monster. Branagh (who also coauthored the screenplay) may have followed Shelley's novel, in the sense of including the main characters and the major episodes, but his film can hardly be called faithful to the spirit of Shelley's novel. Shots of incisions, the hanging of the innocent Justine, amputations, the monster's cutting out the heart of Frankenstein's wife and brandishing it at him, and, worst of all, Robert De Niro's monster makeup, would have appalled the author; today, they elicit two responses the novel never would: derisive laughter or groans of disgust.

A literal adaptation of Shelley's novel does not lend itself easily to film, because it is an epistolary novel, one told through an exchange of letters between a captain and his sister about his encounter with Frankenstein and the monster who has been following his creator. Epistolary novels are virtually impossible to adapt in their original form. Branagh realized that, and although he retained the captain as a minor character, he dispensed with the letters. In film, even when the contents of a letter are crucial to a particular scene, the complete letter cannot be shown unless it is a short note. Usually, most of the letter is masked so that only the relevant text stands out.

Because it is also an epistolary novel, Alice Walker's Pulitzer Prize–winning novel *The Color Purple* was a challenge to its adapter. On one level,

it is a novel about written expression and the need to articulate feelings that, if they cannot be expressed orally, must be committed to paper; and that, if they cannot be addressed to the right person, must be addressed to God. Clearly, it would be difficult to present this philosophy on the screen, yet the film repeats the exact words with which the novel opens: "You better not never tell nobody but God. It'll kill your mammy." These words are addressed to Celie, a fourteen-year-old black girl, by her stepfather who has raped her and taken away the two babies that she bore. Forbidden to speak of her suffering and shame to another person, Celie begins a series of letters to God. Thus, *The Color Purple* consists of Celie's letters to God, her sister Nettie's letters to her, and Celie's letters to Nettie.

When Steven Spielberg decided to make the film version of *The Color Purple* (1985), he could not ignore the importance of the letters. Screenwriter Menno Meyjes had to make certain choices, one of which was to give Nettie's letters a purely narrative function so they could fill in details that Celie would not have known. Since Nettie's letters are for the most part nondramatic, Spielberg generates some drama by having them visualized while Celie is reading them. While Celie is on her porch reading Nettie's description of life in Africa, an elephant appears in the background. When Celie is in church reading about the destruction of an African church, a bulldozer comes through the altar of the church where she is sitting. Concurrent visualization at least suggests the effect of language on the imagination, which is one of the novel's main points.

Movies, it should be remembered, originated as mass entertainment for audiences. The preamble to the Production Code did not equivocate about the function of film being "primarily . . . entertainment without any explicit purpose of teaching or propaganda." In truth, movies both teach and propagandize—but they do so entertainingly. Often this means supplying an upbeat ending where a play or novel might not. When Warner Bros. decided to produce the movie version of the controversial Tennessee Williams play *A Streetcar Named Desire*, the ending had Stella leaving Stanley after she learned that he has raped her sister Blanche. The studio felt that audiences would want Stanley to pay for what he had done. However, in the play Stella stays; it is evident that Stella and Stanley need each other and that Blanche's institutionalization will restore their marriage to what it was before she arrived.

David Lean's film version of Charles Dickens's *Great Expectations* has Pip and Estella rushing off together at the end, which is completely contrary to Dickens's intentions. John Ford's *The Grapes of Wrath* scuttles Steinbeck's original ending and instead has Ma Joad extol "the people" for their ability to survive any crisis, including the Great Depression. Yet, strangely, both films capture the essence of their sources, while providing more optimistic endings for audiences that could accept the spirit of the novel but not the complete body in which that spirit resides.

Adaptations of Novels

One way of coming to an understanding of the nature of film adaptation is to study the novel and then its subsequent movie version. Jane Austen's *Emma* inspired a film set in the late twentieth century that is a totally faithful re-creation of the novel.

Jane Austen's **Emma,** *Amy Heckerling's* **Clueless** *(1995), and Doug Mc-Grath's* **Emma** *(1996).* Jane Austen's 1815 novel *Emma* depicts a decent but self-absorbed and manipulative heroine, Emma Woodhouse, who lives with her widower father in class-conscious Highbury, not far from London. Emma's social status guarantees her a privileged existence spent, for the most part, in meddling in other people's lives. Emma decides to play matchmaker for the illegitimate Harriet Smith, who idolizes her and never questions her judgment. When a farmer, Robert Martin, shows an interest in Harriet, Emma discourages the relationship. Instead, she steers Harriet toward the vicar, Mr. Elton, who is interested in Emma, not in Harriet. When Elton expresses his true feelings, Emma is shocked. The Emmas of the world do not live in parsonages. Elton eventually finds a wife, and Emma becomes more understanding after she realizes the consequences of interfering in other people's lives.

Emma's foil is her brother-in-law (the brother of her sister's husband), Mr. Knightley, some sixteen years older than she and capable of seeing her faults as well as reminding her of them. Knightley seems to be the least likely partner for Emma. Austen, however, knows better. Throughout the novel, Austen keeps readers wondering who will pair off with whom. Harriet—for

Alicia Silverstone (left) as Cher, the Emma figure in *Clueless* (1995); and Stacy Dash as Dionne, Amy Heckerling's substitution for Jane Austen's Jane Fairfax. *(Courtesy Paramount Pictures and MOMA/FSA)*

whom Emma had singled out Elton, and then Frank Churchill—ends up with the man who wanted her from the beginning: Robert Martin. And Frank Churchill, who did not seem especially interested in Jane Fairfax, ends up marrying her. That leaves only Knightley and Emma, whose marriage brings the novel to its conclusion.

For this kind of plot to succeed, each potential relationship must also be probable. One could, for example, imagine the union of Jane and Knightley, or even of Harriet and Knightley; when Elton snubs Harriet at a ball, Knightley saves her from embarrassment by dancing with her. One could also imagine the union of Harriet and Churchill, who rescues her from a band of gypsies. Austen creates situations that are so realistic that any of these pairings is possible; she also convinces us that the marriage partner each character chooses is the right one.

Amy Heckerling, who both wrote and directed *Clueless*—an unusually intelligent and occasionally touching version of *Emma*—moves the time ahead to the 1990s and the setting to Beverly Hills. Emma becomes Cher (Alicia Silverstone), who is about five years younger than Austen's heroine and still a high school student. Mel, her father, is an affluent lawyer, who indulges Cher's passion for designer clothes and Rodeo Drive shopping sprees. Cher's mother, like Emma's, died soon after she was born; but, unlike Emma, Cher has no sister. She does, however, have a slightly older stepbrother (not thirty-seven but around twenty)—Josh, the son of Mel's second wife from a previous marriage. Although Mel and Josh's mother are divorced, Josh is attending UCLA and often visits with Mel and Cher. Thus Cher and Josh see each other frequently—like Emma and Knightley. Moreover, as the script emphasizes, they are not blood relatives. Josh, like Knightley, calls Cher's attention to her own shortcomings.

In Cher's high school, no one is poor, but there is the right racial, social, and ethnic mix to suggest a microcosmic society in which distinctions are made according to dress, grades, sexual orientation, and behavior. In this world, Cher and her friend Dionne, with their fashionable clothes and cell phones, legislate for those who are too insecure to be themselves.

Just as Harriet was unable to assert her individuality in *Emma*, so, too, is Tai, her equivalent in *Clueless*. Tai, the new student—a gawky but sexually experienced young woman—is the perfect candidate for a Cher and Dionne makeover. Tai becomes their creation, with hairstyle, makeup, and clothes selected by them. Just as Harriet was attracted to the farmer Robert Martin in the novel, Tai is drawn to someone like herself—the class clown and skateboarder, Travis. And just as Emma discouraged a relationship with Martin and directed Harriet to Elton, Cher steers Tai toward a popular student also named Elton. Heckerling's Elton is solicitous of Tai because he wants to impress Cher, and later he expresses his feelings for Cher in a car, as his nineteenth-century namesake did in a carriage.

Heckerling realized that Austen's Jane Fairfax and Frank Churchill, a talented but financially dependent woman and an affluent but self-indulgent man, could never meet in the setting she had created. Instead, she substitutes an African American couple, Murray and Dionne; Murray is a chauvinist who insists on calling Dionne "woman," and Dionne is a feminist who resents sexist language. Murray and Dionne become mirror images of Josh and Cher. Each couple must change, abandoning misconceptions in favor of a deeper awareness of the partner's uniqueness—failings included.

Once Heckerling had substituted Dionne and Murray (who clearly have eyes only for each other) for Jane and Churchill, she could suggest nothing between Tai and Murray. Instead, she created the character of Christian, on whom Cher develops a crush. In a scene that further reveals Cher's lack of insight, Murray explains to her that Christian is gay, using language that is both street-smart and literary (he explicitly refers to Oscar Wilde). To Heckerling's credit, there is no trace of homophobic contempt in his remarks. Murray—and Dionne as well—can accept what Cher cannot even comprehend.

Any version of *Emma* should include three weddings, which poses a problem if the three heroines are still in high school. What Heckerling has done instead is to take two of Austen's characters—Emma's tutor and Mr. Weston, who have just married as the novel begins—and turn them into two unmarried teachers at the high school. Motivated partly by her desire to get better grades and partly by her mania for matchmaking, Cher, with

Gwyneth Paltrow (Emma) and Jeremy Northam (Mr. Knightley), in *Emma* (1996). *(Courtesy Miramax Films and the Margaret Herrick Library of the Academy of Motion Picture Arts and Sciences)*

Dionne's help, keeps bringing the two teachers closer together until the inevitable occurs. Present at their wedding are the three couples who will be having their own weddings in a few years.

Clueless offers many rewards for those who are able to view it as less a youth-oriented film than a modern version of a classic that takes liberties with the original but always remains faithful to its spirit.

A year after *Clueless* was released, a literal adaptation of *Emma* arrived on the screen. In adapting *Emma*, Doug McGrath, who also directed the film, remained faithful to the novel in both spirit and letter, going so far as to use much of Austen's own language. He has also succeeded in re-creating the novel on the screen, insofar as it is possible for film to do this with a third-person narrative and an omniscient point of view. Austen used omniscience judiciously in *Emma*, preferring to present as much of the action as she could from Emma's point of view. Heckerling realized this and thus used voice-over narration in *Clueless*—but only from Cher, who comments on her own behavior and gradually reaches some level of self-knowledge. McGrath also uses voice-over, but he has succeeded in making it more than a film convention; for the most part, voice-over occurs when Emma (Gwyneth Paltrow) writes in her diary—the closest any adapter can come to evoking Austen's reflections on her characters. Toward the end of the film, in a scene that does not exist in the novel, we even hear Emma's silent prayer in a chapel.

True to Austen, McGrath portrays Highbury as a world unto itself, insulated from anything as mundane as international affairs. Highbury's parochialism is apparent in the credits, during which a planet spins in the galaxy, growing larger as it moves closer into the frame. We soon recognize it as Earth, but not the planet to which we are accustomed. This planet consists of one country, Britain, which is made up of only London and Highbury; soon London disappears, leaving only Highbury.

McGrath also succeeds in having the actors play the potential couples in such a way that any union might be possible. When Frank Churchill joins Jane Fairfax for a duet, he sings with far greater enthusiasm than he did with

Emma, who had accompanied him at the piano earlier. On the other hand, when Harriet lies on the ground after being robbed by gypsies, Churchill extends his hand to her; McGrath cuts to a close-up of their clasped hands. Are they clasped because he is literally bringing her to her feet? Or is this a sign of a budding romance? And why does Knightley, who tells Emma that he cannot dance, dance so well with Harriet?

Like Austen, McGrath makes the picnic at Box Hill the turning point. Churchill insists upon a game in which everyone makes one or two witty remarks or three dull ones. When the garrulous Miss Bates jokes that whatever she says will be dull, Emma replies that, at least on this occasion, her dull comments will be limited in number. Knightley realizes the pain that Emma's words have caused Miss Bates and reproaches her for lack of consideration. It is at this point in both the novel and the film that Emma's remorse makes her determined to rise in Knightley's estimation—something one does only if the other party is worth the effort.

As well-written and directed as both *Clueless* and *Emma* are, audience reaction depends, to a great extent, on the performances of the leads. Neither Cher nor Emma can be just the typical spoiled brat or "Daddy's little girl," although each is a bit of both. Nor can they be vicious. Glib, insensitive, self-centered, haughty—yes; but deliberately cruel—no. That each moves from the extremes of self-love to love of other is a tribute to the directors and the writers but also to the talents of Alicia Silverstone and Gwyneth Paltrow.

Virginia Woolf's Mrs. Dalloway *and Marleen Gorris's* Mrs. Dalloway *(1996).*   Virginia Woolf's 1925 novel, *Mrs. Dalloway*, poses a problem for any filmmaker. How do you make a movie out of a novel about one day in the life of a woman planning a dinner party? Woolf's answer is simple: the woman's life is part of a fabric in which other lives besides her own are interwoven. The novel opens with the line, "Mrs. Dalloway decided to buy the flowers herself." Clarissa Dalloway's decision not to entrust the flower buying to her maid becomes a catalyst that sets off the reaction between past and present, as memory and desire intermingle. Although Clarissa is the wife of a member of Parliament and the mother of a grown daughter, she continually drifts back to the golden days of her youth, when she was wooed by Peter Walsh, who would have given her a more exciting, if less stable, life.

If Woolf had limited herself to depicting the preparations for a dinner party, without the ebb and flow of past and present, she would have produced a gemlike short story. But Woolf had something else in mind: a third-person narrative in which the omniscient narrator moves back and forth between the characters, exploring their consciousness, while at the same time connecting them with Clarissa's reflections during that single day. In short, Clarissa's mental soliloquies mesh so seamlessly with the narrative that the entire novel seems to be totally from her point of view—as if she were the author.

Woolf interweaves three stories in *Mrs. Dalloway*. The first is Clarissa's—her rather uneventful present as the wife of an M.P., whose only function in life is to give parties where most of the guests are her husband's friends. The second, interwoven with the first, is Clarissa's past—her youth at Bourton, where the future held such promise for her and her close friend, Sally Seton; where Peter Walsh courted her; and where she met Richard Dalloway, whom she married, much to Peter's regret. The third concerns a character whom Clarissa never meets—although their paths cross on the morning of that June day—but who becomes very much a part of her life. He is Septimus Warren Smith, a World War I veteran suffering from postwar trauma, who is in London with his Italian wife Lucrezia ("Rezia") and who, before the day is over, will commit suicide by jumping out of a window onto a spiked fence.

Eventually all three stories are resolved. Peter, who has returned from India, and Sally, now Lady Rosseter, arrive at the party, bringing with them memories of a happier time. Dr. Bradshaw is also a guest; however, his announcement that one of his patients has committed suicide causes Clarissa to reflect on the sort of person who would do such a thing. The reader knows that the patient is Septimus, whose deteriorating mental condition prefigures Woolf's; sixteen years after the publication of *Mrs. Dalloway*, Woolf placed a stone in her coat pocket and walked into the River Ouse.

Adapting *Mrs. Dalloway* for the screen posed enormous problems for screenwriter Eileen Atkins, a stage and screen actress who had written and starred in a one-person theater piece, *A Room of One's Own*, based on Woolf's writings. Atkins realized there was no other way to preserve the novel's brief internal monologues (or mental soliloquies) except to use voice-over. However, with Vanessa Redgrave as Clarissa speaking in slow, measured cadences—the spoken equivalent of recalling a past so precious that every moment had to be savored—the soliloquies truly seemed as though they were coming forth from her unconscious. The chief problem was not the flashbacks to Clarissa's youth; those could be accomplished by straight cuts or dissolves. Director Marleen Gorris preferred the former to replicate the speed with which Clarissa can return to a time when she was happiest. The chief problem was introducing the Septimus plot, so that, visually, it is integrated with the others.

The integration occurs in the credits sequence. Immediately after the cast is listed in alphabetical order, a title appears: Italy 1918. The setting is a battlefield. A soldier in a foxhole looks out through a loop of barbed wire at a figure advancing toward him. "Evans, don't come," he cries, but it is too late. The death of Evans will continue to haunt him until, unable to bear the weight of the memory, the soldier—Septimus Warren Smith—ends his life. Gorris dissolves from the soldier's face to another title: London, June 13, 1923.

The *mise-en-scène* is completely different. We are in Clarissa Dalloway's bright and airy bedroom. The credits continue as Clarissa admires herself in front of the mirror. Although she is only planning to buy flowers for her

Vanessa Redgrave as Clarissa Dalloway in *Mrs. Dalloway* (1996). *(Courtesy First Look Films)*

dinner party that evening, she is wearing an elegant aqua ensemble, with a flowing scarf and a yellow-feathered hat. There are a few more credits, as Clarissa descends the stairs saying, "I'll buy the flowers myself, Lucy." She then rhapsodizes about the glorious weather that augurs well for her party. As she leaves her home, she thinks, "What a lark! What a plunge!" For Mrs. Dalloway, "lark" is right. But "plunge?" Into what?

Atkins understands the distinction. "What a lark!" becomes Clarissa's thought, delivered by voice-over. But at that moment in the novel, "the morning—fresh as if delivered to children on the beach"—instantly brings Clarissa back to her youth when, on a similar morning, she threw open the French doors and rushed outside to "plunge" into whatever the day would bring. To capture that seamless interweaving of present and past, and to establish the fact that two time frames are operating in the film, Gorris cuts from Clarissa thinking "What a lark!" in 1923 to her younger self exclaiming, "What a plunge!" as she embraces the new day. The past then dissolves to the present, as Clarissa makes her way to the florist. Now the credits sequence has ended; each of the three plots—the older Clarissa, the younger Clarissa, and Septimus—has been set in motion and will develop incrementally until they come together at the end.

The technique of cutting, and occasionally dissolving, from present to past, has also been established and will continue throughout the film. It is natural for anyone to think of the sequences involving the young Clarissa as flashbacks. It would be more accurate to think of them as scenes from the past, integrated with the present. The scenes are occasioned by some incident or comment that propels the present into the past. The first person Clarissa meets in the film, as in the novel, is the obsequious Hugh Whitbread, who survives by currying favor with those in authority. They no sooner encounter each other than a voice is heard saying, "I can't stand him." The voice belongs to neither character, but to the young Peter Walsh, admonishing the equally young Clarissa for being sympathetic to Hugh, who was stuffy even in his youth. When the florist suggests sweet peas for the table, Clarissa is transported to the past when her closest friend, Sally Seton, cut the heads off flowers and dropped them into a bowl. After making her purchase, Clarissa muses about being Mrs. Dalloway, the party giver, and no longer "Clarissa." At that moment Gorris cuts to the young Clarissa, being told by Peter that she would grow up to be the perfect hostess.

Clarissa's selection of the dress for the party leads to a reverie in which her younger self, in white (as the young Clarissa is generally attired), is with Sally as she is about to experience "the most exquisite moment of her whole life," as Woolf describes it in the novel. Sally and Clarissa kiss on the lips, with a strangely erotic chasteness—neither virginal nor sexual, but a combination of both that leaves Clarissa dazed but ecstatic. The moment is short-lived in both the novel and the film. Peter witnesses the kiss, but does not voice the disapproval expressed in his face. Although his stern look momentarily causes Clarissa to question the kiss, she does not allow his displeasure to mar a privileged moment. If there is any incident in both the novel and film that makes it clear why Clarissa preferred a past where a kiss could be innocent, despite the currents of desire that it generated, to a present where it would be branded as "unnatural," it is this one. If the kiss was "the most exquisite moment," it is because the act itself was exquisite—purged of anything that would reduce it to mere passion.

Throughout the film, Atkins and Gorris imaginatively interlink present and past. Richard Dalloway's decision to buy red flowers for Clarissa is succeeded by a cut of the young Peter bringing white roses to her. When Richard, who knows that Peter was once his rival for Clarissa, learns that he is back from India, he muses, "If Peter Walsh is in town, Clarissa will know," as the scene shifts to the moment in the past when Richard first became aware of Peter's infatuation with Clarissa.

Atkins took a sensible approach to the Septimus subplot: she fragmented it, introducing it piecemeal, sometimes intercutting it with another incident—for example, the luncheon at Lady Bruton's is juxtaposed with Septimus and Rezia's visit to the psychiatrist, Dr. Bradshaw.

Woolf makes it clear that Clarissa never sees Septimus, although they are both in the vicinity of the florist shop when a car backfires, producing an explosive sound that terrifies Septimus. Atkins and Gorris felt that Clarissa should see him, even though she has no idea who he is. In the film, at the moment of the explosion, Clarissa glances at the window and sees Septimus's face pressed against it. She looks as if somehow she knows him, but obviously not by name. Atkins knew that Woolf always believed that Septimus and Clarissa were doubles. He plunges, while she remains wedded to routine; he chooses to act rather than be institutionalized, forced to conform to the role of "mental patient."

Septimus is both the extreme form of Clarissa and the mirror image of Woolf. When the Bradshaws arrive at the party and speak of the patient who has committed suicide, Clarissa's thoughts, rendered in voice-over, are only about the effect the news will have on her party, which actually has been going well. To Clarissa, death is the equivalent of an uninvited guest, as Gorris shows with close-ups of the mouths of Dr. Bradshaw and his wife, as they break the news that brings Clarissa close to fainting. Clarissa then retires to another room, where she looks out the window at her own spiked fence. As in the novel, her inner self is heard, pondering the death of someone she has never met but with whom she feels some vague kinship, questioning his act and comparing what she imagines to have been his life to her own. Clarissa eventually concludes that he will always stay young and will never have to worry about the heat of the sun or the furious winter; that his life, about which she knows nothing, will become, like her youth, a memory—but someone else's.

It is her realization that in a way the young man has triumphed—that he has taken his plunge and is at peace—that allows her to return to her party, resuming her hostess role and moving the film toward its conclusion. Atkins and Gorris knew the film could not end like the novel, in which Peter waits for Clarissa to return, and finally seeing her, says, "It is Clarissa. . . . For there she was." That is literature; it is also uncinematic.

Having made the decision to interweave present and past throughout the film, Atkins and Gorris could not end their *Mrs. Dalloway* in the present. Instead, there is a dissolve from Peter and Clarissa dancing together, slowly and decorously like two middle-aged people, to a group shot of Clarissa, Sally, and Peter on the lawn at Bourton, looking as if the future held unbounded promise and each day would be a lark or a plunge.

Michael Cunningham's The Hours *and Stephen Daldry's* The Hours (2002).

Michael Cunningham's 1998 novel *The Hours* is itself an adaptation. Cunningham could never have written *The Hours* without a thorough knowledge of *Mrs. Dalloway* and Virginia Woolf's life. "The Hours" was the working title of Woolf's *Mrs. Dalloway*, one theme of which is the passage of time. Like *Mrs. Dalloway*, Cunningham's novel interweaves present and past, but in a totally different way. *The Hours* tells three stories: Virginia Woolf's struggle to write *Mrs. Dalloway* in a London suburb in 1923; Clarissa Vaughan's preparations for a reception in honor of a poet dying of AIDS in New York at the end of the twentieth century; and Laura Brown's attempt to read *Mrs. Dalloway* in Los Angeles in 1949, while struggling, like the title character, to find some meaning in her life.

The novel begins with a 1941 prologue—specifically March 28, 1941, when Virginia Woolf, after leaving notes for her husband Leonard and sister Vanessa, waded into a river and drowned herself. The prologue is like a flash-forward; Cunningham has given Virginia Woolf her own year—not 1941, but 1923.

In the modern section, Clarissa Vaughan is a New York book editor who sets out one morning to buy flowers for a party in honor of Richard (whose last name is not revealed until the end), a terminally ill and suicidal poet, who calls her "Mrs. Dalloway" because she resembles Woolf's character. Richard is the incarnation of the Septimus figure and commits suicide in the same way.

While Woolf's Clarissa and Richard Dalloway are married, Clarissa Vaughan and Richard are former lovers, products of the sexual revolution of the 1960s, where there was no distinction between unsafe and protected sex. Woolf's Clarissa could recall a youth at Bourton where the closest thing to an erotic experience was the kiss between herself and Sally Seton. Clarissa Vaughan lived in an open relationship in Wellfleet with Richard and his lover Louis.

Cunningham envisions what a contemporary Clarissa might have been like, unfettered by the conventions and moral codes that Mrs. Dalloway had to observe. Clarissa has now settled into a relationship with a television producer, Sally Lester, obviously modeled after Sally Seton. We can also consider Cunningham's Clarissa a combination of Woolf's Clarissa and Rezia, Septimus's wife. Cunningham seems to be imagining what might have happened if Clarissa Dalloway had met Septimus; if she had, she would have sensed a kindred spirit, especially since Woolf had originally planned to end the novel with Clarissa's suicide. If Septimus and Clarissa are doubles, they would have understood each other. Yet if *The Hours* is any indication, Clarissa Dalloway could no more have prevented Septimus from killing himself than Clarissa Vaughan could have prevented Richard from doing the same. The voices that drove each of them to suicide were louder than any human's.

When appropriate, Cunningham echoes Woolf's language, sometimes literally in italics and sometimes allusively. *The Hours*'s opening line, "There are still the flowers to buy," recalls "Mrs. Dalloway decided to buy the flowers herself." Before going out to buy the flowers, Clarissa Vaughan feels as if she is about to "plunge" into a pool. Clarissa remembers rushing out of the glass doors in Wellfleet at eighteen, just as Woolf's Clarissa did at Bourton at the same age. Mrs. Dalloway ended up living in London's fashionable West End; Clarissa Vaughan, in New York's West Village.

En route to buy flowers, Clarissa Vaughan first meets Walter Hardy, a hack writer, whom she invites to her party, just as Mrs. Dalloway encountered Hugh Whitbread, reminding him of her party. Walter has a lover, Evan, in poor health; Hugh Whitbread has a wife, Evelyn, in a nursing home. At the florist, Clarissa hears a loud noise, just as Mrs. Dalloway did; but it is not a car backfiring, as it is in Woolf's novel, but a movie crew getting ready for a shoot. And just as the skywriting plane spelled out "Kreemo Toffee" in *Mrs. Dalloway*, providing a diversion for the onlookers, the thought of a movie in production excites Clarissa.

The counterpart to Peter Walsh, who returns from India to tell Mrs. Dalloway that he is in love with a married woman, is Louis, Richard's former lover, who returns from San Francisco to inform Clarissa that he is in love with a student. Lady Bruton's luncheon invitation to Richard Dalloway is echoed in the luncheon to which a gay actor, Oliver St. Ives, has invited Sally to interest her in a script with a gay action hero.

Cunningham's re-creation of the year 1923 in the "Mrs. Woolf" chapters is the result of extensive scholarship. Naturally, he takes liberties with some of the details, but only to make his narrative more dramatic. For example, in September 1923, the historical Virginia Woolf was at the Richmond station waiting for her husband Leonard to arrive from London. Tired of living in seclusion, she suddenly felt the urge to purchase a ticket to London. When Leonard arrived and learned what Virginia had done, she immediately requested a refund. Cunningham offers an alternative version. Out for a walk, Virginia suddenly decides to travel to London. "What a lark! What a plunge!" Cunningham does not italicize these lines, indicating that they are not from the novel but from within Virginia's consciousness. She is not waiting to meet her husband; rather, she has escaped from his tutelage. However, when Virginia sees him rushing toward her, rather than explain or get a refund, she simply keeps the ticket, never informing Leonard of what she had planned.

The Laura Brown narrative may seem original, but it too has its basis in both *Mrs. Dalloway* and Woolf's life. Laura, the name of Virginia's half-sister from her father's first marriage, was mentally unstable and was eventually institutionalized. Laura Brown has not quite reached that stage but is approaching it. Desperately trying to finish *Mrs. Dalloway*, and knowing a good deal about the author's life (especially her suicide), she contemplates the same, checking into a hotel with a copy of the novel, which she plans to read before ending her own life. Laura eventually decides against suicide, since she is pregnant with a second child.

Even more so than Clarissa Vaughan, Laura is the true stand-in for Virginia Woolf: a married woman with an adoring husband and a young son ("Richie") but who is still unsatisfied. When Kitty, a neighbor, confides in her about the major surgery she must undergo for the removal of a tumor, Laura consoles her as only she can: with an embrace and a kiss. The inspiration was the kiss between Clarissa and Sally Seton in *Mrs. Dalloway*. But there is a major difference. Laura is giving herself to Kitty, but in a manner that is both maternal and sensual. In their embrace, Laura feels she has discovered "the depths of Kitty," something for which Kitty's husband has searched but never found—the implication being that no man ever could. And in discovering Kitty's depths, Laura seems to have discovered her own, which will eventually cause her to abandon her family and forge a new life for herself.

Near the end of the novel, Richard, like Septimus, frames himself in the window of his apartment and slides off the sill to his death. He bids farewell to Clarissa with the same words that Virginia Woolf used in her suicide note to Leonard—"I don't think two people could have been happier than we've been." In the final chapter, set "at the end of the twentieth century," Richard's mother, an eighty-year-old woman, arrives at Clarissa's apartment after being informed of her son's suicide. Richard's actual name is Richard Worthington Brown. His mother is Laura Brown, who left her husband and "Richie" after her second child, a daughter, was born. The reason is the same that prompted Virginia Woolf to buy a ticket to London in September 1923: to return to a life that, for all its dangers and enticements, provided opportunities for a "lark" and a "plunge" that the suburbs could not. Unlike Virginia, who yielded to her husband's wishes, Laura Brown did what she felt she must. Once her daughter was born, she left her family and went on to a life of her own, eventually becoming a librarian in Canada.

Laura's husband, we learn, died of liver cancer; a drunk driver killed her daughter; and Richie grew up to be a distinguished poet, who has also written a novel with a female protagonist who commits suicide. The novel, however, was Richard's revenge on his mother, who was apparently the model, although the few who had read it assumed the character was inspired by Clarissa. But this may have been Cunningham's way of suggesting that Virginia Woolf, Clarissa Vaughan, and Laura Brown are not that different, since each has made a free choice. Virginia Woolf yearned to plunge into life, but her madness brought her to a plunge of a different and tragic kind; Clarissa Vaughan accepts life on its own terms, knowing that there will always be a day that signals a plunge, but that it will also be "followed by others, far darker and more difficult"; and Laura Brown's plunge is the most difficult of all, since it involved severing connections with the past, including a husband, a son, and a daughter, in order to preserve her own sanity.

Although the characters in *The Hours* are interlinked by name and allusion to Virginia Woolf's novel as well as her life, the novel can stand on its own as a masterpiece of literary fiction.

In adapting *The Hours*, screenwriter David Hare retained Cunningham's tripartite narrative, fragmenting it in a way more suited to film than to fiction. Because *The Hours* was a 2002 release, the Clarissa Vaughan and Laura Brown narratives were moved up to 2001 and 1951, respectively.

The Virginia Woolf segment (1923, 1941) remained intact, since it was anchored in fact.

The film has a prologue in the form of a credits sequence that, like the novel, begins with Virginia Woolf's suicide. First we hear the sound of rushing water, followed by a tracking shot of a river; the location is identified by a title: Sussex, England, 1941. A woman puts on her coat, leaves her home, and makes her way through a stretch of woods. Intercut with her walk to the river—the River Ouse, in which Virginia Woolf drowned herself—are excerpts, spoken in voice-over, from the letter that Woolf had written to her husband Leonard, informing him that she can no longer continue in life. Arriving at the embankment, she finds a large rock and places it in her coat pocket. Then she wades into the water, eventually sinking beneath the surface. The shot of her submerged body is followed by the film's title, *The Hours*.

Director Stephen Daldry then cuts to a setting that looks comparatively modern. A man pulls up in his car and enters a house, carrying a bouquet of roses: "Los Angeles 1951." The man is Dan Brown, whose wife Laura is still sleeping. More credits follow, as another time frame is introduced: Richmond, England, 1923, eighteen years before Virginia Woolf's suicide. Leonard is speaking with a doctor about his wife's condition. The credits continue; Virginia is seen lying in bed but awake—a subtle way of connecting her with the sleeping Laura Brown, both of whom are experiencing a similar emptiness.

There is a sudden cut to a woman in a leather jacket entering an apartment and getting in bed with another woman, who is only partially asleep. "New York City 2001." The two women are Sally Lester and Clarissa Vaughan. Alarm clocks—or, in Virginia Woolf's case, chimes—go off, awakening Laura, Virginia, and Clarissa, as they prepare to face the new day with the customary rituals: ablutions, the hair, the mirror inspection. Compared with Virginia and Clarissa, Laura is listless, preferring to stay in bed a bit longer to read *Mrs. Dalloway*. Within minutes, three women have become a triptych; although they exist in different time periods, they share the common experience of a single day, in which everything affecting each of them seems to be happening at the same time, making us believe that each woman would have understood the other.

As the credits sequence comes to an end, we see Clarissa discarding a bunch of dead flowers, Dan placing the yellow roses in a vase, and a maid arranging the blue cornflowers in the Woolf house at Richmond. At that point, Virginia descends the stairs, as the final credit "Directed by Stephen Daldry" comes on the screen, and the film proper begins.

Unlike the novel, with its 1941 prologue, the film has a prologue peculiar to cinema: a credits sequence in which three time frames (four, counting the 1941 suicide) and three lives unroll before our eyes. The intercutting, established in the credits sequence, predominates throughout. As Virginia finally decides upon *Mrs. Dalloway's* opening sentence, spoken in voice-over, Laura reads it aloud, and Clarissa announces, "Sally, I think I'll buy the flowers myself."

In adapting the novel, David Hare chose to focus exclusively on the essential characters from Cunningham's book, omitting Walter Hardy and Oliver St. Ives along with episodes involving them. The Wellfleet scenes are alluded to, not dramatized. Daldry also made choices, one of the more important being the doubling of Laura and Virginia. In addition to the unfulfillment that they share, they are so much alike, even in such physical details as hairstyles, that they seem to be aware of each other's presence. Virginia's decision to have Mrs. Dalloway kill herself is followed by Laura's attempt to bake a birthday cake for her husband. Although the two incidents don't seem to be related, they really are. Baking the cake is another diversion Laura uses to avoid confronting her own fate, which seems to point toward suicide. What Hare and Daldry have done is connect two decisions, one involving the end of a novel; the other, the end of a life. Neither, however, actually happens as originally planned: Virginia decides against Mrs. Dalloway's suicide, and Laura will find another way of dealing with a marriage that has reached a dead end. Virginia's decision to let Mrs. Dalloway live is intercut with Laura's checking into a hotel to commit suicide. Before taking the pills she had laid out, Laura drifts off into sleep as a flood seems to materialize beneath her bed, engulfing her, as the River Ouse did Virginia. In Laura's case it is only a dream. And just as Virginia made her choice, so does Laura when she awakens. "I can't. I can't," Laura cries.

The film version of *The Hours* depends as much on the visual as the verbal to clarify with a few images what can only be accomplished by a close reading of the novel. Perhaps a detective-fiction buff might have picked up on the fact that "Richie" Brown became Richard the AIDS-afflicted poet. And when his full name is finally given, Richard Worthington Brown, the close reader might wonder if this is indeed the case. In the film, after Laura decides against suicide, she picks up Richie at Mrs. Latch's house where she had left him. "You're my guy," she tells him consolingly. Daldry then cuts to a black-and-white wedding photo of a woman who looks like, and actually is, Laura Brown. The camera zooms back to Richard, who was obviously looking at his mother's picture. Richard goes to the window and draws aside the curtain. We expect a POV shot, and we get one—but not of the street below. Instead, Daldry repeats an earlier shot of Richie calling to his mother from the window of Mrs. Latch's house. Only an unobservant film viewer would miss the connection.

Early in the writing of *Mrs. Dalloway*, Woolf envisioned a kiss between Clarissa and another woman, the equivalent of "the enchanted kiss in fairy tales." She succeeded in the scene when Clarissa and Sally Seton kiss. For a film that tells three stories, there will be three kisses, not one. Laura kisses Kitty on the lips because it is the only way she knows to console a woman who has all the symptoms of ovarian cancer. It is an ambiguous kiss, because Laura is an ambiguous character. The kiss is demure yet sensuous, ethereal but physical. She kisses Kitty to assuage her anxiety and at the same time to experience some kind of union with a fellow sufferer, whose marriage is also unfulfilling.

When Vanessa Bell leaves after visiting Virginia at Richmond, Virginia embraces her sister hungrily, as if she were trying to enfold Vanessa into herself, so they could be inseparable. She kisses her passionately, but not sexually.

After the ordeal of Richard's suicide, Clarissa, exhausted, kisses Sally. Again, there is nothing erotic about the kiss; it is an unspoken sign of Clarissa's gratitude for Sally's support and love, without which she would not have been able to function.

Although each kiss is different, each is motivated by need—the need to comfort another, to unite oneself with another, and to express one's devotion to another.

Unlike Cunningham's novel, which only has a prologue, the movie has an epilogue as well, bringing it full circle. Again Virginia wades into the river, as we hear her voice instructing Leonard to remember their years together, their love for each other, and above all "always the hours." When her head sinks beneath the surface, the film ends.

The Hours is as faithful an adaptation as any novelist could desire. As an audiovisual medium, the film is able to provide, through Philip Glass's score, a recurring theme common to all three narratives, first heard when we see the River Ouse, rushing along inexorably—the music, a series of rapid chords, echoing the same inevitable movement toward each woman's personal destiny. The color scheme, with its alternations of browns and blues, has already been discussed, but it too works to make three lives into one. Like any successful film adaptation, *The Hours* achieves a new life on the screen quite different from the one it had on paper.

Adaptations of Plays

Although they are written to be performed, plays also present challenges to filmmakers who want to adapt them for the screen. Playwrights are limited in ways novelists are not. In the theater, the action is advanced through dialogue, embellished by whatever accoutrements (sets, costumes, makeup, lighting) have been chosen for the production, and performed within a space such as an auditorium, an amphitheater, a theater-in-the-round, a loft, or even a parking lot.

In order for a play to successfully translate into a movie, it must be "opened up" for the screen; this is particularly important in the case of single-set plays, many of which are among the theater's finest: *The Little Foxes*; *A Streetcar Named Desire*; *Come Back, Little Sheba*; *Long Day's Journey into Night*; and others. Musicals like *The King and I* and *Gypsy* pose fewer problems because of their multiple settings. Filmmakers can use a variety of techniques to open up a play in which the action is limited to one or two places.

Filmmakers can take advantage of their medium by dramatizing or visualizing material that could only be narrated on the stage. William Inge's play *Picnic* (1953) takes place in a yard between two houses in a small Kansas town. Thus the Labor Day picnic, which inspired the title and is a vital element of the plot, is never seen. Since the play dramatized the way a stranger's arrival on a Labor Day morning altered the lives of all the characters, for the 1956 film version screenwriter Daniel Taradash transferred the most dramatic scenes in the play to the picnic, where the characters revealed their true nature and innermost thoughts. And director Josh Logan used the picnic to provide audiences with a vivid depiction of an end-of-summer ritual in rural America.

Gore Vidal, who adapted Tennessee Williams's *Suddenly, Last Summer* (1958) for the screen, added more scenes, since the play had only one set: a garden. In the play, Catherine Holly had been committed to Lion's View State Asylum because she was considered insane. By showing Catherine (Elizabeth Taylor) at Lion's View, Vidal and director Joseph L. Mankiewicz were also able to portray the horrible conditions that existed there. Since the plot hinges on whether Catherine will be lobotomized, the film opens with a lobotomy being performed in an operating room. Most important, as Catherine delivers her climactic monologue, in which she recounts the hideous death of her cousin Sebastian, details of the incident and the events leading up to it are shown on the screen.

Filmmakers can also visualize symbols so that they cease to be abstract. The "streetcar" in *A Streetcar Named Desire* is both symbolic and real. It is the mode of transportation that takes Blanche DuBois to her sister's home, where she hopes to escape from a sordid and painful past. Film allows us to see the streetcar, which, from the outset, is associated with Blanche, since it was instrumental in bringing her into an environment in which she would eventually be destroyed. In another Tennessee Williams play that became a successful film, *The Night of the Iguana* (1962), the iguana, which is tied to a rope and kept under the porch, could not be seen on the stage; yet it is a symbol of the nonconformist (perhaps the artist), whose movements society tries to restrict because those who deviate from the norm often threaten those who have sworn to uphold it. While it is not really necessary to see the iguana, John Huston, who directed the 1964 movie version, obviously knew that audiences expected it; and seeing the iguana, which does not conform to the traditional notion of beauty, highlights the point that Williams was making.

Plays can also be opened up by moving some incidents to other locations to achieve variety. Lillian Hellman had no choice but to have the villain of her play *Watch on the Rhine* (1941) killed in the living room, since the entire action was set there. The 1943 movie version transfers the murder to the garage. In the play *Streetcar*, Blanche tells Mitch about her husband's suicide after they return from the Moon Lake Casino. The film allows Blanche to tell Mitch at the Casino itself.

In film, Shakespeare's soliloquies or asides can be rendered in voice-over. Voice-over is perfect for both, which are simply the character's thoughts spoken aloud. In the 1948 film version of *Hamlet*, Laurence Olivier frequently used voice-over to make these stage conventions more natural. What the character is thinking, the audience should hear.

Sometimes in adapting a play, a screenwriter will create a character from a name merely mentioned in the play or create a new character to pair off with one who does appear in the play. In the film version of *Tea and Sympathy*, not only does Ellie — who in the play is known only as the prostitute with whom Tom Lee failed so abominably that he attempted suicide — appear as a character, but the encounter between her and Tom is depicted as well. At the end of the play *The Little Foxes* (1939), Alexandra knows that her mother, Regina, was responsible for her father's death. When the 1941 film version was released, the Production Code required some kind of retribution; thus the original ending, in which Alexandra stays on to remind Regina of what she has done, might make it seem that Regina has not been punished. In the film, therefore, Alexandra leaves home with a young man, David Hewitt, who did not exist in the play but was created for the film so that Alexandra could be paired off with him — and Regina would be left alone with her guilt.

Not every major play has been adapted for the screen as successfully as *Streetcar*, *Picnic*, and *The Little Foxes*.

In Marsha Norman's Pulitzer Prize–winning one-act play *'Night, Mother* (1983), a daughter tells her mother that she plans to commit suicide that night. The play observes the three unities of Greek tragedy: unity of action (one main plot), unity of place (one setting), and unity of time (the time covered in the play is identical to the time required to perform it). The plot of *'Night, Mother* is structured in such a way that a film version would also have to observe the unities. In the 1986 film version, the action was opened up a bit, but not enough to keep the moving images from becoming static pictures. Paul Newman's 1986 film version of Tennessee Williams's *The Glass Menagerie* had similar problems. Because of his great respect for the text, Newman scarcely opened up the action at all, and the result was like watching a photographed play.

Thus, strict fidelity to a work of literature does not necessarily result in a good film. Purists may be delighted that the text is intact, but moviegoers expect "moving pictures."

Adaptations of Short Stories

Short stories are notoriously difficult to adapt because of their brevity. Thus, when Twentieth Century-Fox decided that O. Henry's short stories would be ideal for film, the studio realized that because of the author's great popularity, it would be better to use an anthology approach rather than to select one and expand it into a full-length movie that would bear only a slight resemblance to the original. Thus *O. Henry's Full House* (1952) consisted of five different O. Henry stories by five different directors.

Other filmmakers have taken on the challenge of creating a film from a single short story, even if it is only a few pages long. This brevity can make it impossible to produce a feature-length film that remains completely faithful to the original story. The best movie versions of short stories, such as Robert Siodmak's *The Killers* (1946) and Hitchcock's *The Birds*, use their sources purely as points of departure.

Daphne du Maurier's "The Birds" and Alfred Hitchcock's* The Birds (1963). Daphne du Maurier's *Kiss Me Again, Stranger* (1952), a collection of eight short stories, included one called "The Birds." Set in Cornwall, in the extreme southwest of England, where du Maurier spent most of her life, "The Birds" was inspired by two actual experiences in which seagulls attacked the author and her dogs, and, later, a farmer as he was plowing.

The story is told from the point of view of Nat Hocken, a farm worker, who lives on an island with his wife and two children. On a day in early December, Nat notices birds circling overhead but pays no attention. That night, they mass at his window, pecking at it—and then at him, when he opens it. They then enter the children's room through an open window, colliding with one another and littering the floor with their dead bodies.

The unprovoked attacks continue, but the official reason seems to be a sudden climactic change that has sent hordes of birds into Britain. Because du Maurier wrote the story in the early years of the Cold War, the townspeople blame the plague of birds on the Russians. Next, a state of emergency is declared in Britain after the birds start attacking RAF planes. Isolated in his home with his wife and family, without telephone service or radio reception, Nat lights his last cigarette and waits. "Won't America do something?" his wife asks. The question is never answered, and Nat wonders "how many million years of memory were stored in those little brains, giving them the instinct to destroy mankind with all the deft precision of machines."

Hitchcock bought the rights to "The Birds" shortly after *Kiss Me Again, Stranger* was published but was interested in only two aspects of the story: the coastal setting, suggesting isolation; and the birds' unprovoked attacks. Changing the setting was easy; it became Bodega Bay in northern California. The attacks were another matter. In the film, they are explained neither scientifically nor politically; Hitchcock would not resort to pseudo-science or Cold War hysteria.

Fresh from making *Psycho*, Hitchcock conceived of a *Psycho*-like plot with an unmarried son, Mitch; his widowed mother, Lydia; and a female intruder, Melanie. It is not coincidental that the women's names, Melanie and Lydia, begin with the same letters as those of the sisters in *Psycho*, Marion and Lila. In both films, a car trip becomes a rendezvous with destiny, a real mother-son relationship replaces a ghostly one, and a female arrives to threaten that relationship.

Visually, Melanie (Tippi Hedren) and Lydia (Jessica Tandy) are doubles, right down to their hairstyles. One could easily see Melanie as a younger version of Lydia; both are born to be grandes dames. Neither can love. Melanie pursues Mitch (Rod Taylor) with a pair of lovebirds, offering symbolically what she cannot give naturally. At the beginning of the film, Mitch is looking for a pair of lovebirds as a birthday present for his kid sister, Cathy. The gift is appropriate. Cathy needs all the love she can get, since she does not receive it from her mother and sees her brother only on weekends. Cathy was a late child. Lydia was so paranoid about being left alone (perhaps because she rightly sensed that her husband would predecease her) that she ignored the basics of family planning and had Cathy some twenty years after Mitch. Cathy, who was six when her father died, has just turned eleven; Mitch is in his early thirties. No wonder Cathy regards Mitch as a surrogate father; it's no wonder, too, that Cathy is attracted to Melanie, who looks more like her mother than Lydia does. Lydia, in fact, could pass for Cathy's grandmother. Similarly, Melanie is attracted to Cathy, in whom she sees herself as a child — a child whose own mother walked out on the family when Melanie was eleven. However, Melanie does not realize that, by pursuing Mitch to Bodega Bay, she will inherit a mother. Lydia, who has sabotaged every one of Mitch's relationships with a woman in order to keep him for herself, has no fears about Melanie. The birds will see to it that Melanie is no longer a threat to Lydia's matriarchy.

If *The Birds* is taken as an allegory, there is no reason to explain the attacks except as an external manifestation of something within the characters.

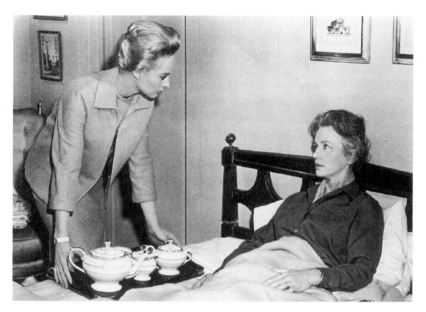

Doubles: The intrusive blonde (Tippi Hedren) serving breakfast to the fearful matriarch (Jessica Tandy) in Hitchcock's *The Birds* (1963), a total reworking of Daphne du Maurier's short story. *(Courtesy MOMA/FSA)*

With the exception of Cathy, they are loveless and self-absorbed people, who, had they been birds, would have clawed at each other; had Cathy been a bird, she would have been a lovebird.

It is evident from the film's ironic ending that Mitch, Lydia, and Cathy get—and do not get—what they want. As Mitch, Cathy, Lydia, and the bandaged and traumatized Melanie prepare to leave for San Francisco, conceding victory to the birds, Lydia holds Melanie against her breast. For the first time, Lydia looks benign and strangely happy, knowing that Melanie, who will need plastic surgery, if not psychotherapy, will never marry Mitch. Cathy has a surrogate mother in Melanie, but from the look on Melanie's face, it is hard to imagine her being able to function normally again. Mitch lived up to Lydia's expectations that he act as the "man of the family," like his father, by driving all of them out of Bodega Bay. On the other hand, Mitch and Cathy have both lost: Mitch has lost a potential mate, and Cathy, a mother figure. Lydia, however, has triumphed—thanks to the birds. All that Lydia has lost is her house; she might have to live in San Francisco.

Philip K. Dick's "Minority Report" and Steven Spielberg's Minority Report (2002).

Just as Hitchcock used only the basic premise of du Maurier's "The Birds" for his own examination of the mystery of evil, Spielberg did pretty much the same when he decided to bring Philip K. Dick's

1954 story, "Minority Report," to the screen. Dick's story is set in a futuristic New York, where an organization called Precrime has succeeded in reducing the number of violent acts through information gleaned from three mutants or "precogs" capable of predicting crimes before they occur, resulting in the arrest of the "perpetrators" and their internment in detention camps. The "babbling" of the precogs is first analyzed and then transcribed on punchcards with the name of the potential criminal and his or her victim.

The head and founder of Precrime, Tom Anderton, is proud of his organization, believing it has proved successful (even though men and women are arrested on the basis of intention rather than deed), until a punchcard comes up with Anderton's name on it. Dick wrote "Minority Report" during the first stages of the Cold War, when there was real fear of a third world war with the Soviet Union and/or its ally, Communist China. Dick asks the reader to envision an America after an Anglo-Chinese War that has devastated vast sections of New York. The country is now at peace, and interplanetary travel is possible for those who prefer to live elsewhere than on Earth. With the creation of Precrime, the military has been rendered virtually powerless.

Anderton finds himself in a similar situation; he suspects that Ed Witwer, his assistant and eventual replacement when he retires, has framed him, hoping to edge him out of Precrime and run the operation himself. After Anderton learns of the existence of a minority report from one of the precogs that contradicts the majority report of the other two, he resolves to find it. When he does, he discovers that the minority report has Anderton changing his mind once he knew he would commit a murder. Anderton also discovers that Kaplan, a retired army general and head of a right-wing veterans' organization, has a copy of the minority report that he plans to read at a rally. Kaplan hopes that by proving Precrime is error-ridden, he will restore the army to its pride of place (and eventually create a military dictatorship).

Realizing that the release of the report would spell the end of Precrime, and believing that Precrime is preferable to fascism, Anderton shoots Kaplan and goes into voluntary exile on another planet.

By the time Steven Spielberg decided to make a film based on "Minority Report," the world had changed so dramatically that it would have been impossible to adhere strictly to Dick's plot, which had a political subtext: the determination of right-wing militarists to regain the power they lost with the end of a war that heralded the collapse of communism and deprived the army of any meaningful role in the new order. The police stepped into the vacuum and created Precrime, which was equally right-wing in its attempt to tamper with free will. Since the screenwriters, Scott Frank and Jon Cohen, were carrying out Spielberg's intentions, they reduced Dick's story to a skeletal scenario, consisting of the characters of Anderton, his assistant Wally, Witwer, and the three precogs—all of whom have undergone

Tom Cruise as the "precriminal" Tom Anderton and Samantha Morton as the "precog" Agatha, whose minority report can clear him, in Steven Spielberg's *Minority Report* (2002). *(Courtesy Dream Works and Twentieth Century-Fox)*

a major change. The turning point—Anderton's discovery that two of the precogs have identified him as a potential murderer—was retained, leading to a labyrinth of involvement considerably more complex than Dick's story.

Dick's setting has also been changed, from New York to Washington, D.C. No longer are we in some nebulous future, but in a specific year: 2054, which was perhaps Spielberg's way of acknowledging his source—Dick's short story, published in 1954—and suggesting that had the writer lived to witness the high-tech revolution of the 1980s and 1990s, along with the historical changes that have occurred since 1954, he might have applauded the way Spielberg made his story meaningful to the twenty-first century.

Spielberg has always shown the greatest compassion for "others," whether they are aliens in *E.T.* and *A.I.* or humans drawn to aliens because their own societies, even their own families, are "alien" to them, as in *Close Encounters*. The precogs have been given the distinctive names of Agatha, Dashiell, and Arthur, perhaps Spielberg's way of connecting them with two of the great practitioners of detective fiction (Agatha Christie and Dashiell Hammett) and the eminent science-fiction writer Arthur C. Clarke, who coauthored the script of *2001: A Space Odyssey* with director Stanley Kubrick. Spielberg's precogs no longer sit in "high-backed chairs"; rather, they float in a nutrient-enriched pool, seemingly inert until they envision a precrime. Here is the clearest departure from Dick's story, necessitated both by the nature of film, which favors the visual over the verbal, and the technology of the twenty-first century, which makes it possible for the precogs to envision a crime before it occurs, rather than experience it as babble in need of decoding. Thus, Agatha (Samantha Morton) can see a crime of passion as it would have occurred without Precrime.

The names of potential perpetrators are no longer stamped on punchcards, but inscribed on red balls that roll down a chute, ready to be retrieved. Once Anderton sees the ball with his name on it, he becomes a man on the run.

In the film, Anderton's odyssey has darker overtones than Dick's story. The palette in *Minority Report* is often bathed in a steely blue light, like a color film drained of its hues, with Tom Cruise, as Anderton, looking in need of a shave or a dermatologist. Cruise has never looked less handsome, yet his is the face of a man who understands street life because he is drug-dependent and thinks nothing of venturing into Washington's netherworld to support his habit.

This addition to Anderton's character provides him with a flaw that humanizes him. When we discover that Anderton's only child, Sean, was abducted and killed, Anderton's role in enforcing Precrime is even more understandable, as is the bond that develops between Anderton and Agatha, whose minority report is crucial to his clearing himself.

In view of Spielberg's devotion to liberal causes, the director could never have accepted Dick's ending. In the film, Precrime has proved so successful in Washington, where the murder rate has dropped by ninety percent, that it is about to go national, resulting in an America in which the exercise of free will would be restricted to good, or at best neutral, acts. Although some medieval theologians believed that sin exists first in the order of intention, there is an enormous difference between contemplating a crime, or even preparing for one, and actually committing it. Free will is uniquely human. Precrime does not acknowledge that distinction.

Unlike Dick, Spielberg cannot allow Precrime to continue, because it is both a threat to freedom of choice and a form of totalitarianism. In the film, Precrime's founder, Lamar Burgess (Max von Sydow), has devised a monstrous plan to ensure Precrime's existence. The three precogs were abandoned children, subjected to some form of experimentation that robbed them of their original personalities and made them the equivalent of psychics. Lacking any sort of a life, they lie in a pool like human pods. Agatha, the most intelligent of the precogs, was the daughter of an addict who, once out of rehab, wanted her daughter back. Since Agatha was invaluable to Precrime, Burgess killed her mother, forgetting that within Agatha's consciousness was a visual transcript of the incident that could be downloaded. Agatha's is the minority report that includes her mother's murder and the murderer's identity.

Burgess went to such extremes to preserve Precrime that he arranged for Anderton's only child, Sean, to be kidnapped and killed. Eventually, Agatha's minority report is downloaded and Burgess's villainy is revealed, but the film does not end with his death (really suicide).

An epilogue reveals Spielberg's enormous compassion for others—specifically the precogs, who had been used in such an inhumane experiment. Once Precrime had been discontinued, the precogs, obviously unable to function as members of society, were sent to "an undisclosed place"—a storybook house where they could spend their days at peace—hardly compensation for what they had endured. All that has happened is that one form of isolation has been exchanged for another. The precogs are last seen reading books, as if they were catching up with an activity of which they were deprived when they were made the servants of a deviant technology.

The Nature of Screenwriting

As we have seen, successful adaptations are often the result of skillful screenwriting. Screenwriting is an art unto itself. Distinguished authors like William Faulkner and F. Scott Fitzgerald tried to write for the screen, but what they produced pales in comparison with their fiction. Fitzgerald's film scripts either contained dialogue the actors found impossible to speak or were so cluttered with description that they had to be pruned drastically. Fitzgerald's talent lay in fiction, where he could narrate or describe without dramatizing, rather than in screenwriting, where he would have to suppress the urge to tell everything through words and would need to delegate some authority to the camera.

The ideal screenplay advances the plot in two ways: verbally, through dialogue; and visually, through action. If a screenplay were total dialogue, there would be no difference between a screenplay and a stage play. Screenwriters must visualize the action as they write it. When the visual might be more effective than the verbal, the writer must suppress the desire to rely on dialogue and, instead, must indicate how the action can be visualized.

Julia (1977) has a literate—that is, well-written and intelligently executed—script by Alvin Sargent, yet there are parts of the film that contain no dialogue at all. Sargent knew when language was necessary to advance the plot, and when images were. For example, the scene in which Lillian is watching a performance of *Hamlet* in Moscow is crosscut with Julia's murder in Frankfurt. Sargent realized that it would be more effective to have the murder take place without any dialogue at all so there would be a contrast with the performance of *Hamlet*, where dialogue is essential. Thus a further contrast results: verbalized stage violence and nonverbal real violence.

Although it is obvious that a screenplay is intended to be visualized, the consequences of visualization may not be so obvious. One such consequence is the kind of language with which the screenplay is written. Audiences expect both the photographed image and the characters' dialogue to be realistic. In real life, we point to an object and call it a "this" or a "that." In film, a demonstrative can have a visual antecedent, so that a "this" or a "that" is something the audience sees. When Ellen (Claudette Colbert) sees the blanket partition that Peter (Clark Gable) has arranged between their beds in *It Happened One Night*, she says, "That makes it all right," glancing in the direction of the blanket. It is the glance that makes the grammar and the line all right, too. A screenwriter who is not thinking visually might have written: "The fact that you've put up a blanket between the beds makes it all right." That would be stage dialogue, which tends to be more precise and grammatical than film dialogue; it can also turn off moviegoers.

Screen dialogue is often truncated—that is, sentences are frequently left unfinished, and speech is fragmentary. For this reason, screen language is closer to actual conversation than any other kind of dialogue, even that of the most naturalistic kind of theater. An example of stage dialogue is Nick's lines in Lillian Hellman's play *The Autumn Garden*: "These are my oldest friends. I think as one grows older it is more and more necessary to reach out your hand for the sturdy old vines you knew when you were young and let them lead you back to the roots of things that matter." Even though these lines are supposed to sound pompous, they would sound doubly so in a film if they were delivered in close-up or even medium shot. The audience might even laugh. *The Autumn Garden* has never been filmed, even though it is considered Hellman's finest play. Yet if it were, and the screenwriter decided to retain these lines, they would have to be changed to something like this: "These are my oldest friends. You might call them the vines that bring me back to my roots."

Movie dialogue is more like the exchange between Butch and Sundance in *Butch Cassidy and the Sundance Kid*:

BUTCH: How long you figure we been watching?
SUNDANCE: Awhile.
BUTCH: How much longer before you think they're not after us?
SUNDANCE: A while longer.
BUTCH: How come you're always so talkative?
SUNDANCE: Born blabby.

To appreciate the way a screenwriter economizes on language, compare the dialogue in a novel with that in the movie based on the novel. Often a screenwriter will incorporate dialogue from the novel into the screenplay if the dialogue is appropriate. However, spoken dialogue is not necessarily the same as written dialogue; screen dialogue has to be made compatible with the rhythms of human speech. In both Raymond Chandler's novel *The Big Sleep* and the 1946 film version directed by Howard Hawks, General Sternwood asks the detective Philip Marlowe about himself. Here is what Marlowe says in the novel:

> I'm thirty-three years old, went to college once and can still speak English if there's any demand for it. There isn't much in my trade. I worked for Mr. Wilde, the District Attorney, as an investigator once. His chief investigator, a man named Bernie Ohls, called me and told me you wanted to see me. I'm unmarried because I don't like policemen's wives.

Compare Marlowe's reply in the film:

> I'm thirty-eight years old, went to college once. I can still speak English when there's any demand for it in my business. I worked for the District

Attorney's office once. It was Bernie Ohls, his chief investigator, who sent
me word you wanted to see me. I'm not married.

Since Humphrey Bogart was playing Marlowe, the character's age had to be
changed from thirty-three to thirty-eight. But the real difference is the suc-
cinctness of the screen dialogue, which imparts the same information as the
novel but more concisely.

Economy of language, which is at the heart of screenwriting, is not
the same as ellipsis, in which words are omitted for the sake of balance or
parallelism. Ellipsis is rhetorical rather than dramatic, artificial rather than
real. In a scene from Elia Kazan's 1976 movie version of F. Scott Fitzgerald's
unfinished novel *The Last Tycoon*, the producer Monroe Stahr (Robert De
Niro) watches the rushes of a highly sophisticated 1930s movie in which
the hero says to the heroine, "I love you," and she replies, "And I, you." Stahr
is furious: " 'And I—you!' Who talks like that?" Claudius in *Hamlet* does, for
one: "And he to England shall along with you." But that is stage dialogue;
in particular, Elizabethan stage dialogue. And nobody talked like that in Elizabethan England, either.

People talk in strands, in words and phrases strung together in a kind
of beaded syntax, much the way Neff talks in *Double Indemnity*—in units of
thought, where the ideas generate their own rhythm and their own grammar. Consider the scene in *Double Indemnity* when Neff first meets Phyllis;
the dialogue is charged with undercurrents of sexual innuendo:

PHYLLIS: There's a speed limit in this state, Mr. Neff. 45 miles an hour.
NEFF: How fast was I going, officer?
PHYLLIS: Around 90.
NEFF: Suppose you get off your motorcycle and give me a ticket.
PHYLLIS: Suppose I let you off with a warning this time.
NEFF: Suppose it doesn't take.
PHYLLIS: Suppose I whack you over the knuckles.
NEFF: Suppose I burst out crying and put my head on your shoulder.
PHYLLIS: Suppose you try putting it on my husband's shoulder.
NEFF: That tears it.

Sometimes movie characters speak in epigrams, but these are movie,
not stage, epigrams. They are memorable because they compress a complex
idea into an easily remembered line that is natural for the character to speak
and is not merely an occasion for the writer to wax clever. At the end of
Now, Voyager (1942), Charlotte (Bette Davis) says to Jerry (Paul Henreid),
"Oh, Jerry, don't let's ask for the moon. We have the stars." By using images
(moon, stars) that everyone readily understands, she sums up with marvelous
precision humankind's perennial desire to overreach. Yet what Charlotte says

is appropriate to the circumstances: Charlotte is happy just to take care of Jerry's daughter, even though Jerry can no longer be her lover.

Movie epigrams are not stage epigrams, which tell us more about the playwright's gift for language than about the character's motivation or psychology. In Oscar Wilde's *The Importance of Being Earnest*, Lady Bracknell's line "Hesitation of any kind is a sign of mental decay in the young, of physical weakness in the old" is a stage epigram because it functions not so much as dialogue as an expression of Wilde's wit. While we may enjoy that wit, we sense that we are hearing the author, not the character.

In *All About Eve*, when Margo Channing (Bette Davis) says, "Fasten your seat belts; it's going to be a bumpy night," she is parodying the airline cliché, "Fasten your seat belts; it's going to be a bumpy flight." Margo's line is not a turn of phrase but a variation on a phrase already turned. Unlike Oscar Wilde's epigrams, which can be quoted out of context and still sound witty, Margo's "Fasten your seat belts" is the closing line of a specific sequence. Realizing that Eve is now her rival, Margo drinks too much at a party and becomes progressively more ill-tempered. Downing one last martini, she sweeps across the room, turns, delivers the line, and exits in the grand manner. The camera, which has been tracking her the whole time, exits in a huff with her. As a curtain line, "Fasten your seat belts" might have fallen flat; as an exit line in a movie, it is ideal, particularly given Bette Davis's memorably corrosive delivery. (Nobody ever says, "Do you remember when Lady Bracknell said, 'Hesitation of any kind is a sign of mental decay in the young, of physical weakness in the old?' " They do say, "Do you remember when Bette Davis said, 'Fasten your seat belts; it's going to be a bumpy night' in *All About Eve*?")

Just as the movie epigram differs from the stage epigram, the movie monologue — an extended speech in which a character reveals important information — differs from the stage monologue. In *All About Eve*, Eve (Anne Baxter) delivers a monologue about her dreary childhood and tragic marriage, playing on the sympathies of her five listeners. Even if Joseph L. Mankiewicz had not directed his own screenplay, a director would have no other choice but to cut to the listeners on certain lines, as Eve either calls her listeners by name or alludes to something about them that causes them to respond. There are some seven cuts in Eve's monologue, yet they are so unobtrusive that by the time Eve finishes speaking, the audience feels it has heard a monologue, while it has really witnessed a scene. In the theater, the speech could never be a true monologue, since Eve poses rhetorical questions to her listeners or makes references that necessitate a reaction from them, and these reactions demand close-ups. In the movie there is no question that one listener is moved, another is close to tears, a third is attentive, a fourth is concerned, and a fifth is mildly skeptical but ultimately convinced. It is important that we see, and see clearly, each listener's reaction, since Eve is winning each of them over by her tale of woe—a tale that, incidentally, is fabricated.

By its nature, a screenplay is best appreciated after one has seen it brought to the screen. *Patton* (1970) is best remembered for Patton's (George C. Scott) opening monologue; yet, taken simply as a monologue, it is not on a par with such great stage monologues as Hickey's in Eugene O'Neill's *The Iceman Cometh* or Blanche's in *A Streetcar Named Desire*. However, if, while reading it, you try to imagine Patton growing progressively larger as he becomes more outrageous, which is what happens on-screen, you can then appreciate how the words were translated into images. Patton progresses from a tiny figure against a gigantic American flag to a face that fills the screen to a tiny figure again. It is like watching the ego inflate itself and then lose air.

A novel can span several hundred pages without adhering to a strict code, with the text broken up into chapters or chapter equivalents. Writing a play requires division into acts and, if necessary, scenes within those acts. If the setting changes in a novel, it can be indicated by a phrase ("Meanwhile, in London . . ."); in a play, a change of location is marked by an act or scene change, as in Lillian Hellman's *The Searching Wind*: act 1, scene 1, the drawing room of the Hazen house, Washington, D.C.; scene 2, a room in the Grand Hotel, Rome. In a screenplay, structuring the narrative and designating scene changes are even more complicated.

A screenplay follows a specific format. Every professional screenplay (although not always published ones) begins with the same two words in capital letters: FADE IN. Fade in on what? Suppose you wanted to fade in on a cabin in the woods. That would be your first shot. How you indicate it depends on whether you are writing a spec script—one for which you have no firm commitment from a studio—or a shooting script—one that is being prepared for filming. In a shooting script, shots or scenes are numbered. So far, we are fading in on a cabin in the woods. But that instruction is incomplete; shots have to be described in terms of place (INTERIOR or EXTERIOR) and time (DAY or NIGHT). Thus, an incomplete opening might be:

FADE IN:
1. INT—CABIN—NIGHT

What is going on in the cabin? Suppose the first shot is to be of Elise, the heroine, standing anxiously at the window, waiting for her husband to return. How is she to be shown? What will be the size of her image: CU, LS, MS? To convey anxiety, a CU is necessary. How will the audience know that she is waiting for her husband? Voice-over narration (V.O.) will be used to reveal her thoughts. In screenwriting, characters' names or designations (ELISE, CROWD), camera movements (PAN TO), transitions

(DISSOLVE TO), the word sound (SOUND of laughter), and sound effects (SF or SFX) are capitalized. Thus, the shooting script might begin as follows:

FADE IN:
1. INT—CABIN—NIGHT

CU of ELISE standing anxiously at window. A storm rages outside.

> ELISE (V.O.)
> John said he'd be back by nightfall, but it's close to midnight. Dear God, not now . . . please, not now.

To show John, the screenwriter would start a new shot.

2. EXT—MAINE WOODS—NIGHT

ELS of JOHN trudging through snow. SLOW ZOOM IN to reveal face, weather-beaten but confident.

Note, for example, how Alan Alda observes the rules in this brief excerpt from the credits sequence in his *Four Seasons* screenplay:

7. EXT—VILLAGE STREET—DAY
HIGH SHOT—station wagon makes its way down the street. Over this we HEAR:

> DANNY'S VOICE
> Who ate the bread? What the hell is this?
> You started without me?

8. EXT—13TH STREET—DAY
The station wagon pulls up to the curb. CLAUDIA ZELLER is waiting for them, holding a large unfinished painting and a box of supplies. She waves and smiles. Claudia is an Italian from the Bronx. Earthy, intelligent, and strong. She gets in the car with the painting, passing it with difficulty over everybody's head as she gets into the back of the car.

> DANNY
> You brought your work?

> CLAUDIA
> It's almost finished. I'm hot. I'm cooking.
> I can't stop for a whole weekend.

The vacationing couples in Alan Alda's *The Four Seasons* (1981). Left–right, Jack Weston, Alan Alda, Carol Burnett, and Rita Moreno (foreground); Bess Armstrong and Len Cariou (background). *(Courtesy Universal Pictures)*

> DANNY
> I stopped my work for the weekend.

> CLAUDIA
> Danny, please, you're a dentist.

> DANNY
> (to Anne)
> You hear this? I can sculpt a bicuspid that would fool God himself, but I'm just a dentist.

> CLAUDIA
> I'll go out in the fields with the cows.
> I'll stay out of everybody's way.

She accidentally sticks the painting in Nick's face. Nick grabs at his eye and winces.

> CLAUDIA (cont'd.)
> Oh, Nick, I'm sorry. Are you all right?

NICK
Fine.
(to Danny)
I'm glad you didn't bring your dentist's chair.

JACK
You hear about Janice and Hal?

CLAUDIA
I just got off the phone with her. It's a nightmare.
Drive. Let's get as far away from the whole damn thing as we can.

The station wagon takes off.

CUT TO:

9. EXT — MERRIT PARKWAY — DAY
The station wagon moves down the highway past the greens and reds and yellows of spring.

SPRING MONTAGE:
Crabapple trees spraying blossoms like fountains.

Lilac branches sagging with purple buds.

Dark rain clouds passing over the sun.

Forsythia shimmering in a spring rain, its buds dropping under the weight of the fresh water.

Small wet birds in a nest shaking water drops from nearly featherless wings.

And finally, sunset in the woods. New leaves are everywhere. A rabbit crawls slowly out of its hole and surveys the place.

10. EXT — THE BARN — NIGHT
In the distance the station wagon pulls up to a barn that has been made into a house.

END OPENING TITLES.
Screenwriting is an art that film history — which emphasizes the development of film as a medium, the studio system and the stars that came out of it, and the role of the director in the filmmaking process — has tended to ignore, perhaps because the script is pre-filmic. Even though most narrative films start with a script, the script recedes into the background as it changes

from a verbal to a visual text, so that by the time the film has been completed the words have been translated into images. Thus, moviegoers associate dialogue not with the writer but with the actors speaking the lines or with the scenes in which they are spoken. Understandably, writers bristle when films are advertised as "A Film by (director's name)" or "A (director's name) Film," while their names are at the end and generally in smaller type. Nevertheless, anyone who is serious about film will always look for the screenwriter's name in the credits. Understanding the screenwriter's role is integral to understanding the film medium, in which the script is a blueprint for the edifice that emerges.

NOTES

1. Ingmar Bergman, "Film Has Nothing to Do with Literature," in *Film: A Montage of Theories*, ed. Richard Dyer MacCann (New York: E. P. Dutton, 1966), 144.
2. The terms used throughout the rest of this chapter come from Wayne C. Booth, *The Rhetoric of Fiction* (Chicago: University of Chicago Press, 1961).

CHAPTER 9
Film Analysis

Film provides an experience that cannot be found elsewhere. Film can crystallize an emotion or an idea into a visual image. When language is used, the words are integrated with the images so that they become inseparable. Once we see *Casablanca*, a line like "Here's looking at *you*, kid" is forever linked with the speaker, Humphrey Bogart, and the one to whom it is spoken, Ingrid Bergman. We remember the look in their eyes.

Films, when remembered, appear as images—sometimes with sound, words, or music. Those images, with or without sound or music, become the touchstone by which we tend to define the nature of film. Films must be analyzed on their own terms. In other words, they are works that could never have been possible, or have reached their level of excellence, in any other medium.

Sometimes a particular scene seems to capture the essence of film. For example, the ending of *The Third Man* movingly depicts a moment using only image and sound—the basic elements of moviemaking. Anna (Alida Valli) walks down a Vienna road through a drift of leaves—her face expressionless, her gaze fixed. Holly Martins (Joseph Cotten) leans against a cart and lights a cigarette, waiting to be recognized. As the autumn leaves fall in a silent shower, Anna moves out of the frame—and out of Martins's life—without so much as a glance in his direction. Martins grows progressively smaller, until he is

The ultimate snub: the ending of *The Third Man* (1949), in which Anna (Alida Valli) walks past Martins (Joseph Cotten) without even a nod in his direction. *(Courtesy MOMA/FSA)*

nothing but a tiny figure by the side of a road, ready to disappear like the smoke from his cigarette. The ending achieves what only film can: eloquence without words. Not one line of dialogue is spoken: the zither alone speaks, as it plays with restrained sadness the famous "*Third Man* Theme."

Isak Borg's final vision in Bergman's *Wild Strawberries* offers another beautiful moment in film. In this scene, Sara, Isak's boyhood love, leads him through a meadow to a bay. Across the bay, Isak sees his mother knitting while his father fishes, apparently with some success, for the rod is beginning to curve over the water. They wave at their son, and he smiles back at them. Isak's vision of his parents has the texture of an impressionist painting. Not only is the shot perfectly composed but it also captures the essence of its subject: eternity objectified as a state into which we do not freeze like figures in a mural but, rather, melt imperceptibly, the way spring softens into summer or summer ripens into autumn.

It is natural to have a favorite scene; yet scenes are parts of a whole, a fact that we tend to forget when we single out scenes for special consideration. When analyzing films, viewers should ask if a single moment in a movie can crystallize the film experience. Or is there such a thing as a work that, in its totality—not merely in part—epitomizes the art of film?

Let us analyze five films that can truly be considered film art. Although they are all rich texts, with many scenes that can be looked at individually, we will examine each film as a whole and draw on the topics we have discussed in previous chapters to analyze the choices that the filmmakers have made to realize their visions.

Casablanca (MICHAEL CURTIZ, 1942)

Michael Curtiz's *Casablanca* has become a classic in part because of its mythic subtext, its sense of history, its timeless plot, and its extraordinary performances.

Humphrey Bogart and Ingrid Bergman as the legendary lovers in *Casablanca* (1942). *(Courtesy MOMA/FSA and Warner Bros., Inc.)*

Casablanca is an unusual example of film adaptation. Before there was a *Casablanca*, there was a play called *Everybody Comes to Rick's* by Murray Burnett and Joan Alison, which Warner Bros. purchased in December 1941; the play, however, never reached Broadway and is rarely staged. Even if the play had managed to open in New York, it would have been poorly reviewed and then forgotten. *Casablanca*, on the other hand, is one of the most popular films ever made, even though the plot is not that different from the plot of *Everybody Comes to Rick's*. In the play, Rick Blaine is the jaded owner of a café in Casablanca. One evening, a woman from his past, Lois Meredith, appears with the Czech freedom fighter Victor Laszlo. Although Rick and Lois resume their relationship, Rick begins to develop a political conscience; realizing that Laszlo must continue to fight fascism and that Lois must go with him, Rick makes it possible for the two of them to fly to Lisbon while he stays behind in Casablanca to meet an uncertain fate at the hands of the Nazis.

Everybody Comes to Rick's furnished the *Casablanca* screenwriters (and there were several) with the main characters and plot points: the African

American pianist, Sam, Rick's confidant; the Nazi general, Strasser; Victor Laszlo and Lois (renamed Ilsa in the film, because Swedish-born Ingrid Bergman was cast in the role); the prefect of police, Reynaldo (called Renault in the film); Ugarte, who traffics in stolen visas and whose letters of transit provide the denouement; and the Bulgarian couple, Jan and Annina, whom Rick helps to leave Casablanca. The Production Code precluded Ilsa's sleeping with Rick as Lois did in the play. The World War II setting dictated the film's ending: Laszlo and Ilsa board the plane, while Rick goes off to join the Free French with Captain Renault, who, like Rick, was once apolitical but now wants to do his part to stop fascism.

If the plot sounds far-fetched, it is. Yet generations have fallen under *Casablanca's* spell because a solid mythic foundation lies beneath the rickety plot. While there is no particular myth to describe the subtext, there is a universal one: the myth of regeneration. *Casablanca* insists that as long as there are uncommitted people like Rick, who are capable of change, there is hope for the world. And once the uncommitted have changed, they make it possible for the Victor Laszlos to do what most of us cannot: make the world a better place.

We identify with Rick because we, too, may be more concerned about ourselves than about the world; we also identify with Laszlo, because we aspire to his idealism. We even empathize with the patrons of Rick's Café, a true cross section of humanity, who show the kind of courage we envy. As the Germans bellow their anthem, the patrons respond defiantly with "La Marseillaise" and drown them out. When Rick tells Ilsa that "the problems of three little people don't amount to a hill of beans in this crazy world," he is admitting that there are times when individual needs must be subordinated to the common good. Yet this is not any man speaking to any woman but Humphrey Bogart speaking to Ingrid Bergman, one icon to another. Each is the perfect embodiment of the character: Bogart, the cynic in need of regeneration; Bergman, the woman with the power to regenerate him.

With two other actors the effect could never have been the same. George Raft was considered for the role of Rick; Ann Sheridan, Michele Morgan, and Hedy Lamarr for Ilsa; but Bogart and Bergman have such powerful screen personas that when they play characters like Rick and Ilsa, a coinciding of persona and character results, so that when we think of *Casablanca*, we think of Humphrey Bogart and Ingrid Bergman and not merely of Rick Blaine and Ilsa Lund.

Yet we also think of *Casablanca* as a peculiarly American film, whose subtext is America's commitment to the oppressed peoples of the world, particularly during the early years of World War II when the film was released. Rick's Café is Europe in microcosm. Casablanca was a French colony in December 1941, the time in which the main action is set, as evident from Rick's line, "If it's December 1941 in Casablanca, what time is it in New York?" And his next lines—"I bet they're asleep in New York. I bet they're asleep all over America"—would have resonated with 1942–1943 audiences, who realized that on December 7, when the Japanese bombed Pearl Harbor, America was roused from the sleep of isolationism and forced to wake up to a world war that had begun two years earlier in Europe and that now America had no choice but to enter.

America's entry into the war necessitated many changes in the script, including the nationalities of the characters. Although Ingrid Bergman was Swedish, her character became Norwegian. Sweden was neutral during the war, and it would not have served the film's interest for a woman from a neutral country to be a freedom fighter's wife. Instead, Ilsa became Norwegian, since Norway had fallen to the Nazis in 1940, thus making her country one of the victims of Nazism. Berger is also Norwegian, as well as being a member of the underground, which he indicates by showing Laszlo his Cross of Lorraine ring. The Cross of Lorraine, a crucifix with a smaller transverse piece above the larger one, was also the symbol of the French Resistance.

It is understandable that Victor Laszlo is a freedom fighter; his country, the former Czechoslovakia, was overrun by the Nazis in 1938. Major Strasser is a Nazi, who, as a visitor to Casablanca, is really in "unoccupied France," as Captain Renault delicately reminds him. Most 1942–1943 audiences would have understood the reference. When France fell to the Nazis in 1940, France's president, Marshal Pétain, eager to prevent a total takeover that would have humiliated the French people, agreed to an arrangement in which the Germans occupied northern France, meaning that more than half of the country, including Paris, was under Nazi occupation. As a colony, however, Casablanca was "unoccupied France"—but by the end of 1942 the distinction hardly mattered.

Although Captain Renault is the prefect of police in what is theoretically part of "unoccupied France," he is unwilling to alienate Major Strasser because of the victories the Nazis had been scoring since 1938. Thus we never know where Renault's allegiance lies until the end. With the other characters, there is little doubt. For example, the Leuchtags, an elderly couple delighted to be able to leave Casablanca for America, are German; so, it seems, is the kindly waiter, Carl (played by the lovable S.Z. Sakall, who was actually Hungarian). The police officer Tonelli is Italian, and so, perhaps, is Signor Ferrari, owner of the Blue Parrot, who is quite knowledgeable about the black market in stolen visas. Ugarte, who makes his living selling those visas, would seem to be Spanish; if so, it is a subtle way of alluding to Franco's Spain, which, while not a member of the Axis, came close to being a fascist country. Jan and Annina Brandel, who are so eager to come to America (and will, thanks to Rick's munificence), are Bulgarian. They have no wish to return to their country, which joined the Axis in 1941. Sascha, the bartender, is Russian; his country became one of the Allies for the duration of the war after the Nazis attacked the former Soviet Union in June 1941. Yvonne, Rick's ex-lover, fraternizes with the Nazis until the singing of the "Marseillaise" makes her realize she has been behaving like a French collaborationist. The characters' names alone suggest a cross section of Europe: Norway, Czechoslovakia, Italy, France, Spain, Bulgaria, Russia, and of course, Germany.

America is represented by Rick Blaine. By letting Jan Brandel win at roulette, he makes it possible for the Brandels to leave Casablanca; he does the same for Victor and Ilsa by allowing them to use the letters of transit. But that gesture of commitment is not enough. Renault suggests that Rick, now a wanted man, might consider joining the Free French in Brazzaville. And since Renault has also developed a political conscience, becoming a patriot instead of a neutral, he will join Rick, thus contributing two new members to the French Resistance, which, historically, was never as big as Hollywood led the world to believe. But myth and history often diverge, and sometimes history disappears into the subtext. *Casablanca's* subtext is multileveled: Europe in miniature during the early years of World War II, a call for commitment as well as a criticism of neutrality and isolationism, and an affirmation of America's responsibility to the "huddled masses yearning to breathe free." Rick's establishment, a haven for the Brandels and the Laszlos of the world, was not called Rick's Café Américain for want of a better name.

Raging Bull (MARTIN SCORSESE, 1980)

Martin Scorsese's skillful use of black and white, rhythm, intertitles, and music makes *Raging Bull* a masterpiece in itself, even while it echoes films from earlier decades.

The credits begin with the intermezzo from Mascagni's opera *Cavalleria Rusticana*; it is soothing, tranquil music, coming midway in an opera about betrayal, adultery, and murder. The credits are in color, with the title in flamboyant red. During the credits, a boxer in a hooded robe is seen limbering up in the ring in slow motion. The combination of Mascagni's serene music and the eerie sight of a boxer in an otherwise empty ring, moving with the speed of a puppet, prompts us to wonder if this is the raging bull of the title. And if we know that the film is based on the life of Jake La Motta (Robert De Niro), who lost the title of middleweight champion of the world to Sugar Ray Robinson in 1951 (and who was also known to be ill-tempered and violent), we might also ask why Scorsese has created such dreamlike credits and scored them with music that is similarly restful.

Anyone who has learned to read visuals and correlate them with the accompanying soundtrack would sense that perhaps Scorsese is asking the viewer to feel some compassion for the title character, as one might for a once raging bull that now rages alone because he has become too slow-moving to be a threat.

Robert De Niro as middleweight champion Jake La Motta in *Raging Bull* (1980). *(Courtesy MOMA/FSA)*

But poignancy fades as the film begins. Not only does the bull rage but he rages in black and white—and at a pace that is at odds with that of the credits, which look lethargic in comparison. Those who were expecting a sentimental biopic in color must have been taken aback by the changeover to black and white and the opening shots of pounding fists and battered faces. Scorsese has made four artistic choices: to tell La Motta's story in black and white, the way the great boxing pictures of the past—*Body and Soul* (1947), *The Set-Up* (1949), *Champion* (1949)—were filmed; to quote as a subtext the movie *On the Waterfront* (1954), in which boxing is an important theme; to provide a chronological and historical framework through titles introducing each sequence—"New York, 1964"; "The Bronx, 1941"; "La Motta vs. Robinson, 1943"; and, finally, to use a framing device, beginning and ending with La Motta, now a nightclub performer capitalizing on his former fame, rehearsing a monologue in his dressing room. Everything else—La Motta's career from 1941 on—is enclosed between the prologue and the epilogue, like a series of texts between two bookends.

Segmenting the action requires variations of rhythm, which poses problems, since Scorsese has to shuttle back and forth between La Motta's professional, domestic, and social life. Yet all of these scenes have one common note: violence. La Motta can be almost as violent at home or in a club as he is in the ring. The turbulence of the first sequence, which includes a bloody fight as well as a riot among the spectators, seems to have abated at the beginning of the second, set in the Bronx, where La Motta and his first wife live. However, we soon discover that only the rhythm is different.

An argument over the way a steak should be cooked throws La Motta into such a rage that he almost trashes the kitchen. Violence is violence; the occasion determines the manner in which it is expressed.

Scorsese, with the assistance of his extraordinary editor, Thelma Schoonmaker, varies the rhythm so successfully that no two scenes — regardless of where they are set — are the same. When La Motta sees Vicky (Cathy Moriarty), soon to be his second wife, she is at the local pool, looking like a 1940s pinup. The pace slows down, as La Motta fixes his gaze on her. Other men are also aware of her, and Scorsese conveys a men's club atmosphere by having us hear only the men as they speak. Vicky just moves her lips; to the men, she is only an object. They do not hear her because they do not think of women as human beings enjoying the same freedom of speech as men. Women are meant to be silent; if they speak their mind, a slap across the face ends the conversation.

While *Raging Bull* may seem to be sexually explicit, the love scenes between La Motta and Vicky are antiseptic. She behaves robotically, planting kisses on his face or chest and removing articles of clothing as requested. But there is no real passion; the only lust is on La Motta's part, and that is short-lived. Because he has a fight coming up, he cools himself by emptying a pitcher of ice water down his shorts. This is clearly a male universe; there is far more affection between the men, who embrace and kiss freely, than there is between the men and the women. When Jake brings Vicky to his apartment for the first time, Scorsese uses a three-shot to illustrate La Motta's hierarchy of love. La Motta, left of frame, and Vicky, right, stand in profile at the dresser, on which there is a picture of La Motta and his brother, Joey (Joe Pesci). The picture stands between them, as does the bond between the brothers after they marry.

Scorsese frequently uses slow motion, but not to give a blow-by-blow breakdown of a fight, as one might expect in a boxing film. Slow motion is used in the fight sequences primarily to reflect the point of view of the boxer, who is so disoriented after a round that nothing looks or moves as it normally would. But Scorsese also uses slow motion outside the ring. When La Motta sees Vicky in a club, it is as if his vision were temporarily altered as she turns into the golden girl of his imagination, moving in a rhythm that is different from that of the real world. It happens again at the Copacabana when she spots some old friends and makes her way to their table.

Segmenting the narrative poses another set of problems: no matter how the rhythm is varied, certain events must be either omitted or telescoped. Scorsese does both. Most of 1944–1947 is reduced to a montage of stills from La Motta's fights and home movies of his and his brother's marriages. But the fact that the films are in color indicates that Scorsese was trying to suggest some of the changes in the media that occurred in the 1941–1964 period — such as color home movies.

The brief switch to color is not accidental, nor are later sequences, set in the 1950s, that show a television set in La Motta's home. Significantly, the set doesn't work. Jake's days in the ring are over; likewise, sporting events, once available only on radio, can now be seen by anyone who can afford a television set. Jake can afford one, but television will never be his medium, which was evident in 1951 when viewers saw him lose his title to Sugar Ray Robinson.

Like Steven Spielberg and Woody Allen, Scorsese has an astounding knowledge of movie history. Sometimes he refers to past films by evoking an image of the past; Vicky wears a white turban and a white two-piece swim-suit, looking like Lana Turner in *The Postman Always Rings Twice* (1946). Other times he makes a direct reference—Terry's (Marlon Brando) famous speech in *On the Waterfront*, in which he chastises his brother Charley for making him throw a fight and thus lose his chance to become a contender, saying, "I could have been somebody. I could have been a contender."

At the end of the film, La Motta, a would-be entertainer, sits at his dressing table, staring into the mirror as he rehearses the speech. He is think-ing not of Terry or Charley but of his own brother, Joey, from whom he became estranged when, in a moment of irrational jealousy, he accused Joey of committing adultery with Vicky. In both *On the Waterfront* and *Raging Bull*, the brothers were mirror images—similar and opposite, as reflections are. *On the Waterfront*, then, becomes a subtext for *Raging Bull*—another film about brothers who never saw in each other what they should have seen and therefore could never do more than bond in the most primitive way.

Scorsese does not ask us to sympathize with Jake La Motta; he asks us to view La Motta as we might any protagonist who has experienced a tragic fall. Certainly, none of the classical tragic figures (Oedipus, Hamlet, Lear, Othello) were blameless; frankly, one would not want to be around them very long, given their penchant for rage. But La Motta's fall is as real within the context of *Raging Bull* as Othello's is within that of Shakespeare's play.

The end title is an excerpt from the Gospel of Saint John. After Jesus cures a man who was born blind, the Pharisees summon the man a second time, insisting that his sight was restored by a sinner. The man replies that he does not know whether Jesus was a sinner; he knows only that once he was blind and now he can see.

The next title is a dedication: "Remembering Haig R. Monoogian, Teacher, May 23, 1916–May 28, 1980, with love and affection, Marty." This is a personal reference to a professor at New York University under whom Scorsese studied. Perhaps Monoogian encouraged Scorsese to look for qual-ities in La Motta—or someone like him—that would elude others. The dedication aside, the end title suggests that *Raging Bull* might open the eyes of those who expect to find tragic figures only in the classics but not in

Jim Carrey as Truman Burbank, whose life has been turned into a television series without his knowledge in *The Truman Show* (1998). *(Courtesy MOMA/FSA)*

everyday life. Perhaps they will say, like the man who was formerly blind, "Now I can see."

With its variations of mood, tone, and rhythm; popular songs as background music, reflecting the changing tastes of the American public over a twenty-year period; intertitles that identify characters and specify time and place; and an end title that exhorts the viewer to see human beings whole before judging them, *Raging Bull* is inconceivable in any form other than film.

The Truman Show (PETER WEIR, 1998)

In some ways a reflexive film, and in some ways an allegory, *The Truman Show* is both visually remarkable and intellectually interesting.

The Truman Show is a study in media control, depicting the way Christof (Ed Harris), an all-powerful television producer, has managed to turn the life of an ordinary citizen, Truman Burbank (Jim Carrey), into a television series viewed by millions without Truman's being aware of it. For thirty years, Truman's life, including his prenatal state, has been unfolding on television screens. Truman, however, has no idea that Seahaven, the idyllic island community where he lives, is really a set honeycombed with hidden cameras that record his activities (except the most intimate ones); and that everyone, including his wife and his closest friend, is an actor. While *The Truman Show* seems to be the forerunner of reality television, there is a significant difference: in reality television the performers know they are participating in a narrative that is, to a great extent, their own creation in the sense that their actions constitute the plot; Truman, however, has no idea he is the star of a series created by someone else.

It is easy to imagine the movie's ending with Truman's being killed off the way soap opera characters are when they have served their purpose as plot catalysts and are no longer needed, or when viewers no longer like them. *The Truman Show*, however, does not end with death but with discovery.

The faithful viewers (and there seem to be no other kind) long for the day Truman learns the truth, knowing that his emancipation will be theirs. Basically, the viewers look forward to being free to live their own lives without having to tune in to somebody else's.

Even though it is essentially about television, *The Truman Show* could only take place in the movies. The television series portrayed in the film could never air. No network could authorize a series that violates the Ninth Amendment, which has been extended to include the right of privacy; nor would any network have the technical capabilities to produce such a series. Movie studios can transform their lots into whatever a script dictates. The Twentieth Century-Fox lot became a Welsh village for *How Green Was My Valley* and the village of Lourdes in *The Song of Bernadette*; it also served as both Yonkers and Manhattan in *Hello, Dolly!* (1969). The set in *The Truman Show* allows us to step back and analyze the differences between the two media: television, which can seduce a nation into voyeurism; and film, which is doubly voyeuristic by allowing viewers to watch a movie about a television series watched by others. The film also succeeds in re-creating a world so like our own, yet so different, that we must leave the one before we can appreciate the other.

That is what film does: for a couple of hours we are immersed in a world that has been staged, edited, and musically scored. *The Truman Show* erases the line between illusion and reality. Viewers see a reality that is really an illusion, although the die-hard Trumanians have made it such a part of their lives that they see Truman Burbank as both a real person and a character—in other words, a "real character," the way soap opera fans can confuse the actors with their characters, sometimes berating the performers in public for doing something in a particular episode that disturbed them.

Unlike a typical network series, *The Truman Show* dispenses with commercial interruptions. The sponsors' products are incorporated into the scenes, and the commercials into the dialogue. When Truman is gardening, his wife, Meryl (Laura Linney), returns from shopping. "Look at this," she exclaims, holding up one of her purchases, as she looks into a hidden camera lens. "It's a Chef's Pal. Dicer, slicer, and peeler in one. Never needs sharpening. Dishwasher safe." Truman, unaware that his wife has just done a product-placement commercial, replies, "Gee, that's great," sounding like the husband in a typical commercial. Later, Truman's friend Marlon appears brandishing a six-pack, with the beer label clearly displayed.

Although *The Truman Show* demonstrates television's (and film's) ability to create a world that seems as real as our own, it also suggests that it is only by testing the fundamental principles of reality, which we tend to take for granted, that the difference between the artificial and the real can be understood. One of the most extraordinary moments in the film is Truman's discovery that the sky is a cyclorama, which he can actually touch. It is that realization, or epiphany, that frees him from the clutches of Christof, who not only chose Truman for the lead in the series when

Truman was in his mother's womb but also adopted him through his corporation, Omnicam.

Some films require a greater suspension of disbelief than others; *The Truman Show*, however, just asks us to accept this premise and not subject it to the rigors of logic by asking such questions as how a corporation was allowed to adopt a child, how Truman obtained a Social Security card, whether his teachers were all actors, and whether the federal government has become a tool of the media, which has now achieved the ultimate in control: complete control of a person's destiny, turning free will into an illusion, life into a script, and relationships, including marriage, into narrative strategies that can be altered whenever the plot needs a new angle or a new character.

These concerns, however, are irrelevant if the film is taken allegorically. Common to allegory are emblematic or transparent names (Christof, Truman, Omnicam, Seahaven) and a two-tiered narrative, which suggest that there is something beyond the literal level of meaning. "Christof" suggests Christopher (literally, "Christ bearer" in Greek), the third-century saint who, supposedly, discovered that the child he was carrying across a river was really Christ. Through his organization, Omnicam ("all camera"), Christof becomes the father or surrogate "bearer" of Truman, the "true man," the only voice of truth in a community built on deception. His surname, Burbank, is a media reference, evoking Burbank, California, the home of NBC-TV, the Walt Disney Studios, and Warner Bros. The true man has been made into a television character because Christof was looking for someone as free of malice as Christ, whom he could protect from the "lies and deceit" of the real world by providing him with an ideal one, where deception is no more harmful than a painted backdrop.

Truman's emancipation leaves him free to pursue a real relationship with the woman who once played a minor character in the series (Natascha McElhone). Her name was Sylvia, although the character's name was Lauren. Sylvia was so determined to alert Truman to the web of deception being spun around him that she forgot her character's name in one episode and used her own. Sylvia was on the verge of exposing Christof's hoax when her "father" arrived on the set and whisked her off in his car, leaving viewers thinking it was part of the plot, while it was really an improvised attempt to keep Truman in a state of ignorance. It is Sylvia to whom Truman rushes when he leaves the fake set, about to emerge into reality. Yet Truman's exit from the world of artifice is not that different from our own departure from the haven of the movie theater. Like Truman, we awaken from the "daylight dream," as the critic Parker Tyler called film, into whatever reality awaits us when the lights come up. The reality to which Truman awakened was the reality of love, based on another equally important reality: truth.

A.I. Artificial Intelligence (STEVEN SPIELBERG, 2001)

With its fairy-tale subtext, *A.I.* becomes more than a science-fiction film. Steven Spielberg draws on universal themes to tell a story that poses challenging questions.

Like any science-fiction film, *A.I.* starts from a premise. We are asked to envision a future after the greenhouse effect has caused the ice caps to melt, submerging major cities such as New York. Famine has decimated the populations of many countries, thus creating the need for robots and new categories to distinguish them from humans. A robot is now a "mecha"; a human, an "orga." Since orgas believe they alone are "real," they feel superior to the artificial mechas. With the limiting of pregnancies, Dr. Allen Hobby (William Hurt) and his team have invented a child robot, "a robot that dreams," who, although a mecha, is capable of love. *A.I.* then becomes Spielberg's *Pinocchio*, with a sentient robot, as opposed to a wooden puppet that first had to be animated if it were ever to become human.

Despite Spielberg's dependence on *Pinocchio*, *A.I.* goes as far beyond the Disney film as *Pinocchio* went beyond the Pygmalion myth, in which the sculptor Pygmalion falls in love with the statue he made. When Pygmalion implores Venus to bring the statue to life, the goddess grants him his wish. *Pinocchio* is more complex, involving not one, but several, transformations. After Geppetto fashions a puppet that he names Pinocchio, he prays that his creation will become real, so that Pinocchio can join his family, which at present consists of a cat, Figaro, and a goldfish, Cleo. The Blue Fairy answers Geppetto's prayer, animating the puppet but not transforming wood into flesh. Incarnation is more difficult; it has to be earned. Pinocchio, who yearns to be a "real boy," achieves his wish after he embarks on a rescue mission proving he is "brave, truthful, and unselfish."

Pinocchio is *A.I.*'s point of departure, followed by other Spielberg films dealing with otherness (*E.T.*, *Close Encounters*, *Schindler's List*) and the lost child (*Close Encounters*, *E.T.*, *Hook* (1991), *Empire of the Sun*). Thus such vital episodes in *Pinocchio* as Stromboli's traveling marionette show, the Pleasure Island adventure, the underwater quest for Geppetto, and the Blue Fairy's climactic transformation of Pinocchio appear in radically altered form in *A.I.* It is as if Spielberg is warning his audience (and the PG-13 rating should be an indication) that his film is a fairy tale for the twenty-first century where dreams may come true, but not just by earning merit points in bravery, honesty, and selflessness. This is not a world where the Blue Fairy turns robots into humans with a touch of a wand.

With the invention of a sentient robot, Dr. Hobby's Cybertronics has become the equivalent of an adoption agency, able to fulfill a couple's need for a child. Monica and Henry Swinton (Frances O'Connor and Sam Robards) had a son, Michael, who, for some unexplained reason (illness or accident), has been cryogenically preserved. Through his position at Cybertronics,

Haley Joel Osment as David and Jude Law as Gigolo Joe in Steven Spielberg's *A.I. Artificial Intelligence* (2001). *(Courtesy Dream Works and Warner Bros.)*

Henry becomes eligible for a sentient robot, David (Haley Joel Osment). Monica, who at first finds David's presence intrusive, gradually develops feelings for him similar to, but not identical with, a mother's for her child.

When Michael revives, sibling rivalry results, forcing the parents to take sides—Monica becoming more protective of David; and Henry, of Michael. Eventually, David's behavior convinces Henry that he is dangerous, which is by no means the case. Unwilling to bring David back to Cybertronics, where he would be destroyed, Monica chooses to abandon him in the forest. The abandoning of David recalls the scene in *Snow White and the Seven Dwarfs* in which the hunter, unable to carry out the Queen's order to kill Snow White, leaves her in the woods. What Monica senses, but cannot express, is that David is too real to be a robot, and not human enough to qualify as a son.

If *A.I.* seems thematically top-heavy, the reason is Spielberg's attempt to forge parallels between his film and *Pinocchio*. Spielberg frames the moral of the Disney movie (true humanity is not achieved by lying or shirking responsibilities, but by truthfulness and commitment) within an ethical context: the obligations of the dominant class to minorities, regardless of how different they may appear. Spielberg appears to be pondering, but not developing, another theme: If a puppet or a mecha were to become "real," thereby acquiring a human nature, the puppet/mecha would also be subject to death. *Pinocchio* stops short of depicting the consequences of incarnation; except for *A.I.*'s ambiguous final scene, Spielberg also avoids the issue, preferring to grapple with another question: "What is real, as opposed to artificial?"

Spielberg synthesizes Stromboli's traveling marionette show, where Pinocchio was the star attraction, with the Pleasure Island adventure, in which irresponsible boys enjoy themselves—drinking, smoking, and even vandalizing a model home—until the hour of reckoning comes when they are turned into donkeys and shipped off to the mines. The result is the Flesh Fair sequence. Having exposed us to a world of a dwindling human population and a falling birth rate, Spielberg asks us to imagine what might happen when the orgas realize that mechas will outnumber them. Some families will keep their robots, purely for the services they provide; others will discard them, creating a homeless and rootless underclass. The abandoned mechas have been marginalized, restricted to certain areas—in effect, ghettoized. If found in orga zones, mechas are rounded up and exhibited in Flesh Fairs, "celebrations of life," where the orgas can vent their hatred at those who epitomize the artificial and threaten their numerical superiority. After David has been abandoned, he is captured by mecha hunters and is about to be exhibited at a Flesh Fair, where robots are shot through cannons and doused with boiling liquid for the amusement of humans. Within the context of Spielberg's films, the Flesh Fair, where robots are victimized for their otherness, recalls his Holocaust film, *Schindler's List*, in which "others"—labeled "*Untermenschen*" or subhumans—were sent to death camps. When David asks one of the robots why they are being subjected to such mistreatment, the robot replies, "History is repeating itself."

The Flesh Fair is the film's turning point. When David realizes he may be burned, he cries, "Don't burn me!" A woman in the audience senses that David is not an ordinary mecha; "Mechas don't plead for their life," she cries out. It is clear that David possesses consciousness. Here the parallels between David and Pinocchio start to diverge. Ever since Monica read *Pinocchio* to David, he was obsessed with finding the Blue Fairy, who could make him into a "real boy," thus ensuring Monica's love. Pinocchio, on the other hand, never doubted Geppetto's love. David's goal, then, is not so much to be real as to be regarded as real by Monica, who has become the equivalent of his mother.

David is a sentient robot; as such, he can reason. After he and the love robot, Gigolo Joe (Jude Law) escape from the Flesh Fair, they head for Rouge City, a Pleasure Island for adults, to learn the whereabouts of the Blue Fairy from Dr. Know. The Dr. Know sequence is a parody of a quiz show like *Jeopardy*; instead of answering questions from various categories, Joe and David have to pose them. David figures correctly that by combining two categories, Flat Fact and Fairy Tale, he will be able to learn where the Blue Fairy can be found: at "the end of the world where the lions weep," which turns out to be Manhattan.

Except for a few skyscrapers, New York is under water. David makes contact again with Dr. Hobby, who tells him he *is* a "real boy." Although David cannot eat, sleep, or perform bodily functions, he can love, think, reason, and express emotion. Dr. Hobby puts it another way. He reminds David that humans have the ability to "chase down" their dreams, which is what David has done. The question Spielberg seems to be posing is, "What truly characterizes a human being? Eating and sleeping—activities we share with animals? Or the ability to think, reason, and pursue a goal?" "You found a fairy tale and followed your dream," Dr. Hobby tells David. But the dream has not yet become a reality. One final adventure is necessary, and like Pinocchio's, it will take place under water—this time in an amphibicopter.

Pinocchio's underwater quest for Geppetto, who along with Cleo and Figaro are in the belly of the whale Monstro, was enhanced by fascinating animation as various forms of aquatic life passed before us. In *A.I.*, we see something quite different: the remains of what was once New York City. Radio City Music Hall is at the bottom of the ocean; all that is visible of the Statue of Liberty is her torch-bearing hand. The first phase of the underwater adventure ends in a submerged Coney Island, where David sees what he thinks is the Blue Fairy, but is just a plaster statue, the kind one might see at the entrance to an amusement park attraction.

Many moviegoers thought the film was about to end at this point, until the narrator reminded us that David remained in the amphibicopter for two thousand years, while the ocean froze, staring all the while at the statue. The human race has become extinct, and the frozen world belongs to the aliens, one of whom releases David from the amphibicopter, allowing him to approach the statue, which falls apart before his eyes.

It is hard to know how Stanley Kubrick, who had originally intended to make *A.I.*, would have ended the film. One suspects he would not have chosen Spielberg's ending, which was ambivalent enough to satisfy anyone desiring closure and willing to offer an interpretation. Another director-screenwriter might have ended *A.I.* with David's seeing his dream crumble and realizing his quest was in vain. *A.I.* would then have been an anti-*Pinocchio*, in which dreams come true only for the dominant class, but not for others.

Spielberg's ending is an attempt to retain the film's mythic quality and resolve the plot by bringing David into the Blue Fairy's presence. After an alien frees David from the amphibicopter, we see a close-up of David's face, transfigured and luminous. Spielberg then cuts to a less-than-transfigured David, looking like someone in a home video. The home David is in, however, is a simulacrum—a copy that looks like Monica and

Henry's house. We are seeing a version of that home, a study in blue — the appropriate place for the appearance of the Blue Fairy against a blue-paneled window.

David can now make his request, but he does not receive the answer he expected. "I cannot make you a real boy," the Blue Fairy explains. David's, however, is a two-part wish: to become a real boy, so Monica will love him. The Blue Fairy can grant the second — and more important — part of his wish and bring Monica back, if there were some vestige of her person such as a fingernail or a piece of bone. Fortunately, Teddy, the super-toy that accompanied David on his odyssey, has a lock of hair that David clipped from Monica's head.

The Blue Fairy cannot reunite David and Monica unless authorized; she serves an alien with superior intelligence. "Give him what he wants," the alien commands. The Blue Fairy obeys: "Your wish is my command." The alien informs David that Monica can only be brought back for one day. David is more fortunate than Emily in Thornton Wilder's play *Our Town*, in which Emily is able to return to earth for a single day, but only as an observer unable to be seen or heard. David and Monica spend their day together, at the end of which Monica grows tired and lies down to sleep. David does likewise, holding her hand. Before Monica falls into an eternal sleep, she says, "I love you, David. I have always loved you." Then a benevolent voice informs us that David also went to sleep, and then to "that place where dreams are born."

In the stage musical of James M. Barrie's *Peter Pan* (1954), with which Spielberg is obviously familiar, Peter sings about "a place where dreams are born/And time is never planned./It's not on any chart/You must find it in your heart/Never Never Land."

Spielberg would like to leave us with the image of David going to that mythical nowhere. Will David experience the peace that passeth understanding? And where exactly will that be? Is David entering the afterlife along with Monica, or will they be entering two different afterlives? David may have been created, but he has not been born. Thus David cannot die, as humans do. If the resolution of *A.I.* is not entirely satisfying (we should remember that Spielberg also wrote the screenplay), it may be that the problem the film poses — our responsibilities to "others" — is ongoing and has yet to achieve closure.

Perhaps, in the end, "the place where dreams are born" is Dream Works SKG, the studio that Spielberg co-founded in 1996 with Jeffrey Katzenberg and David Geffen. Certainly, Spielberg dreamed a dream, a *Pinocchio* for the new century, but he did not achieve it alone: *A.I.* was a co-production between DreamWorks, Amblin Entertainment (Spielberg's independent production company), and Warner Bros.

Crouching Tiger, Hidden Dragon (ANG LEE, 2001)

The artistic success of *Crouching Tiger, Hidden Dragon* was due to Ang Lee's ability to combine various genres and motifs, with which western audiences were already familiar, within an exotic setting that was both alien and fascinating to them. Set in nineteenth-century China, *Crouching Tiger* suggests a Hong Kong martial arts film; characters run up walls, duel in mid-air, and glide over treetops, defying gravity and verisimilitude but at the same time dazzling the eye by their balletic grace.

Just as the woman's film is sometimes called a "weepie," the martial arts film is frequently labeled "chopsocky," implying that it is simply a display of feats, moves, and stunts. However, no martial arts film has ever won the kind of critical acclaim that *Crouching Tiger* has: four Oscars (best foreign film, musical score, art direction, and cinematography). Another reason that the film is so highly esteemed is that the martial arts sequences are integral to the plot, not just choreographed combat. Ang Lee is a serious director who has had no difficulty adapting to the Hollywood mode of moviemaking. Lee has his own way of "Hollywoodizing" the material: he interweaves motifs from various genres that are universally recognizable.

For example, *Crouching Tiger* in many ways resembles a western. When Lo ("Dark Cloud") leads a raid on a caravan, he is photographed on horseback at the top of a hill—a familiar composition in westerns signaling the beginning of an Indian attack. With a cry, he leads his followers down the hill, riding in front of the coach carrying Jen (Zhang Ziyi), whose comb he takes. Jen, a martial artist herself, does not behave like the typical female passenger during an Indian attack; she is no Mrs. Mallory of *Stagecoach*, who says her prayers while the bullets fly. Since the comb is an heirloom, Jen takes off on horseback to reclaim it, only to fall in love with the thief. The terrain that she crosses in her pursuit of Lo looks like John Ford's Monument Valley or a typical Southwest landscape with red earth, cliffs, and mesas.

When Jen arrives at a frontier outpost, she encounters the same unsavory types that many a western hero has. She is no Destry (*Destry Rides Again*, 1939), whose initial meekness makes him an object of ridicule. Jen does not suffer fools. Like the title character in *Shane*, she does not take lightly to taunts; when menaced, Jen retaliates, sending the thugs crashing through the railing and landing on the floor below. The entire sequence is reminiscent of a barroom brawl, a common occurrence not just in westerns but in other kinds of films as well—for example, the musical *Wabash Avenue* (1950), the romantic film *Till the End of Time* (1946), and the dynasty film *Giant* (1956).

Crouching Tiger is also a love story, contrasting the spiritual but doomed relationship between Li Mu Bai (Chow Yun Fat) and Yu Shu Lien (Michelle Yeoh), and the distinctly physical one between Jen and the desert bandit

Jen (Zhang Ziyi) and the Green Destiny in Ang Lee's *Crouching Tiger, Hidden Dragon* (2001). *(Courtesy Sony Pictures Classics)*

Lo. Shu Lien had been engaged to a Wudan warrior, who was killed by one of Li's enemies. To preserve his memory, Shu Lien and Li refrain from expressing their true feelings for each other, although their eyes tell a different story. Jen, a government official's daughter, yearns for a life of adventure of the sort she has read about in novels where women fight alongside men. Lo is an orphan who found acceptance in a gang, although he yearns for respectability. The Li–Shu Lien subplot culminates in Li's death; the resolution of the Jen-Lo subplot is not so easily interpreted.

Although *Crouching Tiger* is less opaque in retrospect than it may have seemed during a first viewing, it is the kind of film that is best examined thematically, since it embodies so many generic and mythic elements.

One such theme is "the return of the hero." The film begins with Li's arrival, which is not as stylized as Ethan's at the beginning of *The Searchers*, but still has the look of a mythic return. A famous martial artist, Li had been at Wudan, a mountain retreat similar to Monsalvat, where, in the grail legends, the Knights of the Holy Grail lived a monastic type of life. Li was seeking enlightenment, which can only come with the cessation of desire. Li recalls the retired gunfighters of *The Gunfighter* and *Unforgiven*, who cannot escape from their past; or characters from crime movies, like Roy Earle in *High Sierra*, who would like to go straight, until the prospect of pulling "one last job" becomes too tempting to ignore. Li would also like to put the past behind him, yet he must avenge his master's death at the hands of Jade Fox.

Crouching Tiger also explores the theme of "the failed quest and never-to-be-fulfilled love." Li failed to find the enlightenment he was seeking. His master never told him about the "dark place" he would encounter — his personal dark night of the soul. He cannot achieve the inner peace he seeks because he has not overcome his desire for Shu Lien. There is "something I can't let go of," Li explains to her. The "something" is Shu Lien. In *The Searchers* and *Shane*, there is also an unspoken love between a man and a woman. In *The Searchers*, Ethan is in love with his brother's wife, Martha; and she with him. But neither can express it verbally; Ethan plants a chaste kiss on Martha's forehead, and she folds his jacket tenderly as one would a special article of clothing. In *Shane*, Shane and Marion suppress their feelings for each other and bid farewell with a handshake.

The film draws on the "talisman" theme as well. Li is torn between abandoning the warrior's life and avenging the murder of his master, who was poisoned by Jade Fox. He plans to leave his sword, the Green Destiny that had so often dripped with blood, with his friend Sir Te.

The sword is a ritual object common to many myths. In Scandinavian mythology, Frey, god of the fruits of the earth, had a magical sword that could destroy an enemy. The sword often has a name. In Richard Wagner's *Ring of the Nibelungs*, the sword that Wotan has plunged into an ash tree can only be retrieved by Siegmund, who names the sword *Nothung* ("Needful"). In the Arthurian tradition, Arthur proves he is of royal stock by drawing a sword from a rock; when the sword is shattered in battle, Arthur is given Excalibur by the Lady of the Lake. In J.R.R. Tolkien's *The Hobbit* (filmed as *Lord of the Rings: The Fellowship of the Ring*, 2001), Bilbo slays the giant spider with his sword, which he then names "Sting."

The theft of the sword is an important plot point in *Crouching Tiger*, in which Jen is oblivious to the significance of the Green Destiny. Her theft of the sword is an act of daring, inspired by her dreams of becoming a warrior like Li and Shu Lien. The theft is also Jen's form of self-liberation from a society where her prearranged marriage would ensure her father's job.

The theft of the talisman is also common in myth. The fall of Troy was presaged by the theft of the Palladium, an ancient statue of the goddess Pallas Athena. In Wagner's *Parsifal*, based on the grail legend, the wicked magician Klingsor has gained possession of the spear that pierced Christ's side at the crucifixion; the guileless Parsifal manages to restore the spear to the Knights of the Holy Grail and heal the grail king, Amfortas, who had been suffering from a wound inflicted by Klingsor. Klingsor, who once aspired to be a grail knight but was rejected, understood the significance of the spear, without which the knights could not function as a community.

"The battle between good and evil" is a common theme that appears in the film. Jen's governess, the infamous Jade Fox, stole the Wudan manual, hoping to master its contents. Jade Fox, who could never aspire to Wudan's ideals, remained a member of Giang Hu, martial artists portrayed somewhat simplistically in the film as members of the criminal underworld espousing a "kill or be killed" philosophy. Jen, anxious to achieve the highest form of selfhood possible, masters the manual, causing Jade Fox to realize that her protégée has outstripped her. It is hard not to view the Wudan–Giang Hu dichotomy in terms of the familiar western scenario of hero versus villain.

Crouching Tiger employs the "battle for a soul" motif as well. Just as the Good and the Bad Angels in Christopher Marlowe's *Dr. Faustus* fought for Faust's soul, so do Li and Jade Fox for Jen's. Li senses a potential Wudan warrior in Jen, who, he hopes, will break the gender barrier at Wudan, making her the first of her sex. He knows that Jen lacks even the rudimentary form of enlightenment. Martial arts, to her, means emancipation, an escape from her dull world into the realm of high adventure. One thinks of Barbara Worth (Margaret Lockwood) in *The Wicked Lady* (1945), who disguises herself as a highwayman, robbing wayfarers to pay her gambling debts, and then becoming so excited by her new role (a welcome relief from playing wife to a boring husband) that she embraces it wholeheartedly.

Jen is unwilling to commit herself to Wudan, feeling her independence will be restricted. She may have surpassed Jade Fox, but she is still under her influence. However, if Jen continues on the reckless path she has set for herself, she will be no different from the hoods who make up the Giang Hu, except that her skills will be superior to theirs.

Crouching Tiger also features an "interrupted wedding." Although Jen is in love with Lo, she rejects him, knowing that their backgrounds are too dissimilar for anything other than a desert fling. Lo interrupts the bridal procession by begging her to join him in the desert. One thinks of the wedding ceremony in Charlotte Bronte's *Jane Eyre*, in which an uninvited guest reveals that the bridegroom has a wife; and of Donizetti's opera *Lucia di Lammermoor*, in which the heroine's lover interrupts the marriage that her deceitful brother has arranged for her.

Additionally, Ang Lee includes the "death of the hero" theme. Just as hero and villain square off in the traditional western, Li must confront Jade Fox, who, lacking the skills of a true Wudan warrior, uses a poisoned needle to kill Li. The death scene, which recalls works in which the lover dies in the beloved's embrace or at his or her side, provides the only opportunity for Shu Lien to express her true love for Li. One thinks of Tristan's dying in Isolde's embrace in Wagner's *Tristan und Isolde*, Antony in Cleopatra's in Shakespeare's *Antony and Cleopatra*, and Othello's falling over Desdemona's body in Shakespeare's *Othello* or Verdi's operatic version. Sometimes it is the reverse— the hero admitting his love to the dying heroine, as in *Camille* (1937), or giving her the big send-off because he is too macho to express his true feelings, as in *Dead Reckoning* (1947).

Myths are usually resolved, happily or otherwise. Earlier Lo had told Jen about an old proverb: "A faithful heart makes wishes come true"; he recounts the story of a young man who threw himself from a mountain so that his parents' health could be restored. The wish came true, but the son never returned. When Jen asks Lo what his dream is, he replies that it is to be in the desert with her. In an image of great purity, Jen leaps from the mountain, floating into space. Is she trying to achieve the peace that Li was seeking? If so, it would be in death. Or is she so gifted that she can soar into the air, like the young man in the story, to make Lo's wish a reality? But the young man never returned. Does Jen now feel differently about Lo, whom she had earlier rebuffed, knowing that their love, like Li and Shu Lien's, was futile, but for reasons of class rather than honor? Is Jen's a sacrificial act in atonement for Li's death? Jen is indirectly responsible for Li's death; if she had not been so bored and self-absorbed that as soon as she heard about the Green Destiny she decided to steal it, Li would never have been put in a position where he had to reclaim it. And if she had chosen the path that Li offered her, Wudan with its synthesis of external prowess and internal discipline, she might have become Wudan's first woman warrior.

The ending is unresolved; optimists could argue that love conquers all, and that leaping from a mountain is not that different from leaping from a parapet. Realists would respond by claiming that Lo's parable about the young man does not fit their situation, since Lo's wish is not for another but for himself and Jen. And, to complete the analogy between their situation and the young man's, whoever leaps from the mountain never returns. A realist would also consider *Crouching Tiger* a study in contrast between the sacred and the profane—spiritual love and physical love, neither of which can be held up as the ideal (which is a combination of the two). The first extreme ended in death: the death of a man who could not act on the love he felt for a woman; the second, in the ambiguously motivated act (redemptive or sacrificial) of a young woman who pursued one way of life over another and resolves her dilemma by leaping into the void.

Analyzing Films

If there is a movie that you believe embodies everything film should be, ask the following questions:

- What techniques did the filmmaker use to create the feeling of a complete film rather than a mere collection of scenes?
- Could it have been anything other than a film—a novel, a short story, a play, for example—and still have been as effective; or was film the medium in which it reached its level of excellence?
- How much of the film is told through images or camera movement, without recourse to dialogue?
- Does the use of film deepen or enhance the story being told?

- Do the camera and the script work together, each doing what it does best, so that word and image are allies rather than enemies?
- What is the subtext, or infranarrative? How does it enrich the film?

Looking for the answers to these questions will allow you to analyze a movie, while making your filmgoing experience more meaningful. Filmmakers strive to use their medium to create effects that cannot be achieved in another form. If a film remains entirely on a superficial level, with visuals to match, and whatever it has to offer can be absorbed in one viewing, it is just a diversion. Film art does not exhaust itself in a single viewing. Using an analytical eye, you can return to movies again and again, developing an understanding of and appreciation for the art form.

CHAPTER 10

Film Theory and Criticism

Most criticism from Aristotle to John Dryden is really the theory of literature. Students reading Aristotle's *Poetics* for the first time may be disappointed if they expect a detailed analysis of a Greek tragedy. In the *Poetics*, Aristotle was practicing legislative criticism. He was setting forth certain principles (art as imitation, plot as soul, the tragic hero as midway between perfect goodness and utter depravity) and establishing various categories and distinctions (the simple versus the complex plot, the kinds of recognition). But he was not explicating a text or exploring its levels of meaning.

In *On the Sublime*, Longinus analyzed one of Sappho's poems, but most of the work is also legislative: how to achieve the sublime, how not to achieve it, what elements of the sublime can be learned, what elements are innate. Horace's *Ars Poetica* also ignores practical criticism, as does Sir Philip Sidney's *An Apology for Poetry*, which by its very title is a defense of an art rather than an interpretation of it.

Descriptive criticism, the analysis of a literary work, is relatively new; it began in 1688 with John Dryden's *An Essay of Dramatic Poesy*, and not very successfully at that. Dryden was superb when he championed the cause of English drama, but deficient when he tried to analyze a particular English play, Ben Jonson's *The Silent Woman*. The kind of criticism to which most of us are accustomed, where a text is examined in detail—for example, image by image in a poem—started with the New Critics (John Crowe Ransom, Cleanth Brooks, Robert Penn Warren, and others), who focused almost exclusively on the work, ignoring the historical milieu out of which it came as well as the author's biography.

Early film criticism was also theoretical and reflected the basic premises of literary criticism—namely, that criticizing a medium requires a knowledge of what the medium can and cannot do, and that this knowledge is obtained through theory.

The History of Film Criticism

Film criticism began not long after the advent of film itself. Over time the Russians, grammarians, apologists, realists, auteurists, mythographers, semioticians, feminist critics, ideological critics, reception theorists, and reviewers have all contributed to our understanding of film.

The Russians

Film criticism really began in Russia with the Revolution of 1917. It is true that before that time newspapers had reviewers, that in 1915 Vachel Lindsay published *The Art of the Moving Picture*, and that in 1916 Hugo Munsterberg's *The Photoplay: A Psychological Study* appeared. But no filmmaker attempted to explain the nature of his craft until Lev Kuleshov started writing in 1917. In the famous Kuleshov Workshop at the State Film School in Moscow, which included such pupils as V. I. Pudovkin and, briefly, Sergei Eisenstein, Kuleshov performed various experiments in **montage,** which he defined alternately as "the joining of shots into a predetermined order," "the alternation of shots," and "the organization of cinematic material." To show how editing can alter the face of objective reality, Kuleshov intercut a close-up of an actor's neutral face with three different shots: (1) a bowl of soup, (2) a woman in a coffin, and (3) a little girl with a toy bear. Audiences marveled at the actor's "versatility" in expressing (1) hunger, (2) sorrow at his mother's death, and (3) joy at the sight of his daughter.

Pudovkin continued in his teacher's footsteps. He idolized Kuleshov, and made the extravagant claim that while others made films, Kuleshov made cinematography. Kuleshov was not infallible; although much of his theory still has value, some of it is misleading. His belief that the shot is the equivalent of the word has led to a misunderstanding of what the shot can and cannot say; his comparison between a sentence and a sequence limits the sequence to imparting only the information of which a sentence is capable; his view that the way a film is put together is more important than what it means is equivalent to the fallacy that form is more significant than content.

To his credit, Kuleshov was critical of the way Russian directors shot scenes. A great admirer of American films, he contrasted American "fast montage" with Russian "slow montage." He envisioned a suicide scene in which a despondent man would sit down at his desk, remove a pistol from the drawer, press it to his forehead, and pull the trigger. The American director would fragment the scene by breaking it up into its components: a close-up of the man's agonized face, a shot of his hand reaching into the drawer, an extreme close-up of the man's eyes, and, finally, the firing of the pistol. The Russian director would simply film the scene as if it were taking place on the stage.

What Kuleshov meant by "montage" in this example was nothing other than the editing technique that D. W. Griffith had perfected. Thus, when Kuleshov said montage developed in America, he was speaking the truth. Pudovkin continued to explore the implications of montage, which at this stage still meant editing. He argued that the foundation of film art is editing and that a film is not "shot" but "built" from individual strips of celluloid. Pudovkin was intrigued by what happens when two different shots are combined within the same narrative context. For example, in *Tol'able David* (1921), a tramp enters a house, sees a kitten, and immediately wants to drop a stone on it. Pudovkin reads the scene in this way: Tramp + Kitten = Sadist.

To Eisenstein, Pudovkin was incorrect: the equation was not $A + B = C$, but $A \times B = Y$. Shots are meant to collide, not join together. With Eisenstein, montage was no longer a matter of combining shots or of alternating them but of making them collide with each other: $A \times B = Y$; fox $\times$ businessman = cunning. In *Tol'able David*, when director Henry King cuts from the tramp to the kitten, both the tramp and the kitten are part of the same scene; in *Strike* (1924), when Eisenstein juxtaposes the face of a man and the picture of a fox, the fox is not an integral part of the scene as the kitten is in *Tol'able David*. To King, the kitten is a character; to Eisenstein, the fox is a metaphor.

The Grammarians

As new terms like *montage, dissolve, wipe*, and so on entered the vocabulary of film, definitions became necessary to explain their functions. In 1935 Raymond Spottiswoode published *A Grammar of the Film*, whose purpose was "to make as precise as possible the language and grammar of film."[1] Spottiswoode was critical of some of the ways in which film expressed itself. He had little use for the wipe because, unlike the cut, which is imperceptible, the wipe calls attention to itself. He believed that while dissolves could be justified, they generally interfered with the film's rhythm because they slurred over the bridge between shots and altered the tone of a scene. Although *A Grammar of the Film* was a serious attempt to analyze film techniques, much of it is outdated by today's standards. We no longer speak of "credit titles," and what were once known as "strip titles" are now "subtitles."

The Apologists

Spottiswoode combined a study of film terminology with a defense of the medium, arguing that movies can become an art only if they first become part of a nation's cultural life and that critics must help film to develop a national character. He was forced to defend film, as Sir Philip Sidney was forced to defend poetry 350 years earlier, against its detractors, who called moviegoers "celluloid nitwits." However, few defenses of the filmmaker are as eloquent as Rudolf Arnheim's in *Film as Art*:

> [The filmmaker] shows the world not only as it appears objectively but also subjectively. He creates new realities, in which things can be multiplied, turns their movements and actions backward, distorts them, retards or accelerates them. . . . He breathes life into stone and bids it move. Of chaotic and illimitable space he creates pictures . . . as subjective and complex as painting.[2]

To Arnheim, the fact that photography is limited is precisely what makes film an art. Because photography is incapable of perfect reproduction, film ceases to be a mere replica of reality. Film is the art of partial illusion, the same illusion that exists on the stage, where we accept a room that has only three walls. In a silent film, we accept characters who speak but cannot be heard; in a black-and-white film, we ignore the absence of color.

Because film is capable of distortion, it is not a purely realistic medium. To the doubters who think the camera reproduces the object as it is, Arnheim explains how the camera's ability to approach an object from different and unusual angles creates effects that are ordinarily found in great painting: "Art begins where mechanical reproduction leaves off."[3] And Arnheim had no doubt that film was art.

The Realists

Since the first film critics based their theories on silent films, they were more sympathetic to montage than the critics who came of age with the talkies. Sound brought spoken dialogue, and once the pictures learned to talk, they were not as docile as they had been when they were silent. Russian montage was not well suited to the narrative sound film, in which the combination of happy face and flowing brook could break dramatic continuity or destroy verisimilitude.

"There are cases in which montage far from being the essence of cinema is indeed its negation," wrote André Bazin,[4] whose untimely death in 1958 was an irreparable loss to film criticism. What bothered Bazin about montage was its inability to offer more than a limited and, frequently, distorted view of reality. Bazin discerned two main traditions in film: montage and mise-en-scène, or the cut as opposed to the long take. It was mise-en-scène that he championed, and it was the mise-en-scène directors like Jean Renoir, William Wyler, and Orson Welles whom he favored.

Although mise-en-scène was discussed in chapter 3, it is worthwhile to review the meaning of a phrase that has now become enshrined in the vocabulary of film. It is impossible to define *mise-en-scène* as succinctly as one would a *dissolve* or a *wipe*. The French expression, which derives from the theater, is difficult to translate because it means staging a film with the same feeling for style and detail that a theater director (*metteur-en-scène*) brings to a play, in the sense that the film director "stages" the action, positions the actors within the frame, sees that they are dressed in costumes typical of the era and suited to the characters, and works with the director of photography and the production designer to create the proper visual style. Mise-en-scène is the result: the blending of all the elements of filmmaking, from acting and makeup to the composition of the shots, into a whole to produce as close an approximation of reality as possible.

Directors who work within the mise-en-scène tradition achieve a high degree of realism by shooting certain scenes in long take. In fact, some of the finest camera work in film is a result of the long take. The opening of Orson Welles's *Touch of Evil* derives its power from being an uninterrupted tracking shot. The long take was particularly evident in William Wyler's *The Best Years of Our Lives* (1946), a 172-minute movie with 190 shots per hour; the average film has between 300 and 400 per hour. Wyler filmed several scenes without making a single cut, creating action and reaction within the same shot. Bazin justly admired the famous ending: the wedding of Wilma (Cathy O'Donnell) and Homer (Harold Russell). All of the principals are present: Al and Milly Stephenson (Fredric March and Myrna Loy); their daughter, Peggy (Teresa Wright); and Fred Derry (Dana Andrews), Homer's best man. Fred and Peggy are in love, but his inability to find a job has prevented their marriage. As Homer and Wilma exchange vows, Fred turns in the direction of Peggy, who is standing with her parents. At that moment, Wyler brings everyone into the frame. The vows seem equally applicable to Fred and Peggy; the result is the illusion of a double wedding. A cut at any point during the scene would have shattered that illusion.

Another scene Bazin praised was the one in which Fred phones Peggy to terminate their relationship. Fred, Al Stephenson, and Homer are in a bar, where Homer is playing the piano. In one unbroken movement, the camera goes from the piano to the phone booth, pausing only for a quick look at Al. Another director might have used several cuts or allowed us to overhear the conversation between Fred and Peggy. The fact that Wyler did neither reinforces Bazin's thesis that Wyler did not have imitators, only disciples.

Bazin wanted film to encompass as much reality as possible, but mise-en-scène cannot produce realism by itself; it needs **deep focus,** a technique in which background and foreground are in focus at the same time. Thus, mise-en-scène and deep focus are allies. Deep focus has three other advantages

In the celebrated long take from *The Best Years of Our Lives* (1946), William Wyler brings all the principals into the frame for the wedding of Homer (Harold Russell) and Wilma (Cathy O'Donnell). *(Courtesy Samuel Goldwyn Productions)*

for Bazin: it brings spectators into closer contact with the image; it is intellectually more challenging than montage, which manipulates spectators and annihilates their freedom of choice by making them see only what the filmmaker wants them to see as opposed to deep focus, which presents spectators with the entire image, from which they may choose to see only a part, such as the foreground; and it allows for ambiguity, which is absolutely essential to works of art, whereas montage reduces a scene to one meaning.

Bazin never expressed his theory of film in a full-scale critical work, only in the form of essays and articles. Yet it is clear that he was moving toward an aesthetics of realism. Bazin was especially impressed by the neorealistic Italian films that appeared after World War II — for example, Roberto Rossellini's *Open City* (1945) and *Paisan* (1946), and Vittorio De Sica's *The Bicycle Thief*. He saw these films as showing the same respect for reality that deep focus does. Neorealism and deep focus have the same purpose: to keep reality intact. In a neorealistic film, Eisensteinian montage is impossible; nothing can be added to the existing reality. The cutting must follow the script, which cannot tolerate juxtapositions.

Initially, it was film's realism that caused its adversaries to regard it as a copy of nature. To Siegfried Kracauer, film's ability to capture reality, far from being a handicap, is its greatest asset. Just as in the *Poetics* Aristotle determined the nature of art before he discussed the nature of tragedy, Kracauer began his epochal *Theory of Film* not with film itself but with its parent—photography.

Kracauer is unwilling to call photography an art for the same reason that he is unwilling to call film an art: the photographer lacks the artist's freedom to create his or her own inner vision. Both the photographer and the filmmaker are more dependent on the material world than either the painter or the poet. In art, the raw material of nature disappears; in film, it remains.

Kracauer's reluctance to elevate film to an art form inevitably follows from his belief that film is better equipped than any other medium to record physical reality. Consequently, film should stay on the surface of reality, for when it tries to penetrate the surface it becomes uncinematic. Parker Tyler challenged Kracauer's thesis by showing that film has successfully explored such themes as split personality, e.g., *Persona*, and the impossibility of certitude, e.g., *Blow-Up* (1966) by moving from the surface into the realms of human consciousness, where the camera once feared to tread. Kracauer would probably agree with Tyler but then add, "*Persona* and *Blow-Up* are uncinematic," meaning not that they are inferior films (quite the contrary) but that they deal with a form of reality that is better suited to the novel. Kracauer's position is thoroughly classical. Each form reaches its highest stage of development when it accomplishes what no other form can.

To Kracauer, films are either cinematic or uncinematic. The more they reflect the material world, the more cinematic they are; as soon as they forsake physical reality for spiritual reality, they become less cinematic. He would therefore call the historical film uncinematic by nature because it is an artificial reproduction of a bygone age; the fantasy film uncinematic, because of its otherworldliness; and the literary adaptation uncinematic, because in a novel or a drama the physical world is not the only one that matters—there is the inner world of the characters, which the camera has difficulty entering.

Because film evolved from photography, it shares four characteristics with this medium: an affinity for unstaged reality, a penchant for the fortuitous and the random, a sense of endlessness, and a preference for the indeterminate. A fifth characteristic is peculiar to film alone: an ability to capture the open-ended flow of life as it appears in the stream of situations and occurrences that constitute human existence. Kracauer is not saying that film must never attempt to stage reality or that it must always deal with such themes as chance encounters and unpredictable events. He means only that film favors nature in the raw and resists the artificial; thus, film balks at being made to resemble a play. As we have seen, shooting a film from the point of view of a spectator in an orchestra seat is entirely different from shooting it from the point of view of the camera eye, which can look up, down, around, over, under, and beyond what it sees. Naturally, photography favors the fortuitous; some of the most memorable pictures ever taken were the result of the photographer's being in the right place at the right time.

The camera does not have to record whatever passes in front of its lens for film to have a liking for the fortuitous. Kracauer means that many movies involve chance occurrences on streets, in the badlands of the West, on ships, in airports, railroad stations, hotel lobbies, and so forth. Film tends toward the endless because physical reality is seemingly without end; thus, in a movie a change of scene may be a change of continent. The filmmaker had to learn how to bridge vast distances by creating such transitions as the fade and the dissolve.

Film is indeterminate because physical reality is indeterminate. The juxtaposition of laughing face and flowing brook evokes the same response the world over. But what of the meal of wild strawberries and milk that Mia offers the Knight in *The Seventh Seal* (1958)? Bergman has not falsified reality by making the strawberries and milk other than what they are. The context of the scene changes the strawberries and milk from picnic food to food for a eucharistic meal; it also changes those who eat the food into communicants. Reality's indeterminacy is one of the glories of film, in that an object can be both itself and a symbol at the same time. The strawberries and milk never cease to be what they are: a means of sustenance. The scene determines the *kind* of sustenance: spiritual as well as physical.

Toward the end of *Theory of Film*, Kracauer distills the essence of his thesis into the myth of Perseus and Medusa's head. Because the sight of Medusa's head turned men to stone, Athena warned Perseus not to look directly at it but only at the reflection on the shield:

> Now of all the existing media the cinema alone holds up a mirror to nature. Hence our dependence on it for the reflection of happenings which would petrify us were we to encounter them in real life. The film screen is the polished shield.[5]

Hence the complete title of Kracauer's book: *Theory of Film: The Redemption of Physical Reality*. Kracauer does not believe that film deals only with nature in the raw as opposed to nature transfigured. Nature in the raw, of course, is film's starting point, as it must be; for nature in the raw—physical reality—is to film what language in the raw—words—is to literature: the means by which the work comes into being. Yet how does film redeem physical reality? The very fact that Kracauer speaks of holding a mirror up to nature—a polished mirror at that—provides the answer. A polished mirror will not catch a reflection of the physical universe as it is but as something better than it is; it catches a higher form of reality, one that is no less real than what we see around us but is superior to it. How can art imitate nature and improve it? Aristotle never tells us. How can film mirror reality and redeem it? Kracauer never tells us. For the answer, we must examine the works of artists who knew the secret of working within the material universe without becoming mired in it.

The Auteurists

It was in the late 1950s that the cult of the director arose, resulting in a spate of books on great and not so great auteurs. Presently, there is a book, a section of a book, an encyclopedia entry, or a monograph on every director who has made some contribution to the art of film, even if it was only directing a Republic western with verve and style, as Joe Kane did. That contribution might be revolutionary, as in the case of D. W. Griffith, or minor, as in the case of Edgar G. Ulmer. Yet if there can be critical studies of minor authors, there can be critical studies of minor directors. Minor does not mean mediocre; one's influence on a particular art form may not be pervasive, but it can nonetheless be noteworthy.

As we saw in Chapter 7, auteurism is merely *one* way of looking at film. It enables those who need a "handle," so to speak, on film to have one. Certainly it is much simpler to deal with a work of known than unknown authorship; among other things, it affords a sense of control and security. Even though it is common knowledge that Shakespeare wrote *Hamlet* and Dickens wrote *Great Expectations*, we still speak of "Shakespeare's *Hamlet*" and "Dickens's *Great Expectations*." To be able to say "Hitchcock's *Psycho*" means we can approach *Psycho* in the same way we might approach *Hamlet*; just as a literary scholar can discuss *Hamlet* within the broader context of Shakespeare's plays, we can approach *Psycho* within the context of Hitchcock's work instead of viewing it merely as a horror film or as the prototype of the modern slasher film.

There are, of course, drawbacks to auteurism. The auteurist approach cannot be applied unilaterally. It would be something of a joke to write, "Edward Bernds's *The Bowery Boys Meet the Monsters* (1954)," although confirmed auteurists would think nothing of it. Whatever one may think of Edward Bernds (a competent director) or the film, such a designation is bound to strike nonauteurists as laughable.

Auteurists can teach us something about the way directors repeat compositions, framings, and certain types of shots. Frank Capra's love of bells, which ranges from the tolling bells in *Lost Horizon* (1937) to the bell on the Christmas tree in *It's a Wonderful Life*, led to his using the bell as the logo of his short-lived production company, Liberty Films. No doubt Capra associated bells with the spirit of freedom and a feeling of joy. Hitchcock's high shots, or God's eye shots, may be a vestige of his Roman Catholicism or merely an attempt to suggest an unseen, omnipotent presence peering down at the world. At any rate, the high shot is a favorite Hitchcockian device, as is irising in D. W. Griffith, double framing in John Ford, long takes in Orson Welles and William Wyler, and a claustrophobic atmosphere in Edgar G. Ulmer. If writers in the auteurist tradition can deepen our understanding of a director's style, they have served film well. However, auteurism can be considered only as a way of approaching film, specifically of approaching the films of selected directors.

The Mythographers

Parker Tyler was the first film critic to understand how mythic the movies are. In *The Hollywood Hallucination* (1944), Tyler explained the extraordinary appeal of stars like Greta Garbo and Marlene Dietrich: they were mystery women, phantom ladies, moon goddesses like Diana. Their inaccessibility made them more desirable than they really were. If they ever loved a man, they could love him only in **myth,** where they would never have to yield. Even if a man broke down their resistance, we could never believe these goddesses could offer him anything more than fairy-tale love.

To Tyler, even Mickey Mouse cartoons had mythic underpinnings. Intelligent moviegoers watch an animated mouse without feeling that their intelligence has been insulted because they instinctively recognize some myth, some universal pattern of experience, behind the cartoon. Tyler identified it as the Frankenstein myth, which is based on an even older myth of the artist who creates a human being out of inert matter (e.g., Prometheus, who molded man from earth; Pygmalion, who carved Galatea out of marble). We understand intuitively that Mickey Mouse is someone's creation. Tyler cited other similarities between Mickey Mouse and the Frankenstein monster: both are mechanized beings; both are factory products—Mickey, the product of the Disney factory; the monster, of Frankenstein's laboratory; both obey their masters. There is also a difference between them: in *Frankenstein*, the monster turns on his maker, but Mickey always remains an amiable mouse.

We identify with the underdogs in animated cartoons because they have the same problems we have. We forget that they are ducks, mice, or pigs and think of them as humans, running the same obstacle course as ourselves and encountering the same frustrations. Yet, Tyler asks, is it not the same situation in gangster films? Don't we empathize with the Little Caesars, the Dillingers, the Bonnies and Clydes? Many moviegoers find gangsters sympathetic, for various reasons: gangsters are nonconformists who flout morality; their lives are colorful; they are upwardly mobile, often beginning at the bottom with petty crime and moving up the ladder of notoriety to bank heists and bloodbaths. Hollywood tends to humanize its gangsters, and to Tyler, humanization equals glorification. Interestingly, Tyler makes no distinction between Superman and the gangster. Who gave Superman the right to take the law into his own hands? He is only a newspaper reporter, not a police officer. Yet we look the other way when Clark Kent ducks into a phone booth and emerges as Superman; or, rather, our unconscious looks the other way as a reporter becomes a disrupter of the normal order.

In *Magic and Myth of the Movies* (1947), Tyler continued to explore the ways in which the unconscious sees films and to show how we accept certain actions in a movie that we would not tolerate in real life. Physical pain is never humorous, yet we laugh when comics slip on banana peels or get pies thrown in their faces. We do not laugh because we are sadistic; the comics give us the right to laugh by becoming scapegoats for our sake and suffering indignities on our behalf. It is the same with comics who distort their faces and mock themselves: they laugh at themselves first so that we can laugh with them. Yet if we read their actions correctly, the rubber-faced clowns are really asking for our approval, our love. They humiliate themselves in order to win our applause.

Tyler saw the stars of the 1930s and 1940s as gods and goddesses. Because the screen made them immortal, they could not die; they underwent only a ritual death, like the vegetation deities who die in winter and are resurrected in spring. A star can never really die, because divinity makes death impossible. The almost universal interest in films of the past supports Tyler's thesis. Humphrey Bogart will live as long as his films are shown, and there is little likelihood that the world will call a moratorium on movies. To see Bogart in *Casablanca* is to see a man in his prime, not a man who died of cancer in 1957. In *The Happy Ending* (1969), the heroine's husband accuses her of mooning over *Casablanca* whenever it is on television. When he reminds her that practically the entire cast is dead, she replies that Humphrey Bogart, Peter Lorre, Sidney Greenstreet, and Claude Rains are more alive than either of them.

The Semioticians

Semiotics emphasizes the way a film transmits its meaning through signs and codes.[6] Its approach is similar to that of the myth critics, who search out universal patterns and archetypal themes. Semiotics is also the theoretical side of structuralism, which is not so much a new discipline as a new approach to older disciplines such as linguistics, anthropology, psychoanalysis, and rhetoric — disciplines that are more concerned with signs than with objects. Thus structuralists are invariably attracted to myth because myths are the first structures, the first messages of a culture.

But myths are coded; they are invisible patterns, "offstage voices," as French literary critic Roland Barthes might call them. The structuralist tries to bring the voice from the wings to center stage. Myths remain coded until they become transparent; then society discards them as clichés. The reason myths were such unifying forces in ancient societies is that they resisted decoding. Frequently they appeared in binary form, reflecting the dualism inherent in nature (spirit/matter, male/female, life/death) and in culture (urban/rural, endogamy/exogamy, freedom/imprisonment). The great myths are inexhaustibly bipolar; they resist any attempt to reduce them to a single meaning. Oppositeness is at the heart of Greek mythology, which is one reason it is constantly being reinterpreted. The Oedipus myth, for example, embodies the polarities knowledge/ignorance, wife/mother, old order/new order, rationalism/mysticism, sight/blindness. Myths such as this are deathless because they are founded on natural, not artificial, opposites.

It is understandable that semiotics has become fashionable. Semiotics is studied in universities and in adult-education centers, where courses in semiotics for the layperson teach students how to translate the signs they encounter in daily life, such as the body language spoken at parties but not always understood, and clothing ads that suggest that a romantic future is in store for the wearer.

In his collection of essays, *Mythologies* (1972), Roland Barthes sees signs everywhere. A person's hairstyle can designate the class and era to which he or she belongs. To use an obvious example, in Joseph L. Mankiewicz's *Julius Caesar* (1953), the fringed hair of the characters is a sign of their "Roman-ness." Professional wrestling abounds in signs. The wrestler with the fleshy, sagging body telegraphs certain messages to the spectator: repulsiveness, cru-elty, cowardice. The wrestler's body determines the way he acts in the ring. The conventions of wrestling, such as the armlock and the twisting of the leg, are all parodies of tragedy. Just as the mask of tragedy is an exaggeration of the human face, so, too, is wrestling an exaggeration of human suffering. The opponent who lies flat on his back with his arms outstretched has been crucified. In wrestling, defeat reaches the nadir of humiliation — crucifixion.

Even our detergents speak to us, according to Barthes, whose exam-ples derive from late 1960s and early 1970s television commercials. Chlori-nated detergents proclaim they are absolute; as liquid fire, they blaze a path through the dirt and annihilate it. Powdered detergents are more selective; they liberate the dirt. Foam detergents, on the other hand, are useless; they are luxury items, airy and immaterial, as impractical as bubble bath.

If detergents talk, so does food. Fish-and-chips speaks of nostalgia, of the British bearing up under the Blitz; steak speaks of virility and, if it is served rare and swimming in blood, of an ambrosia that produces godlike strength. In Jacques Tourneur's *Experiment Perilous* (1944), a woman on a train orders steak for a male passenger because she assumes that steak is a "man's" dish.

On the surface, semiotics seems rather easy to understand. There is a signifier (say, a gold band) and the signified (marriage); there is **denotation,** by which a word keeps its literal meanings ("He lit the *fire*"), and **conno-tation,** by which it takes on other meanings ("He was consumed by the *fire* of passion"); there is *langue*, a language system that can be verbal (English, German, and so on) or nonverbal (the "language" of poker, falconry, and so on); and there is *parole* (speech), the actual practice of a language system.

The problems begin when one attempts to apply this terminology to film. In film, what are the signifiers? Can a movie denote and connote, or in film does denotation become connotation? There is also the haunting question, Is film a language system? To Christian Metz, the best known of the film semioticians, film is not *langue*.[7] In language, a word can acquire a different meaning merely by the addition of a single letter—for example, *d* or *r* added to the end of *love*. But film has no words. Metz rightly rejects the shot-as-word theory and compares the shot to the sentence. Like a gifted child, film skipped the parts of speech and moved to a higher grade. But if film has no parts of speech, then it has no grammar. We know that "He see the man" is ungrammatical in standard English; but what is ungrammatical in a movie? Using a dissolve instead of a cut?

Another difference is that in words there is a distance between the signifier and signified. *Sadness* can be broken up into its signifier (the sound *sad-nes*) and its signified (the concept of unhappiness). But in film the signified cannot be disengaged from the signifier. In a movie, sadness is not *sad-nes* but a child weeping, a man wailing, an American secretary sitting alone at an outdoor café in Venice while couples stroll past her. In a movie, sadness is not a concept but an actual situation (a sad family) or an attribute of a specific person (a sad man). For the same reason, denotation and connotation are not distinct in film. A movie denotes and connotes at the same time. When Isak Borg raises a glass of wine in Bergman's *Wild Strawberries*, he is Isak Borg who at that moment is having lunch with his daughter-in-law and some young hitchhikers; he is also Isak Borg the priest figure, officiating at a communion service and elevating not a wineglass but a chalice.

Metz claims that film is "like" language because it communicates. But how does it communicate? In two ways: syntagmatically and paradigmatically. A **syntagma** is a unit of actual relationship; thus **syntagmatic relationships** result when the units of a statement or the units in a filmic chain follow each other in order. If we analyze the way the subplots of *Nashville* interconnect, or we trace the rise of a character such as the title character of *Mildred Pierce* from housewife to restaurant owner, we are approaching the film syntagmatically.

A **paradigm** is a unit of potential relationship; thus **paradigmatic relationships** are associative, not sequential. They are not concerned with the order of the links in the chain but with the meanings we associate with them. If we associate the title character of *Serpico* with Jesus Christ, or the madness that erupted at the Hollywood premiere in *The Day of the Locust* with the outbreak of World War II, we are approaching the film paradigmatically. Because paradigmatic relationships are independent of the order in which the events occur, they can also exist between scenes taking place at different times within the film. Shane's ride of vengeance at the end of George Stevens's film of the same name should, by its horizontal movement, recall the first appearance of Wilson the gunfighter, who also rode horizontally across the frame; yet it also contrasts with the way Shane rode down into the valley at the beginning of the film. If we associate descent with something positive (the desire to reform) and horizontal movement with something negative (the desire to murder), then we have made a paradigmatic connection.

It is not enough for the semiotician simply to isolate syntagmas and paradigms; the movie relays its messages through codes that the filmmaker used and that the semiotician must now reconstruct. There are all kinds of codes: codes of dress, color, lighting, and so forth. In certain simplistic westerns, we may discover that white and black attire mean hero and villain, respectively; in other westerns, the dress code will yield to a landscape code, in which the signifier (Monument Valley) becomes the signified (America in microcosm).

Transportation codes are particularly meaningful in discovering a filmmaker's intentions. Karel Reisz saw the car as a vehicle charged with associations of death in *Isadora* (1969); in *Two for the Road*, the particular car in which the couple is traveling is related to a particular stage in their marriage. In *The Wild One* (1954), the motorcycle is the embodiment of raw virility, fascism, and arrested sexuality; but in *Easy Rider* (1969), the motorcycle epitomizes young, disenchanted America in the late 1960s. The yuppies of the 1980s, however, do not travel by motorcycle; they go cross-country in a motor home in *Lost in America* (1985), in which *Easy Rider* is mentioned so reverentially that the idealistic sixties becomes the yardstick by which to measure the materialistic eighties.

Cigarettes in the movies of the 1930s and 1940s were the epitome of cool and sophistication: Humphrey Bogart in a trench coat and a fedora, speaking with a cigarette between his lips; Bette Davis, brandishing her cigarette as if it were a scepter. The sight of so many stars smoking, which made cigarettes an essential part of one's wardrobe, influenced countless moviegoers to take up the habit.

His Girl Friday (1940) is one of the few films in which the cigarette is not just an accessory but a sign of belonging to a special group. The film is a reworking of the famous stage play *The Front Page*, in which a newspaper editor, Walter Burns, resorts to all kinds of devious tactics to keep his star reporter, Hildy Johnson, from getting married. For *His Girl Friday*, Howard Hawks turned Hildy, a male in the play, into a woman (played by Rosalind Russell) with the same name. Although Hawks's Hildy insists that she wants to give up the newspaper business and marry an insurance salesman, Walter knows otherwise. There are many ways in which Hawks makes it clear that Hildy belongs in Walter's world — her striped suits, for example, which make her look more like a "newspaper man" (which is what she calls herself) than a female journalist. But cigarettes are another sign of belonging. When Walter, Hildy, and Hildy's fiancé, Bruce, are at a restaurant, Hildy and Walter keep blowing their cigarette smoke in his face, making him distinctly uncomfortable. When Hildy interviews a prisoner, she offers him a cigarette, which the prisoner declines. The prisoner does not belong to the newspaper world, in which the cigarette is almost like a badge or a press card.

Sometimes codes are not quite so easy to decipher. Whenever Marlene Dietrich wore a tuxedo in a movie, as she did in *Morocco* and *Blonde*

Marlene Dietrich looking androgynous in *Blonde Venus* (1932). *(Copyright © Paramount Pictures. Courtesy MCA Publishing Rights, a Division of MCA, Inc.)*

Venus, both directed by Josef von Sternberg, 1930s audiences were taken aback at the sight of such a sensuous woman in men's clothes. A dress code was operating, but what did it mean? In *Morocco*, it meant that a strange form of defeminization had taken place by which Dietrich had become the essence of Hollywood Woman (seductive, smoldering) decked out with the trappings of Hollywood Man (debonair, aggressive). Thus the Dietrich figure in a tuxedo became androgynous.

Critics who are influenced by semiotics use a specialized vocabulary. For example, they do not think of film narrative solely in terms of plot. They distinguish between plot, diegesis, and discourse. The **plot,** or what Aristotle in the *Poetics* called the *mythos*, is the ordered arrangement of the incidents in terms of a beginning, a middle, and an end. The **diegesis** is the story that is recounted, embodying everything that pertains to it regardless of how much of it actually appears on the screen. The party in *Notorious* is an all-evening affair, but on the screen it lasts only ten minutes. Thus there is a difference between diegetic time (all evening) and film time (ten minutes). The **discourse** is the manner in which the story reaches the audience. That story includes what is dramatized as well as what is implied; it is based on a script that is brought to the screen by a team that has broken the action down into various codes (color codes, dress codes, lighting codes, codes of manners); it is the result of the interaction between an "I" and a "you," between the one telling the story (the filmmaker) and the one perceiving it (the filmgoer); it is the result of decisions made before, during, and after production. Thus the main title and the end credits would be very much a part of the film's discourse; a credits sequence, which is visualized action, is part of the plot (the film's structure) and diegesis (the film's world).

While semioticians have shown how complex film narrative is, one should remember that it is perfectly possible to write good film criticism without resorting to critical jargon. If it is understood properly, Aristotle's concept of plot is as applicable to film narrative as it is to literary narrative. "Plot is the structure of events," Aristotle wrote. Note that he does not call the plot the story line, as many would, but the *shape* of the story line and the *form* it takes. To Aristotle, the plot is the soul of the work—the source of its life. Remove the plot from a work of fiction and it ceases to be a work of fiction; remove it from a narrative film and it ceases to be a narrative film. Soul is structure; it is the harmony that exists when all the parts work together. Once plot is understood as the nucleus around which the incidents, the characters, the theme, and the setting gather, and the source from which they draw their life, it can then be perceived as the soul of the work and as something quite distinct from the story line, which is a bodily part.

Semiotics is to film what linguistics is to literature. A knowledge of linguistics can be helpful in reading dialect literature or in interpreting poetry, since poets coin new words and use old ones in startlingly new ways. However, literature can be analyzed quite successfully without the terminology of linguistics. Similarly, semiotics can enhance our perception of a film by disclosing the way signs and codes operate in it, yet film can be discussed intelligently without resorting to the vocabulary of semiotics.

Feminist Criticism

Feminist film criticism, whose practitioners include Laura Mulvey, Julia LeSage, Annette Kuhn, and E. Ann Kaplan, is indebted to the work of the French psychologist Jacques Lacan, particularly his theory of the mirror stage of development. Briefly stated, the theory holds that the image a child sees reflected in a mirror produces ambivalent feelings. The child is attracted to the image because it is an ideal image but is repelled by it, too, because the real can never be the ideal; the ideal is *other than* real. The Hollywood studio system, a male-created and male-dominated industry, seems never to have gone beyond the mirror stage, according to radical feminists. In the classic Hollywood film, the separation of real and ideal made woman other, an object rather than a subject. Specifically, the woman was an object of the male gaze; she was an exhibit or a spectacle rendered in terms of anatomy (bosom, legs, mouth, posterior) and fractured representation (close-ups, extreme close-ups). The idealization of woman (soft focus, front lighting, lenses smeared with Vaseline or covered with gauze to give the face a glow) originated in the fear of castration. It was as if the male had unconsciously struck a bargain with the female: if she would not deprive him of his potency, he would glorify her image. In this way, the universe would remain phallocentric, dominated by the symbol of male potency, the phallus, which, according to Lacan, is a signifier. The phallus represents male power as well as male presence, as opposed to female helplessness and female absence. Since the female lacks the organ on which the signifier depends, she denotes absence—the absence of power, authority, and speech. Speech is phallocentric, the prerogative of the male; speechlessness is the state of the female. Thus, even when women speak, they are passive; it might be more accurate to use the passive voice.

Although the woman's film of the 1930s and 1940s placed women at the center of the action, feminists would still argue that, despite the woman's pivotal role, it is the male who sets the plot in motion. *Dark Victory*, a key woman's film, is ostensibly the story of Judith Traherne's acceptance of death from brain cancer. After Dr. Steele, a neurosurgeon, diagnoses Judith's condition, she reluctantly submits to surgery. Later she falls in love with Steele, who cannot bear to tell her that the operation was unsuccessful and her condition is terminal. Judith learns the truth by accidentally coming upon her medical record. Embittered, she turns on Steele, indulges in self-pity and drink, but finally returns to him, begging his forgiveness. Forgiveness for what, one might ask? She is the one who is going to die, not he. Judith even goes to his apartment and admits that she has been a "fool." That visit, however, results in her marriage to Steele, without which the plot cannot be resolved. Judith knows that blindness will precede death. When her eyesight suddenly fails, she does not tell Steele, who must depart for an important medical meeting, but manages to help him pack while continuing to behave normally. The ending of *Dark Victory* would have been impossible without the character of Steele, for it is Judith's marriage to him that gives her the courage to face not just death but death alone.

Like all theories, phallocentrism and the mirror stage cannot be proved scientifically. As a result, they may strike one as either probable or bizarre. One can also argue that women were depicted as goddesses endowed with an aura denied to men because Hollywood believed that attractive women were "good box office." Women liked seeing themselves on the screen, and men liked seeing women on the screen. When moviegoers of both sexes were happy, the studios thrived.

Still, Hollywood's ambivalence toward women cannot be ignored. As Laura Mulvey states in her seminal article, "Visual Pleasure and Narrative Cinema," "woman . . . stands in patriarchal culture as signifier of the male other."[8] Mulvey goes on to argue that the male, trained to avoid gazing at himself (thereby becoming an object), instead makes the female the object of the gaze—the male gaze. Mulvey obviously does not mean that men avoid mirrors or refrain from checking their appearance in them. Her thesis is that the male is expected to be a doer (subject), not a receiver; thus he relegates the receiving or passive role to the female (object). In terms of moviemaking, such transference leaves the male free to control the action, allowing him to become more complete than the gazed-upon female. The screen then replaces the mirror, and just as the ideal ego is conceived in a moment of recognition in front of the mirror, the feminine ideal is conceived on the mirror-screen. However, it is an ideal created by a male, who looked into that mirror and saw not himself but woman and rendered her in accordance with his image. As far as movies are concerned, God may have created the world but it was man who created woman.

When woman is the object of the male gaze, she is given the full treatment; she is exquisitely gowned and impeccably coiffed. Her face is bathed in a light that cleanses it of imperfections. A close-up transforms her image into a portrait. Woman as movie star is Other as Ideal, and the ideal should be idealized. However, other is also not-I, and in a phallocentric world what is not-I is not male. As not-male, woman is often relegated to a subordinate position in the frame. In westerns, she is frequently behind the hero, serving him or standing in the background looking terrified as he takes on the villain. When the hero rides off at the end, she becomes a part of the landscape in the extreme long shot that concludes the film.

Like any theory, Mulvey's is difficult to prove. Men will say they are as concerned with their image as women are, adding that they express this in a different way: shaving, combing their hair, tightening the knot on their tie. Mulvey, however, isn't talking about good grooming but about that stage known as the "mirror-moment" and its manifestation in film. In a typical Hollywood movie, it is generally the male who controls the narrative. In *Vertigo*, the narrative is controlled by Scottie; we see what he sees, and once he makes Judy over into Madeleine we see what he wants to see. It is as if Judy's point of view—or, for that matter, the real Madeleine's—does not exist; or, if it does, it is not worth considering. The real Madeleine isn't even a character; the only time we ever catch a glimpse of her—fleetingly, at that—is when Elster throws her corpse from the bell tower.

Since Hollywood has traditionally been a patriarchy, with comparatively few women ever reaching the executive suite, feminists have wondered if women might have been portrayed differently in the woman's film if the directors—and, ideally, the writers as well—had been female. There have been male directors (for example, George Cukor, Edmund Goulding, Irving Rapper) who were known as "woman's directors" because of their ability to make movies with which female audiences could identify. Cukor's *Camille*, Goulding's *Dark Victory*, and Rapper's *Now, Voyager* may be classics, yet they perpetuate the image of woman as sufferer—a saintly creature who

Jerry (Paul Henreid) in *Now, Voyager* (1942), lighting the cigarette of Charlotte Vale (Bette Davis), who ends up as mother surrogate to his daughter—but not as his wife. *(Courtesy Warner Bros.)*

must tolerate abuse, place her lover's happiness before her own, and die nobly when her time comes. We will never know what, if anything, a female director would have done with *Dark Victory*—a death and transfiguration script, in which the protagonist is required to go through a cycle of self-pity and drink before she can accept her terminal illness, after which she has the strength to die alone.

Like *Dark Victory*, *Autumn in New York* (2000) features a young woman (Winona Ryder) facing terminal illness. Yet anyone looking for a distinctly feminine sensibility in *Autumn*, directed by Joan Chen, that would make it different from *Dark Victory* would be hard-pressed to find it. If Edmund Goulding had the reputation of being a woman's director, it was because he could project that sensibility (the feminine side of himself, perhaps) into the material. *Thelma and Louise* is considered a feminist film; the script was written by a woman, Callie Khouri, but directed by a man, Ridley Scott, who also directed one of the most "masculinist" movies ever made, *Gladiator*. Likewise, Penny Marshall showed great compassion for male adolescents (and adolescent males) in *Big* (1988). She showed the same compassion for women in *A League of Their Own* (1992), not only treating each of the women on the baseball team as an individual but also portraying the main male character, an alcoholic ex-ballplayer (Tom Hanks) as a failure worthy of sympathy rather than contempt. Amy Heckerling has a knack for depicting adolescents of both sexes sympathetically in such films as *Fast Times at Ridgemont High* (1982) and *Clueless* (discussed in Chapter 8). In Gillian Armstrong's remake of *Little Women* (1994), Marmee and her daughters look and act as if they can survive a father's absence. On the other hand, *Julia*, one of the best films ever made about friendship between women, was directed by a man, who was also responsible for *The Men* (1950) and *High Noon*: Fred Zinnemann. In *Julia*, Lily (Jane Fonda) and Julia (Vanessa Redgrave) are depicted as women in control of their lives and also of their narrative.

The best one can do is look at two film versions of the same source—one directed by a woman, the other by a man—and try to reach some conclusions. George Kelly's Pulitzer Prize–winning play *Craig's Wife* was filmed twice—in 1936 and 1950. The title character is Harriet Craig, whose obsession with making her home into a spotless but lifeless showpiece alienates everyone around her, including her husband, Walter, who finally leaves her. The play proved enormously popular with women, many of whom sympathized with Harriet, whose need for security began when her father walked out on his family, leaving Harriet's mother with a mortgage and two daughters to support.

The play's title remained the same in the first version, *Craig's Wife* (1936), directed by Dorothy Arzner, who was known in the industry as a "woman picture director" because the idea of a woman behind the camera was unusual, even though there had been several others before her. The script was also written by a woman, Mary McCall, Jr. The result was a sympathetic portrait of a woman so determined to avoid her mother's fate that she experiences a similar one—the difference being that Harriet was left with a house without a mortgage. McCall structured the screenplay so that the other characters left the house in pairs, until Harriet was completely alone. Rosalind Russell played Harriet in such a way that one pitied rather than despised her, particularly at the end, when, deserted by everyone, she learns of her sister's death.

Although the second version, *Harriet Craig* (1950), took considerable liberties with Kelly's play, the basic theme—a woman's valuing her house over her husband—remained the same. In this version, the director was a male, Vincent Sherman, who specialized in melodrama; the star was Joan Crawford, who excelled at playing tough-minded women; and the script was by Ann Froelich and James Gunn. Froelich, whose sympathy for socialism was well known in Hollywood, could hardly have been expected to be sympathetic to Harriet, who represented the worst features of capitalism. Even if the writers wanted to humanize Harriet, they would have had to contend with Crawford's persona: the tough-as-nails woman who fought her way to the top and had every intention of staying there. Crawford's Harriet interferes with her cousin's marital plans, almost manages to convince Walter's boss that her husband is too irresponsible to be sent to Japan (where

John Boles and Rosalind Russell as the Craigs in the first version of George Kelly's play *Craig's Wife* (1936), directed by Dorothy Arzner. *(Courtesy MOMA/FSA)*

The Craigs again: Wendell Corey and Joan Crawford, sporting a severe hairdo and manacle-like bracelets, in the remake, *Harriet Craig* (1950), directed by Vincent Sherman. *(Courtesy MOMA/FSA)*

she could not accompany him), and coldly rejects her next-door neighbor's offer of friendship even after everyone has left her. Harriet gets what she deserves: an empty house. With a script that made it difficult to empathize with Harriet, and a star like Crawford, who made it impossible, no director, male or female, could have won an audience over to Harriet's side. Even if Arzner, who left the industry in 1943, had been coaxed into directing *Harriet Craig*, she could never have accomplished what she did in *Craig's Wife*, where she had the benefit of McCall's script and Russell's subtle acting.

One can only conclude that the script, the subject matter, the actors, and, especially, the director's vision of the material determine how the sexes are portrayed on the screen.

Ideological Criticism

This kind of criticism is not quite so simple as interpreting a film as a reflection of the filmmaker's ideology in the sense of a belief system, political or economic, that the filmmaker has embraced and that may be detected in his or her work. If you know that Italian director Gillo Pontecorvo is

Father, son, and the crucial bicycle in Vittorio De Sica's *The Bicycle Thief* (1947). *(Courtesy Movie Star News)*

a committed communist, you might want to approach his *La grande strada azzurra* (*The Wide Blue Sea*, 1957) in terms of his view of capitalism as a dehumanizing force that exploits the masses and creates an underclass whose members might have to break laws in order to survive. While Pontecorvo's radicalism is very much in evidence in the film, it is only one aspect of his art. So is the Marxism of Cesare Zavattini, who wrote the original story that became the basis of Vittorio De Sica's *The Bicycle Thief*, which portrayed the devastating effect of the theft of a bicycle on a husband and father. We can clearly understand the father's plight, since his job depends on the bicycle. But we are also expected to understand the thief, who had been reduced to such straits that he stole from someone only slightly better off than himself.

The Hollywood product is not quite so radical; still, it is true that many Hollywood movies have a political subtext or even a political philosophy. Films that glorify empire builders (*Pittsburgh*, 1942; *An American Dream*, 1944); self-made Americans (*East of Eden*; *Lucy Gallant*, 1955; *Giant*); pioneers (most American westerns); and rugged individualists (*The Fountainhead*, 1949) are clearly pro-capitalist. Leo McCarey's *My Son John* (1952) is blatantly anticommunist, reflecting the director's own loathing of communism as an insidious force that seduces American intellectuals like the title character.

Other films are more difficult to pigeonhole. Billy Wilder's *The Apartment* is certainly not anticapitalist, although it deals with the way senior executives exploit those under them—a situation that can exist in any profession or in any society. Joseph L. Mankiewicz's *No Way Out* (1950), one of the first films to deal openly with racism in America, is the work of a liberal but not left-wing filmmaker. Spielberg's *Schindler's List* is antifascist, but not left-wing. *Reds* (1981), Warren Beatty's three-hour epic about the American communist writer John Reed set against the background of the Russian Revolution, is a sympathetic account of American radicalism but takes a dim view of the Soviet brand of communism. Although you cannot ignore ideology in a film, it would be a mistake to base an entire discussion on it. If you find yourself spending more time writing about ideology than about structure, either the film is a political tract—and if so, is propaganda—or you have become so caught up in the filmmaker's ideology that you are ignoring its narrative form.

Analyzing a film in terms of the film's or the filmmaker's politics is only one kind of ideological criticism. Included in the same edition of *Film Theory and Criticism* in which Laura Mulvey's article appeared is Robin Wood's "Ideology, Genre, Auteur" (668–678), which shows just how complex this kind of criticism can be. Capra's *It's a Wonderful Life* and Hitchcock's *Shadow of a Doubt* (1943) are two of the most respected films in American cinema. On the surface, they appear to be anything but ideological. *It's a Wonderful Life* seems to be about an archetypal American town, Bedford Falls. Yet there are three communities portrayed in the film: Bailey Park, named after the family that founded the building and loan company where the needy find help because the Baileys believe in people helping people; nearby Pottersville, home of the ogre-like Potter, who wants to get all of Bedford Falls under his control, which he could only do if there were no building and loan company; and Bedford Falls as it might have been if Potter had had his way—as George Bailey (James Stewart) learns when he attempts suicide and is rescued by the angel Clarence (Henry Travers), who shows George what the town would have been like if he had never been born. Bedford Falls would have looked like a film noir set, where harsh lighting exposes everyone's dark side, which is all that is left in the absence of charity and love. This is the Bedford Falls that Potter would have created, a testimonial to his inhumanity. *It's a Wonderful Life* is no valentine to America, despite its frequent appearance on television at Christmastime. It suggests there is the America to which we should aspire, which is Bedford Falls in macrocosm, as opposed to the America that would have resulted if the Potters of the land had refashioned it in their own image.

Wood also reminds us that there are three distinct worlds in *Shadow of a Doubt*, even though the film is a study in doubles, one of Hitchcock's favorite themes. The chief doubles (they are ubiquitous in the film) are an uncle and his niece, who share the same name, Charlie. Uncle Charlie (Joseph Cotten) is a serial killer who preys on wealthy widows; Little Charlie (Teresa

Wright) is the one who discovers his criminal past. At the beginning of the film, Uncle Charlie is hiding out in a seedy boardinghouse in a Philadelphia slum. To avoid suspicion, he pays a visit to his unsuspecting sister and her family in Santa Rosa, California. Like Bedford Falls, Santa Rosa seems to be idyllic; like Uncle Charlie, it also has its dark side, which is seen in the Til Two sequence. Realizing his niece has discovered his identity as the "Merry Widow murderer," Uncle Charlie induces her to go into a bar, the Til Two, with him. Til Two is straight out of film noir—dimly lit and sleazily seductive. A waitress, sluggish and zombielike, saunters into view; one of Little Charlie's former classmates, the waitress is shocked to find her in a dive. Is Hitchcock suggesting that the Til Two would have become the norm in Santa Rosa if Uncle Charlie had stayed on, infecting the community with his nihilism? Is Uncle Charlie, who believes "the world's a hell," representative of the Nazis who were making the world a hell in 1943 when *Shadow of a Doubt* was released and who, if they had triumphed, would have reduced it to a film noir nightmare? Although Hitchcock was not a political filmmaker, he always believed that nothing is what it seems to be, including people and countries. America is many things; it is like Henry Jekyll's house in Stevenson's *Dr. Jekyll and Mr. Hyde*, which has a back door that leads to a totally different world.

Approaching a film through the filmmaker's politics is easy. More difficult is finding and resolving the ideological tension that drives the film and gives it a complexity that defies political labels.

Reception Theory

How does an audience "receive" a film in the sense of responding to it? This is the question that practitioners of reception theory, such as Janet Staiger, Timothy Corrigan, and Miriam Hansen, have attempted to answer. According to Janet Staiger's *Perverse Spectators: The Practices of Film Reception*, reception is a complex matter, since the way one reacts to a film or interprets it depends on a number of factors, including:

1. **Type of film** (action-driven, plot-driven, Hollywood product, international film with subtitles, beginning-middle-end narrative with closure, open-ended narrative that leaves the viewer with questions about the outcome of the plot or the fate of the characters)
2. **Mode of exhibition** (theater, classroom, tape, DVD, network television, cable television)
3. **The nature of the viewer** (knowledgeable and cooperative; uncritical and indifferent; attentive and quiet; unruly and talkative)
4. **The makeup of the audience** (racially homogeneous/racially heterogeneous—for example, a predominantly black audience with

a few whites in attendance at a movie about African American life; a predominantly white audience with a few blacks in attendance at a movie featuring practically no African Americans at all; in general, being a minority member at a movie aimed at a majority, or vice versa)

5. **Level of identification** (the extent to which the audience cannot only differentiate between the characters and their relationship to each other and to the plot but the extent to which they can see themselves or others in these characters)

6. **Ideological perspective** (a feminist at a male-oriented movie where women are demeaned or treated as sex objects; a socialist at a film that extols capitalism/a capitalist at a movie that is sympathetic to left-wing causes; a politically homogeneous audience at a movie that is completely in tune with their beliefs)

7. **Aesthetic considerations** (audiences sensitive to mise-en-scène, appreciative of the artful use of lighting and color and able to see how these elements function in the film, even if the narrative is murky or confused; audiences familiar with the work of a particular director who can see stylistic traces or thematic repetition in the director's latest film; moviegoers who consider a film's technique to be more important than the plot)

8. **Marketing strategies** (newspaper ads, radio and television commercials, and trailers, which can affect audience response positively if there is a correlation between the strategy and the kind of film that the audience has been led to expect; or negatively, if there is none and the audience feels cheated). Although *Jaws* was an excellent example of commercial moviemaking, it profited from a provocative ad with very little text: "The horrifying motion picture from the terrifying No. 1 best seller" preceded the title, JAWS, followed by "She was the first." Then the image: the "she" was a female swimmer, perhaps even nude, beneath whom lurked a shark with jagged teeth, its beady eyes raised upward as if at the swimmer. The ad promised sex (little) and scares (many) within a PG format. The box office receipts suggested that few, if any, viewers were disappointed. If *Me, Myself and Irene*, one of the summer of 2000's contributions to grossout comedy, proved less profitable than *There's Something About Mary*, the reason might be the wholesomely dopey picture of Jim Carrey in the ad, which implied another *Ace Ventura: When Nature Calls* (1995) or maybe an R-rated *Truman Show*.

As movie audiences grow increasingly diverse, there is little likelihood that there will ever be an all-embracing theory of film reception—only more studies, both sociological and psychological, on spectator response. As Janet Staiger has astutely observed, there is, in addition to the knowledgeable

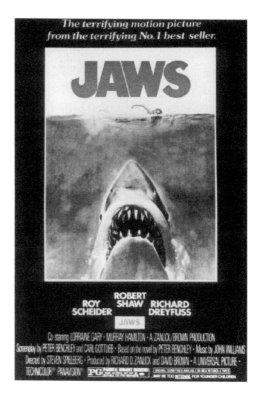

The famous ad for Steven Spielberg's *Jaws* (1975) that promised—and delivered—a bit of sex and a multitude of chills. *(Courtesy Universal Pictures)*

and cooperative spectator, the "perverse spectator," who does the unexpected and is not influenced by hierarchies or criteria created by academics (and who may actually believe a farce is more of a "movie" than is a drawing-room comedy); far from identifying with the hero, the perverse spectator reassembles—or maybe reshoots—the film in his or her imagination, making the villain the real protagonist. Such spectators may be experiencing film on a much deeper level than the knowledgeable elites.

The Reviewers

A film reviewer is not necessarily a film critic; few reviewers can be considered critics if by critic we mean a representative of the most insightful approach possible. If Alexander Pope's standards are applied to contemporary reviewers, only a handful would qualify as critics. Pope expected the critic to know everything about the work under evaluation:

> You then whose judgment the right course would steer,
> Know well each ancient's proper character;

His fable, subject, scope in every page;
Religion, country, genius of his age:
Without all these at once before your eyes,
Cavil you may, but never criticise.

— *An Essay on Criticism* (I, 118–123)

Film reviewers write for newspapers and magazines or deliver their reviews on television and radio. Film reviewing, then, is a branch of print and broadcast journalism. Movies are a form of news; thus they should be covered. The question is, by whom? Ideally, by someone who is knowledgeable about film. However, it often happens that the film reviewer of a local newspaper is a reporter who was assigned to the movie beat because there happened to be an opening in that department. A major newspaper, on the other hand, is likely to have several reviewers who know film and have a wholeness of vision that is reflected in their reviews. They can relate the film being reviewed to other films of its kind, to the director's or the stars' previous work, to the writer's former scripts. Their reviews are not valentines studded with superlatives; rather, they offer a reasoned and balanced judgment of a film so that if they use words like "greatest" or "best," we know they aren't being hyperbolic.

Television critics are a special breed: limited sometimes to a mere minute of air time, they are almost forced to be glib to keep the viewer from switching channels. Thus, to base one's knowledge of film criticism on television reviewing is to limit criticism to one-liners and sound bites. If you look at the newspaper ads for movies, you will notice endorsements from so-called critics from entertainment-oriented magazines and the less prestigious newspapers or from cable networks, whose function is to promote popular entertainment. Respectable critics can therefore trash a movie, and the distributors will be able to find enough positive-sounding phrases ("flawless," "unpredictable," "energetic," "hilarious," "dazzling," "two thumbs-up") for a full-page ad.

The best film critics, such as Stanley Kauffman, Richard Corliss, David Denby, David Ansen, and Anthony Lane, write for magazines. They are essentially essayists, who write reflective pieces and whose reviews never appear on the day that a movie opens. Anyone who needs guidance for the movie of the weekend will have to depend on newspaper or television critics. A magazine review may appear several weeks after the film's opening. One reads David Denby in *The New Yorker* not to decide what to see but to encounter a mind at work—a mind that's trying to grapple with what the critic has experienced and hopes to share it with concerned readers, some of whom may already have seen the film and want to compare their reaction with his.

Film reviewing in America goes back to the turn of the century, when readers were so hungry for reviews that they even accepted plot summaries and naïve accounts of the wonders of celluloid. By 1904, the *Philadelphia*

Inquirer was reviewing movies: its review of *The Great Train Robbery* (1903) was superficial ("There is a great amount of shooting"), but at least it was a beginning. By 1906, the first film journals had been started. In 1909, the *New York Times* ran its first movie review, an archly written piece on D. W. Griffith's *Pippa Passes*; from that time on, film reviewing became a regular department in the *Times*. Since there were no special qualifications for reviewing films, anyone could write about them, and often did. Frank Woods, an advertising salesperson for the *New York Dramatic Mirror*, wrote a movie column in the *Mirror* under the pseudonym "The Spectator" from 1908 to 1912; he went on to become a leading screenwriter.

Before he became a major playwright, Robert E. Sherwood served as film critic for *Life* magazine from 1920 to 1928. Men of letters such as Edmund Wilson, Joseph Wood Krutch, and Mark Van Doren also wrote occasional film criticism. However, Wilson, Krutch, and Van Doren made their reputations in literary criticism, not movie reviewing. The first writer to achieve a national reputation for movie reviewing was James Agee, who between 1941 and 1948 reviewed for both *Time* magazine and *The Nation*. In addition to being a critic, Agee was also a novelist, a poet, and a screenwriter; his reviews therefore had a literary tone not usually found in movie columns. Agee could be vicious, but generally he was honest and regarded himself as an amateur conversing with his readers.

Agee's death at forty-five prevented him from leaving behind a fully developed theory of film; yet he demonstrated in outline, if not in detail, what a critic should be. It is clear from his review of Michael Curtiz's *Mission to Moscow* (1943), made when Russia was an American ally, that he sensed the film's importance, not as art but as pro-Soviet propaganda. Although *Mission to Moscow* justified Stalin's purge trials, Agee was unmoved by the film's rationalizations. Instead, he wrote:

> About the trials I am not qualified to speak. On surface falsifications of fact and atmosphere I might, but on the one crucial question, whether Trotsky and Trotskyists were or were not involved with Germany and Japan in a plot to overthrow the government and to partition the country, I am capable of no sensible opinion. I neither believe it nor disbelieve it.[9]

One imagines that Agee would have been the kind of critic who could take a film on its own terms, however political those terms may be. His charge that *Mission to Moscow* indulges its audience is more damning than five paragraphs of invective. Agee was not the kind of critic who catered to prejudices and yearned to make his audience a reflection of himself but, rather, one who believed that readers have the right instincts within them and need only the proper guidance to bring them forth.

Whether Agee would have become an auteurist is problematic. He was certainly conscious of the role of the director, as is evident from his review of Preston Sturges's *Hail the Conquering Hero* (1944). Sturges's mother was a free spirit who gave her son a charmed life: private schools and early exposure to opera, theater, and ballet. His foster father was a down-to-earth Chicago millionaire. Agee saw Sturges as a man torn between his mother's love of the arts and his foster father's love of making money. Thus in his films Sturges was always floundering between art and popular entertainment, tending more toward the latter than the former. Agee realized that he was doing something unusual when he invoked a director's life as background for his films, thus giving us a glimpse into the kind of critic he might have become. Agee understood Sturges's dilemma: does one make movies to make statements or to make audiences happy? In Sturges's *Sullivan's Travels*, John L. Sullivan (Joel McCrea), a liberal director who may well be Sturges's persona, abandons social-consciousness films for comedies because "there's a lot to be said for making people laugh." In *The Palm Beach Story*, Sturges showed his ambivalence toward money, satirizing gold diggers and the frivolous rich alike but resolving their problems before the fade-out.

Agee was not afraid to express admiration for B-films. He must have known that producer Val Lewton's movies would someday be classics, for he hailed *The Curse of the Cat People* and *Youth Runs Wild*, also a Lewton production, as the best "fiction films" of 1944. He also wrote favorably of Robert Siodmak's *Phantom Lady* (1944), which is now regarded as a model of film noir.

Another important reviewer was Bosley Crowther.[10] Of all the newspaper reviewers of his era, he carried the greatest weight because from 1940 through 1967 he wrote for the *New York Times*. Since Crowther reviewed for the most prestigious paper in America, he did not waste his time on what he deemed to be "junk." Whereas Agee saw more in Val Lewton films than calculated fright, Crowther saw nothing in them. *Cat People*, he felt, was "labored and obvious"; and although he found *The Curse of the Cat People* sensitive, it did not make his Ten Best list.

Crowther wrote for that anomaly known as the *New York Times* reader: someone who was educated but not pedantic, conservative but not a book burner, liberal without endorsing every cause as right, a believer in human values without being a teary sentimentalist. Crowther had these qualities himself. When the National Legion of Decency condemned Roberto Rossellini's *The Miracle* (1948) as an affront to the Virgin Birth, Crowther praised it as a work of art. But in the 1960s his influence began to wane. Movies were changing, and so were audiences. One of the last reviews Crowther wrote before his retirement was of *Bonnie and Clyde*. The review gave no indication of the sane judgments of which he was capable. Unable to see the film as a commentary on the Great Depression, he branded it as cheap, pointless, and marred by violence.

Dwight Macdonald, who devoted more than forty years of his life to movie reviewing, defined the concept of *film critic*: A critic will judge the film's quality, prove its quality, and compare the film with other films, giving it its proper place within the history of motion pictures.[11]

Naturally, not all reviewers can fulfill Macdonald's criteria. Pauline Kael, however, could.

The best of Pauline Kael's criticism has been collected in *For Keeps: 30 Years of Movies*. Because she identifies with the moviegoer, she is sometimes forced to assume an egalitarian, even an anti-intellectual pose. She constantly laments the way film is taught in universities, claiming that an overly scholarly approach will kill "movies" (her favorite term for the medium, because in America we never say "I'm going to the films" but "I'm going to the movies"). She scorns pretentiousness, believing that movies like *Last Year at Marienbad* (1961) can drive audiences away, although that has not happened because there were enough viewers and critics who found its lack of narrative clarity a metaphor for the unknowable. Kael championed American movies, yet she was not chauvinistic; she merely felt that they come closer to what movies ought to be than do most European films. Although she scorned auteurism, she had favorite directors, among them Robert Altman and Sam Peckinpah. Kael may have written for *The New Yorker*, but there is no wordiness in her style; there is wit, however, which may explain her long association with the magazine.

If Pauline Kael sounds like a mass of contradictions, it is because, on the one hand, she wrote about an art form that, in its inception, was not taken seriously (movies were "flickers" and nothing more). On the other hand, she wrote about an art form that is now taken seriously and is the subject of undergraduate and graduate study as well. Thus, Kael maintained a "one of the people" stance by addressing the reader as "you." As a critic whose knowledge of the other arts is on a par with her knowledge of film, Kael was more than just one of the people; she was the people at their most perceptive. David Denby, who has always acknowledged the influence Kael had on him, often speaks directly to the reader. At the end of his *New Yorker* review of Anthony Minghella's *Cold Mountain* (2003), Denby wrote: "You either shut [the film] out or go all the way into it and come out feeling both shaken and wildly happy."

Despite her formidable intelligence, Kael could err; no critic is infallible. We should remember that Tolstoy refused to consider Shakespeare a classic, and T. S. Eliot made the extravagant claim that Virgil's *Aeneid* was the only true classic of Western literature. Kael could also be hyperbolic when she felt strongly about a movie: she once compared the evening *Last Tango in Paris* closed the 1972 New York Film Festival with the evening Igor Stravinsky's *The Rite of Spring* premiered, calling each date a cultural landmark. Because she disapproved of auteurism, she set out to discredit Orson Welles as the auteur of *Citizen Kane* in her essay "Raising Kane," which first appeared in *The New Yorker* and then as the introduction to *The Citizen Kane Book*. Subsequent criticism, notably by Robert Carringer, has shown that Kael was not entirely correct in attributing the script wholly to Herman J. Mankiewicz. Kael certainly had her blind spots; she either failed, or refused, to see how Welles imposed his personality on *Citizen Kane* by drawing on his stage and radio experience (especially overlapping dialogue and musical bridges) to combine the best of both media in the film.

To her credit, Kael at least had a philosophy of film: it is a people's art form. Moviegoers loathe sham; they prefer "movies" to "cinema"; they want theorizing kept to a minimum; they cannot bear to see their values mocked. Thus, Kael reacted negatively to *A Clockwork Orange* because it argued that humankind's capacity for evil is never exhausted. Kael, who believed in people (or, at least, in moviegoers), could not accept that. Consequently, she accused its director, Stanley Kubrick, of "sucking up to the thugs in the audience."[12]

Pauline Kael wrote what are really essay-reviews. Her method was to reconstruct the film, incorporating her own impressions, comparisons with other films, and frequently comparisons with other art forms. Those who dislike Kael claim that in reconstructing the film she created an anti-film that bore little resemblance to the original. If Kael did this, and it was not often, readers were at least afforded an X-ray of her thoughts so that they could experience what was going on in her mind when she saw the film and later, when she was writing about it. We may not always be able to see every movie we read about. What reviewers as critics can do is suggest how we might have reacted during the film and when reflecting on it. Pauline Kael provided this vicarious experience better than most of her colleagues.

Practical Criticism: Interpreting *Citizen Kane*

If fiction is a house with many windows, as Henry James alleged, then criticism is a house with many doors, each with its own key. No school of literary criticism has a monopoly on interpretation; each offers its own peculiar access to the work. The New Criticism stresses the text; historical criticism places the text within its time; biographical criticism, within the context of the author's life; Marxist criticism, within the framework of the class struggle; psychoanalytic criticism, within the workings of the unconscious; myth criticism, within the universal dreams of humankind.

That criticism is an applied art is evident from the various ways in which a film historian, an auteurist, a myth critic, and a social historian might interpret *Citizen Kane*.

The Film Historian

The history of *Citizen Kane* is filled with so many untruths and half-truths that uncovering the real truth about the film is as complex as the attempt of the reporter, Thompson, to solve the enigma of "Rosebud." The popular assumption that RKO was in such a state of financial instability that its president, George J. Schaefer, wooed Orson Welles, the boy wonder of stage and radio, to Hollywood in the hope of working wonders for the studio, is one such untruth. In "A History of RKO Radio Pictures, Incorporated, 1928–1942," Richard B. Jewell has shown that in 1940, the year RKO signed Welles, its finances were in good shape.[13] Furthermore, the studio had a tradition of hiring stage personalities such as Katharine Hepburn, George Gershwin, and the director Garson Kanin; RKO's hiring of Welles, therefore, was not inconsistent with studio policy, although his being given the right of final cut was inconsistent with Hollywood policy in general.

Although one may never know whose idea it was—Welles's or Herman J. Mankiewicz's—to make a movie based on the life of newspaper tycoon William Randolph Hearst, films about the rise of an entrepreneur from obscurity to renown were not unknown. Since Mankiewicz, who wrote the first two drafts of *Citizen Kane* (which he entitled *American*), had been writing for the movies since 1926, he may well have been influenced by the script Preston Sturges wrote for *The Power and the Glory* (1933), which dealt with a Kane-like railroad magnate. Thomas Garner (Spencer Tracy) in *The Power and the Glory* is as enigmatic as the master of Xanadu. Moreover, there are points of contact between the two films: the Horatio Alger theme, the flashbacks following the tycoon's death, violations of chronology, and the extremes of admiration and contempt that both men inspired.

Mankiewicz, however, was not wholly responsible for the script of the film that ultimately became *Citizen Kane*. Pauline Kael's "Raising Kane" is in error on this point.[14] In an attempt to refocus attention on Mankiewicz, whom Welles had eclipsed, Kael downplayed Welles's contribution even to the point of undermining its originality. What other critics consider Wellesian, she attributes to Gregg Toland's cinematography. Kael invites us to compare *Kane* with *Mad Love* (1935), a Peter Lorre "mad doctor" movie, which Toland photographed and which has certain features in common with *Kane*: gothic sets, a physical resemblance between the bald Lorre and the bald Welles in *Kane*'s final scenes, cavernous rooms, and even a white cockatoo.

"Raising Kane," which has occasioned controversy since its publication, has been superseded by what appears to be the definitive work on the subject, Robert L. Carringer's *The Making of Citizen Kane*. Consequently, we now know that "Mankiewicz . . . wrote the first two drafts. His principal contributions were the story frame, a cast of characters, various individual scenes, and a good share of the dialogue. . . . Welles added the narrative brilliance—the visual and verbal wit, the stylistic fluidity, and such stunningly original strokes as the newspaper montages and the breakfast table sequence."[15] Unlike Kael, who exalted Mankiewicz at the expense of Welles, Carringer is perfectly willing to credit Mankiewicz for a contribution of

The glass paperweight in *Kitty Foyle* (1940), which probably inspired the one in *Citizen Kane*. *(Courtesy WCFTR)*

"fundamental importance," but, knowing what he does about the film's genesis, he cannot attribute the script solely to him.

Nor can Carringer allow the myth to persist that Gregg Toland determined how *Citizen Kane* would be photographed. Carringer proves that Welles and Toland were in total agreement as to how the film would be shot; it was not to resemble a typical Hollywood movie but, rather, would display all the techniques at which Toland excelled (low angles, deep focus, high-contrast photography, and the like). Deep focus, long takes, and a paucity of close-ups would also serve Welles's purpose. One must never forget that Welles came from the theater; hence, deep focus and long takes would be as close as he could come to duplicating stage drama. Since stage actors project more forcefully than film actors, a preponderance of close-ups would reveal their lack of film experience. One must also never forget that the leading roles were played by members of Welles's Mercury Theatre. Finally, it should be remembered that the Mercury Theatre had a weekly radio series, *The Mercury Theatre on the Air*, which Welles hosted and in which he frequently appeared. *Citizen Kane* contains examples of a common radio-drama device, the cross-fade, in which a character begins a sentence in one place and someone else finishes it in another.

Although *Citizen Kane* is not always thought of in terms of RKO, it was an RKO product. In fact, a cable TV movie about the making of *Citizen Kane* has been aptly entitled *RKO 281* (1999) because that was the film's production number. Carringer even demonstrates that the glass paperweight, so crucial to the plot, is not that different from a similar paperweight that appeared in an earlier RKO film, *Kitty Foyle*. In both films, the paperweight has a snow motif that conjures up memories of childhood. Since both paperweights were made by the RKO property department, it is unlikely that Mankiewicz or Mankiewicz/Welles hit upon the paperweight idea without some prior knowledge of *Kitty Foyle*.

Knowledge of a film's production history makes it possible to speak authoritatively about the film. Without such knowledge, one runs the risk of crediting individuals with contributions that others have made.

The Auteurist

Like many a first film, *Citizen Kane* contains within it the director's major themes and preoccupations. Here it is Welles's ambivalence toward wealth and his fascination with corruption. Welles's world is full of potentates—men who are larger than life: Kane, Bannister of *The Lady from Shanghai*, Gregori Arkadin of *Mr. Arkadin* (1955), and their alter egos in the director's Shakespearean films (*Macbeth*, 1948; *Othello*, 1952; and *Chimes at Midnight*, 1967).

Wealth assumes various forms in Welles's films: Kane's Xanadu, the Amberson mansion in *The Magnificent Ambersons*, the yacht in *The Lady from Shanghai*, the castle of Dunsinane in *Macbeth*, the castle at San Tirso in *Mr. Arkadin*, and Henry IV's court in *Chimes at Midnight*. Conversely, symbols of squalor also recur: Mary Kane's boardinghouse, the boardinghouse to which George and Aunt Fanny retreat in *The Magnificent Ambersons*, the Mexican fleabag in *Touch of Evil*, K's flat in *The Trial* (1963).

There are certain Wellesian artifacts that characterize the rich, the corrupt, and the guilty: mirrors (*Kane*, *The Lady from Shanghai*, *Othello*); corridors (*Kane*, *Macbeth*, *The Trial*); staircases (*Kane*, *The Magnificent Ambersons*); chauffeured cars (*Kane*) and private planes (*Mr. Arkadin*).

Another Wellesian theme is one that might be labeled the "war of the worlds." The extraordinary world encroaches on the ordinary, and the fortuitous and the irrational confront the stable and the orderly. In *Kane*, Susan Alexander (Dorothy Comingore) gives up a secure but mediocre existence to enter Kane's erratic world, in which she clearly does not belong. In Welles's other films, the two worlds are reflected in various ways: the automobile confronts the horse and buggy in *The Magnificent Ambersons*; Nazism brings disorder to a quiet Connecticut town in *The Stranger* (1946); an Irish sailor is exposed to the idle but murderous rich in *The Lady from Shanghai*; an ordinary couple is thrown into a nightmarish world of drugs and violence in *Touch of Evil*; the little man is introduced to fascist bureaucracy in *The Trial*. Even in the Shakespearean cycle, worlds collide: Macbeth's and Lady Macbeth's, Macbeth's and Macduff's (*Macbeth*); Othello's and Iago's, Othello's and Desdemona's (*Othello*); Falstaff's and Henry's, Falstaff's and Hal's (*Chimes at Midnight*).

The Wellesian king figure dies as he lived—in style: Kane's arms solemnly folded on his breast, Othello's bier carried aloft, Henry IV expiring on his throne. Even the Wellesian villain goes out in the grand manner: from the top of a tower (*The Stranger*, 1946), in a maze of mirrors (*The Lady from Shanghai*), plunging through space (*Mr. Arkadin*).

As Welles's first film, *Kane* represents the beginning of the Wellesian style, which would continue to manifest itself visually (long takes, dichotomy of light and darkness, recurring mirror and snow imagery) and aurally (overlapping dialogue, cross-fades) in his later work. The three-minute-long take that begins *Touch of Evil* had its origin in the camera's moving up the gate of Xanadu at the opening of *Citizen Kane* and in the camera's craning up the billboard advertising Susan Alexander Kane's appearance at El Rancho, moving over to the skylight, then shooting down at Susan seated at a table. Kane's multiple image reflected in the panels of the mirrored corridor anticipates the multiple images of Elsa and Bannister in the climax of *The Lady from Shanghai*. Welles's ambiguous attitude toward light (source of knowledge and sign of its absence; symbol of innocence and illusion as well as the glare of reality) runs throughout his films. Susan, a study in white with her blond hair and gleaming white skin, is a symbol of innocence exploited. The light that floods her face makes her even more pathetic; so does the light that masks the face of the doomed Isabel in *The Magnificent Ambersons*. Conversely, the light that hardens the face of the already hardened (and blond) Elsa Bannister in *The Lady from Shanghai* mocks the symbol of innocence by its profusion.

Like *Kane*, other Welles films open in darkness or semidarkness (*The Lady from Shanghai, The Stranger, Macbeth, Touch of Evil*). Darkness can suggest a womblike withdrawal (the dimly lit Xanadu), as well as a universe unilluminated by grace or providence (*The Lady from Shanghai, Touch of Evil*).

For a true appreciation of *Kane*, one must know how, as the first expression of Welles's visual and aural style, it foreshadowed themes and techniques that reappear in his subsequent films.

The Myth Critic

Every leading character in *Citizen Kane* is the incarnation of a mythological figure. Kane himself is a Zeus type. Zeus, who never had a childhood, was whisked off to Crete by his mother so that his wicked father, Cronos, would not devour him as he had his other children. Charles Foster Kane was also deprived of a normal boyhood. When he was a child, his mother entrusted him to a guardian so that he could enjoy a lifestyle that she could never give him.

Neither Zeus nor Kane was happily married. Zeus's marriage to Hera may have been made on Olympus, but it was not blessed with tranquility. Kane's marriage to the cool, patrician beauty Emily Norton (Ruth Warrick) was no different. A president's niece, Emily was socially superior to her husband and showed it by her demeanor. Kane therefore looked for love elsewhere, finding it briefly in an aspiring but untalented singer, Susan Alexander. Zeus also sought other women, rarely appearing to them as himself but rather taking other forms (a bull, a swan, a husband away from the war). Kane also conceals himself by diluting his importance when he describes his job to Susan, preferring that she love him for himself: "I run a couple of newspapers. How about you?"

When Kane tries to make Susan into an opera star, he steps out of the role of Zeus and into that of Pygmalion. But he becomes a Pygmalion in reverse. The sculptor Pygmalion fell in love with his own creation, which miraculously came to life. Welles inverts the myth, making Kane into an anti-Pygmalion who fashions a puppet for himself out of a living woman.

Zeus replaced his father's tyranny with the enlightened rule of the Olympians. Kane must fight his surrogate father (Thatcher, his guardian), who embodies the worst qualities of the privileged class. When Thatcher asks Kane what he would have liked to be, Kane replies, "Everything you hate." In fact, Kane is always fighting Cronos in some form: Thatcher, the elderly owner of *The Inquirer*, which he takes over; the political boss Jim Gettys. When he is not clashing with Cronos, he is battling Prometheus in the person of Leland (Joseph Cotten), who sees him for what he is: "You don't care about anything except you."

Ultimately, Zeus became another Cronos: authoritarian, misanthropic, vindictive, fearful of having his power usurped, and, finally, aloof. Kane gradually grows more and more like Thatcher-Cronos; although he wants to benefit humanity, he has become too corrupted by wealth to do so. In the *Iliad*, Zeus, weary of all the infighting among the Olympians, frequently retires to the topmost peak of Mount Ida; Kane, disillusioned by political defeat, broken friendships, and Susan's failure as an opera star, retires to the seclusion of Xanadu.

If it is viewed as myth, *Kane's* universality is more evident than it would be if the film were studied as a historical artifact or as the work of an auteur.

The Social Historian

As Machiavelli noted in *The Prince*, half of our affairs are governed by fortune (*fortuna*); the other half, by personal endeavor (*virtù*). It was by pure chance that Mary Kane (Agnes Moorehead), the owner of a boardinghouse, acquired the Colorado Lode. A boarder, unable to pay his rent, gave her a deed to an abandoned mine shaft that turned out to be the world's third-richest gold mine. Once *fortuna* places something in our path, *virtù* must take over. Unfortunately, Mary Kane's *virtù* was misdirected; married to a failure, she did not want her son, Charles, to become a replica of his father. She therefore entrusted the boy's care to Walter P. Thatcher, a noted financier; in so doing, she deprived Charles of a normal childhood so that he could enjoy a life befitting a millionaire.

The American dream can become a nightmare. Charles Foster Kane first tries to redeem himself. When he assumes control of the *New York Inquirer*, he begins exposing trusts and slumlords. He tells his guardian, "It is my duty — I'll let you in on a secret, it is also my pleasure — to see to it that decent, hard-working people of this community aren't robbed blind by a pack of money-mad pirates!"

The Three Faces of Kane

The republican Kane flanked by Leland, his drama critic (Joseph Cotten), and Bernstein, his managing editor (Everett Sloane). *(Courtesy MOMA/FSA)*

Kane is a principled muckraker. He also refuses to run the newspaper as if it were his private enterprise; instead, he delegates authority. He even writes a Declaration of Principles, promising his readers an honest newspaper. However, while he is writing it, his face is shrouded in darkness. Kane is clearly irredeemable.

There is no salvation for Kane because he is heir to his mother's belief that the purchasing power of money is infinite. Just as his mother bought him a privileged life, Kane buys his second wife an operatic career as well as an opera house, forcing her into a role for which she has no talent—in effect, doing to her what her mother might have done, if she had had Kane's wealth. All Kane needs to hear is that Susan's mother wanted her daughter to be an opera singer; he immediately launches Susan's career, completely disregarding the fact that she will never be anything but an amateur. Since Susan has become a public figure, Kane expects her to be able to take harsh criticism. When Leland is too drunk to finish his review of Susan's performance, Kane takes over and writes the same kind of negative notice that Jedidiah would have written—a review ending with the word "weak." Having failed as a politician and as an opera impresario with his wife as his only client, Kane retires to his pleasure dome on the Florida Gulf Coast.

Who is Charles Foster Kane? After his death, the press called him a plutocrat; his guardian branded him a communist; the Union Square demagogues labeled him a fascist. Then there is Kane's view of himself: "I am, always will be, and always have been one thing: an American."

The popular conception of Kane, confused and contradictory, is no different from the popular conception of America: the republic to which we pledge allegiance, the democracy we claim we are, the empire others perceive us to be. The three faces of America become Kane's three faces. First, he is the republican editor who delegates authority to his representatives; then, he is the democratic leader, promising in his Declaration of Principles to be a champion of human rights; finally, he is the imperialist, bald and gowned, an Oriental potentate living in splendor at Xanadu. *Citizen Kane* forces us to watch the transformation of the country through the transformation of one man.

While each interpretation is valid as far as it goes, one could easily write an essay combining all of them by recounting details about the film's production history, showing how *Kane*'s visual style is repeated in Welles's other films, relating its archetypal plot to well-known myths, and noting its ambivalence about a society that encourages "rags-to-riches" optimism and places material values before spiritual ones.

Guidelines for Film Criticism

There is no single way to criticize film. After a lifetime of reviewing, Dwight Macdonald wondered whether the norms that had once served him were still valid. Since Macdonald's guidelines are among the best that a contemporary critic can offer us, it is worthwhile to repeat them here. They represent ways of approaching film; however, they are not ironclad laws. For this reason, there will be exceptions; some of the guidelines may not be applicable to a particular film, as Macdonald is the first to admit. Still, it is easier to deal with exceptions when we have standards by which to measure them than if we had no standards at all. The following excerpt from Macdonald's work *Dwight Macdonald on Movies* summarizes his guidelines succinctly:

> I know something about cinema after forty years, and being a congenital critic, I know what I like and why. But I can't explain the *why* except in terms of the specific work under consideration, on which I'm copious enough. The general theory, the larger view, the gestalt—these have always eluded me. Whether this gap in my critical armor be called an idiosyncrasy or, less charitably, a personal failing, it has always been most definitely there.
>
> But people, especially undergraduates hot for certainty, keep asking me what rules, principles or standards I judge movies by—a fair question to which I can never think of an answer. Years ago, some forgotten but evidently sharp stimulus spurred me to put some guidelines down on paper. The result, hitherto unprinted for reasons which will become clear, was:
> (1) Are the characters consistent, and in fact are there characters at all?
> (2) Is it true to life?
> (3) Is the photography cliché, or is it adapted to the particular film and therefore original?
> (4) Do the parts go together; do they add up to something; is there a rhythm established so that there is form, shape, climax, building up tension and exploding it?
> (5) Is there a mind behind it; is there a feeling that a single intelligence has imposed his own view on the material?

The democratic Kane as Man of the People. *(Courtesy MOMA/FSA)*

The last two questions rough out some vague sort of meaning, and the third is sound, if truistic. But I can't account for the first two being there at all, let alone in the lead-off place. Many films I admire are not "true to life" unless that stretchable term is strained beyond normal usage: *Broken Blossoms, Children of Paradise, Zéro de conduite, Caligari, On Approval,* Eisenstein's *Ivan the Terrible.* And some have no "characters" at all, consistent or no: *Potemkin, Arsenal, October, Intolerance, Marienbad, Orpheus, Olympia.* The comedies of Keaton, Chaplin, Lubitsch, the Marx Brothers and W. C. Fields occupy a middle ground. They have "consistent characters" all right, and they are also "true to life." But the consistency is always extreme and sometimes compulsive and obsessed (W. C., Groucho, Buster), and the truth is abstract. In short, they are so highly stylized . . . that they are constantly floating up from terra firma into the empyrean of art, right before my astonished and delighted eyes.[16]

If philosophy begins with wonder, as Plato claimed, so, too, does film criticism—with a sense of amazement that pictures can move, and the desire to explain how the moving picture can be a work of art. Even though you know the pictures do not move miraculously, never lose that childlike sense of wonder that you felt when you saw your first movie. Realize that when you are asked to write about a movie you are sharing in an ancient art,

The Imperial Kane as Master of Xanadu. *(Courtesy MOMA/FSA)*

the art of criticism, which goes back to the fourth century B.C.E. Although film criticism is in its infancy compared to literary criticism, it works from the same principle: the desire to explain structurally, descriptively, psychologically, or ideologically how a work of art functions. The papers you write will be on limited topics; they always are: "Deep Focus in *Citizen Kane*," "The Chronology of *Citizen Kane*," "Expressionism vs. Realism in *Citizen Kane*." Yet if you peruse scholarly journals such as *Film Criticism*, *Film Quarterly*, and *Literature/Film Quarterly*, you will discover articles by film scholars that are equally specific. One would have to write a book in order to articulate a philosophy of film. Still, when you write your papers, at least try to relate your particular topic to the entire film, showing how deep focus figures in the film's overall meaning, how the alternation between expressionism and realism is part of the film's tension, or how the jumbled chronology reflects the film's attitude toward Kane's life and biography in general.

Think of the parts in relation to the whole. This is what *Anatomy of Film* has attempted to do: to proceed from the components of narrative film to the total film and, finally, to ways of interpreting film. Whether you pursue film criticism professionally or simply as a moviegoer, remember that a work of art possesses integrity, or wholeness. A film is a totality; even if it is approached piecemeal, it does not lose its integrity, although that integrity may be hard to discern unless the parts are reassembled.

Alexander Pope was quoted earlier in this chapter because Pope, who was not even twenty when he wrote *An Essay on Criticism*, formulated principles that are still relevant. As you might expect, he also had something to say about focusing on the whole rather than the parts:

'Tis not a lip or eye we beauty call,
But the joint force and full result of all.

— An Essay on Criticism (II, 45–46)

No matter what kind of critic you become or what kinds of critics you read, relate your approach and theirs to the film as a total work of — one hopes — art.

NOTES

1. Raymond Spottiswoode, *A Grammar of the Film: An Analysis of Film Technique* (Berkeley: University of California Press, 1969), 29.
2. Rudolf Arnheim, *Film as Art* (Berkeley: University of California Press, 1974), 133.
3. Ibid., 57.
4. André Bazin, *What Is Cinema?* Vol. 1, trans. Hugh Gray (Berkeley: University of California Press, 1967), 50.
5. Siegfried Kracauer, *Theory of Film: The Redemption of Physical Reality* (New York: Oxford University Press/Galaxy Books, 1965), 305.
6. One of the best general studies of semiotics is Kaja Silverman, *The Subject of Semiotics* (New York: Oxford University Press, 1983); on film semiotics, see J. Dudley Andrew, *The Major Film Theories: An Introduction* (New York: Oxford University Press, 1976), 212–241. Also recommended is the structuralism issue of *College English* (October 1975).
7. Christian Metz, *Film Language: A Semiotics of the Cinema*, trans. Michael Taylor (New York: Oxford University Press, 1974), 105.
8. Laura Mulvey, "Visual Pleasure and Narrative Cinema," in *Film Theory and Criticism*, 5th ed., ed. Leo Braudy and Marshall Cohen (New York: Oxford University Press, 1999), 834.
9. James Agee, *Agee on Film: Reviews and Comments by James Agee* (New York: Grosset & Dunlap, 1969), 39.
10. On Crowther's career, see Frank E. Beaver, *Bosley Crowther: Social Critic of the Film* (New York: Arno Press, 1974).
11. Dwight Macdonald, *Dwight Macdonald on Movies* (Englewood Cliffs, N.J.: Prentice-Hall, 1969), 471.
12. Pauline Kael, *Deeper into Movies* (Boston: Atlantic–Little, Brown, 1974), 378.
13. Richard B. Jewell, "A History of RKO Radio Pictures, Incorporated, 1928–1942" (Ph.D. diss., University of Southern California Press, 1978).
14. Pauline Kael, "Raising Kane," *The Citizen Kane Book* (Boston: Little Brown, 1971), 1–84.
15. Robert L. Carringer, *The Making of Citizen Kane* (Berkeley: University of California Press, 1985), 35.
16. Macdonald, *Dwight Macdonald on Movies*, ix–x.

APPENDIX I
List of Films Referenced and Directors

Film	Director
About Schmidt (2002)	Alexander Payne
Abraham Lincoln (1930)	D. W. Griffith
The Accused (1948)	William Dieterle
Ace Ventura: When Nature Calls (1995)	Steve Oedekerk
Across the Pacific (1942)	John Huston
Adam's Rib (1949)	George Cukor
Address Unknown (1944)	William Cameron Menzies
The African Queen (1951)	John Huston
Against All Odds (1984)	Taylor Hackford
The Age of Innocence (1993)	Martin Scorsese
A.I. Artificial Intelligence (2001)	Steven Spielberg
Alice Doesn't Live Here Anymore (1974)	Martin Scorsese
All About Eve (1950)	Joseph L. Mankiewicz
All About My Mother (1999)	Pedro Almodóvar
All the President's Men (1976)	Alan J. Pakula
All Quiet on the Western Front (1930)	Lewis Milestone
All That Heaven Allows (1955)	Douglas Sirk
American Beauty (1999)	Sam Mendes
An American in Paris (1951)	Vincente Minnelli
An American Romance (1944)	King Vidor
American Pie (1999)	Paul Weitz

*Films chosen for the Library of Congress's National Film Registry (1989–), created to single out films of historical and cultural significance.

Film	Director
Amistad (1997)	Steven Spielberg
The Amityville Horror (1979)	Stuart Rosenberg
And the Band Played On (1993)	Roger Spottiswoode
And Now Tomorrow (1944)	Irving Pichel
And Then There Were None (1945)	René Clair
Angels with Dirty Faces (1938)	Michael Curtiz
Anne of the Thousand Days (1969)	Charles Jarrott
Another Woman (1988)	Woody Allen
À nous la liberté (1931)	René Clair
Anything Else (2003)	Woody Allen
Anywhere but Here (1999)	Wayne Wang
Apache (1954)	Robert Aldrich
**The Apartment* (1960)	Billy Wilder
**Apocalypse Now* (1979)	Francis Ford Coppola
Apollo 13 (1995)	Ron Howard
Arise, My Love (1940)	Mitchell Leisen
Armageddon (1998)	Michael Bay
**The Asphalt Jungle* (1950)	John Huston
Autumn in New York (2000)	Joan Chen
Avanti! (1972)	Billy Wilder
**The Awful Truth* (1937)	Leo McCarey
Back to the Future (1985)	Robert Zemeckis
Back to the Future Part II (1989)	Robert Zemeckis
The Bad and the Beautiful (1952)	Vincente Minnelli
**Badlands* (1973)	Terrence Malick
Ball of Fire (1941)	Howard Hawks
The Band Wagon (1953)	Vincente Minnelli
The Barkleys of Broadway (1949)	Charles Walters
Barry Lyndon (1975)	Stanley Kubrick
Becket (1964)	Peter Glenville
Bed and Board (1970)	François Truffaut
Beginning of the End (1957)	Bert I. Gordon
Bend It Like Beckham (2002)	Gurinder Chadha
Beloved (1998)	Jonathan Demme
Berkeley Square (1933)	Frank Lloyd
**The Best Years of Our Lives* (1946)	William Wyler
Betsy's Wedding (1990)	Alan Alda
The Bicycle Thief (1947)	Vittorio DeSica
Big (1998)	Penny Marshall
The Big Carnival (Ace in the Hole) (1951)	Billy Wilder

The Big Heat (1953)	Fritz Lang
The Big Picture (1989)	Christopher Guest
The Big Sleep (1946)	Howard Hawks
A Bill of Divorcement (1932)	George Cukor
The Birds (1963)	Alfred Hitchcock
★The Birth of a Nation (1915)	D. W. Griffith
The Bishop's Wife (1947)	Henry Koster
Bitter Rice (1948)	Giuseppe De Santis
Bitter Sweet (1940)	W. S. Van Dyke II
The Blackboard Jungle (1955)	Richard Brooks
Black Hand (1950)	Richard Thorpe
The Blair Witch Project (1999)	Daniel Myrick, Eduardo Sanchez
Blazing Saddles (1974)	Mel Brooks
Blind Husbands (1918)	Erich von Stroheim
The Blob (1958)	Irving S. Yeaworth, Jr.
Blonde Venus (1932)	Josef von Sternberg
Blow-Up (1966)	Michelangelo Antonioni
The Blue Angel (1930)	Josef von Sternberg
Bluebeard (1944)	Edgar G. Ulmer
Body and Soul (1947)	Robert Rossen
Body Heat (1981)	Lawrence Kasdan
Bombardier (1943)	Richard Wallace
Bonnie and Clyde (1967)	Arthur Penn
Boomerang! (1947)	Elia Kazan
The Bowery Boys Meet the Monsters (1954)	Edward Bernds
Boys Don't Cry (1999)	Kimberly Peirce
The Bravados (1958)	Henry King
Breathless (1959)	Jean-Luc Godard
Brewster's Millions (1985)	Walter Hill
★Bride of Frankenstein (1935)	James Whale
The Bridge on the River Kwai (1957)	David Lean
Brief Encounter (1946)	David Lean
Brigadoon (1954)	Vincente Minnelli
★Bringing Up Baby (1938)	Howard Hawks
Broadway Danny Rose (1984)	Woody Allen
Broken Arrow (1950)	Delmer Daves
★Broken Blossoms (1919)	D. W. Griffith
Broken Lance (1954)	Edward Dmytryk
The Brotherhood (1968)	Martin Ritt
Brute Force (1947)	Jules Dassin
Buddy Buddy (1981)	Billy Wilder

Film	Director
Bullets over Broadway (1994)	Woody Allen
Burnt Offerings (1976)	Dan Curtis
Butch Cassidy and the Sundance Kid (1969)	George Roy Hill
Bwana Devil (1952)	Arch Oboler
The Cabinet of Dr. Caligari (1919)	Robert Wiene
California Suite (1978)	Herbert Ross
Camille (1937)	George Cukor
Cape Fear (1991)	Martin Scorsese
Capturing the Friedmans (2002)	Andrew Jarecki
Carrie (1976)	Brian De Palma
Casablanca (1942)	Michael Curtiz
Casino (1995)	Martin Scorsese
Cast Away (2000)	Robert Zemeckis
Casualties of War (1989)	Brian De Palma
Catch Me If You Can (2002)	Steven Spielberg
Cat People (1942)	Jacques Tourneur
Caught (1949)	Max Ophüls
Celebrity (1998)	Woody Allen
Champion (1949)	Mark Robson
Chaplin (1992)	Richard Attenborough
Cheyenne Autumn (1964)	John Ford
Chicago (2002)	Rob Marshall
The Children's Hour (1962)	William Wyler
Chimes at Midnight (1966)	Orson Welles
Chinatown (1974)	Roman Polanski
Citizen Kane (1941)	Orson Welles
A Clockwork Orange (1971)	Stanley Kubrick
Close Encounters of the Third Kind (1977)	Steven Spielberg
Clueless (1995)	Amy Heckerling
Cold Mountain (2003)	Anthony Minghella
Colorado Territory (1949)	Raoul Walsh
The Color of Money (1986)	Martin Scorsese
The Color Purple (1985)	Steven Spielberg
Colors (1988)	Dennis Hopper
Come Back, Little Sheba (1952)	Daniel Mann
Coming Home (1978)	Hal Ashby
Coney Island (1943)	Walter Lang
Contact (1997)	Robert Zemeckis
The Corn Is Green (1944)	Irving Rapper
The Corn Is Green (1979)	George Cukor

The Country Girl (1954)	George Seaton
Cover Girl (1944)	Charles Vidor
Craig's Wife (1936)	Dorothy Arzner
Crash Dive (1943)	Archie Mayo
The Creature from the Black Lagoon (1954)	Jack Arnold
Crimes and Misdemeanors (1989)	Woody Allen
Criss Cross (1949)	Robert Siodmak
Crouching Tiger, Hidden Dragon (2001)	Ang Lee
The Crying Game (1992)	Neil Jordan
Cry of the City (1948)	Robert Siodmak
The Curse of the Cat People (1944)	Gunther von Fritsch, Robert Wise
Curse of Frankenstein (1957)	Terence Fisher
Dancer in the Dark (2000)	Lars von Trier
Dances with Wolves (1990)	Kevin Costner
Dark City (1950)	William Dieterle
Dark Passage (1947)	Delmer Daves
Dark Victory (1939)	Edmund Goulding
Darling (1965)	John Schlesinger
A Day at the Races (1937)	Sam Wood
Day for Night (1973)	François Truffaut
The Day of the Locust (1975)	John Schlesinger
★The Day the Earth Stood Still (1951)	Robert Wise
The Dead (1987)	John Huston
Dead End (1937)	William Wyler
Dead Men Don't Wear Plaid (1982)	Carl Reiner
Dead Reckoning (1947)	John Cromwell
Death Becomes Her (1992)	Robert Zemeckis
Deconstructing Harry (1997)	Woody Allen
The Deer Hunter (1978)	Michael Cimino
Destry Rides Again (1939)	George Marshall
Detective (1985)	Jean-Luc Godard
★Detour (1946)	Edgar G. Ulmer
Dial M for Murder (1954)	Alfred Hitchcock
Dirty Harry (1972)	Don Siegel
Dishonored (1931)	Josef von Sternberg
Dog Day Afternoon (1975)	Sidney Lumet
A Doll's House (1973)	Patrick Garland
★Double Indemnity (1944)	Billy Wilder
Down with Love (2003)	Peyton Reed
Dracula's Daughter (1936)	Lambert Hillyer
Dr. Cyclops (1940)	Ernest Schoedsack
Dream Street (1921)	D. W. Griffith

Film	Director
Dressed to Kill (1980)	Brian De Palma
The Driver (1978)	Walter Hill
Dr. Jekyll and Mr. Hyde (1932)	Rouben Mamoulian
Dr. Strangelove or:	Stanley Kubrick
How I Learned to Stop Worrying and	
Love the Bomb (1964)	
Dr. Zhivago (1965)	David Lean
Duck Soup (1933)	Leo McCarey
Duel in the Sun (1947)	King Vidor
Dumb & Dumber (1994)	Peter Farrelly
Easter Parade (1948)	Charles Walters
East of Eden (1955)	Elia Kazan
Easy Living (1937)	Mitchell Leisen
Easy Rider (1969)	Dennis Hopper
Edge of Darkness (1943)	Lewis Milestone
8½ (1963)	Frederico Fellini
Emma (1996)	Doug McGrath
The Emperor Waltz (1948)	Billy Wilder
Empire of the Sun (1987)	Steven Spielberg
Escape from Alcatraz (1979)	Don Siegel
E.T.: The Extra-Terrestrial (1982)	Steven Spielberg
Everyone Says I Love You (1996)	Woody Allen
The Exorcist (1973)	William Friedkin
Experiment Perilous (1944)	Jacques Tourneur
The Extraordinary Seaman (1969)	John Frankenheimer
Eyes Wide Shut (1999)	Stanley Kubrick
Face to Face (1976)	Ingmar Bergman
Fall of the Roman Empire (1964)	Anthony Mann
Family Plot (1976)	Alfred Hitchcock
Fantasia (1940)	Ben Sharpsteen
Far from Heaven (2002)	Todd Haynes
Fast Times at Ridgemont High (1982)	Amy Heckerling
Fatal Attraction (1987)	Adrian Lyne
Father of the Bride (1950, 1991)	Vincente Minnelli, Charles Shyer
Fedora (1979)	Billy Wilder
The File on Thelma Jordan (1949)	Robert Siodmak
The First Time (1952)	Frank Tashlin
Five Graves to Cairo (1943)	Billy Wilder
Fixed Bayonets (1951)	Samuel Fuller

Flying Down to Rio (1933)	Thornton Freeland
Follow the Boys (1944)	Edward Sutherland
Foolish Wives (1921)	Erich von Stroheim
A Foreign Affair (1948)	Billy Wilder
Foreign Correspondent (1940)	Alfred Hitchcock
Forever Amber (1947)	Otto Preminger
Forrest Gump (1994)	Robert Zemeckis
Fort Apache (1948)	John Ford
The Fortune Cookie (1966)	Billy Wilder
48 Hours (1982)	Walter Hill
★42nd Street (1933)	Lloyd Bacon
The Fountainhead (1949)	King Vidor
The Four Hundred Blows (1959)	François Truffaut
The Four Seasons (1981)	Alan Alda
Four Weddings and a Funeral (1994)	Mike Newell
★Frankenstein (1931)	James Whale
Frankenstein Meets	Ray William Neill
the Wolf Man (1943)	
French Kiss (1995)	Lawrence Kasdan
Frenzy (1972)	Alfred Hitchcock
Frequency (2000)	Gregory Hoblit
The Freshman (1990)	Andrew Bergman
Friday the 13th (1980)	Sean S. Cunningham
The Front (1975)	Martin Ritt
The Front Page (1974)	Billy Wilder
Full Metal Jacket (1987)	Stanley Kubrick
Gangs of New York (2002)	Martin Scorsese
The Gangster (1947)	Gordon Wiles
Gentlemen Prefer Blondes (1953)	Howard Hanks
Geronimo: An American Legend (1993)	Walter Hill
Ghost (1990)	Jerry Zucker
Giant (1950)	George Stevens
The Giant Claw (1957)	Fred S. Sears
Gigi (1958)	Vincente Minnelli
Gilda (1946)	Charles Vidor
Gladiator (2000)	Ridley Scott
The Glass Menagerie (1986)	Paul Newman
★The Godfather (1972)	Francis Ford Coppola
★The Godfather, Part II (1974)	Francis Ford Coppola
★Gold Diggers of 1933 (1933)	Mervyn LeRoy
Gold Diggers of 1935 (1935)	Busby Berkeley
The Golden Bowl (2001)	James Ivory
★Gone with the Wind (1939)	Victor Fleming

Film	Director
*GoodFellas (1990)	Martin Scorsese
*The Grapes of Wrath (1940)	John Ford
The Greatest Story Ever Told (1965)	George Stevens
Great Expectations (1946)	David Lean
The Great Lie (1941)	Edmund Goulding
*The Great Train Robbery (1903)	E. S. Porter
Greed (1924)	Erich von Stroheim
The Green Berets (1968)	John Wayne, Ray Kellogg
The Grifters (1990)	Stephen Frears
Guadalcanal Diary (1943)	Lewis Seiler
*Gun Crazy (1949)	Joseph H. Lewis
The Gunfighter (1950)	Henry King
Hail the Conquering Hero (1944)	Preston Sturges
Halloween (1978)	John Carpenter
Hamlet (1948)	Laurence Olivier
Hannah and Her Sisters (1986)	Woody Allen
The Happy Ending (1969)	Richard Brooks
Hard Times (1975)	Walter Hill
Harriet Craig (1950)	Vincent Sherman
The Haunting (1963)	Jan De Bont
The Haunting (1999)	Robert Wise
Hello, Dolly! (1969)	Gene Kelly
Hello Frisco, Hello (1943)	H. Bruce Humberstone
Hennessy (1975)	Don Sharp
He Ran All the Way (1951)	John Berry
He Walked by Night (1948)	Alfred L. Werker
*High Noon (1952)	Fred Zinnemann
High Sierra (1941)	Raoul Walsh
High Society (1956)	Charles Walters
Hilda Crane (1956)	Philip Dunne
Hiroshima, Mon Amour (1959)	Alain Resnais
*His Girl Friday (1940)	Howard Hawks
Hold Back the Dawn (1941)	Mitchell Leisen
Holiday (1938)	George Cukor
Holiday Inn (1942)	Mark Sandrich
The Hollow Man (2000)	Paul Verhoeven
Hollywood Canteen (1944)	Delmer Daves
Hollywood Ending (2002)	Woody Allen
Hook (1991)	Steven Spielberg
Horse Feathers (1932)	Norman Z. McLeod
Hour of the Wolf (1968)	Ingmar Bergman

The Hours (2002)	Stephen Daldry
House of Wax (1953)	André de Toth
The House on Carroll Street (1988)	Peter Yates
The House on 92nd Street (1945)	Henry Hathaway
*How Green Was My Valley (1941)	John Ford
How to Marry a Millionaire (1953)	Jean Negulesco
Human Desire (1954)	Fritz Lang
Humanité (1999)	Bruno Dumont
The Hurricane (1937)	John Ford
Husbands and Wives (1992)	Woody Allen
Hustle (1975)	Robert Aldrich
I Confess (1953)	Alfred Hitchcock
I Died a Thousand Times (1955)	Stuart Heisler
I Married a Monster from	Gene Fowler, Jr.
Outer Space (1958)	
Indiana Jones and	Steven Spielberg
the Last Crusade (1989)	
Indiana Jones and	
the Temple of Doom (1985)	Steven Spielberg
In the Company of Men (1997)	Neil LaBute
In the Good Old Summertime (1949)	Robert Z. Leonard
In the Mood for Love (2000)	Wong Kar-wai
*Intolerance (1916)	D. W. Griffith
*Invasion of the Body Snatchers (1956)	Don Siegel
The Invisible Man (1933)	James Whale
Invitation to the Dance (1956)	Gene Kelly
Irma la Douce (1963)	Billy Wilder
Isadora (1969)	Karl Reisz
It Came from Beneath the Sea (1955)	Robert Gordon
It Came from Outer Space (1953)	Jack Arnold
*It Happened One Night (1934)	Frank Capra
It's Always Fair Weather (1955)	Gene Kelly, Stanley Donen
*It's a Wonderful Life (1946)	Frank Capra
I Walked with a Zombie (1943)	Jacques Tourneur
Jane Eyre (1944)	Robert Stevenson
Jaws (1975)	Steven Spielberg
Jezebel (1938)	William Wyler
Johnny Guitar (1954)	Nicholas Ray
The Jolson Story (1946)	Alfred E. Green
Jules and Jim (1961)	François Truffaut
Julia (1977)	Fred Zinnemann
Juliet of the Spirits (1965)	Federico Fellini

Film	Director
Julius Caesar (1953)	Joseph L. Mankiewicz
Jurassic Park (1993)	Steven Spielberg
Keeper of the Flame (1943)	George Cukor
Key Largo (1948)	John Huston
The Kid Stays in the Picture (2002)	Nanette Burstein, Brett Morgen
King and Country (1964)	Joseph Losey
The King and I (1956)	Walter Lang
The King of Comedy (1983)	Martin Scorsese
King Kong (1933)	Merian C. Cooper, Ernest B. Schoedsack
Kismet (1955)	Vincente Minnelli
Kiss Me, Stupid (1964)	Billy Wilder
Kitty Foyle (1940)	Sam Wood
Knock on Any Door (1949)	Nicholas Ray
Kundun (1997)	Martin Scorsese
Lacombe, Lucien (1974)	Louis Malle
L.A. Confidential (1997)	Curtis Hanson
La dolce vita (1960)	Federico Fellini
The Lady and the Monster (1944)	George Sherman
Lady Be Good (1941)	Norman Z. McLeod
The Lady Eve (1941)	Preston Sturges
The Lady from Shanghai (1948)	Orson Welles
Lady in the Dark (1944)	Mitchell Leisen
Lady in the Lake (1946)	Robert Montgomery
Lady in White (1988)	Frank LaLoggia
La grande strada azzurra (The Wide Blue Sea) (1957)	Gillo Pontecorvo
Lake Placid (1999)	Steve Miner
The Last of the Mohicans (1992)	Michael Mann
The Last Picture Show (1971)	Peter Bogdanovich
La strada (1954)	Federico Fellini
Last Tango in Paris (1972)	Bernardo Bertolucci
The Last Temptation of Christ (1988)	Martin Scorsese
Last Train from Gun Hill (1956)	John Sturges
The Last Tycoon (1976)	Elia Kazan
Last Year at Marienbad (1961)	Alain Resnais
Lawrence of Arabia (1962)	David Lean
A League of Their Own (1992)	Penny Marshall
The Letter (1940)	William Wyler

*Letter from an Unknown Woman (1948)	Max Ophüls
A Letter to Three Wives (1949)	Joseph L. Mankiewicz
Lifeboat (1944)	Alfred Hitchcock
Little Big Man (1970)	Arthur Penn
Little Caesar (1930)	Mervyn LeRoy
The Little Foxes (1941)	William Wyler
The Little Mermaid (1988)	John Musker, Ron Clements
Little Women (1933)	George Cukor
Little Women (1994)	Gillian Armstrong
The Locket (1946)	John Brahm
The Lonely Villa (1909)	D. W. Griffith
Long Day's Journey into Night (1962)	Sidney Lumet
Look Who's Talking (1989)	Amy Heckerling
Lost Horizon (1937)	Frank Capra
Lost in America (1985)	Albert Brooks
The Lost Weekend (1945)	Billy Wilder
The Lost World: Jurassic Park (1997)	Steven Spielberg
Love Among the Ruins (1975)	George Cukor
Love in the Afternoon (1957)	Billy Wilder
Love Is a Many-Splendored Thing (1955)	Henry King
M (1931)	Fritz Lang
Macbeth (1948)	Orson Welles
Mad Love (1935)	Karl Freund
*The Magnificent Ambersons (1942)	Orson Welles
The Major and the Minor (1942)	Billy Wilder
Malcolm X (1992)	Spike Lee
The Maltese Falcon (1941)	John Huston
The Man from Colorado (1948)	Henry Levin
The Man from Laramie (1955)	Anthony Mann
Manhattan (1979)	Woody Allen
Manhattan Murder Mystery (1993)	Woody Allen
Man of the West (1958)	Anthony Mann
The Man Who Knew Too Much (1956)	Alfred Hitchcock
The Man Who Shot Liberty Valance (1962)	John Ford
The Man Who Wasn't There (2001)	Joel Coen
Marnie (1964)	Alfred Hitchcock
Mary, Queen of Scots (1971)	Charles Jarrott
Mary Shelley's Frankenstein (1994)	Kenneth Branagh
*M*A*S*H (1970)	Robert Altman

Film	Director
The Matrix (1999)	Larry and Andrew Wachowski
The Matrix Reloaded (2003)	Larry and Andrew Wachowski
The Matrix Revolutions (2003)	Larry and Andrew Wachowski
McCabe and Mrs. Miller (1971)	Robert Altman
Mean Streets (1973)	Martin Scorsese
*Medium Cool (1969)	Haskell Wexler
Meet John Doe (1941)	Frank Capra
*Meet Me in St. Louis (1944)	Vincente Minnelli
Meet Nero Wolfe (1936)	Herbert Biberman
Me, Myself and Irene (2000)	Bobby Farrelly, Peter Farrelly
The Men (1950)	Fred Zinnemann
The Merry Widow (1925)	Erich von Stroheim
The Merry Widow (1934)	Ernst Lubitsch
Metropolis (1926)	Fritz Lang
Midnight (1939)	Mitchell Leisen
A Midsummer Night's Sex Comedy (1982)	
Mighty Aphrodite (1995)	Woody Allen
*Mildred Pierce (1945)	Michael Curtiz
Minority Report (2002)	Steven Spielberg
The Miracle (1948)	Roberto Rossellini
Miracle on 34th Street (1947)	George Seaton
Mission to Moscow (1943)	Michael Curtiz
*Modern Times (1936)	Charlie Chaplin
Monkey Business (1931)	Norman Z. McLeod
Monsoon Wedding (2002)	Mira Nair
Moon over Miami (1941)	Walter Lang
Moonstruck (1987)	Norman Jewison
*Morocco (1930)	Josef von Sternberg
Moulin Rouge (2001)	Baz Luhrmann
Mr. Arkadin (1955)	Orson Welles
Mr. Deeds Goes to Town (1936)	Frank Capra
Mrs. Dalloway (1996)	Marleen Gorris
Mrs. Doubtfire (1993)	Chris Columbus
Mr. Skeffington (1944)	Vincent Sherman
Mrs. Miniver (1942)	William Wyler
*Mr. Smith Goes to Washington (1939)	Frank Capra
Mulholland Falls (1996)	Lee Tamahori
Murder, My Sweet (1944)	Edward Dmytryk
Murder on the Orient Express (1974)	Sidney Lumet
My Big Fat Greek Wedding (2001)	Joel Zwick
*My Darling Clementine (1946)	John Ford

My Life (1993)	Bruce Joel Rubin
My Little Chickadee (1940)	Edward Cline
My Man Godfrey (1936)	Gregory La Cava
My Reputation (1946)	Curtis Bernhardt
My Son John (1952)	Leo McCarey
Mystic River (2003)	Clint Eastwood
The Naked City (1948)	Jules Dassin
The Naked Dawn (1955)	Edgar G. Ulmer
The Naked Spur (1953)	Anthony Mann
Nashville (1975)	Robert Altman
Natural Born Killers (1994)	Oliver Stone
The Net (1995)	Irwin Winkler
A New Life (1988)	Alan Alda
New York, New York (1977)	Martin Scorsese
Nickelodeon (1976)	Peter Bogdanovich
A Night at the Opera (1935)	Sam Wood
A Night in Casablanca (1946)	Archie Mayo
Nightmare on Elm Street (1984)	Wes Craven
'Night, Mother (1986)	Tom Moore
The Night of the Hunter (1955)	Charles Laughton
The Night of the Iguana (1964)	John Huston
The Night Porter (1974)	Liliana Cavani
Ninotchka (1939)	Ernst Lubitsch
Nora Prentiss (1947)	Vincent Sherman
North by Northwest (1959)	Alfred Hitchcock
No Sad Songs for Me (1950)	Rudolph Maté
Nothing Sacred (1937)	William Wellman
Notorious (1946)	Alfred Hitchcock
No Way Out (1950)	Joseph L. Mankiewicz
Now, Voyager (1942)	Irving Rapper
O Brother, Where Art Thou? (2000)	Joel Coen
Of Mice and Men (1939)	Lewis Milestone
Old Acquaintance (1943)	Vincent Sherman
The Old Maid (1939)	Edmund Goulding
Olympia (1936)	Leni Riefenstahl
One Flew over the Cuckoo's Nest (1975)	Milos Forman
One True Thing (1998)	Carl Franklin
One, Two, Three (1961)	Billy Wilder
On the Town (1949)	Gene Kelly, Stanley Donen
On the Waterfront (1954)	Elia Kazan
Open City (1945)	Roberto Rossellini

Film	Director
Open Range (2003)	Kevin Costner
Othello (1952)	Orson Welles
The Others (2001)	Alejandro Amendâbar
Out of the Past (1947)	Jacques Tourneur
Paid in Full (1950)	William Dieterle
Paisan (1946)	Roberto Rossellini
Pale Rider (1987)	Clint Eastwood
The Palm Beach Story (1942)	Preston Sturges
The Passenger (1975)	Michelangelo Antonioni
Passion Fish (1992)	John Sayles
A Passion of Anna (1969)	Ingmar Bergman
The Passion of the Christ (2003)	Mel Gibson
Pat and Mike (1952)	George Cukor
Paths of Glory (1957)	Stanley Kubrick
Patton (1970)	Franklin Schaffner
Pearl Harbor (2001)	Michael Bay
Peggy Sue Got Married (1986)	Francis Ford Coppola
Penny Serenade (1941)	George Stevens
The Perfect Storm (2000)	Wolfgang Petersen
The Perils of Pauline (1947)	George Marshall
Persona (1966)	Ingmar Bergman
The Petty Girl (1950)	Henry Levin
Phantom Lady (1944)	Robert Siodmak
The Philadelphia Story (1940)	George Cukor
Phone Call from a Stranger (1951)	Jean Negulesco
The Pianist (2002)	Roman Polanski
Picnic (1955)	Joshua Logan
Pillow Talk (1960)	Michael Gordon
Pinocchio (1940)	Ben Sharpsteen, Hamilton Luske
Pippa Passes (1909)	D. W. Griffith
The Pirate (1948)	Vincente Minnelli
Pirates of the Caribbean: The Curse of the Black Pearl (2003)	Gore Verbinski
Pitfall (1948)	André De Toth
Platoon (1986)	Oliver Stone
The Player (1992)	Robert Altman
Pleasantville (1998)	Gary Ross
Possession (2002)	Neil LaBute
Postcards from the Edge (1994)	Mike Nichols
The Postman Always Rings Twice (1946)	Tay Garnett

Potemkin (1925)	Sergei Eisenstein
The Power and the Glory (1933)	William K. Howard
The Preacher's Wife (1996)	Penny Marshall
Prelude to War (1942)	Frank Capra
Pretty Woman (1990)	Gary Marshall
Priscilla, Queen of the Desert (1994)	Stephen Elliott
The Private Life of	
Sherlock Holmes (1970)	Billy Wilder
The Prowler (1951)	Joseph Losey
Psycho (1960)	Alfred Hitchcock
Psycho (1998)	Gus Van Sant
The Public Enemy (1931)	William Wellman
The Purple Heart (1944)	Lewis Milestone
The Purple Rose of Cairo (1985)	Woody Allen
Pursued (1947)	Raoul Walsh
The Quiet Man (1952)	John Ford
Radio Days (1987)	Woody Allen
Raging Bull (1980)	Martin Scorsese
Raiders of the Lost Ark (1981)	Steven Spielberg
Rashomon (1950)	Akira Kurosawa
Rear Window (1954)	Alfred Hitchcock
Rebecca (1940)	Alfred Hitchcock
Rebel Without a Cause (1955)	Nicholas Ray
Red Mountain (1951)	William Dieterle
Red River (1948)	Howard Hawks
Reds (1981)	Warren Beatty
The Red Shoes (1948)	Michael Powell
Rhapsody in Blue (1945)	Irving Rapper
Road to Morocco (1942)	David Butler
Road to Perdition (2002)	Sam Mendes
Road to Singapore (1940)	Victor Schertzinger
Road to Utopia (1945)	Hal Walker
The Roaring Twenties (1939)	Raoul Walsh
Rooster Cogburn (1975)	Stuart Millar
Rope (1948)	Alfred Hitchcock
Rope of Sand (1949)	William Dieterle
Rosemary's Baby (1968)	Roman Polanski
The Rose Tattoo (1955)	Daniel Mann
Roxie Hart (1942)	William Wellman
The Runaway Bride (1999)	Gary Marshall
Run Lola Run (1998)	Tom Tykwer

Film	Director
Russian Ark (2003)	Alexander Sokurov
Saboteur (1942)	Alfred Hitchcock
Sabrina (1954)	Billy Wilder
Sahara (1943)	Zoltan Korda
Sands of Iwo Jima (1949)	Allan Dwan
Saving Private Ryan (1998)	Steven Spielberg
Scarface (1932)	Howard Hawks
Scarlet Street (1945)	Fritz Lang
Scenes from a Marriage (1973)	Ingmar Bergman
Schindler's List (1993)	Steven Spielberg
Scream (1995)	Wes Craven
Scream 2 (1997)	Wes Craven
Scream 3 (2000)	Wes Craven
Sea of Grass (1947)	Elia Kazan
The Searchers (1956)	John Ford
Searching for Debra Winger (2002)	Rosanna Arquette
The Searching Wind (1946)	William Dieterle
Seduction of Joe Tynan (1979)	Jerry Schatzberg
September (1987)	Woody Allen
September Affair (1950)	William Dieterle
Serpico (1973)	Sidney Lumet
The Set-Up (1949)	Robert Wise
Seven Brides for Seven Brothers (1954)	Stanley Donen
The Seventh Seal (1957)	Ingmar Bergman
The Seven Year Itch (1955)	Billy Wilder
Shadow of a Doubt (1943)	Alfred Hitchcock
Shadows and Fog (1992)	Woody Allen
Shakespeare in Love (1998)	John Madden
The Shame (1968)	Ingmar Bergman
Shane (1953)	George Stevens
Shanghai Express (1932)	Josef von Sternberg
She Wore a Yellow Ribbon (1949)	John Ford
The Shining (1980)	Stanley Kubrick
Shock Corridor (1963)	Samuel Fuller
Shoeshine (1946)	Vittorio De Sica
The Shop Around the Corner (1940)	Ernst Lubitsch
Show Boat (1936)	James Whale
The Sign of the Cross (1933)	Cecil B. De Mille
The Silence of the Lambs (1991)	Jonathan Demme
Silk Stockings (1957)	Rouben Mamoulian
Singin' in the Rain (1952)	Gene Kelly, Stanley Donen

The Sixth Sense (1999)	M. Night Shyamalan
Sleep, My Love (1948)	Douglas Sirk
Small Time Crooks (2000)	Woody Allen
Smiles of a Summer Night (1955)	Ingmar Bergman
Snow White and the Seven Dwarfs (1937)	Ben Sharpsteen
Soldier Blue (1970)	Ralph Nelson
Some Like It Hot (1959)	Billy Wilder
The Song of Bernadette (1943)	Henry King
Sorry, Wrong Number (1948)	Anatole Litvak
The Sound of Music (1966)	Robert Wise
Sous les toits de Paris (Under the Roofs of Paris) (1930)	Marcel Carné
The Spanish Earth (1937)	Joris Ivens
Spellbound (2002)	Jeffrey Blitz
The Spiral Staircase (1946)	Robert Siodmak
The Spirit of St. Louis (1957)	Billy Wilder
Stagecoach (1939)	John Ford
Stage Door Canteen (1943)	Frank Borzage
Stage Fright (1950)	Alfred Hitchcock
Stalag 17 (1951)	Billy Wilder
Stardust Memories (1980)	Woody Allen
A Star Is Born (1954)	George Cukor
A Star Is Born (1976)	Frank Pierson
Star Wars (1977)	George Lucas
The Steel Helmet (1951)	Samuel Fuller
Stella Dallas (1937)	King Vidor
Stepmom (1998)	Chris Columbus
The Sting (1973)	George Roy Hill
Stolen Kisses (1968)	François Truffaut
The Story of Adele H. (1975)	François Truffaut
The Strange Love of Martha Ivers (1946)	Lewis Milestone
The Stranger (1946)	Orson Welles
Strangers on a Train (1951)	Alfred Hitchcock
Strangers When We Meet (1960)	Richard Quine
A Streetcar Named Desire (1951)	Elia Kazan
The St. Valentine's Day Massacre (1967)	Roger Corman
Suddenly, Last Summer (1959)	Joseph L. Mankiewicz
The Sugarland Express (1974)	Steven Spielberg
Sullivan's Travels (1941)	Preston Sturges
A Summer Place (1959)	Delmer Daves
Sunset Boulevard (1950)	Billy Wilder
Sunshine State (2002)	John Sayles
Suspense (1946)	Frank Tuttle

Film	Director
Suspicion (1941)	Alfred Hitchcock
Sweet and Lowdown (1999)	Woody Allen
Sweet Liberty (1986)	Alan Alda
Sylvia Scarlett (1935)	George Cukor
Take a Letter, Darling (1942)	Mitchell Leisen
A Tale of Two Cities (1935)	Jack Conway
Tarantula (1955)	Jack Arnold
Taxi Driver (1976)	Martin Scorsese
Tea and Sympathy (1956)	Vincente Minnelli
Tell It to the Judge (1949)	Norman Foster
The Terminal (2004)	Steven Spielberg
Thelma and Louise (1991)	Ridley Scott
Them! (1954)	Gordon Douglas
There's No Business Like Show Business (1954)	Walter Lang
There's Something About Mary (1999)	Bobby Farrelly, Peter Farrelly
These Three (1936)	William Wyler
They All Kissed the Bride (1942)	Alexander Hall
They Died with Their Boots On (1941)	Raoul Walsh
They Shoot Horses, Don't They? (1969)	Sydney Pollack
They Were Expendable (1945)	John Ford
The Thing (1951)	Christian Nyby
Things to Come (1936)	William Cameron Menzies
The Thin Man (1934)	W. S. Van Dyke
The Third Man (1949)	Carol Reed
The 39 Steps (1935)	Alfred Hitchcock
This Island Earth (1955)	Joseph Newman
Three Days of the Condor (1975)	Sydney Pollack
Three Kings (1999)	David O. Russell
Three Little Words (1950)	Richard Thorpe
Through a Glass, Darkly (1961)	Ingmar Bergman
Thunder Birds (1942)	William Wellman
Till the Clouds Roll By (1946)	Richard Whorf
Till the End of Time (1946)	Edward Dmytryk
Time After Time (1976)	Nicholas Meyer
Time Code (2000)	Mike Figgis
The Time Machine (1960)	George Pal
The Tin Star (1956)	Anthony Mann
To Catch a Thief (1955)	Alfred Hitchcock
Tol'able David (1921)	Henry King
Tonight and Every Night (1944)	Victor Saville
Tootsie (1982)	Sydney Pollack

Tora! Tora! Tora! (1970)   Richard Fleischer
★Touch of Evil (1958)   Orson Welles
Treasure of the Sierra Madre (1948)   John Huston
The Trial (1963)   Orson Welles
A Trip to the Moon (1902)   Georges Méliès
Trouble in Paradise (1932)   Ernst Lubitsch
The Trouble with Harry (1955)   Alfred Hitchcock
True Grit (1969)   Henry Hathaway
The Truman Show (1998)   Peter Weir
★Twelve O'Clock High (1949)   Henry King
Two for the Road (1967)   Stanley Donen
The Two Mrs. Carrolls (1947)   Peter Godfrey
Two Rode Together (1961)   John Ford
★2001: A Space Odyssey (1968)   Stanley Kubrick
Two Weeks in Another Town (1962)   Vincente Minnelli

Ulzana's Raid (1972)   Robert Aldrich
The Umbrellas of Cherbourg (1964)   Jacques Demy
The Unbearable Lightness of Being (1988)   Philip Kaufman
Under Capricorn (1949)   Alfred Hitchcock
Une Femme Douce (1969)   Robert Bresson
Unfaithful (2002)   Adrian Lyne
Unforgiven (1992)   Clint Eastwood
The Uninvited (1944)   Lewis Allen
An Unmarried Woman (1978)   Paul Mazursky
The Untouchables (1987)   Brian De Palma

The Vagabond King (1956)   Michael Curtiz
★Vertigo (1958)   Alfred Hitchcock
Victor/Victoria (1982)   Blake Edwards
Viridiana (1961)   Luis Buñuel

Wabash Avenue (1950)   Henry Koster
Wag the Dog (1997)   Barry Levinson
Wagon Master (1950)   John Ford
A Walk in the Sun (1945)   Lewis Milestone
War of the Worlds (1953)   Byron Haskins
The Warriors (1979)   Walter Hill
Waterworld (1995)   Kevin Reynolds
The Westerner (1940)   William Wyler
When Willie Comes Marching Home (1950)   John Ford
While You Were Sleeping (1994)   Jon Turteltaub
★White Heat (1949)   Raoul Walsh
Who Framed Roger Rabbit (1988)   Robert Zemeckis

Film	Director
The Wicked Lady (1945)	Leslie Arliss
The Wild One (1954)	Laslo Benedek
Wild Strawberries (1957)	Ingmar Bergman
Witness for the Prosecution (1957)	Billy Wilder
★The Wizard of Oz (1939)	Victor Fleming
The Woman in the Window (1944)	Fritz Lang
A Woman of Affairs (1928)	Clarence Brown
★Woman of the Year (1942)	George Stevens
The Woman on the Beach (1947)	Jean Renoir
The Wrong Man (1957)	Alfred Hitchcock
Wuthering Heights (1939)	William Wyler
X-Men (2000)	Bryan Singer
Yolanda and the Thief (1945)	Vincente Minnelli
You've Got Mail (1998)	Nora Ephron
You Were Never Lovelier (1942)	William A. Seiter
Zelig (1983)	Woody Allen
Zéro de conduite (1933)	Jean Vigo
Ziegfeld Follies (1946)	Vincente Minnelli

APPENDIX 2
Sample Student Papers

Art vs. Violence in *A Clockwork Orange*
DAVID GOULDSTONE

Stanley Kubrick's adaptation of Anthony Burgess's novel received the New York Film Critics award for the best film of 1971. It was acclaimed as much for its aesthetic qualities as for the moral questions that it raised. Kubrick incorporated music from various classical compositions at critical moments in the film to highlight the tensions and ambiguities that he wanted to illustrate. He used the music of Rossini and Beethoven (which inspires Alex's dreams of mayhem and destruction) as a background for the senseless violence that Alex and his friends commit.

When Alex and his clique fight a rival gang, the violence of both groups is given a perverse beauty through stylish choreography and music from Rossini's "Thieving Magpie." Consequently, the audience is torn between the viciousness of the fight and the beauty of its visualization, experiencing a sense of uncertainty and ambiguity. This is intentional on Kubrick's part; it is his attempt to estrange the audience from the victims of the encounters. Perhaps he is using this tension to illustrate the variety and contradictions of human nature. While society may condemn acts of violence, there is, nevertheless, an innately aggressive aspect of human nature. Kubrick's use of music, therefore, retrieves this tendency from the audience's unconscious, thereby causing moral uncertainty.

Thus, we don't know whether to sing along with Alex to the music of "Singin' in the Rain," kicking our feet in time with his, or to be repelled by his brutality. Kubrick even has the kindness to remind us of our uncertainty at the end, leaving "Singin' in the Rain" resonating in our ears and forcing us to choose between memories of the fleet-footed Gene Kelly dancing across the puddles and of Alex's cruel feet stomping his victim.

Interestingly, Kubrick plays with our attitude toward Alex in a similar way. First he incites our contempt as we witness Alex's relentless cruelty; then our sympathy as he is betrayed and spiritually crucified; and, finally, our uncertainty as he "rises" again. We can detest his adoration of "ultraviolence," yet the undeniable charm of his Elizabethan dialect and his love of "Ludwig van" prevent us from rejecting him completely. Alex is, paradoxically, a cultured barbarian, which is, perhaps, what Kubrick is accusing us all of being.

The film exudes aesthetic appeal. As one critic wrote, "Mr. Kubrick constantly uses . . . a wide-angle lens to distort space relationships within scenes," contending that the director intends to separate people and images from the environment and emphasize their distinctions (Canby 193). Kubrick creates a surreal, dreamlike atmosphere from the start. First, we are greeted by the face of Alex (one eye ringed with fake lashes); then we take in his environment. Kubrick may have used this surreal technique to represent the drug-induced vision of Alex and his gang when they are at the milk bar. Kubrick reverts to a realistic style when they are not high—for example, during the day or when Alex is sent to prison.

On the surface, the film is futuristic, but, in truth, it is a critique of contemporary society. The clothes and the setting have a futuristic look, but Kubrick refuses to comfort the audience by implying that the events are in the distant future.

Alex's final line, "I was cured, all right!" mocks the therapy that society prescribed for him. Alex has returned to his old self with the help of the very people who tried to destroy his soul and his freedom of choice. It is an ironic redemption for Alex, who has risen, fallen, and risen again in a world that is no less sick than he is. Consequently, it is impossible for such a society to offer Alex any salvation. Therefore, when he once again dreams of rape and violence to the music of Beethoven's Ninth Symphony, we accept the fact that he is back to "normal." Quite simply, it was futile to expect that the cause of his condition—society—could also be his cure.

Works Cited

Canby, Vincent. " 'A Clockwork Orange' Dazzles the Senses and Mind."
   Review of *A Clockwork Orange*. *New York Times*, 20 December 1971.
   Reprinted in *The New York Times Film Reviews* (1971–1972). New York:
   New York Times and Arno Press, 1973. 193.
A Clockwork Orange. Directed by Stanley Kubrick. With Malcolm McDowell,
   Patrick Magee, and Adrienne Cori. Warner Bros. 1971.

Run Lola Run: Running to Stand Still

PAUL BELL

"Love can do everything." A statement that is simple, yet strong and direct,
as is Tom Tykwer's *Run Lola Run* (1998). The line is spoken less than five
minutes into the movie, yet it remains a constant throughout. In what may
start a resurgence in the German cinema, *Run Lola Run* is one of the few
German films that have succeeded in the American market. It has a strong
yet simple screenplay that has been transformed into an amazing film.

The film begins with Manni (Moritz Bleibtreu), a low-tiered criminal,
calling his girlfriend, Lola (Franka Potente), from a pay phone to ask why she
has failed to pick him up. After learning that her moped has been stolen,
Manni explains that he has lost the money he was carrying, leaving him with
only twenty minutes to come up with 100,000 DM (roughly $55,000); oth-
erwise, he will be killed by the mob.

What follows are three different versions of the couple's quest for the
money. In the first, when Lola fails to get the money from her banker father,
Manni attempts to rob a supermarket with Lola's belated help. The robbery
almost succeeds, until they turn a corner and are caught. A police officer accidentally shoots Lola, whose refusal to die results in a cut to Lola's hanging
up the phone twenty minutes earlier.

In the second version, Lola holds her father at gunpoint while she
robs the bank. Although she is able to catch up with Manni before he tries
to rob the supermarket, he carelessly walks out into the middle of the
street and is struck by an ambulance. This time it is Manni's refusal to die
that triggers the third version, in which Lola just misses her father at the
bank and instead goes into a casino, where she wins enough to save Manni.
However, at the same time, Manni stumbles upon the vagrant who originally

stole the money, which he is then able to give back to the mob boss. The film ends with Manni's asking Lola what she has in her bag, which we know is the extra 100,000 DM.

The film's main theme is that even the smallest events can have major consequences. The best example occurs in the telephone conversation between Lola and Manni. As Lola is hanging up, Tykwer cuts to a television screen where we see a domino chain in action. There is no clearer example of causality than dominoes. The seemingly irrelevant incident that sets the chain of events in motion is a man with a dog, attempting to trip Lola as she races down the stairs of her apartment building. As she continues to interact with the other characters in her quest for money, the camera will focus on them and then cut to snapshots of them in the future.

One such character is a woman pushing a child in a stroller. Lola nearly collides with the woman, and in each of the three versions they cross each other's path. In the first, the woman becomes destitute, her child is taken from her, and she steals someone else's child. The second imagines a future in which the woman plays the lottery and strikes it rich. In the third, she finds religion.

The fate of the man on the bike, too, differs in each version. The first two versions have him trying to sell the bike to Lola. In the first scenario, the man, after being beaten up by thugs, finds a woman whom he marries; in the second, he becomes a drug addict. The third is tricky: instead of witnessing the man's future, we see him selling the bike to the vagrant who stole Manni's money.

Every character in the film is subjected to different scenarios, including Lola's father, his lover, and the bank's security guard. The lover is pregnant with her husband's child. However, in each version Lola's father does not get the full story. Twice, the lover is only able to admit that she is pregnant before she is interrupted. The second time, her full account precipitates an argument between her and Lola's father just as Lola walks in; in the third version, the lover is cut off again before she can tell Lola's father that the child is not his.

Different scenarios also create different consequences for the security guard, who suffers a heart attack in the third version. In an interesting scene, in which Lola holds the guard's hand, doing her part to resuscitate him, the viewer is left to wonder if the guard, with whom Lola has had many strange altercations, is her real father.

Run Lola Run has moments when dialogue is important, such as the scene in which Lola's father claims that he is not her real father and that he is leaving Lola and her mother to have a child with his lover. These moments, admittedly, are few and far between; but when they occur, Tykwer focuses completely on the conversation. Unnecessary background movement and sound come to a halt, so the viewer can pay attention to the dialogue, despite the fact that the film is primarily visual.

Tykwer's creative use of the medium—for example, the alternation between film and video—is what makes *Run Lola Run* so impressive. Any scene involving Manni or Lola is shot in 35 mm. Those in which they are not involved are shot in video, suggesting that there are two different worlds. In Manni and Lola's world, the real one, "miracles can happen just like in the movies" (Tykwer). Then there is the other world, the synthetic one, which changes to the real one when Lola comes running into it, and Tykwer switches back to 35 mm.

Tykwer's camera not only zooms in on the characters but also moves around them. Lola is constantly in pursuit of the money for Manni. Even when she is standing still, her mind is moving as fast as she is running. The camera is rarely still; it is a constant reminder that Lola has a time limit, and that, as each second ticks by, Manni is closer to dying.

Tykwer uses a variety of film techniques, including animation, perhaps to create a surrealist effect (for example, when Lola runs down the stairs of her apartment building); split screen (Manni on the left waiting for Lola / Lola on the right, waiting to catch up with him before he tries to rob the supermarket); color symbolism (red filter for the love scenes between Lola and Manni); human sound (Lola's scream, which occurs during moments of helplessness and represents her inability to control her destiny); and a musical soundtrack that complements the action (urgent in the first version, more intense in the second, optimistic in the third).

The ending may seem confusing. Tykwer wants us to understand that Lola has gone through all three scenarios, not just the last one. Rather, she has experienced all three, taking a little bit from each with her. For example, she knew the man with the dog was going to try to trip her. How is this possible? Love can do everything: "It is this woman's passion alone that brings down the rigid rules and regulations of the world surrounding her" (Tykwer). Love can move mountains—and does.

Works Cited

Run Lola Run. Directed by Tom Tykwer. With Franka Potente and Moritz
    Bleibtreu. Sony Pictures Classics. 1998.

Tykwer, Tom. As quoted on www.spe.sony.com.classics/runlolarun.

APPENDIX 3
Online Resources and Citation

Video and DVD Rental and Purchase

If you are interested in purchasing or renting tapes or DVDs, you should consult the latest edition of Leonard Maltin's *Movie & Video Guide* (New York: Signet), which is updated annually and includes a complete list of mail-order sources. Two of the best are Critics' Choice Video <www.ccvideo.com> and Facets <www.facets.org>. Another is Movies Unlimited (1-800-4MOVIES), or <www.moviesunlimited.com>.

Web Sites

Just as books can go out of print, Web sites can disappear from the Internet. The newest and best film-related Web sites are currently listed on <www.digital-librarian.com/movies.html>. Another site, which boasts 25,000 links, is <www.cinemedia.org>. Since the information superhighway has so many detours and exit ramps to strange locations, you will waste less time if you have a specific destination or goal in mind. For example:

Ratings

Prior to 1968, the present ratings (G, PG, PG-13, R, and the rarely applied NC-17) did not exist. From the mid-1930s to the mid-1960s, the only ratings that had any significance were those of the National Legion of Decency, established in 1934. The Legion, which was associated with the Roman Catholic Church, classified movies in several categories: General

Patronage, Adults, Morally Objectionable in Part for All, and Condemned. Although the movie industry took these classifications seriously, the Legion was not an arm of the movie industry.

The present ratings, however, are assigned by the Motion Picture Association of America (MPAA). To some moviegoers, these ratings are relative. You might want to consult <www.filmratings.com>, which tries to be as objective as possible about sex and violence. If the phrase used is not just "violence" or "sexuality" but "graphic violence" and "strong sexuality," you might have second thoughts if you have an unusually sensitive child or younger brother or sister. Consider also logging on to <www.critics.com>, which includes reviews that are quite specific about the amount of obscenity, sex, and violence found in new films. Since the MPAA does the ratings, you might consult its Web site:<www.mpaa.org>. Your best bet, however, is a reliable newspaper critic or the Weekend edition of the *New York Times*, which features a column, "Taking the Children," which analyzes recent releases in terms of their suitability to various age levels.

New Films

Usually a film's Web site is some variation on the title. For some films, only the title is needed—e.g., <www.lost-in-translation.com>; for others, the title is followed by "movie" or "film":—e.g., <www.mysticrivermovie.com>, <www.monsterfilm.com>. Still others require the name of the studio or the distributor—e.g.,<www.dreamworks.com/houseofsandandfog>. To be certain, check the movie ads in a major newspaper like the *New York Times*, preferably Sunday's Arts & Leisure section, for specific Web addresses.

Finally, you can always use a keyword search.

Studio Web Addresses

Disney	<www.disney.com>
Universal	<www.universalstudios.com>
Warner Bros.	<ww.movies.warnerbros.com>
MGM/UA	<www.mgmua.com>
Twentieth Century-Fox	<www.FoxMovies.com>
Paramount	<www.paramount.com>
Sony (Columbia)	< www.sonypictures.com>
Miramax	<www.miramax.com>
Castle Rock	<www.castle-rock.com>
Fine Line Features	<www.flf.com>
Fox Searchlight	<www.foxsearchlight.com>

Casts, Credits, and Reviews

The Internet Movie Database (<www.imdb.com>) is a good place to start, although it is not always as complete as one would like. One outstanding feature is under the heading "Awards & Reviews." Click on "external reviews" and then "The Greatest Films—comprehensive analysis of US film." The keyword is "classic." If that is the case, you will discover practically a shot-by-shot analysis of classic films, complete with dialogue excerpts. Of course, even such detailed analyses can never substitute for the actual film experience. You might even want to compare the analysis with the film after you have watched it to see whether the writer has erred in any detail. The Internet Movie Database is also worth perusing for its comments section; there, you'll find responses ranging from the knowledgeable to the uninformed. The All Movie Guide <www.allmovie.com> offers some features similar to imdb.com.

Another resource is the Academy of Motion Picture Arts & Sciences Web site at <www.ampas.org> or <www.oscars.org>. Clicking on "Search" on the Academy's Web site provides a vast amount of information about, among other things, the Fairbanks Center for Motion Picture Study in Los Angeles, a major resource center for film research; lectures and seminars sponsored by the Academy; and student awards and screenwriting fellowships.

If you need a vital piece of information that you cannot find on the Web, you can write to or call the Academy of Motion Picture Arts and Sciences' National Film Information Service (NFIS), the Center for Motion Picture Study, 333 S. La Cienega Boulevard, Beverly Hills, CA 90211-1972 (310-247-3000). You can also visit the Fairbanks Center at 333 S. La Cienega Boulevard in Beverly Hills.

The Library of Congress

Although you may not associate the Library of Congress with films, you will if you log on to <http://lcweb.loc.gov/film>. Go into Film Preservation and Cultural Organization (<http://lcweb.loc.gov/film/orgs.html>), where you will discover links to the National Film Registry, the Academy of Motion Picture Arts and Sciences, the American Film Institute, the British Film Institute, Film Festivals, Film Archives On Line (FAOL), and The Silent Movie Theatre, among many others.

Directors' Sites

These continue to multiply. You might try using the director's name as a URL, e.g., <www.woodyallen.com>. You might also type a director's name into a search engine or else use imdb.com. Using the search engine method, you can decide exactly what aspect of a director's career (his biography, an individual film, an online review or essay) you wish to focus on.

Citing Online Resources

Remember that material from the Internet must be documented when it is used for a research paper or a critical essay. Because the Internet is mistakenly regarded as "free," some may be tempted to think of it as the equivalent of public domain material, unlike books or periodicals. To regard information gleaned from the Internet as different from that derived from books and articles is to disassociate one source of information from another. Any source you use in a report requiring documentation has to be acknowledged.

Let's say you are writing a paper on Clint Eastwood and are aware that he has been profiled on PBS's American Masters series. Go to a search engine, type "American Masters," and locate Eastwood, Clint. When you click on it, you will discover the feature essay, David Kehr's "Eastwood Noir," which you have decided to use. Whether you are quoting directly from Kehr's text or paraphrasing his ideas, you must acknowledge your source and provide such information as author, title, electronic address, and date accessed. If you accessed the essay on January 3, 2004, and are using the MLA style guide, here is how your documentation should look in your Works Cited:

Kehr, David. "Eastwood Noir." Featured Essay. <u>American Masters</u>. PBS.
3 Jan. 2004. <http://www.pbs.org/wnet/americanmasters/database/
eastwood_c.html>.

Ordinarily you would give the air date, or at least the year, of the East-wood program. But the Web site does not provide that information. In a sense, it is not necessary, since you're not quoting from the program, but from the undated essay that came out of that program and was placed online.

In some respects, documenting Internet sources is more complex than documenting books and articles, but it is no less important. Be sure to use a recent reference guide that describes how to cite URLs and electronic resources.

Glossary of Motion Picture Terms

actual sound   Sound from an identifiable sound source, either on- or off-screen.

ambient sound   Noise.

American montage   See **montage.**

anthology film   A feature film consisting of (1) several short, self-contained films or vignettes based on short stories (*O. Henry's Full House, Trio, Quartet*); (2) interrelated narratives with a common theme (*Tales of Manhattan, Flesh and Fantasy*); or (3) excerpts from various films (e.g., the musical sequences from MGM's *That's Entertainment* and *That's Entertainment II*).

A-picture   The main attraction on a double bill during the studio years (1930–1960); the second feature was termed a **B-picture** because it cost less to make.

archetype   A universal theme (quest, odyssey, revenge, love, death), setting (cave, desert, the other world), or character (savior, sorcerer, knight-errant, imperiled maiden) found in the myths and literature of all peoples.

art director   Originally the individual responsible for the design and construction of the sets in accordance with the screenplay and the director's interpretation of it. Presently, someone working under the **production designer (production supervisor),** who is responsible for the film's "look."

artist's cut   A studio-negotiated agreement granting a director editorial autonomy while at the same time adding so many provisos that only films that have succeeded with test audiences would qualify. Not to be confused with the right of **final cut.**

aspect ratio   The ratio of image width to height, formerly 4:3 or 1:33:1 (resulting in an image 1⅓ times wider than high) and now approximately 1:85:1.

asynchronization   Sound related metaphorically or contextually to the next image that we see (for example, the mother calling to her child in *M*, followed by shots of various objects, but not of the child, who is dead).

auteur   French for "author," a term applied to directors such as Hitchcock, Ford, and Welles, whose films are so distinctive that they are regarded as having been "authored" and are designated accordingly (John Ford's *Stagecoach*, Orson Welles's *Citizen Kane*).

auteur theory (auteurism)   The philosophy that the director is the central intelligence behind a film and deserves authorial status and possessory credit (Alfred Hitchcock's *Psycho*). The theory has proved quite controversial, although it can be justified when applied to the work of such auteurs as Billy Wilder, Joseph L. Mankiewicz, John Ford, Hitchcock, and others capable of leaving their personal imprint on their films.

back lighting   Lighting from behind the subject to create a sense of depth.

best boy   Assistant to the **gaffer** (chief electrician).

biopic   A biographical film such as Spike Lee's *Malcolm X* (1992).

Bollywood   The term for the popular cinema of Bombay, India, in which musical sequences are common.

bottom lighting   Lighting from below the subject, leaving part of it in shadow.

B-picture   The second, less expensively made film (B for budget) on a double bill during the studio years (1930–1960), when many theaters featured two movies. Some B-movies are now acknowledged masterpieces (e.g., *Cat People*, *I Walked with a Zombie*, *Detour*).

canted shot   An angled shot, resulting in an asymmetrical, lopsided image to suggest that something is amiss. Also known as a Dutch-angle shot.

close shot (CS)   A head-and-shoulders shot as opposed to a **close-up,** to which it is so similar that the two terms are often considered synonymous.

close-up (CU)   Literally, a shot in which the camera is or appears to be close to the subject (e.g., a shot of the human head).

colorization   Computer-created addition of color to a black-and-white film without the consent of the filmmaker, who is usually dead.

commentative sound   Sound from a source outside the physical setting, such as background music.

composition (composing a shot)   The act of planning a shot or a series of shots as an artist might the details of a painting, with close attention to such matters as lighting, color, camera angles, and spatial relationships.

connotation   The metaphorical meaning of a word ("He was consumed with hatred") or, in film, of an image (the numerous reflections of Eve's successor at the end of *All About Eve*, implying that there will always be newcomers waiting to replace the stars).

continuity editing   The arrangement of the shots in accordance with the director's visualization of the material, resulting in a natural flow of the action and a beginning-middle-end plot.

contrast cut   A transition from one shot to another that is so radically different from the first that it calls attention to the disparity between them.

crane shot   A shot taken when the camera is mounted on a crane (a mechanical arm attached to a trolley, similar to the cherry picker used by utilities crews), enabling the camera to engage in ascending, descending, and lateral movement.

crawl   Credits or titles that move from the bottom of the screen to the top, and occasionally vice versa. Also known as a roll-up title.

credits   The names of the film's creative personnel (actors, writer, production designer, costume designer, director of photography, editor, producer, director), which usually— but not always—appear at the beginning of the film as part of the **main title.**

credits sequence   A narrative segment of the film that unfolds during the credits, often functioning as a prologue and imparting information that is necessary to an understanding of the plot.

crosscutting   Switching back and forth between two actions taking place at the same time, but not necessarily—and, in fact, rarely—in the same place. Also called **parallel cutting.**

cut   (1) The joining of two separate shots so that the first is replaced by the second; (2) the joint connecting two shots; (3) a director's signal ("Cut!") to terminate a scene; (4) a version of a movie **(rough cut, director's cut, final cut).**

deep focus   A type of photography in which foreground, middle ground, and background are clearly visible.

denotation   The literal meaning of a word; in film, the image independent of its symbolic, or **connotative,** meaning (white attire as a mode of dress and not the sign of a white knight).

diegesis   Greek for "narrative" and used by some academics to mean the world of the film, including what happens both on- and off-screen as well as past events that have not been dramatized.

digital cinema   Film created to be computer-readable, shot in digital video with the information stored on a hard drive, and edited digitally with transitions such as **wipes** and **dissolves** (which can be added or deleted without affecting the original footage).

director   The individual ultimately considered responsible for the visualization of the screenplay, although the actual making of the film was a collaborative activity.

director's cut   The film in the form in which the director has envisioned it.

discourse   In linguistics and **semiotics,** speech as personal expression, either verbal or nonverbal; in film, the way in which the story reaches the audience, including all the narrative strategies that have been used, both visualized and implied.

dissolve   A transition in which one shot **fades out** as another **fades in,** sometimes with the two shots overlapping (called a *lap dissolve*).

distribution   The second phase of moviemaking, after **production,** which involves the manner in which a film is marketed and released.

documentary   A nonfiction film.

dolly shot   A moving shot taken on a dolly (a wheeled platform or cart).

dramatic foreshadowing   Early indications of events or actions that will happen later.

editing   The arrangement of the shots in such a way as to create the film's narrative, rhythmic, and tonal structure so that there is variety of image, size, mood, color, texture, and pace.

end credits   A list at the end of the film of virtually everyone, from the stars to the caterer, involved in the production.

end titles   Text that appears at the end of the film and provides the audience with vital information, such as the fate of the characters.

epistolary voice   **Voice-over** narration accompanying the reading or writing of a letter.

establishing shot (ES)   (1) Generally a **long shot** identifying a location, such as a shot of the New York skyline; (2) a **long shot** (for example, a family gathering) that becomes the basis of closer shots of the various components (individual family members).

exhibition   The third phase of moviemaking, after **production** and **distribution,** which refers to the showing of a film in a theater or an auditorium.

extreme close-up (ECU)   A shot in which the camera is so close to the subject that only some aspect of it can be recorded, such as an eye or a monogram.

extreme long shot (ELS)   A shot in which the camera is so far away that the result is a broad, panoramic view.

fade-out/fade-in   The image either disappears as the screen goes dark (fade-out) or materializes out of a dark screen (fade-in).

fiction film   See **narrative film.**

fill light   An auxiliary light placed opposite the **key light,** in conjunction with which shadows are eliminated and a uniform image is produced.

film noir French for "dark film," meaning a film with a discernible dark look characterized by low-key lighting, high-contrast photography, rain-slick streets, flashing neon signs, smoke-filled bars, mirrored cocktail lounges, sunless living rooms, femmes fatales, and easily ensnared males.

final cut The version that audiences eventually see, except for some last-minute fine-tuning, generally of the soundtrack. The **right of final cut,** the goal of most filmmakers, is difficult to achieve in the corporate structure of contemporary Hollywood.

flashback A segment of a film, brief or extended, that dramatizes what has happened in the past.

flash-forward A shot or series of shots depicting an event that will take place at some point in the film but not at the point at which either appears.

focal length The distance in millimeters from the center of the lens to the point where the image is in focus.

Foley artists Sound effects personnel, named after Joe Foley, who synchronize the appropriate sound with the on-screen image (creating the sound of footsteps on a pavement with a shot of someone walking along the pavement, for example).

form cut A cut from one object to a similarly shaped one (for example, from the wheel of a moving vehicle to a spinning roulette wheel).

form dissolve A **dissolve** from one object to a similarly shaped one (for example, from the figure of a ballerina on a music box to a young girl in a ballerina's costume).

frame (1) A single photograph on a strip of film; (2) the borders enclosing the photographed image as if it were placed within a picture frame.

framing The act of composing a shot after the filmmaker has decided on its visual form.

freeze frame A form of **stopped-motion photography,** in which the image is reduced to a still photograph.

front projection Photographing live action in front of a screen, with some kind of background, still or moving, projected onto the screen from the front; the opposite of **rear projection,** in which background is projected from behind the screen.

full shot (FS) See **long shot.**

gaffer The chief electrician.

genre A literary form or type of film in which recurring motifs, stylistic conventions, characters, and plot devices have become so familiar that the work or film is relegated to a category such as tragedy, comedy, or lyric poetry in literature or screwball comedy, horror, or science fiction in film.

God's eye shot A shot taken from above the subject. Sometimes called *birds eye shot.* See **high-angle shot.**

graphics Any combination of print and image, such as a film's **main title.**

grip The individual who oversees everything—props, mostly—except for what falls under the jurisdiction of the **gaffer.**

handheld camera Filming with a portable camera that is either held or attached to the cameraperson.

high-angle shot A shot in which the camera is positioned above (high shot) or at an angle above the subject (high-angle shot). See also **God's eye shot.**

high-contrast photography Sharp contrast between the bright and dark areas of the image; in **film noir,** a white image against a black background.

high-key lighting Lighting that produces uniform brightness (ideal for musicals and comedies) resulting from a low contrast of **key light** to **fill light.**

iconography   Re-creating an image so that it evokes a traditional or familiar pictorial representation, such as a well-known painting or sculpture.

independent film (indie)   (1) A movie made without a studio affiliation; (2) one made by a producer whose production unit is based at a studio that has provided some form of financing and functions as the film's distributor; (3) one distributed through a studio's specialty unit, such as Sony Pictures Classics, Fox Searchlight, or Paramount Classics.

infranarrative   The film's **subtext,** consisting of the various associations made while watching the film (for example, associating the characters with mythic types and archetypal figures, the actors with their previous roles or with other actors with whom they share common traits, and so forth).

insert   A shot, such as a written text (for example, part of a letter), that is edited into the film, not photographed during the particular scene but inserted later.

intercutting   Similar to **crosscutting,** except that in intercutting, switching back and forth from one location to another results in a complete scene (the attempt to sabotage the launching of the battleship in *Saboteur,* for example).

international film   Formerly called a "foreign film." A film produced by any country other than the United States.

intertextuality   Inserting references to other works within one's own, often as a way of acknowledging influences, paying homage, or answering predecessors. Brian De Palma's *Obsession* is a tribute to Hitchcock's *Vertigo,* and Peter Bogdanovich's *The Last Picture Show* pays homage to Howard Hawks's *Red River.*

intertitles   Text that appears on the screen periodically to provide some kind of information; a common technique in silent films. See **titles.**

iris-in/iris-out   The circle-enclosed image keeps expanding until the image is in full view (iris-in); the shot seems to close down as the image is reduced to a circle, which then disappears from the screen (iris-out).

iris shot   A shot in which the image is enclosed within a circle, although rectangular and lozenge-shaped shots also fall under this category.

jump cut   An abrupt transition from one location or time frame to another, sometimes for effect but often because of mediocre editing.

key grip   The head **grip,** who supervises the others.

key light   The primary source of illumination, usually placed above and to the side of the subject.

leitmotif   A recurring musical phrase associated with a character or a theme.

logo   A studio's trademark (e.g., MGM's lion, Universal's globe).

long shot (LS)   A shot in which the camera appears at a distance from the subject (the complete person with some background visible). Also known as a **full shot (FS).**

long take   A take that lasts at least a minute, although there have been instances of shots lasting as long as ten minutes (the eight ten-minute, or thereabouts, shots in Hitchcock's *Rope*). See also **sequence.**

low-angle shot   A shot in which the camera shoots up at the subject from below, making the subject larger than it actually is.

low-key lighting   The result of a **high-contrast** ratio of **key light** to **fill light,** producing dark, shadowy images that are ideal for horror and **film noir.**

main title   The film's title and opening **credits,** often creatively designed and an artistic creation in itself.

masking   Altering the shape of the **frame** so that it can assume a particular shape (a keyhole, peephole). The frame is considered to be masked when everything is blacked out except the shape in which the image will appear.

match cut   A **transition** from one shot to another that is related to it contextually but is often spatially and temporally distinct from it, done so smoothly that there is no break in continuity.

matte shot   A shot created by **masking** out part of the frame, clearing that area for the insertion of another image. In *King Kong*, the scene in which Fay Wray is terrorized by a prehistoric creature is a matte shot; the image of the creature was matted onto the shot of Wray screaming in fear.

medium close-up (MCU)   Midway between a **close-up** and a **medium shot** (chest-to-head).

medium long shot (MLS)   Midway between a **medium shot** and a **long shot**, providing less detail than a long shot.

medium shot (MS)   Midway between a **close-up** and a **long shot** (waist up).

metonymy   The substitution of one term for another to which it is closely related ("crown" for "royalty," "chair" for "chairperson").

miniature rear projection   A technique in which live action (not live actors) is projected onto a screen, in front of which is a scaled set with model figures (for example, a bust of *King Kong*) whose movements are correlated with the live action through **stop-motion photography.**

mise-en-scène   A French theatrical term meaning the staging of a production; in film, composing a shot or a sequence with the same attention to detail (set, lighting, costumes, makeup, positioning of actors within the frame, etc.) that a stage director lavishes on a play.

mobile camera   A general term for the camera in a moving state.

montage   (1) Editing in the sense of assembling the shots to create the complete film; (2) a series of shots that appears in rapid succession; (3) a series of shots linked by **dissolves** and **wipes** to collapse time, often indicated by newspaper headlines or calendar pages dissolving into each other (also known as American montage).

morphing   Suggested by "metamorphosis" and referring to a computer-created transformation of one image into another (for example, human into animal or vice versa, or a fictional character into a historical figure).

Motion Picture Production Code   See **production code.**

myth   A timeless narrative that expresses universal truths about life and death, fate and nature, and the divine and the human.

narrative film   A film with an invented plot. Also known as fiction film and story film.

negative cost   All the expenses incurred in producing the original negative from which positive prints are struck.

New Wave (French New Wave, la nouvelle vague)   A movement in French cinema that began in the late 1950s, when film critics such as François Truffaut, Jean-Luc Godard, and Claude Chabrol became directors who broke with the past, used improvisation, filmed on location (streets, bistros, apartments), deliberately paid homage (*hommage*) to their favorite American directors by repeatedly evoking their films, and upgraded the director from foreman to **auteur** or surrogate author of his or her films.

objective shot   What the camera, as opposed to the character, sees.

omniscient narrator A third-person storytelling technique in which the narrator knows everything about the plot and the characters, including their unconscious desires and innermost thoughts.

opening title Text that appears at the beginning of a film and provides some kind of background information.

optical printer A camera interlocked with a projector to re-photograph images from the original film, so that optical effects such as **wipes, dissolves, fades,** and **freeze frames** can be added.

outtakes Shots eliminated from the final version but sometimes included in the **end credits.**

overlapping dialogue (1) Dialogue in which actors speak over each other's lines, supposedly to sound more realistic; (2) dialogue that carries over from one scene to the next.

overlapping sound Sound that carries over from one scene to the next or anticipates a new scene by starting at the end of the previous one.

over-the-shoulder shot A shot in which the camera is positioned over a character's shoulder, usually from behind, revealing what or whom the character sees. Often used in conversations between two characters.

pan shot A shot in which the camera rotates horizontally on a fixed axis. Not properly a moving shot because the camera itself does not move, only the camera head.

paradigm In **semiotics,** a unit of potential relationship; **paradigmatic relationships** are associative, not sequential, and are concerned with meaning rather than order (for example, associating a scene of fictional violence with a historical incident that resulted in a similar bloodbath).

parallel cut A **transition** from one shot to another occurring at the same time. See also **crosscutting.**

plot A work's narrative structure—not the story line but the arrangement and order of the episodes that make up the work.

point-of-view (POV) (1) A shot from the character's point of view—what the character sees; (2) a shot representing what the character experiences—in a reverie, a memory, a dream—so that we momentarily become the character. See also **subjective camera.**

postproduction The stage following the completion of a film, including the **editing,** the addition of **transitions** and **visual effects,** and musical scoring.

precredits sequence A segment of the film that occurs before the **credits** come on and often contains information that is vital to an understanding of the plot.

preproduction Everything that precedes the actual filming (for example, the preparation of the script, casting, selection of a director and the creative team).

producer The individual who "puts the package together" (cast, writer, director, and so forth) and oversees the entire production from its inception to its completion and, in some cases, oversees its marketing, while also making sure that the film stays within budget.

production The first phase of moviemaking, followed by **distribution** and **exhibition,** and denoting everything involved in the making of the movie prior to its being edited.

production code (Motion Picture Production Code) A self-regulatory policy created in 1930 in response to public pressure to "reform the screen" and replaced in 1968 by the rating system. Unacceptable screen content and language included nudity, homosexuality, drug-taking, vulgarity, obscenity, and blasphemy. White slavery (enforced prostitution) and interracial relationships were cautioned against; crime could not pay, nor could adultery be justified. Rape and seduction could only be suggested.

production designer (production supervisor) The person responsible for the film's "look" as determined by the script and the director's vision of it.

product placement Placing a brand name in a prominent position in the shot so that audiences cannot help noticing it.

rack focus The shifting of focus from one character or area within a shot to another by reducing the character or area to a blur, until such time as the indistinct section is restored to focus.

ratings (the Motion Picture Rating System) A system of rating films inaugurated in 1968 by the Motion Picture Association of America (MPAA) after it became evident that the production code was outdated. The categories, which are now considerably different from those of 1968, presently consist of G (general audiences), PG (parental guidance), PG-13 (parental guidance for children under 13), R (restricted to those 17 or older unless accompanied by an adult), and NC-17 (no children under 17). The R category is especially problematic, since such films as *Schindler's List* and *Saving Private Ryan* have been classified as "R."

rear projection Projecting background footage (for example, a ski slope, a city street) onto the rear of a screen in front of which live action is photographed, so that the characters appear to be skiing or driving down Broadway though they are really in a movie studio.

reflexivity The self-conscious attempt by a novelist, playwright, or filmmaker to call attention to his or her work as a novel, a play, or a film, so that we are reading a novel about the writing of a novel, watching a play about theater, or seeing a film about movies. Sartre's *Nausea* is a novel about the complex process of creating a novel; Jean Anouilh's *Antigone* calls attention to itself as a modern version of Sophocles' tragedy; and Woody Allen's *The Purple Rose of Cairo* makes it clear that it is about movies as the "daylight dream."

right of final cut The director's right, granted by the studio or production company, to have the film released in the form in which he or she intended it to be seen on the screen.

roll-up title See **crawl.**

rough cut An early version of the film as the director had planned it but that is not yet ready for release.

screwball comedy A type of romantic comedy that is noted for witty dialogue, oddball characters, a battle-of-the-sexes plot, and a happy ending in which such barriers as class and profession vanish in the face of true love.

self-reflexive See **reflexivity.**

semidocumentary A fiction film based on fact, photographed and acted in such a way that it resembles both a fiction film and a documentary.

semiotics The study of signs and codes to determine their meaning, especially in such matters as food, color, gesture, dress, and body language.

sequence A segment of a film that, when excerpted, makes a certain amount of narrative sense (*Psycho's* famous shower sequence).

shallow focus Rendering the foreground with greater clarity and sharpness than the background; the opposite of **deep focus.**

shooting script A script prepared for filming, with the scenes numbered and designated in terms of interior/exterior, place, and day/night (for example, INT: Cabin—Day), the camera positions indicated, the **transitions** marked, and the proper spacing observed.

shot What is recorded by a single, uninterrupted run of the camera. See also **take**.

shot/reverse shot Switching back and forth between two characters in conversation so that each one's reaction can be seen.

side lighting Lighting from either side of a subject, leaving it half in light and half in shadow.

special effects See **visual effects**.

spec script A script that is written without any studio commitment and submitted without any guarantee of sale.

Steadicam A camera that is attached to the operator's body, enabling him or her to move easily into, out of, or around areas that cannot accommodate a dolly.

stop-motion photography A type of photography often used in animation in which the camera operates one **frame** at a time so that objects can be adjusted between frames, thereby "coming alive."

story film See **narrative film.**

straight cut The immediate **transition** from one shot to the next.

stream of consciousness The flow of thoughts, memories, and associations, both conscious and unconscious, within a character's mind.

subjective camera A technique in which the viewer stands in for the character, experiencing what the character would have experienced. See also **point-of-view** shot.

subtext See **infranarrative.**

subtitles Print that appears at the bottom of the screen to provide information such as a translation from a foreign language. See **titles.**

swish pan An unusually rapid pan, sometimes resulting in a momentary blur.

synchronization Correlation of sound and image with the sound coming from within the image or from an identifiable source.

synecdoche Similar to **metonymy,** though usually restricted to the substitution of the part for the whole ("law" for "police officer," "deck hands" for "crew").

syntagma In **semiotics,** a unit of actual relationship; **syntagmatic relationships** are those in which the narrative units follow each other in order, allowing the viewer to connect them in a meaningful and coherent pattern.

take Theoretically, the same as **shot,** except that several takes may be necessary before the right one is achieved.

theatrical film A film made for exhibition in a movie theater.

three-dimensional film A type of film briefly popular in the 1950s that provided moviegoers with a sense of depth, but only if they wore Polaroid glasses—a necessary feature because otherwise the film, which had been shot with two lenses, would be a series of overlapping and blurred images.

three-point lighting The standard lighting scheme involving some combination of **back, key,** and **fill lights.**

three-shot A shot with three characters.

tight framing Confining the image, usually a character, within the **frame** lines to suggest entrapment.

tilt shot A shot in which the camera rotates vertically on a fixed axis.

title Any printed text in a film.

top lighting   Lighting from above the subject, capable of producing a glowing effect.

tracking shot   A moving shot, originally with the camera on tracks but now referring to any shot taken when the camera is on some sort of moving vehicle or mechanism, such as a dolly, crane, car, or truck—or even held by or strapped onto a person (e.g., a **Steadicam**).

transition   Device used for bridging scenes, such as **fades, dissolves, wipes,** and **irising.**

two-shot   A shot with two characters.

virtual reality   A computer-simulated environment, which those who have access to it can alter as they wish.

visual effects (special effects)   Effects achieved through special optical and mechanical processes (**wipes, dissolves, freezes, matte shots, stop-motion photography, miniature rear projection,** etc.).

voice of God   Omniscient off-camera narration.

voice-over   Off-camera narration by either a character or a commentator.

wide-angle lens   An angle that has a short **focal length.**

wide-angle shot   A shot taken with a **wide-angle lens,** which, though it can offer a broader view and provide more visual information, also makes the foreground and whatever is in it seem unnaturally larger than the background.

wipe   A transition in which a line appears to move vertically, horizontally, or diagonally across the screen, causing one shot to disappear or close down and another to materialize. Wipes can also appear in the form of clocks, fans, and spirals.

zoom lens   A lens of variable **focal length,** allowing the filmmaker to create the illusion of movement by changing the focal length to move into (zoom in) or out of (zoom out) a scene.

Index

liebestod motif, 217
Lifeboat, 235
lighting, 104–7
Lindsay, Vachel, 321
linear sequences, 62–63
Lions Gate Entertainment, 10
list of films and directors, 361–80
literary techniques used in films, 255–58
    flashbacks, 138–39, 255–56
    flashforwards, 256–57
    point-of-view, 257–60
literature, relationship of film to, 254–96
    film adaptations, 261–88
    literary techniques, 255–58
    screenwriting, nature of, 288–96
Little Big Man, 129
Little Caesar, 29, 135
Little Foxes, The, 90, 217, 281
Little Mermaid, 123
Little Women, 339
Locket, The, 138–39
Logan, Josh, 280
logos, 21–23
Lonely Villa, The, 78
Lone Ranger, The, 218
Long Day's Journey into Night, 36, 59–60
Longinus, 320
long shots (LS), 50–51
long takes, 90–93
Look Who's Talking, 41
Lord of the Flies (Golding), 158
Lorre, Peter, 351
Lost Horizon, 328
Lost in America, 333
Lost Weekend, The, 259
Love for Three Oranges, March from
    (Prokofiev), 218
love motifs, 217
low-angle shots, 53, 86–87
low-key lighting, 105
Lubitsch, Ernst, 95, 156, 211, 212, 236
Lucas, George, 29, 183
Lucia di Lammermoor (Donizetti), 317
Lumet, Sidney, 81, 201–2
Lumière, August, 3
Lumière, Louis, 3
Lysistrata (Aristophanes), 149

M, 38–39
Macbeth (movie), 353, 354
Macbeth (Shakespeare), 113
Macdonald, Dwight, 348–49, 357–58
Machiavelli, Niccolo, 355
Madden, John, 18
Mad Love, 351
Mafia films, 135
magazine reviews, 346
Magic and Myth of the Movies (Tyler), 329–30
Magic Flute, The (Mozart), 219
Magnificent Ambersons, The, 73, 353, 354
main titles, 23–24
Making of Citizen Kane, The (Carringer), 351–52

Malcolm X, 39–40
Mamoulian, Rouben, 57, 72, 76, 110, 262
Man from Colorado, The, 131
Man from Laramie, The, 124–25
Manhattan, 62
Manhattan Murder Mystery, 114
Mankiewicz, Herman J., 349, 351, 352
Mankiewicz, Joseph L., 5, 36, 157, 256, 280,
    291, 331, 342
Mann, Anthony, 124, 126
Man of the West, 124
Man Who Shot Liberty Valance, The, 124, 125,
    235
Man Who Wasn't There, The, 140, 141, 160–62
Marlowe, Christopher, 317
Marnie, 35, 178
    color in, 99
    subjective camera, 54
Marshall, Penny, 338–39
Martin, Dean, 10
Marx Brothers, 150–51, 152, 153
Mary, Queen of Scots, 10
Mary Shelley's Frankenstein, 263
Mascagni, Pietro, 302
*M*A*S*H,* 86
masked frame, 89–90
masking shot. *See* iris
match cut, 67
Matrix trilogy
    Matrix, The, 26, 194–96
    Matrix Reloaded, The, 26, 196–97
    Matrix Revolutions, The, 197–98
    special effects in, 111
    war of the worlds myth in, 194–98
Mayer, Louis B., 228
McCabe and Mrs. Miller, 127
McCall, Mary, Jr., 339, 340
McCarey, Leo, 341
McGrath, Doug, 268, 269
McLuhan, Marshall, 40
Me, Myself and Irene, 152, 344
Measure for Measure (Shakespeare), 152
Medium Cool, 40
medium shots (MS), 50
Meet John Doe, 8
Meet Me in St. Louis, 114
Meet Nero Wolfe, 137
Meistersinger, Die (Wagner), 24
Méliès, Georges, 3, 108
melodramas, 113
Men, The, 339
Menaechmi (Plautus), 149
Mendes, Sam, 82, 89, 101
Menken, Alan, 123
Menzies, William Cameron, 20
Merry Widow, The, 95
metamorphosis, in horror films, 175
Metamorphosis (Ovid), 190
metaphorical dissolve, 69
Method acting, 209
metonymy, 69
Metropolis, 182

rhythm, 77
Richardson, Samuel, 44
Richie, Donald, 191
"Ride of the Valkyries, The" (Wagner), 219
Rimsky-Korsakov, Nikolai, 220
Ring of the Nibelungs, The (Wagner), 194, 316
Rio Grande, 235
Rite of Spring, The (Stravinsky), 349
Ritt, Martin, 27, 103
RKO Radio Pictures, 9
Road to Morocco, 117
Road to Perdition, 82, 88–89
Road to Singapore, 117
Road to Utopia, 117
Roaring Twenties, The, 133, 135, 137
Roberts, Julia, 149
Robinson, Edward G., 134
Rogers, Ginger, 104, 115, 119
Rohmer, Eric, 224
roll-up titles, 29
Romeo and Juliet, 18
Rooster Cogburn, 10
Roots, 142
Rope, 91–92, 97–98, 260
"Rose for Emily, A" (Faulkner), 188
Rosemary's Baby, 178
Rose Tattoo, The, 10
Rossellini, Roberto, 325, 348
Rossini, G., 218
rough cut, 66
Rumble in the Bronx, 27
Runaway Bride, The, 149
Russell, Rosalind, 167, 170, 339, 340
Russian Ark, 90–91
Russian film criticism, 321–22
Ryan, Meg, 149

Saboteur, 36, 51, 66, 157, 235, 257
Sahara, 200
St. Valentine Day's Massacre, The, 135
sample student papers, 381–86
Sands of Iwo Jima, 103, 198
Sant, Gus Van, 28, 158, 178
Santayana, George, 29
Sargent, Alvin, 288
Sarris, Andrew, 224, 225, 226
Sartre, Jean-Paul, 200, 257
satire, 153–54
Satyricon (Petronius), 186
Saving Private Ryan, 143–144
savior myth, in Shane, 191–94
Sayles, John
    Passion Fish, 12–13
    Sunshine State, 26
Scarface (1932), 132
Scarlet Street, 138
scenes and sequences distinguished, 61–62
Schaefer, George J., 351
Scheherazade (Rimsky-Korsakov), 220
Schindler's List, 97, 311, 342
Schlesinger, John, 206
Schoonmaker, Thelma, 304

science fiction films, 180–84
Science Fiction in the Cinema (Baxter), 180
Scorsese, Martin, 74
    Age of Innocence, The. See Age of Innocence,
        The
    Alice Doesn't Live Here Anymore, 167
    Cape Fear, 157–58
    GoodFellas. See GoodFellas
    Kundun, 30
    Last Temptation of Christ, The, 29
    New York, New York, 114
    Raging Bull, 31–32, 302–6
Scott, Ridley, 338
Scream trilogy, 179–80
screen icon, Bogart as, 198–201
screenplays, 4, 255
    format of, 292–96
    literary techniques used in, 255–58
    nature of screenwriting, 288–96
screwball comedies, 145–49
Sea of Grass, 44
Searchers, The, 4, 90, 124, 125, 126, 127, 128,
    129, 198, 315, 316
Searching for Debra Winger, 170
Searching Wind, The (Hellman), 292
Second Piano Concerto (Rachmaninoff),
    218, 219
Seeing is Believing (Biskind), 181
Selznick, David O., 227
semidocumentary, 43–44, 258
semioticians, 330–35
September Affair, 218
sequences, 25–26, 61–65
    associative, 62, 63–64
    credits, 25
    defined, 61
    linear, 62–63
    montage, 62, 65
    precredits, 25–26
    scenes distinguished, 61–62
Serpico, 201–2, 332
Set-up, The, 8, 303
Seven, 202
Seven Brides for Seven Brothers, 114, 116–17,
    122
1776, 142
Seventh Seal, The, 14, 327
Seven Year Itch, The, 23, 181, 218, 219
Shadow of a Doubt, 342–43
Shakespeare, William, 112, 113, 152, 281, 305,
    317, 328
Shakespeare in Love, 11
    examining text of, 17–19
    opening title, 29
shallow focus, 88
Shane, 127, 128, 129, 130, 314, 316, 332
    dissolves in, 69–70
    long shots in, 51
    savior myth in, 191–94
Shelley, Mary, 263
She Loves Me, 214
Sherman, Vincent, 339